Greater
& Fras...

D1004280

Key Maps
2 - 4

Communities Index 5

Area Maps
6 - 9

Downtown Vancouver
10 - 11

101 - 126

142 - 175

182 - 195

202 - 214

222 - 234

242 - 254

262 - 272

301 - 401

Index
500s

TABLE OF CONTENTS

How to Use this Atlas

come see us @ www.mapart.com

MapArt. DIRECTION + DESIGN

PRODUCTION TEAM Malcolm Buchan Brent Carey Michael Foell
Luna Gao Karen Gillingham Mike Grasby
Oksana Kutna Werner Mantei Salina Morrow
Carl Nanders Jameel Ahmed Nizamani Dave Scott
Kyu Shim Samiha Sleiman Shaun Smith
Sam Tung-Ding Ho Matthew Wadley Craig White
Jessie Zhang Marlene Ziobrowski

© mapmobility corp. 2009 Edition
Published by Peter Heiler Ltd.
Distribution by **MapArt Publishing Corp.**
70 Bloor St. E., Oshawa, Ontario L1H 3M2
☎ 905-436-2525 FAX 905-723-6677
Printed in Canada Imprimé au Canada

DESTINATIONS - indicate the town or city the road or highway leads to.

NORTH ARROWS - indicate general direction pointing north.

GRID REFERENCES - are used to locate places, streets or roads in the index. See page 500 for further explanation.

PAGE ARROWS - indicate continued coverage of the map and page.

FIXED PAGE NUMBERING

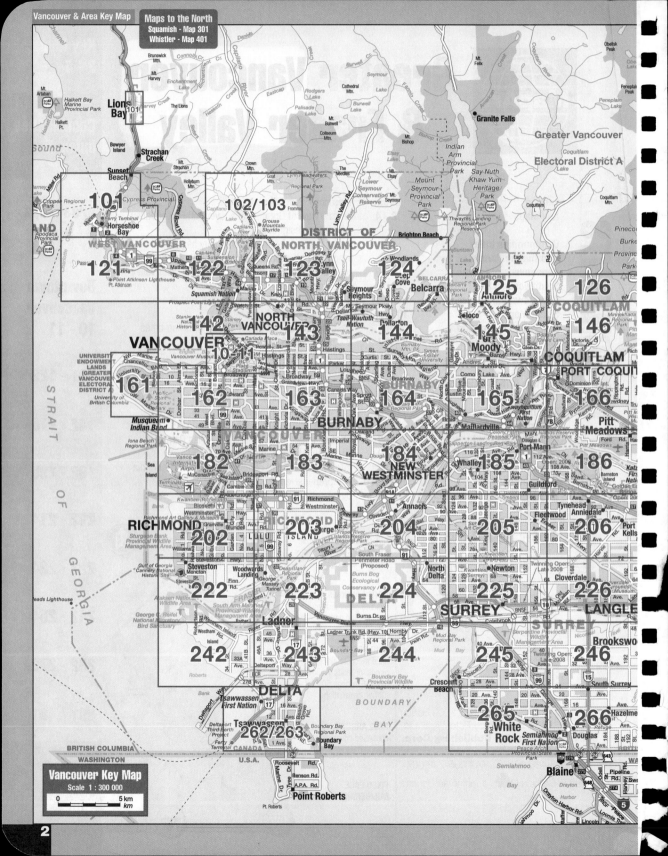

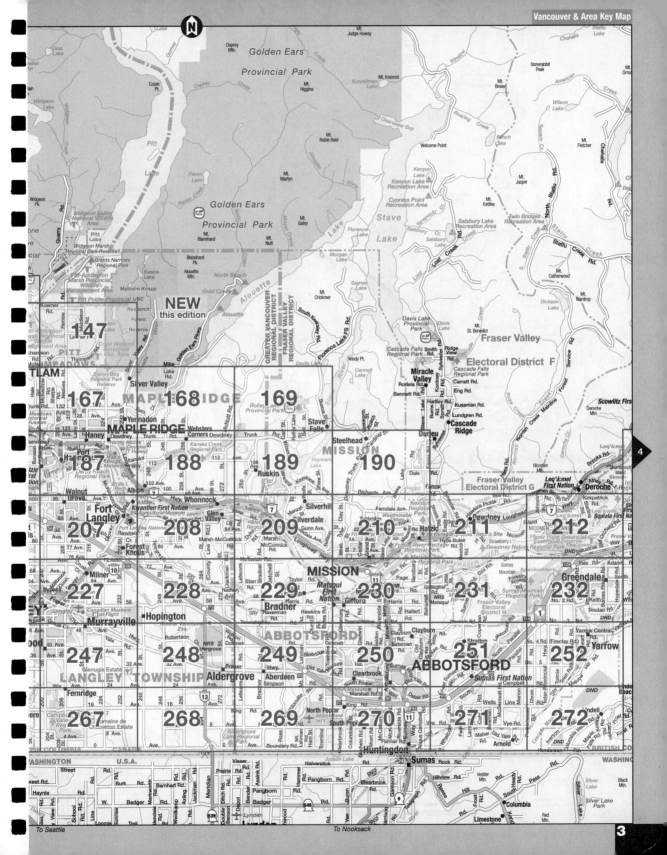

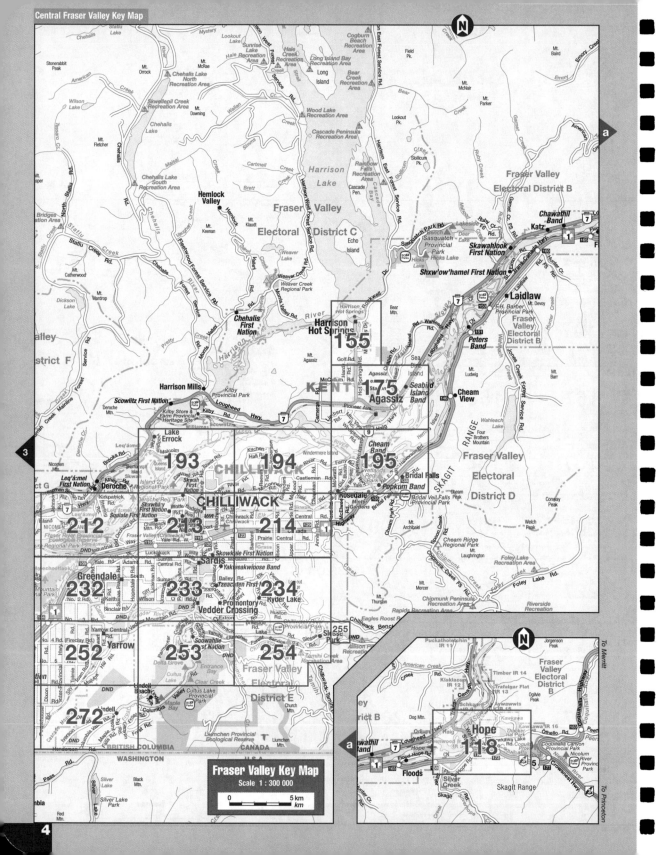

Fraser Valley Key Map
Scale 1 : 300 000
0   5 km
           km

This index is provided to help you locate a community in the atlas.

BOLD TYPE indicates an official municipal name. Blue type indicates a local community name.

Information Panels

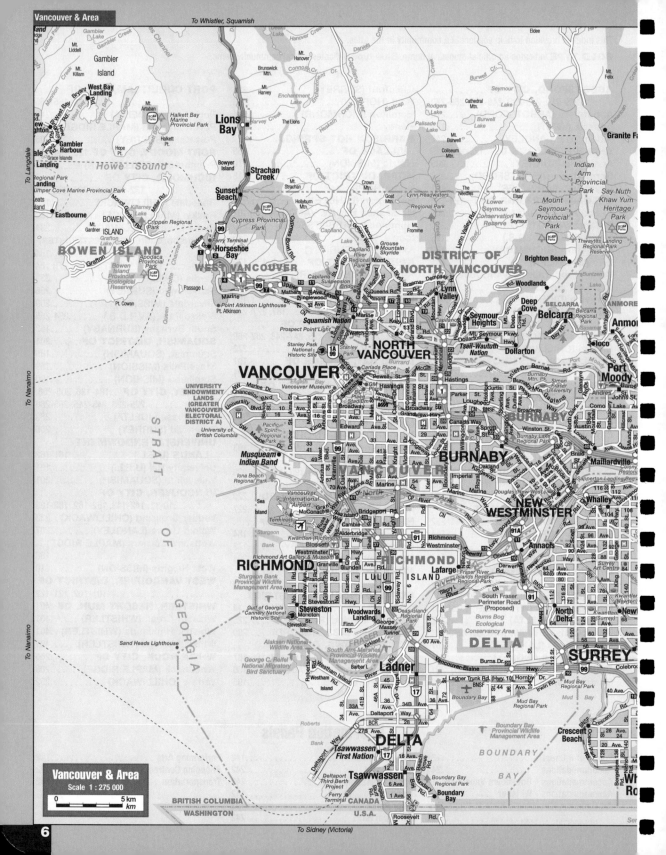

To Whistler, Squamish

To Langdale

To Nanaimo

To Nanaimo

Gambier Island

BOWEN ISLAND

Bowen Island Provincial Ecological Reserve

Lions Bay

Strachan Creek

Sunset Beach

Horseshoe Bay

WEST VANCOUVER

Cypress Provincial Park

DISTRICT OF NORTH VANCOUVER

Brighton Beach

Deep Cove

BELCARRA

Belcarra

Ioco

Seymour Heights

Dollarton

Mount Seymour Provincial Park

Indian Arm Provincial Park

Say Nuth Khaw Yum Heritage Park

Granite Fa

Anmore

Port Moody

NORTH VANCOUVER

Tsleil-Waututh Nation

Stanley Park National Historic Site

Squamish Nation

VANCOUVER

UNIVERSITY ENDOWMENT LANDS (GREATER VANCOUVER ELECTORAL DISTRICT A)

University of British Columbia

Pacific Spirit Regional Park

Musqueam Indian Band

VANCOUVER

BURNABY

Burnaby Lake Regional Park

NEW WESTMINSTER

Maillardville

Whalley

Annacis

Vancouver International Airport

RICHMOND

LULU ISLAND

RICHMOND

Lafarge

Fraser River Islands Reserve Regional Park

South Fraser Perimeter Road (Proposed)

Burns Bog Ecological Conservancy Area

North Delta

DELTA

SURREY

Steveston

Gulf of Georgia Cannery National Historic Site

Woodwards Landing

Deas Island Regional Park

George Massey Tunnel

Crescent Beach

Boundary Bay Regional Park

Alaksen National Wildlife Area

South Arm Marshes Provincial Wildlife Management Area

Ladner

Ladner Trunk Rd. (Hwy. 10)

Mud Bay Regional Park

George C. Reifel National Migratory Bird Sanctuary

Sand Heads Lighthouse

STRAIT OF GEORGIA

DELTA

Tsawwassen First Nation

Deltaport Third Berth Project

Tsawwassen

Ferry Terminal

CANADA

Boundary Bay

BOUNDARY BAY

Boundary Bay Provincial Wildlife Management Area

BRITISH COLUMBIA

WASHINGTON

U.S.A.

Roosevelt Rd.

To Sidney (Victoria)

Gambier Island

West Bay Landing

Gambier Harbour

Grace Islands

Landing

Eastbourne

BOWEN ISLAND

Pt. Cowan

Howe Sound

Queen Charlotte Channel

Passage I.

Point Atkinson Lighthouse
Pt. Atkinson

Prospect Point Light

Marine

English Bay

Vancouver Maritime Museum

Sea Island

Iona Beach Regional Park

Sturgeon Bank

Richmond Art Gallery & Museum

Sturgeon Bank Provincial Wildlife Management Area

Roberts Bank

Westham Island

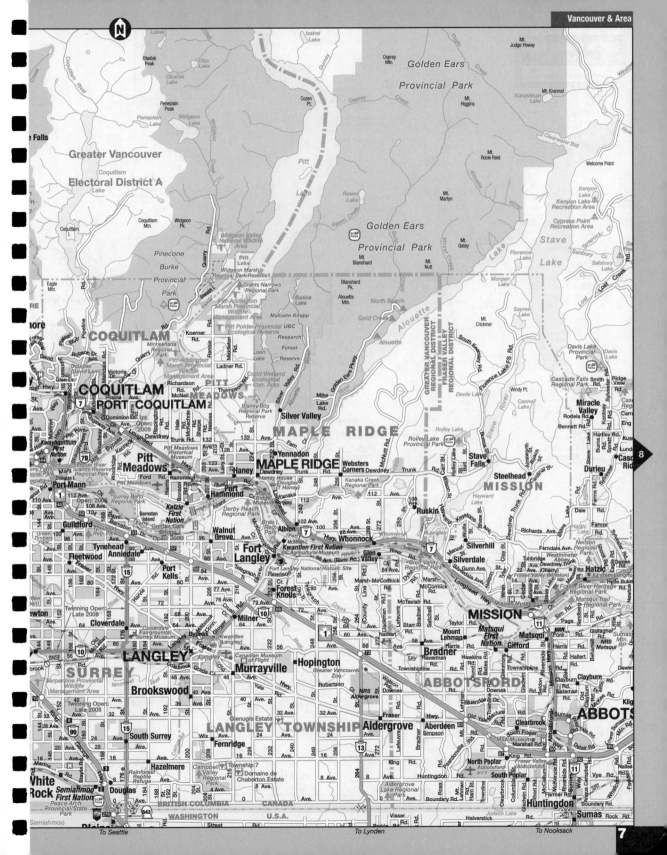

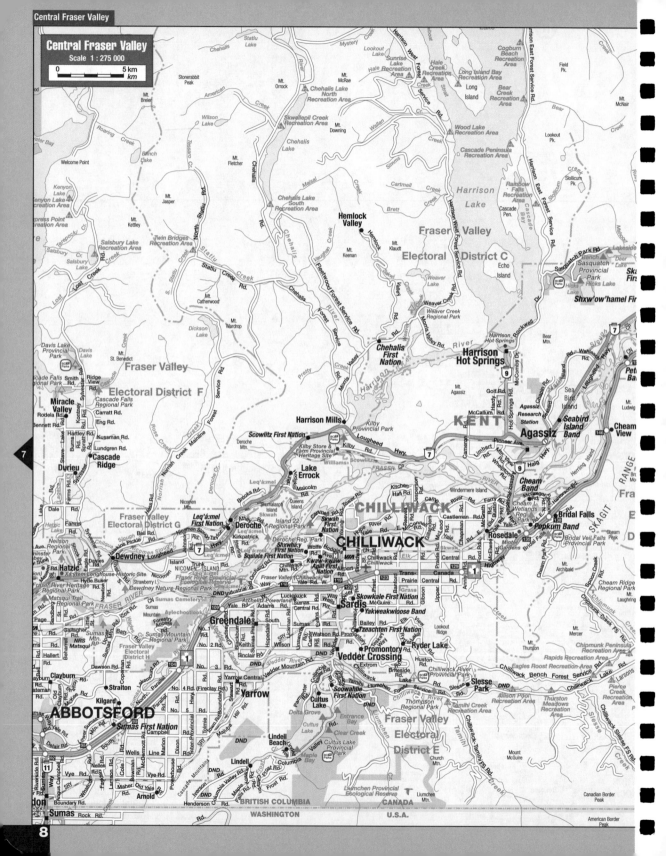

Central Fraser Valley

Scale 1 : 275 000

0   5 km
km

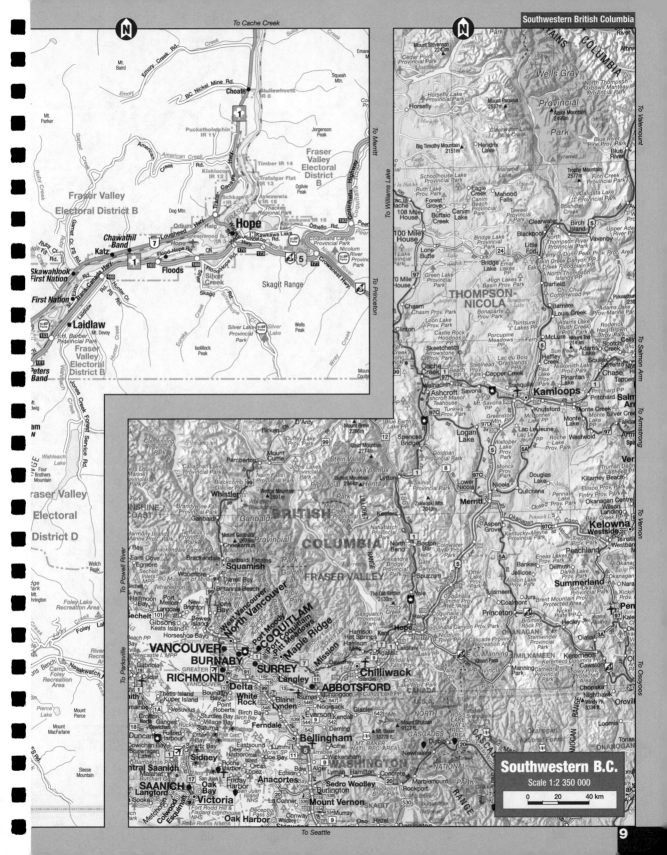

Southwestern B.C.
Scale 1:2 350 000
0   20   40 km

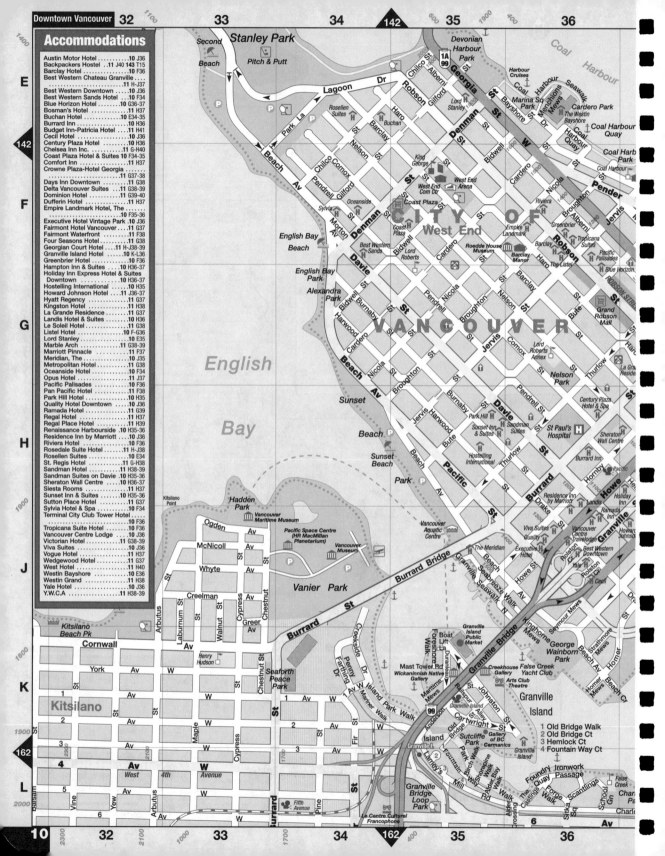

Accommodations

Austin Motor Hotel 10 J36
Backpackers Hostel . . .11 J40 143 T15
Barclay Hotel 10 F36
Best Western Chateau Granville . . . .
. . . . .11 H-J37
Best Western Downtown 10 J36
Best Western Sands Hotel 10 F34
Blue Horizon Hotel 10 G36-37
Bosman's Hotel 11 H37
Buchan Hotel 10 E34-35
Burrard Inn 10 H36
Budget Inn-Patricia Hotel 11 H41
Cecil Hotel 10 J36
Century Plaza Hotel 11 H37
Chelsea Inn Inc. 11 G-H40
Coast Plaza Hotel & Suites 10 F34-35
Comfort Inn 11 H37
Crowne Plaza-Hotel Georgia . . . .
. . . . .11 G37-38
Days Inn Downtown 11 G38
Delta Vancouver Suites 11 G38-39
Dominion Hotel 11 G39-40
Dufferin Hotel 11 H37
Empire Landmark Hotel, The . . . .
. . . . .10 F35-36
Executive Hotel Vintage Park .10 J36
Fairmont Hotel Vancouver 11 G37
Fairmont Waterfront 11 F38
Four Seasons Hotel 11 G38
Georgian Court Hotel 11 H-J38-39
Granville Island Hotel 10 K-L36
Greenbrier Hotel 10 F36
Hampton Inn & Suites 10 H36-37
Holiday Inn Express Hotel & Suites
Downtown 10 H36-37
Hostelling International 10 H35
Howard Johnson Hotel 11 J36-37
Hyatt Regency 11 G37
Kingston Hotel 11 H38
La Grande Residence 11 G37
Landis Hotel & Suites 10 H36
Le Soleil Hotel 11 G38
Listel Hotel 10 F-G36
Lord Stanley 10 E35
Marble Arch 11 G38-39
Marriott Pinnacle 11 F37
Meridian, The 10 J35
Metropolitan Hotel 11 G38
Oceanside Hotel 10 F34
Opus Hotel 11 J37
Pacific Palisades 10 F36
Pan Pacific Hotel 11 F38
Park Hill Hotel 10 H35
Quality Hotel Downtown 10 J36
Ramada Hotel 11 G39
Regal Hotel 11 H37
Regal Place Hotel 11 H39
Renaissance Harbourside .10 H35-36
Residence Inn by Marriott 11 J36
Riviera Hotel 10 F36
Rosedale Suite Hotel 11 H-J38
Rosellen Suites 10 E34
St. Regis Hotel 11 G-H38
Sandman Hotel 11 H38-39
Sandman Suites on Davie .10 H35-36
Sheraton Wall Centre 10 H36-37
Siesta Rooms 11 H37
Sunset Inn & Suites 10 H35-36
Sutton Place Hotel 11 G37
Sylvia Hotel & Spa 10 F34
Terminal City Club Tower Hotel . . . .
. . . . .10 F36
Tropicana Suite Hotel 10 F36
Vancouver Centre Lodge 10 J36
Victorian Hotel 11 G38-39
Viva Suites 10 J36
Vogue Hotel 11 H37
Wedgewood Hotel 11 G37
West Hotel 11 H36
Westin Bayshore 10 E36
Westin Grand 11 H38
Yale Hotel 10 J36
Y.W.C.A 11 H38-39

1 Old Bridge Walk
2 Old Bridge Ct
3 Hemlock Ct
4 Fountain Way Ct

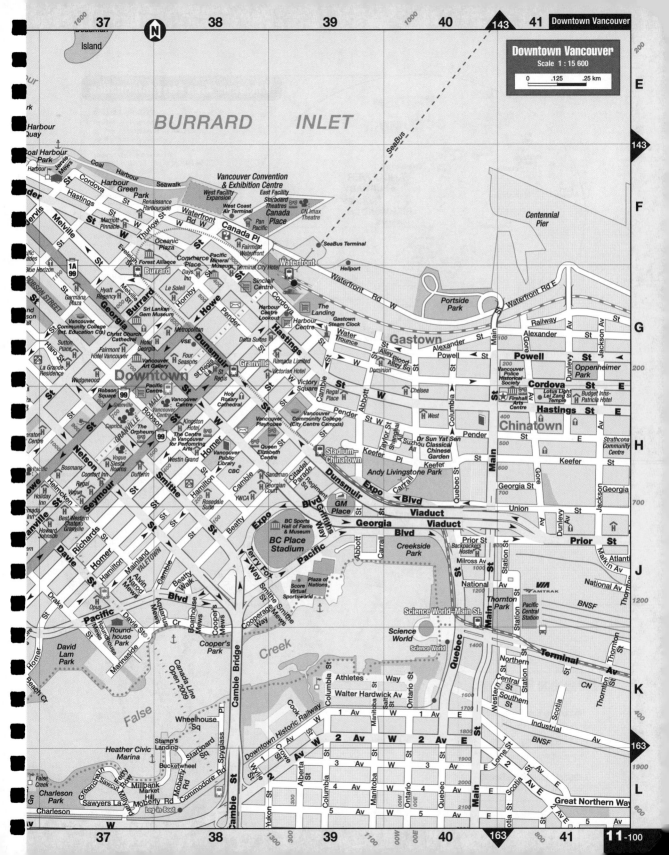

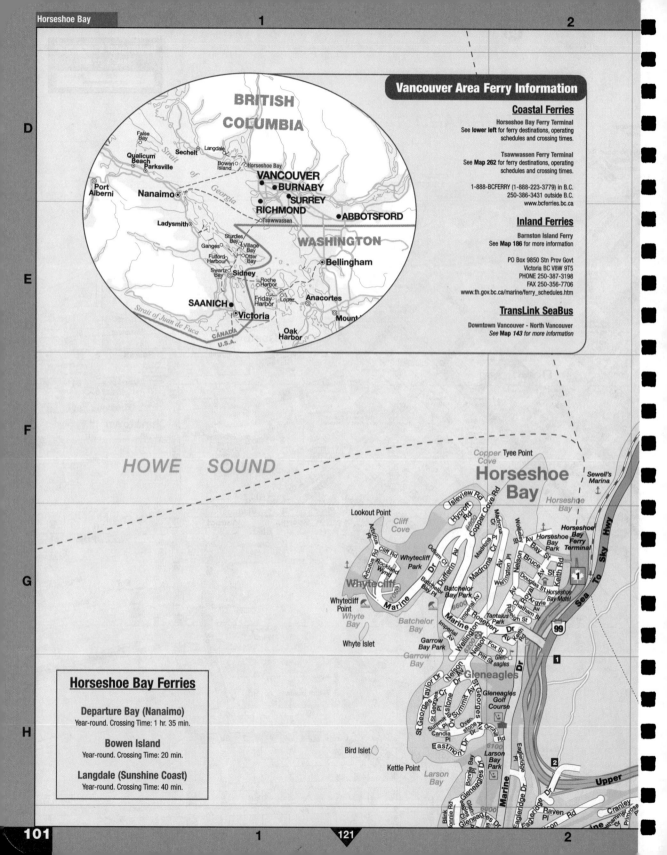

Vancouver Area Ferry Information

Coastal Ferries

Horseshoe Bay Ferry Terminal
See **lower left** for ferry destinations, operating schedules and crossing times.

Tsawwassen Ferry Terminal
See **Map 262** for ferry destinations, operating schedules and crossing times.

1-888-BCFERRY (1-888-223-3779) in B.C.
250-386-3431 outside B.C.
www.bcferries.bc.ca

Inland Ferries

Barnston Island Ferry
See **Map 186** for more information

PO Box 9850 Stn Prov Govt
Victoria BC V8W 9T5
PHONE 250-387-3198
FAX 250-356-7706
www.th.gov.bc.ca/marine/ferry_schedules.htm

TransLink SeaBus

Downtown Vancouver - North Vancouver
See **Map 143** for more information

BRITISH COLUMBIA

False Bay
Qualicum Beach
Parksville
Sechelt
Langdale
Bowen Island
Horseshoe Bay
VANCOUVER
BURNABY
Port Alberni
Nanaimo
SURREY
RICHMOND
ABBOTSFORD
Ladysmith
Tsawwassen
WASHINGTON
Sturdies Bay
Village Bay
Ganges
Fulford Harbour
Otter Bay
Bellingham
Swartz Bay
Sidney
Roche Harbor
Friday Harbor
Lopez
Anacortes
SAANICH
Victoria
Mount
Oak Harbor
Strait of Juan de Fuca
CANADA
U.S.A.
Strait of Georgia

HOWE SOUND

Copper Cove
Tyee Point
Horseshoe Bay
Sewell's Marina
Horseshoe Bay

Lookout Point
Cliff Cove
Isleview Rd
Hycroft Rd
Copper Cove Rd
Madrona Cr
Horseshoe Bay Ferry Terminal

Artburus Pt
Cliff Rd
Whytecliff Park
Odlum Ct
Dufferin Av
Horseshoe Bay Pl
Madrona Pl
Wellesley Av
Bay St
Nelson Av
Bruce St
Keith Rd

Whytecliff
Rockland Wynd
Batchelor Bay Pl
Batchelor Bay Park
Madrona Cr
Wellington Av
Douglas St
Argyle
Horseshoe Bay Motel

Whytecliff Point
Marine Dr
Whyte Bay
Batchelor Bay
Imperial Av
Chatham Av
Haigh St
Tantalus Park

Whyte Islet
Garrow Bay Park
Wellington Av
Marine Dr
Rosebery Dr
Fox St
Imperial Av

Garrow Bay
Nelson
Glen-eagles
Pitt St

Gleneagles
Taylor Dr
St Georges
Gleneagles Golf Course

Nelson
Keystone Av
Summit Av
St Georges Av
Orchill Rd

Bird Islet
St Georges Dr
Summit Av
Candia Pl
Oyster
Eastmont
Larson Bay Park
Eagleridge Dr

Kettle Point
Larson Bay
Bonnie
Gleneagles Dr
Marine Dr
Blink Bonnie Rd
Gleneagles Dr
Eagleridge Pl
Raven Pl
Cranley
Primrose

99

1

Sea To Sky Hwy

Upper

Horseshoe Bay Ferries

Departure Bay (Nanaimo)
Year-round. Crossing Time: 1 hr. 35 min.

Bowen Island
Year-round. Crossing Time: 20 min.

Langdale (Sunshine Coast)
Year-round. Crossing Time: 40 min.

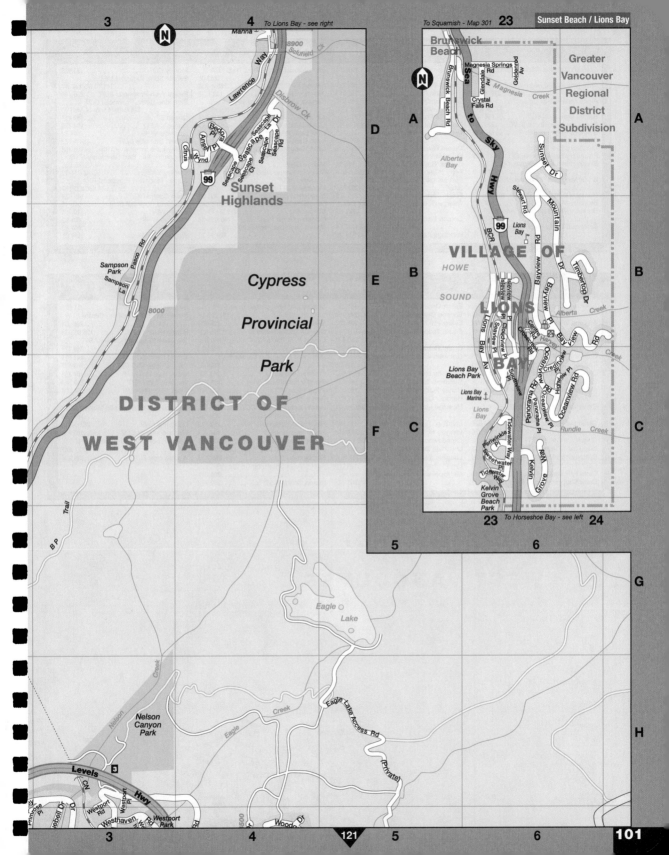

3 **4** To Lions Bay - see right

To Squamish - Map 301 **23**

Marina

Brunswick Beach

Magnesia Springs Rd

Greater Vancouver Regional District Subdivision

D **A**

Sea to Sky Hwy

Crystal Falls Rd

Magnesia Creek

Alberta Bay

Sunset Dr

Stewart Rd

Mountain

99

BCR

Lions Bay

VILLAGE OF

B **B**

HOWE

SOUND

Timbertop Dr

Bayview Rd

Bayview Pl

Alberta Creek

LIONS

Seaview Pl

Crosscreek Rd

Harvey

Oceanview Rd

Crestview

Creanview Pl

Highview Pl

Oceanview Rd

BAY

Panorama Pl

Panorama Rd

Lions Bay Av

Southview

Lions Bay Beach Park

Lions Bay Marina

Lions Bay

F **C** **C**

Penwinkle Way

Tidewater Way

Sweetwater Pl

Tidewater Way

Rundle Creek

Kelvin

Kelvin Grove

Kelvin Grove Beach Park

23 To Horseshoe Bay - see left **24**

5 **6**

3 **4**

N

Lawrence Way

Disbrow Ck

Seiafield Ck

8900

Bedg Pl

Anse Pl

Citrus

Wynd

Seascape Dr

Seascape Pl

Seascape Dr

Seascape Rd

Seascape Ct

Seascape La

99

Sunset Highlands

Sampson Park

Sampson La

Pasco Rd

8000

Cypress

Provincial

Park

DISTRICT OF

WEST VANCOUVER

D

E

F

B P Trail

B P

Eagle Lake

G

Creek

Nelson

Nelson Canyon Park

Eagle Creek

Eagle Lake Access Rd

(Private)

H

Levels Hwy **3**

CN

Primrose Pl

Nebell Dr

Westport Rd

Westport Pl

Westport Rd

Westhaven Rd

Westport Park

1500

Woods Dr

Major Parks

Alaksen National Wildlife Area *DEL* ..	Capilano River Regional *DNV* . .**122** J14	International Ridge Prov. Rec. *FRA*	Mundy *CQT* **165** V35
. . . .**222** N9	Cates *DNV* **144** Q26	. . . .**253** U6	Pacific Spirit Regional *UEL* . . . .
Aldergrove Lake Regional *LGT*	Central Park Pitch & Putt *BUR* **163** Y21	Invergarry *SUR* **185** A-B36	. . . .**161** T5 W6 **162** W7
. . . .**268** Y-Z62	Chineside *PMD* **145** T33	Jericho Beach *VAN* **142** T7-8	Peace Arch Provincial *SUR* . .**266** Z40
Alpha Lake *WHS* **401** H1	Coquitlam River *CQT* **146** S39	Kanaka Creek Regional *MAP*	Pinecone Burke Provincial *CQT* . . . .
Ambleside *WVA* **122** M-N11	Cultus Lake Provincial *FRA* . .**253** T3-6	. . . .**169** Y63-64	. . . .**126** M43-44 N43-44 **146** P43
Barnet Marine *BUR* **144** R28	Cypress Provincial *WVA* **101** D-E4	Kawkawa Provincial *HOP* . . .**118** E47	Queen Elizabeth *VAN* **162** X14
Bear Creek Provincial *SUR* . .**205** G34	Deas Island Regional *DEL* .**223** L17-18	Lighthouse *WVA* **121** L3	Queen's *NEW* **184** Z29
Belcarra Regional *BEL* **124** N28	Derby Reach Regional *LGT*	Lost Lake *WHS* **401** D4	Rainbow *WHS* **401** E2
Blackie Spit *SUR* **245** T31	. . . .**187** A51, C52	Lynn Canyon *DNV* **123** K-L21	Robert Burnaby *BUR* **164** X-Y27
Blueberry Beach *WHS* **401** F2-3	Dream River *WHS* **401** C3-4	Lynn Headwaters Reg. *DNV*	Rolley Lake Provincial *MIS* . .**169** X68
Boundary Bay Regional *DEL* **263** X-Y19	Elgin Heritage *SUR* **245** S34	. . . . .**103** D17-18, E17-18	Serpentine Fen Bird Sanctuary *SUR* .
Brackendale Eagles Provincial *SQM* .	English Bay Beach *VAN* **10** G34	Mahon *CNV* **123** M-N16	. . . .**245** Q35
. . . .**301** D1-2	Ferry Island Provincial *FRA* .**195** A-B19	Malcolm Knapp UBC Research Forest	Stanley *VAN* **142** Q11-12
Bridal Veil Falls Provincial *FRA*	Fort Langley National Historic Site	Reserve *MAP* **168** U55-56	Sumas Mountain Provincial *FRA* . . .
Burnaby Lake Nature *BUR* **164** W25-26	*LGT* **207** F54	Matsqui Trail Regional *ABT* **210** J77-78	. . . .**231** L86 **231** L87
Burnaby Mountain *BUR* **144** S29	Fraser River Heritage *MIS* . . .**210** J76	Meadow *WHS* **401** C3	Town Centre *CQT* **145** R38
Burnaby Mountain Cons. Area *BUR* .	George C. Reifel Bird Sanctuary *DEL*	Minnekhada Regional *CQT* . .**146** Q45	Tynehead Regional *SUR* . .**186** D40-41
. . . .**144** S26-30	. . . .**222** N9	Minoru *RMD* **202** F11-12	Vanier *VAN* **10** J34
Campbell Valley Regional *LGT*	Golden Ears Provincial *MAP*	Mossom Creek Park *PMD* . .**145** Q33-34	Wayside *WHS* **401** G2
. . . .**267** W-X48	. . . .**168** W57-58	Mount Seymour Provincial *DNV*	Wedge *WHS* **401** B3
	Hastings Park *VAN* **143** S19-20	. . . .**124** J-K26	Whytecliff *WVA* **101** G1

Shopping Centres

Aberdeen Shopping Centre *RMD*	Eaton Centre *VAN* **163** Y22	Middlegate Shopping Centre *BUR* . . .	Sinclair Centre *VAN* **11** G38
. . . .**182** D12	Elwood Centre *ABT* **249** T69	. . . .**184** Z25-26	Strawberry Hill Shopping Centre *SUR*
Arbutus Village Shopping Centre *VAN*	Evergreen Mall *SUR* **205** F37	Newton Plaza *SUR* **225** K34	. . . .**205** J31
. . . .**162** W11	Fraser Ridge Shopping Centre *ABT* . .	Newton Town Centre *SUR* . .**225** K34	Surrey Place *SUR* **185** D33-34
Brentwood Mall *BUR* **163** U22	. . . .**250** T77	Ocean Park Plaza *SUR* **265** W32	Ten Oaks Shopping Centre *ABT* . . . .
Bridgepoint Market *RMD* . .**182** B-C13	Grand Robson Mall *VAN* **10** G36	Park Royal *WVA* **122** M12	. . . .**250** T77
Capilano Mall *CNV* **123** N15	Granville Island Public Market *VAN* . .	Peninsula Shopping Centre *SUR*	Tilford Centre *CNV* **143** P19
Cariboo Centre *CQT* **164** W30	. . . .**10** J35	. . . .**245** U37	Town Centre Mall *DEL* **263** X17
Chieftain Centre Mall *SQM* . .**301** G1-2	Granville Mall *VAN* **11** G-H37	Pinetree Village *CQT* **145** T38	Valley Fair Mall *MAP* **187** Z53
Chilliwack Mall *CHL* **213** H-J6	Guildford Town Centre *SUR* . .**185** D37	Plaza International *WVA* **122** N13	Ventura Plaza *ABT* **250** U74
Clearbrook Town Square *ABT* .**250** U73	Haney Place Mall *MAP* **187** Z52	Poco Plaza *PCQ* **145** T38	West Oaks Mall *ABT* **250** U73
Clover Square *SUR* **226** N42	Harbour Centre *VAN* **11** G39	Prairie Mall *PCQ* **146** T40-41	Westminster Mall *NEW* **184** A28
Cloverdale Shopping Centre *SUR* . . .	Heritage Mountain Shoppers Vill. *PMD*	Renaissance Square *CQT* . . .**165** X31	Westminster Quay Public Market *NEW*
. . . .**226** M-N42	. . . .**145** S35	Richmond Centre *RMD* **202** F12	. . . .**184** B29
Columbia Square *NEW* **184** B28	Landing, The *VAN* **11** G39	Richmond Square *RMD* **202** F12	Westview *CNV* **123** L-M16
Co-op Mall *ABT* **250** U76	Langley Mall *LGC* **227** N48	Royal Square *NEW* **184** Z29	Westwood Mall *CQT* **145** T38
Coquitlam Centre *CQT* **145** S-T37	Lansdowne Park *RMD* . . .**202** E12-13	Salish Plaza *CHL* **213** E6-7	Willowbrook Shopping Centre *LGT* . .
Coquitlam Plaza *CQT* **145** T37	Lonsdale Quay Market *CNV* . .**143** P16	Scottsdale Mall *DEL* **224** K30	. . . .**227** M47
Cottonwood Mall *CHL* **213** H-J6	Lougheed Mall *BUR* **164** W30	Semiahmoo *SUR* **265** W37	Woodwards *SUR* **185** C34
Countryside Mall *LGT* **249** T63	Lynn Valley Mall *DNV* **123** L19	Seven Oaks Shopping Centre *ABT* . . .	
Delta Fair Mall *DEL* **263** X17	Metropolis at Metrotown *BUR*	. . . .**250** U74	
Delta Shoppers Mall *DEL* . . .**204** H30	. . . .**163** Y22	Simon Centre *ABT* **250** T73	

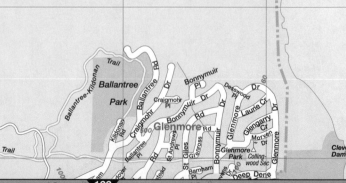

DISTRICT OF

WEST VANCOUVER

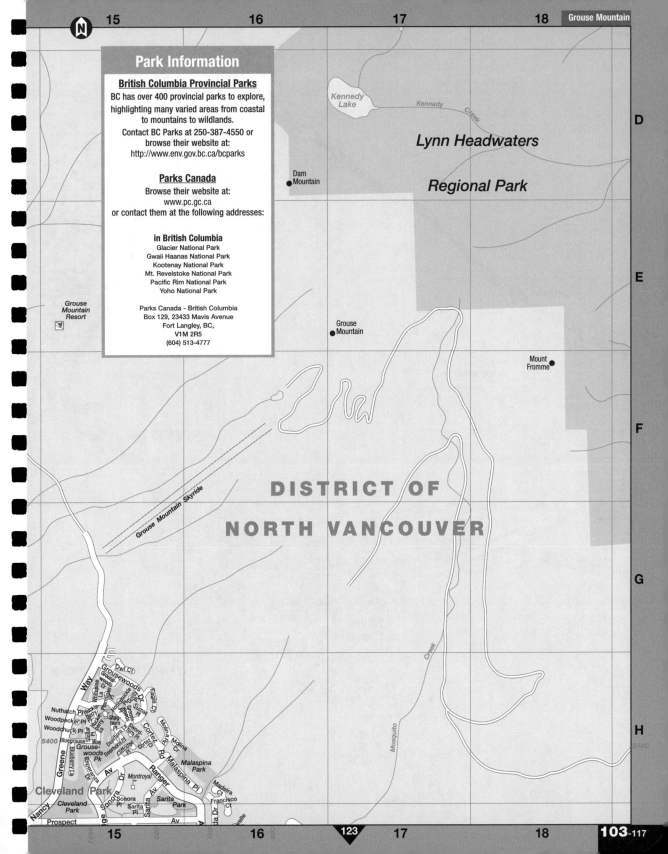

N

D

E

F

G

H

Park Information

British Columbia Provincial Parks

BC has over 400 provincial parks to explore, highlighting many varied areas from coastal to mountains to wildlands.

Contact BC Parks at 250-387-4550 or browse their website at:
http://www.env.gov.bc.ca/bcparks

Parks Canada

Browse their website at:
www.pc.gc.ca
or contact them at the following addresses:

in British Columbia
Glacier National Park
Gwaii Haanas National Park
Kootenay National Park
Mt. Revelstoke National Park
Pacific Rim National Park
Yoho National Park

Parks Canada - British Columbia
Box 129, 23433 Mavis Avenue
Fort Langley, BC,
V1M 2R5
(604) 513-4777

Kennedy Lake

Kennedy Creek

Lynn Headwaters

Regional Park

Dam Mountain

Grouse Mountain Resort

Grouse Mountain

Mount Fromme

Grouse Mountain Skyride

DISTRICT OF

NORTH VANCOUVER

Creek

Mosquito

Owl Ct
Grousewoods Dr
Way
Whitepine
Woods
Eagle Ct
Nuthatch Pl
Woodpecker Pl
Woodchuck Pl
5400
Bluegrouse
Grousewoods Pk
Greene
Blueberry Dr
Staghorn Pl
Sword
Deerhorn Pl
Moina Rd
Cortez Dr
Malaspina Pl
Malaspina Park
Ranger
Montroyal
Av
Madeira Ct
Francisco
Sonora Dr
Sarita Park
Cleveland Park
Nancy
Cleveland Park
Sonora Pl
Sarita Pl
Sarita Av
Prospect
Av

5400

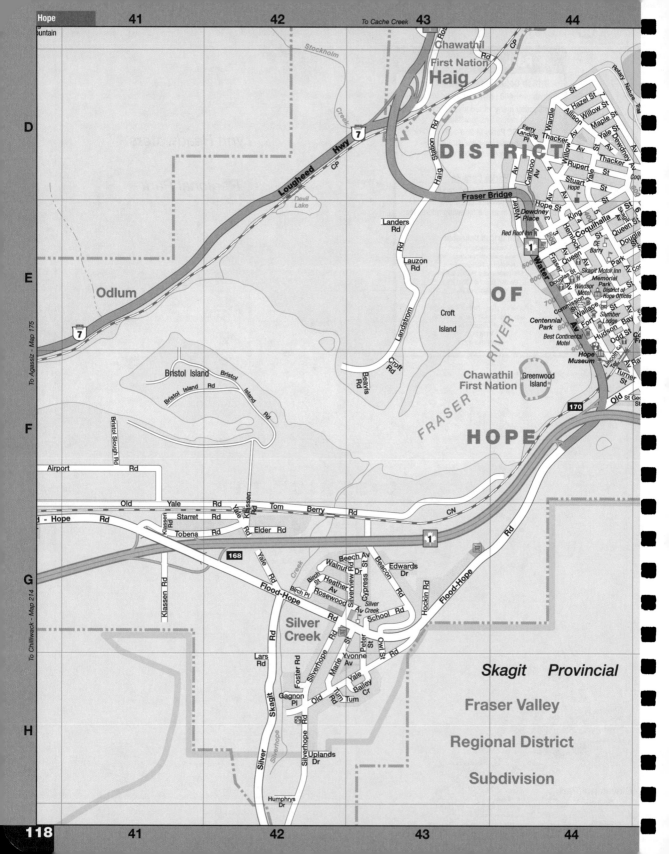

ountain

Stoeknholm

D

Chawathil
First Nation
Haig

Creek

7

Lougheed Hwy

CP

Station Rd

Haig Rd

Chawathil Rd

CP

Rotary Nature Trail

St

Hazel St

Allison St

Willow St

Maple St

Yale Av

Dewdney Av

Thacker Av

Thacker Av

Rupert St

Caribou Av

Ferry Landing Pl

Wardle St

Water

Hope St

Dewdney Place

Stuart Hope St

Yale St

DISTRICT

Coquihalla

King

Fraser Bridge

Landers Rd

Devil Lake

Rd

Lauzon Rd

Landstrom

Landstrom

Red Roof Inn

1

Water

Hemlock

Queen

Park

CE

Barry

Douglas St

Queen

Douglas

Skagit Motor Inn

Memorial Park

District of Hope Offices

E

Odlum

7

Croft Island

OF

Windsor Motel

Commission

Wallace

Ford

Hudson

Slumber Lodge Bay

Odd

Centennial Park

Best Continental Motel

Bristol Island

Bristol Island Rd

Bristol Island Rd

Bristol Island Rd

Beavis Rd

Croft Rd

RIVER

Hope Museum

Chawathil First Nation

Greenwood Island

Lincoln

Turner

Old St Geo St

F

Bristol Slough Rd

Airport Rd

FRASER

HOPE

170

To Agassiz - Map 175

Old Yale Rd

Klassen

Tom Berry Rd

CN

1

d - Hope Rd

Klassen Rd

Starret Rd

Tobena Rd

Yale

Klassen Rd

Elder Rd

Rd

168

Beech Av

Walnut

Silverview Rd

Beacon

Edwards Dr

Hockin Rd

Flood-Hope Rd

G

To Chilliwack - Map 214

Klassen Rd

Creek

Flood-Hope Rd

Birch St

Birch Pl

Heather Av

Rosewood

Cypress Av

Silver Creek School Rd

Silver Creek

Lars Rd

Foster Rd

Silverhope Rd

Marie St

Peter St

Owl St

Yvonne Av

Yale

Bailey Cr

Skagit Provincial

Fraser Valley

Skagit

Gagnon Pl

Old Rd

Tum Rd

Tum Tum

Regional District

H

Silver

Silverhope Rd

Uplands Dr

Subdivision

Humphrys Dr

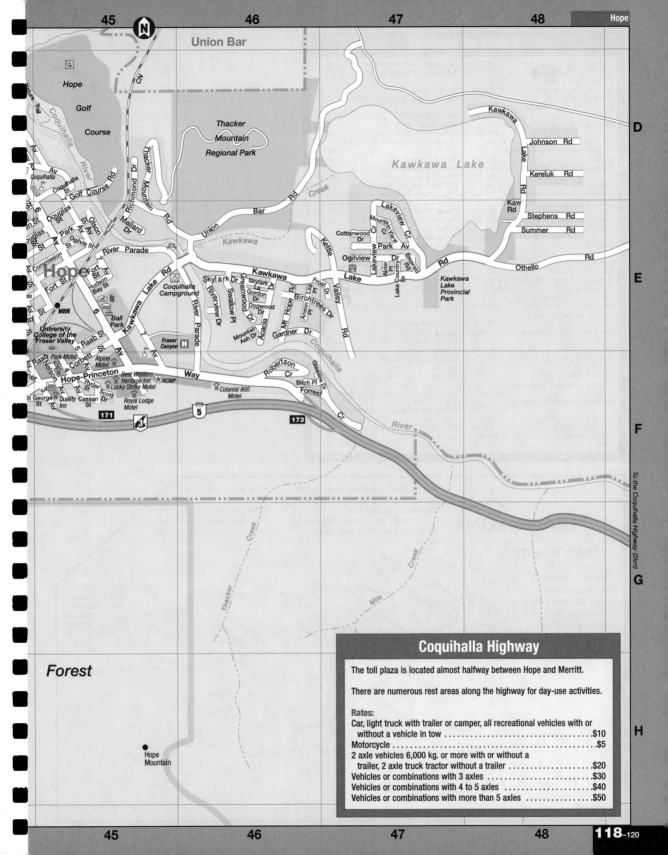

Coquihalla Highway

The toll plaza is located almost halfway between Hope and Merritt.

There are numerous rest areas along the highway for day-use activities.

Rates:
Car, light truck with trailer or camper, all recreational vehicles with or
   without a vehicle in tow $10
Motorcycle $5
2 axle vehicles 6,000 kg. or more with or without a
   trailer, 2 axle truck tractor without a trailer $20
Vehicles or combinations with 3 axles $30
Vehicles or combinations with 4 to 5 axles $40
Vehicles or combinations with more than 5 axles $50

Points of Interest

Atkinson Lighthouse *WVA* 121 M3
B.C. Place Stadium *VAN* 11 J38-39
Bentall Centre *VAN* 11 G37-38
Bloedel Conservatory *VAN* ..162 X14
Brockton Oval *VAN* 142 Q13
Burnaby Heritage Village & Carousel *BUR* 164 X24-25
Burnaby Lake Nature House *BUR* ....
..............................164 W27
Burnaby Sculpture Garden *BUR* 144 S27
Canada Games Pool & Fitness Cen. *NEW* 184 Z29
Canadian Lacrosse Hall of Fame *NEW* 184 Z29
Canada Place *VAN* 11 F39 142 R14
Capilano Salmon Hatchery *DNV* 122 J14
Capilano Suspension Bridge *DNV* .
..............................122 K14
Centennial Ecology Centre *DNV* 123 K21
Centennial Gardens & Pavillion *BUR* 144 S27
Chilliwack Exhibition Grounds *CHL* 213 E5-6
Chinatown *VAN* 11 H41
Cleveland Dam *DNV* 122 J14
Cloverdale Fairgrounds *SUR* 226 M42-43
Cloverdale Race Track *SUR* .226 M42-43
Cultus Lake Water Park *FRA* ..253 R5
Deep Cove Lookout *DNV* 124 M26
Dr. Sun Yat Sen Classical Chinese Garden *VAN* 11 H40
The Centre in Vancouver for Performing Arts *VAN* 11 H38
Gastown *VAN* 11 G40
Gastown Steam Clock *VAN* 11 G39
G.M. Place *VAN* 11 H39
Granville Island *VAN* 10 K35
Greater Vancouver Zoological Centre *LGT* 228 P60-61
Grouse Mountain Skyride *DNV* ......
.......................103 G15 F16
Harbour Centre *VAN* 11 G39
H.R. MacMillan Planetarium *VAN* 10 J34
HMCS Discovery Naval Training Station *VAN* 142 R13

Hyde Creek Nature Centre *CQT* 146 T41
International Boundary Monument *DEL* 262 Z15-16
Lumbermans Arch *VAN* 142 Q13
Lynn Canyon Suspension Bridge *DNV* .
.............................123 K21
Malkin Bowl *VAN* 142 Q12-13
Maplewood Farm *DNV* 143 P21
Miniature Railway *VAN* 142 Q12
Minnekhada Lodge & Nature Centre *CQT* 146 R45
Minter Gardens *FRA* 195 D20
Nat Bailey Stadium *VAN* 162 X14
Nine O'Clock Gun *VAN* 142 Q14
Old Hastings Mill Store *VAN* ..142 T8
Pacific Nat'l Exhibition Grounds *VAN* 143 S19-20
Pacific Space Centre *VAN* 10 J34
Pauline Johnson Memorial *VAN* 142 Q11
Pfitzer Bell Tower *MIS* 210 G77
Provincial Court House *VAN* ..11 H37
Queen Elizabeth Park *VAN* 162 X14
Rainforest Reptile Refuge *SUR* .266 X42
Richmond Oval *RMD* 202 E11
River Rock Casino *RMD* 182 C13
Robson Square *VAN* 11 H37
Royal City Star Riverboat Casino *NEW* 184 B29
S.S. Empress of Japan Figurehead *VAN* 142 Q13
Science World *VAN* 11 J40
Scotia Tower *VAN* 11 G37
Splashdown Park *DEL* 262 W15
Totem Poles *VAN* 142 Q13
UBC Botanical Garden Centre *UEL* ...
.............................161 V3-4
Vancouver Aquarium *VAN* ...142 Q13
Vancouver Aquatic Centre *VAN* .10 J35
Vancouver Convention & Exhibition Centre *VAN* 11 F38-39
VanDusen Botanical Garden *VAN* .....
..............................162 X12-13
West End *VAN* 10 F35

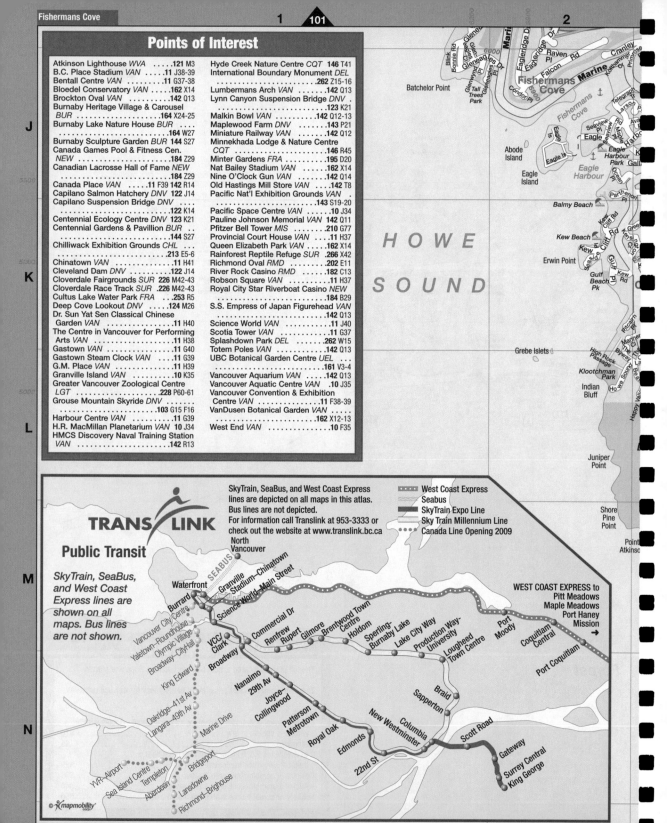

HOWE SOUND

TRANS LINK
Public Transit

SkyTrain, SeaBus, and West Coast Express lines are shown on all maps. Bus lines are not shown.

SkyTrain, SeaBus, and West Coast Express lines are depicted on all maps in this atlas. Bus lines are not depicted.
For information call Translink at 953-3333 or check out the website at www.translink.bc.ca

West Coast Express
Seabus
SkyTrain Expo Line
Sky Train Millennium Line
Canada Line Opening 2009

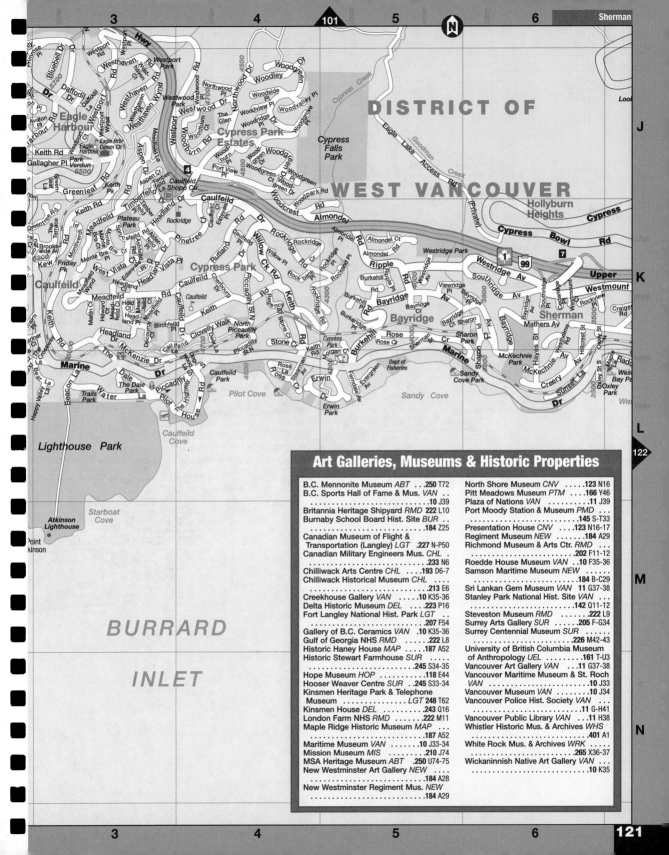

DISTRICT OF

WEST VANCOUVER

Art Galleries, Museums & Historic Properties

B.C. Mennonite Museum *ABT* . . .**250** T72
B.C. Sports Hall of Fame & Mus. *VAN* . .
. . . .**10** J39
Britannia Heritage Shipyard *RMD* **222** L10
Burnaby School Board Hist. Site *BUR* . .
. . . .**184** Z25
Canadian Museum of Flight &
 Transportation (Langley) *LGT* **227** N-P50
Canadian Military Engineers Mus. *CHL* .
. . . .**233** N6
Chilliwack Arts Centre *CHL* **193** D6-7
Chilliwack Historical Museum *CHL* . . . .
. . . .**213** E6
Creekhouse Gallery *VAN* **10** K35-36
Delta Historic Museum *DEL* **223** P16
Fort Langley National Hist. Park *LGT* . .
. . . .**207** F54
Gallery of B.C. Ceramics *VAN* .**10** K35-36
Gulf of Georgia NHS *RMD* **222** L8
Historic Haney House *MAP* **187** A52
Historic Stewart Farmhouse *SUR* . . . . .
. . . .**245** S34-35
Hope Museum *HOP* **118** E44
Hooser Weaver Centre *SUR* . .**245** S33-34
Kinsmen Heritage Park & Telephone
 Museum . . . .*LGT* **248** T62
Kinsmen House *DEL* **243** O16
London Farm NHS *RMD* **222** M11
Maple Ridge Historic Museum *MAP* . . . .
. . . .**187** A52
Maritime Museum *VAN* **10** J33-34
Mission Museum *MIS* **210** J74
MSA Heritage Museum *ABT* .**250** U74-75
New Westminster Art Gallery *NEW* . . . .
. . . .**184** A28
New Westminster Regiment Mus. *NEW* .
. . . .**184** A29

North Shore Museum *CNV* **123** N16
Pitt Meadows Museum *PTM* . . .**166** Y46
Plaza of Nations *VAN* **11** J39
Port Moody Station & Museum *PMD* . . .
. . . .**145** S-T33
Presentation House *CNV* . . .**123** N16-17
Regiment Museum *NEW* **184** A29
Richmond Museum & Arts Ctr. *RMD* . . .
. . . .**202** F11-12
Roedde House Museum *VAN* . .**10** F35-36
Samson Maritime Museum *NEW* . . . . . .
. . . .**184** B-C29
Sri Lankan Gem Museum *VAN* **11** G37-38
Stanley Park National Hist. Site *VAN* . . .
. . . .**142** O11-12
Steveston Museum *RMD* **222** L9
Surrey Arts Gallery *SUR* **205** F-G34
Surrey Centennial Museum *SUR* . . . . . .
. . . .**226** M42-43
University of British Columbia Museum
 of Anthropology *UEL* **161** T-U3
Vancouver Art Gallery *VAN* . . .**11** G37-38
Vancouver Maritime Museum & St. Roch
 VAN **10** J33
Vancouver Museum *VAN* **10** J34
Vancouver Police Hist. Society *VAN* . . .
. . . .**11** G-H41
Vancouver Public Library *VAN* . .**11** H38
Whistler Historic Mus. & Archives *WHS* .
. . . .**401** A1
White Rock Mus. & Archives *WRK* . . . .
. . . .**265** X36-37
Wickaninnish Native Art Gallery *VAN* . . .
. . . .**10** K35

BURRARD

INLET

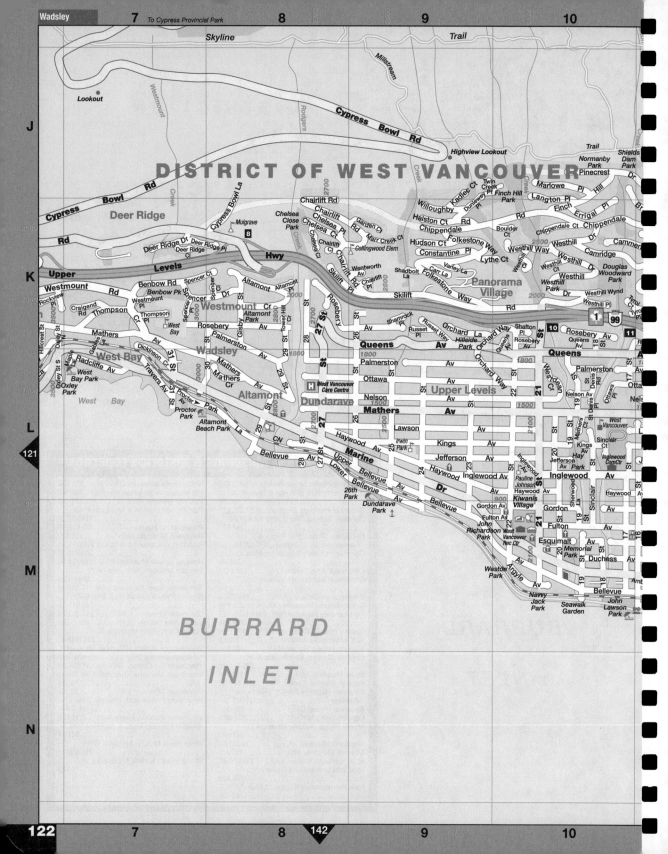

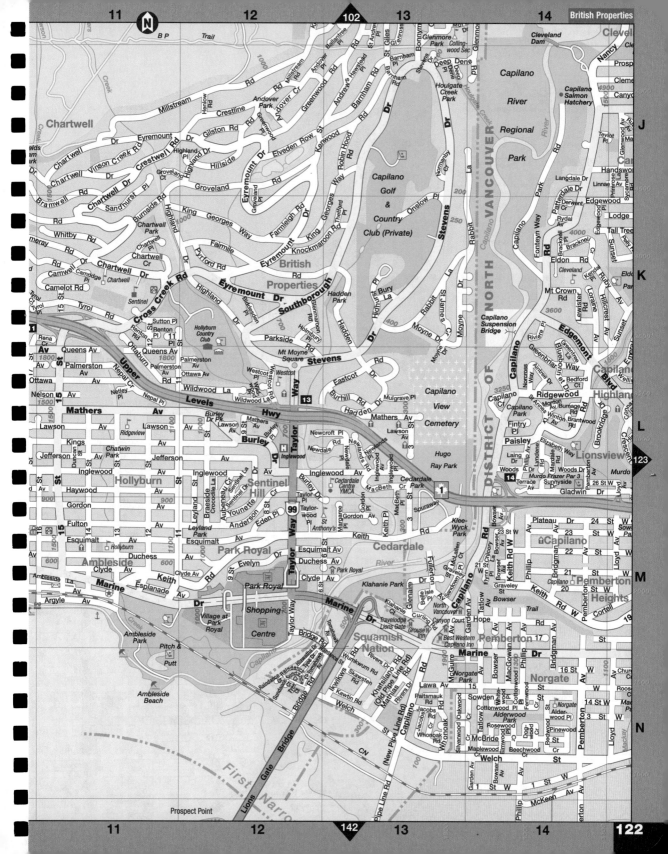

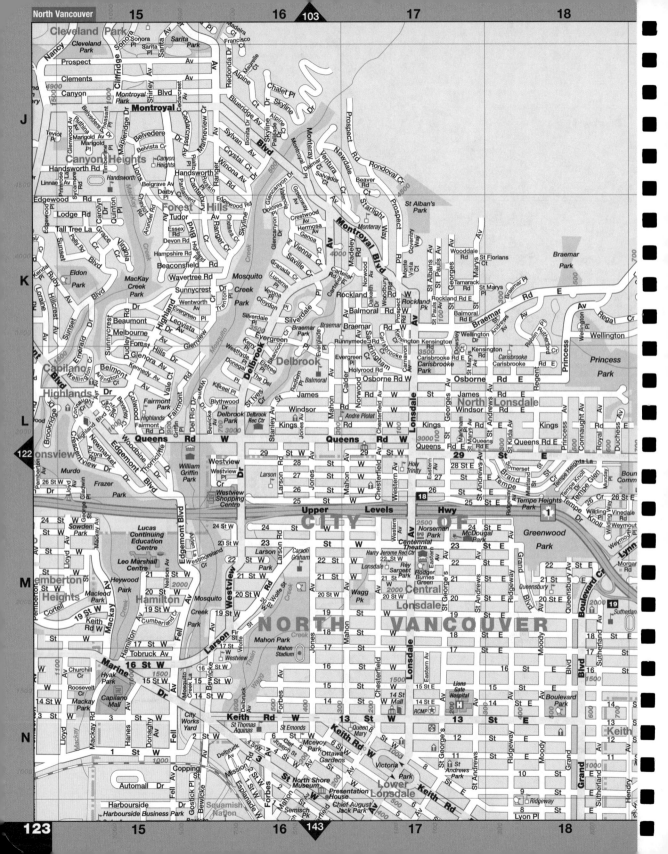

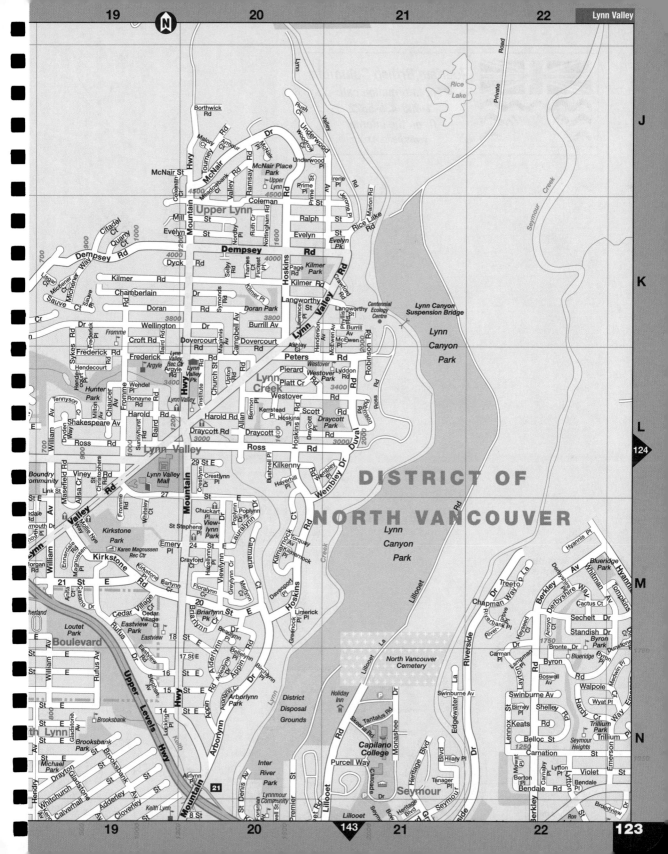

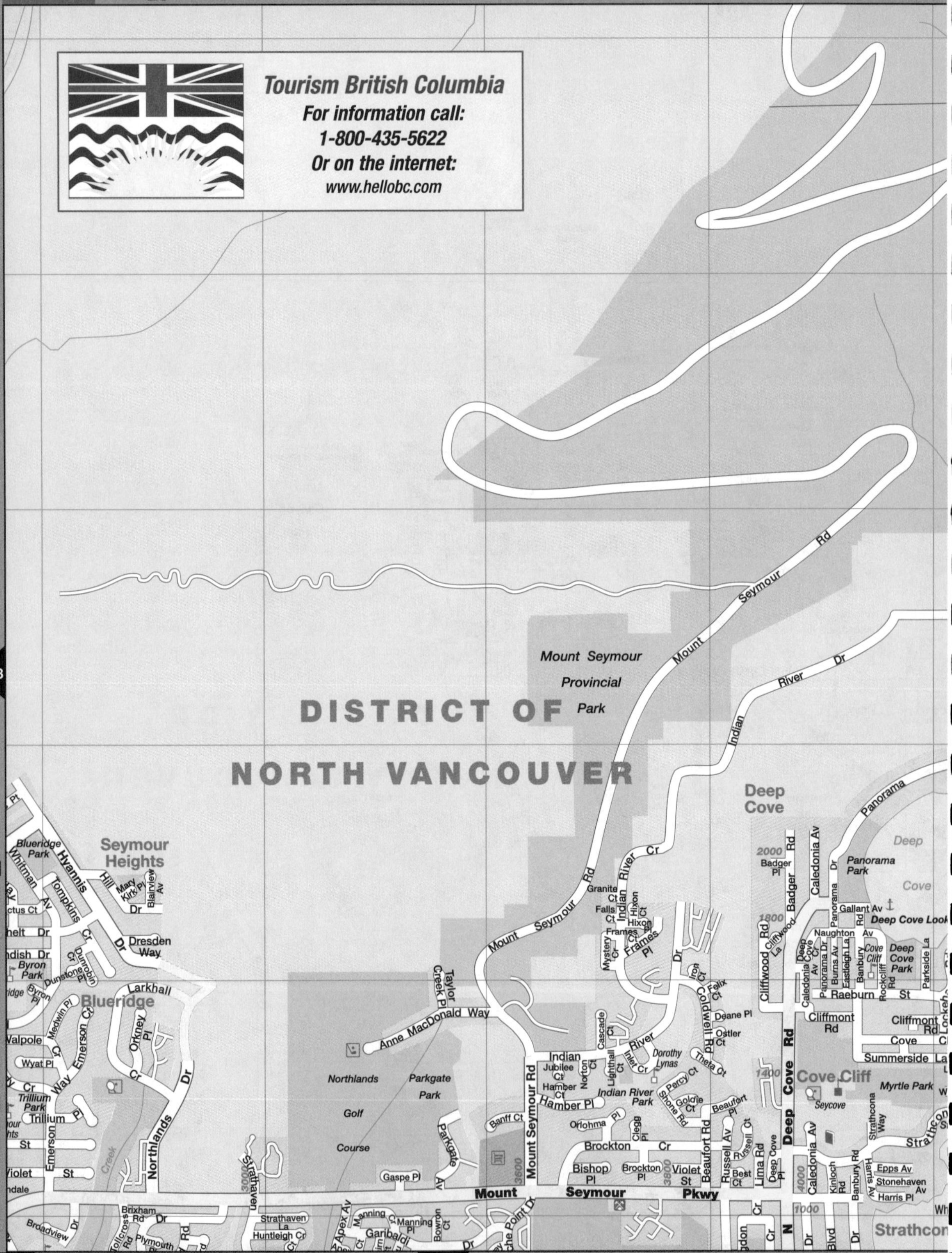

J

K

L

Mount Seymour

Provincial Park

DISTRICT OF

NORTH VANCOUVER

Deep Cove

Deep

Cove

M

Seymour Heights

Blueridge Park

Whitman

Hyannis

Mary Kirk Pl

Blairview Av

Hill

Tompkins

Dr

Cactus Ct

Dresden Way

Dunstone

Candish Dr

Byron Park

Byron

Larkhall

Blueridge

Medkin Pl

Emerson

Okhney

Pl

Dr

Walpole

Wyat Pl

Way

Cr

Cr

Trillium Park

Trillium

Emerson St

Northlands

Violet St

Strathaven

Broadview

Dr

Brixham Dr

Strathaven

Huntleigh Cr

Apex Av

Manning

Manning Pl

Garibaldi

Bowman

The Point Dr

Follcross Rd

Plymouth Dr

Ann

N

Northlands

Golf

Course

Parkgate Park

Anne MacDonald Way

Taylor Creek Dr

Gaspe Pl

Banff Ct

Parkgate

Mount Seymour Rd

3600

Granite Ct

Falls

Indian River Cr

Mystery Cr

Frames

Hixon Ct

Frames

Dr

Indian

Jubilee Ct

Hamber Ct

Hamber Pl

Norton

Lighthart

Cascade

Deane Pl

Ostler

Felix Ct

Theta Ct

Dorothy Lynas

Percy Ct

Goldie

Beaufort

Indian River Park

Oriohma

Pl

Shone Rd

Brockton

Cr

Bishop Pl

Brockton Pl

Violet St

Beaufort Rd

Russell St

Russell Ct

Best Ct

Lima Rd

Deep

Mount   Seymour   Pkwy

3800

Seymour Rd

Mount

Deep Cove Rd

Caledonia Av

2000

Badger Pl

1800

Cliffwood Rd

Cliffwood

Naughton Av

Burns Av

Panorama Dr

Eastleigh La

Caledonia

Av

Deep Cove

Cove Cliff

Rockcliff Rd

Raeburn

Cliffmont Rd

Deep Cove Park

Panorama

Panorama Park

Gallant Av

Deep Cove Look

Deep Cove

Cliffmont Rd

Cove

Summerside La

Myrtle Park

Seycove

Strathcona Way

Cove Cliff

Caledonia Av

1400

Kinloch Rd

Banbury Rd

Harris Pl

Harris Rd

Epps Av

Stonehaven Av

Strathco

Strathcon

Parkside La

Locke

4000

1000

N Dr

Blvd

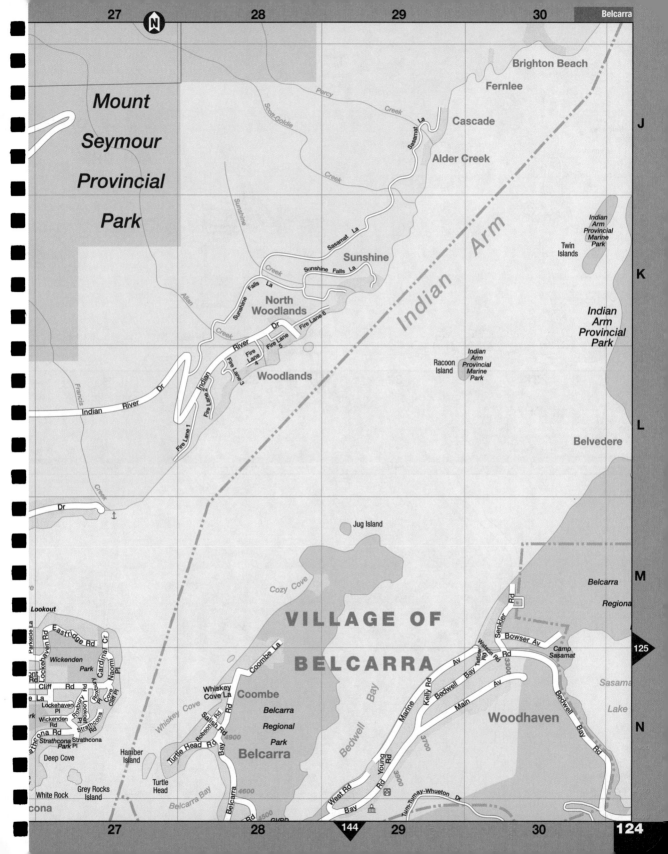

Mount

Seymour

Provincial

Park

Brighton Beach

Fernlee

Cascade

Alder Creek

Percy

Creek

Scott-Goldie

Sasamat La

J

Creek

Sunshine

Sasamat La

Sunshine

Sunshine Falls La

Indian Arm

Indian
Arm
Provincial
Marine
Park

Twin
Islands

K

North
Woodlands

Fire Lane 6

Fire Lane 5

Fire Lane 4

Woodlands

Indian
Arm
Provincial
Park

River

Dr

Indian

River

Racoon
Island

Indian
Arm
Provincial
Marine
Park

Allen

Creek

Sunshine Falls La

Fire Lane 3

Fire Lane 2

Fire Lane 1

Indian River

Francis

Creek

L

Belvedere

Creek

Dr

Jug Island

Cozy Cove

M

Belcarra

Regional

125

Lookout

Eastridge Rd

Parkside Rd

Lockehaven Rd

Wickenden
Park

Cardinal Cr

Naomi
Pl

Cove Cliff Pl

Cliff Rd

Lookout Rd

Roxbury

Strathcona

ont
Rd

Cliff
La

Lockehaven
Pl

Wickenden
Rd

Strathcona Rd

thcona Rd

Strathcona
Park Pl

Strathcona Rd

Deep Cove

Hamber
Island

Grey Rocks
Island

White Rock

cona

VILLAGE OF

BELCARRA

Coombe La

Whiskey
Cove La

Coombe

Belcarra

Regional

Park

Belcarra

Whiskey Cove

Salish Rd

Robson Rd

Turtle Head

Bay

4900

Turtle
Head

Belcarra Rd

Belcarra Bay

4600

4500

GVRD

Bedwell Bay

West Rd

Bay

Young Rd

Marine Av

Bedwell Bay Rd

Kelly Rd

Main Av

Tatlow Av

3700

3900

3000

Tum-Tumay-Whueton Dr

Senkler Rd

Watson Rd

Bowser Av

Camp
Sasamat

3300

Bedwell Bay Rd

Woodhaven

Belcarra

Regiona

Sasama

Lake

N

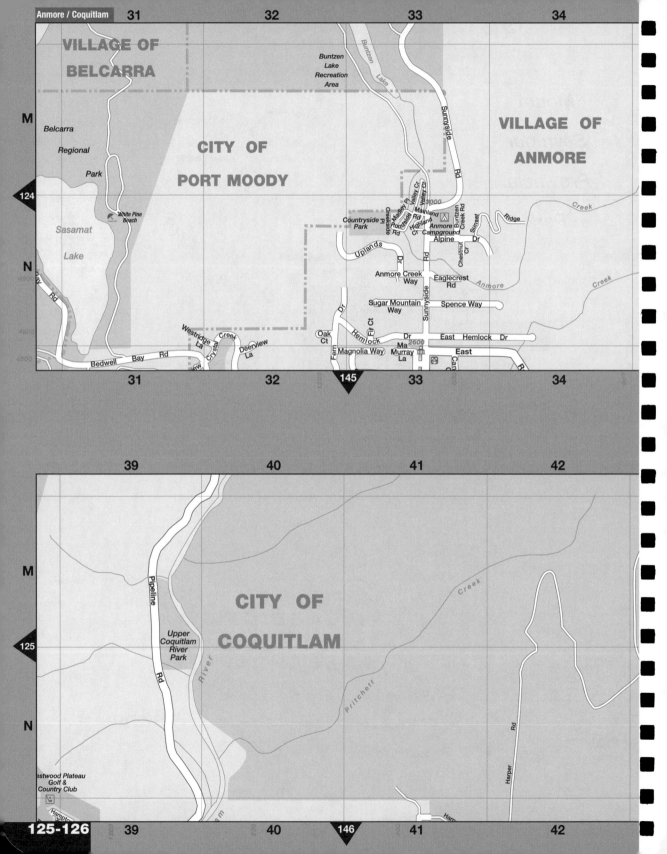

VILLAGE OF
BELCARRA

Buntzen
Lake
Recreation
Area

VILLAGE OF

ANMORE

M

Belcarra

Regional

Park

White Pine
Beach

124

CITY OF
PORT MOODY

Sasamat

Lake

N

Creek

Countryside
Park

Anmore
Campground
Alpine

Ridge

Bay Rd

Uplands

Anmore Creek
Way

Sugar Mountain
Way

Eaglecrest
Rd

Spence Way

Anmore

Creek

Westridge
La

Crystal Creek

Deerview
La

Bedwell Bay Rd

Fern Dr

Hemlock Dr

Oak
Ct

Fir Ct

Dr

Magnolia Way

Sunnyside

East Hemlock Dr

Ma
Murray
La

East

31   32   145   33   34

39   40   41   42

M

CITY OF

COQUITLAM

Creek

125

Pipeline Rd

Upper
Coquitlam
River Park

River

Pritchett

N

Harper Rd

Westwood Plateau
Golf &
Country Club

Hampton

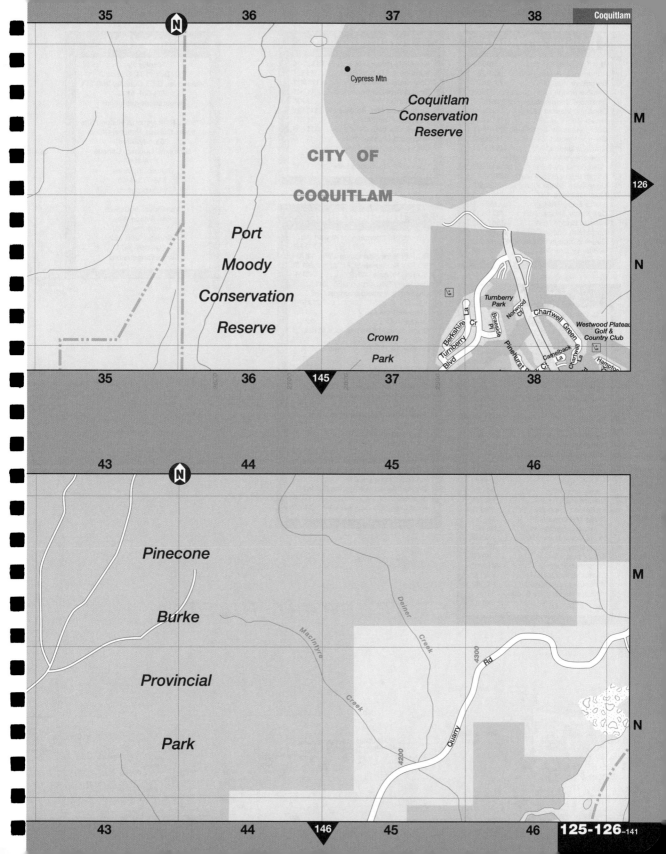

CITY OF

COQUITLAM

Coquitlam
Conservation
Reserve

Cypress Mtn

Port

Moody

Conservation

Reserve

Crown

Park

Turnberry
Park

Berkshire La
Turnberry
Blvd

Cr

Braeside Pl

Norwood Ct

Chartwell Green

Pinehurst

Camelback La

Chartwell La

Westwood Plateau
Golf &
Country Club

Hampton

M

126

N

35   36   37   38

35   36   145   37   38

43   44   45   46

Pinecone

Burke

Provincial

Park

Delner

Creek

Creek

MacIntyre

4300 Rd

Quarry

4200

M

N

43   44   146   45   46

Bridges & Tunnels

Alex Fraser Bridge *DEL* **204** G27
Arthur Laing Bridge *RMD* .**182** B-C12
Burrard Bridge *VAN* **10** J34-35
Cambie Bridge *VAN* **11** K38
Dinsmore Bridge *RMD* **202** E11
Dunsmuir Viaduct *VAN* ...**11** H39-40
Fraser Bridge *HOP* **118** D43-44
George Massey Tunnel *DEL* **223** L16-17
Georgia Viaduct *VAN* **11** H39-40
Granville Bridge *VAN* **10** K35-36
Ironworkers Memorial Bridge
 (Second Narrows Bridge) *DNV* **143** Q-R20
Knight Street Bridge *RMD* .**183** B16-17
Lions Gate Bridge *WVA* **122** N12
Mission Bridge *ABT* **230** K-L74
Moray Bridge *RMD* **182** C12
Oak Street Bridge *RMD* ...**182** B-C13
Pattullo Bridge *NEW* **184** A-B30
Port Mann Bridge *CQT* **185** Z36
Queensborough Bridge *NEW* .**184** C26
Vedder Bridge *CHL* **233** N6

Performing Arts

Arts Club Theatre *VAN* **10** K35-36
Burnaby Art Centre *BUR* **164** X24
Centennial Theatre *CNV* ..**123** M17
Firehall Arts Centre *VAN* **11** H41
Ford Centre *VAN* **11** H38
North Shore Film Studios *CNV* **143** P19
Orpheum, The *VAN* **11** H37
Queen Elizabeth Centre *VAN* ..**11** H38
Starboard Theatres *VAN* **11** F39
Surrey Arts Centre Theatre *SUR* ....
 ....**205** G34
Vancouver Playhouse *VAN* **11** H39

Transportation

Abbotsford International Airport *ABT* .
 ....**270** X71
BC Rail North Vancouver *DNV* **122** N14
BC Rail Squamish *SQM* **301** G1
BC Rail Whistler *WHS* **401** H1
Boundary Bay Airport *DEL* **243** R21-22
Chilliwack Municipal Airport *CHL* ....
 ....**213** G7-8
Delta Air Park *DEL* **244** R27
Deltaport *DEL* **262** U13
Granville Island Ferries *VAN* **10** H34 J35
Heliport *VAN* **11** F-G39
Horseshoe Bay Ferry Terminal *WVA* ..
 ....**101** G2
Langley Airport *LGT* **227** N50
Pitt Meadows Airport *PTM* ..**186** Z44
Roberts Bank Superport *DEL* **262** W12
SeaBus Terminal North Shore *CNV* ..
 ....**143** P16
SeaBus Terminal Vancouver *VAN* ...
 ....**11** F39
Squamish Airport *SQM* **301** A4
Tsawwassen Ferry Terminal *DEL* ....
 ....**262** Z13
Vancouver International Airport *RMD* ..
 ....**182** D8-10
VIA Rail Chilliwack *CHL* **213** F7
VIA Rail Vancouver (Pacific Central
 Station) *VAN* **11** J41
West Coast Air Terminal *VAN* ..**11** F37

Stanley Park

Stanley Park
P.O. Box 1134, Station A
Vancouver, B.C., Canada, V6C 2T1
604-681-5115
www.stanleypark.com

Stanley Park National Historic Site
Parks Canada National Office
25 Eddy Street
Gatineau, Quebec, Canada
K1A 0M5
General Inquiries:
888-773-8888
www.pc.gc.ca

Vancouver Aquarium
845 Avison Way
Vancouver, B.C.
Canada, V6G 3E2
604-659-3474
www.vanaqua.org

Hospitals

B.C. Children's *VAN* **162** W13
Burnaby General *BUR* **163** W21
Carleton *BUR* **163** W21
Chilliwack (General) *CHL* ..**213** E-F6
Delta *DEL* **243** Q18
Eagle Ridge *PMD* **145** S36
Fraser Canyon *HOP* **118** E45-46
George Derby Long Care Centre
 BUR **164** X28
George Pearson Centre *VAN* .**182** Z13
Grace *VAN* **162** W13
Inglewood *WVA* **122** L12
Ladner *DEL* **224** P25
Langley Memorial *LGT* **227** P51
Lions Gate *CNV* **123** N17
Maple Ridge *MAP* **187** Z50
Mission General *MIS* **210** J72
Mount St. Joseph *VAN* ...**163** V15
MSA General *ABT* **270** V75
Peace Arch *WRK* **265** W38
Queens Park *NEW* **184** Z30
Richmond General *RMD* ...**202** F11
Ridge Meadows *MAP* **187** Z50
Riverview Psychiatric *CQT* .**165** W37
Royal Columbian *NEW* **164** Y30
Saint Mary's *NEW* **184** A29
Saint Pauls *VAN* **10** H36
Squamish *SQM* **301** H2-3
Surrey Memorial *SUR* **205** E34
Vancouver General *VAN* ...**162** U13
Whistler Health Care Centre *WHS* ...
 ....**401** A1

Siwash

The Ferguson
Point Tea
House

BURRARD INLET

SEE ENLARGEMENT PAGES 10-11

Locarno
Beach
Jericho Sailing
School
Locarno
Beach Pk
Trimble St
Hostelling
Int'l
Jericho Beach
Park
Discovery St
Royal
Vancouver
Yacht Club
Kitsila
Bea
Simpson Av
Belmont Av
Locarno
Park
Langara Av
Marine Dr
Sasamat St
Bellevue Dr
Jericho
Beach
Old Hastings
Mill Store
Hastings
Mill Park
Point Grey Rd
Cornwa
Pt Grey Rd
Bellevue Dr
Aberthau
Cultural Centre
at Aberthau
W4100
Jericho
Park East
Point
Grey
Rd
Grey
Rd
Point
Grey
Rd
Volunteer
Park
Tatlow
Park
Kitsilano
Tolmie
Av
Trimble
Locarno Crescent
Nautilus
2 Av W
Wallace St
Highbury St
Alma St
W3600
Point Grey
Waterloo St
Av
W
Av
W
W2700
W
4
W
1700
1800
1900
W3400
W3000
W2400
2700

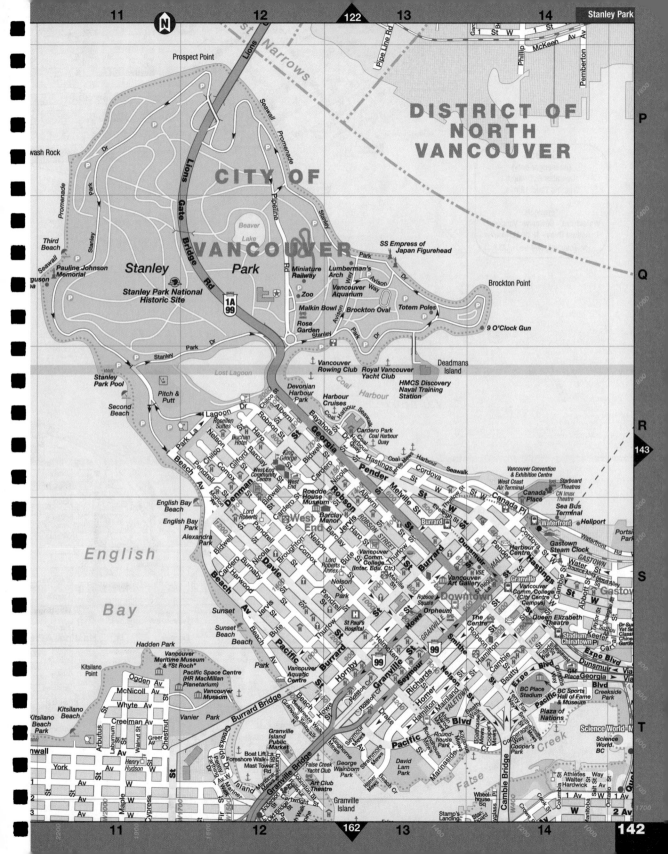

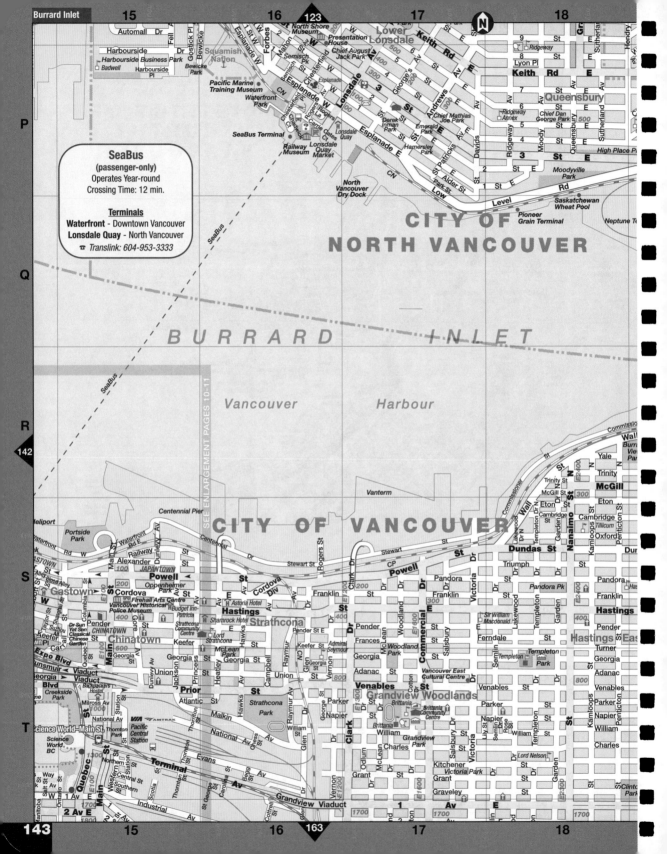

SeaBus
(passenger-only)
Operates Year-round
Crossing Time: 12 min.

Terminals
Waterfront - Downtown Vancouver
Lonsdale Quay - North Vancouver
☎ Translink: 604-953-3333

P

Q

R
142

S

T

**CITY OF
NORTH VANCOUVER**

B U R R A R D   I N L E T

Vancouver   Harbour

CITY OF VANCOUVER

SEE ENLARGEMENT PAGES 10-11

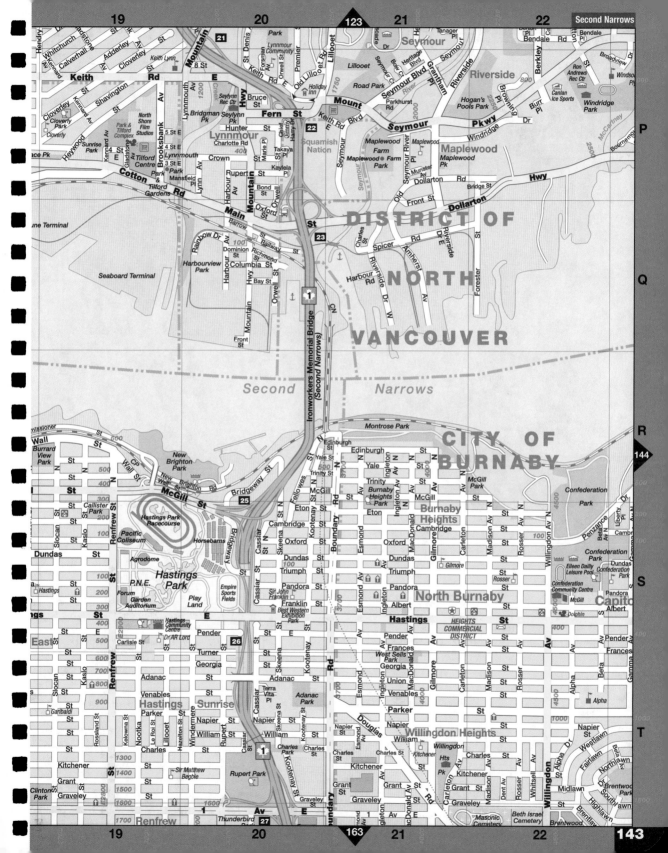

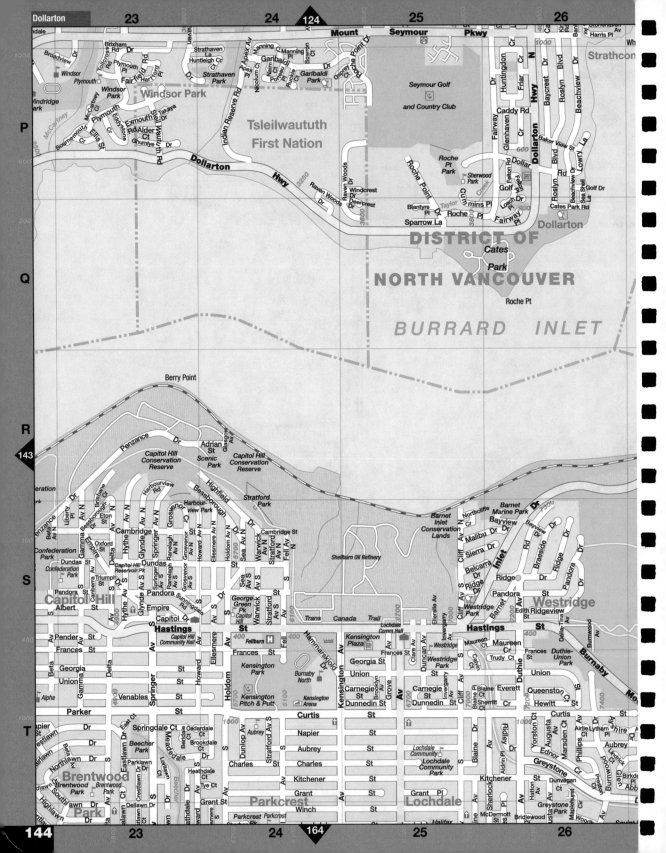

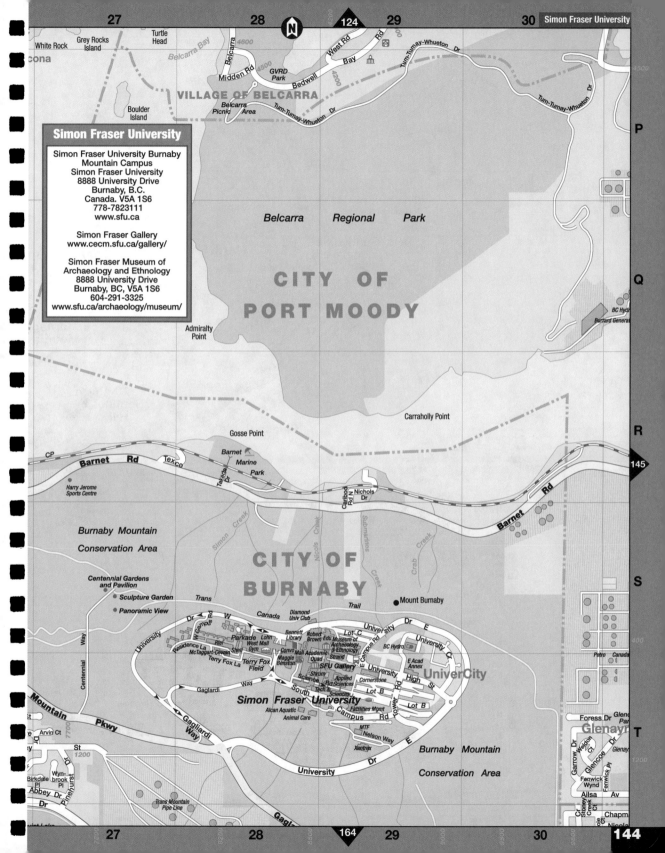

Simon Fraser University

Simon Fraser University Burnaby
Mountain Campus
Simon Fraser University
8888 University Drive
Burnaby, B.C.
Canada. V5A 1S6
778-7823111
www.sfu.ca

Simon Fraser Gallery
www.cecm.sfu.ca/gallery/

Simon Fraser Museum of
Archaeology and Ethnology
8888 University Drive
Burnaby, BC, V5A 1S6
604-291-3325
www.sfu.ca/archaeology/museum/

White Rock
Grey Rocks Island
Turtle Head
Belcarra Bay
Belcarra
Midden Rd
GVRD Park
Bedwell
Bay
West Rd
Tum-Tumay-Whueton Dr
cona

VILLAGE OF BELCARRA
Belcarra Picnic Area
Boulder Island
Tum-Tumay-Whueton Dr
Tum-Tumay-Whueton Dr

Belcarra   Regional   Park

CITY OF
PORT MOODY

P

Q
BC Hydro
Burrard Generat

Admiralty Point

Carraholly Point

R
145

Gosse Point
Barnet
Marine
Park
CP
Barnet   Rd   Texco
Takeda Dr
Cariboo Rd N
Nichols Dr
Barnet   Rd

Harry Jerome Sports Centre

Burnaby Mountain
Conservation Area

S

Simon Creek
Nichols Creek
Submarine Creek
Crab Creek

CITY OF
BURNABY

Centennial Gardens and Pavilion
Sculpture Garden
Panoramic View
Mount Burnaby

Trans
Canada
Trail
University
Dr
E

Diamond Univ Club
Lot C
University
BC Hydro
E Acad Annex
Petro Canada

Dr W
Campus
Rief
Residence La
McTaggart-Cowan
Terry Fox La
Parkade
Lohn
West Mall
Shell
Convo Mall
Maggie Benston
Terry Fox Field
Bennett Library
Robert Brown
Edu
Museum of Archaeology & Ethnology
Strand
SFU Gallery
Shrum
Academic Quad
Applied Sciences
Tech 2
Science
Applied Sciences
Cornerstone
Lot B
Lot B
High St
E Campus Rd
University
University Cr
UniverCity

Way
Gaglardi
Way
South
Campus
Rd
Simon Fraser University
Alcan Aquatic
Animal Care
Facilities Mgmt
Tower Rd

Foress Dr
Glen
Par
Glenayr

Mountain
Pkwy
Arvin Ct
St
Gagliardi
Way
MTF
Nelson Way
Xantrex
Burnaby Mountain
Conservation Area

Garrow Dr
Weldon Ct
Glencoe Ct
Glenay
Fenwick Wynd
Fenwick Pl
Ailsa

Birkdale Pl
Wyn-brook Pl
Pinehurst
Abbey Dr
Dr
Trans Mountain Pipe Line
University
Dr
Gagl

Cr
Stoney Creek
Ct
Chapm
Nicola
Av

Centennial   Way

Gaglardi

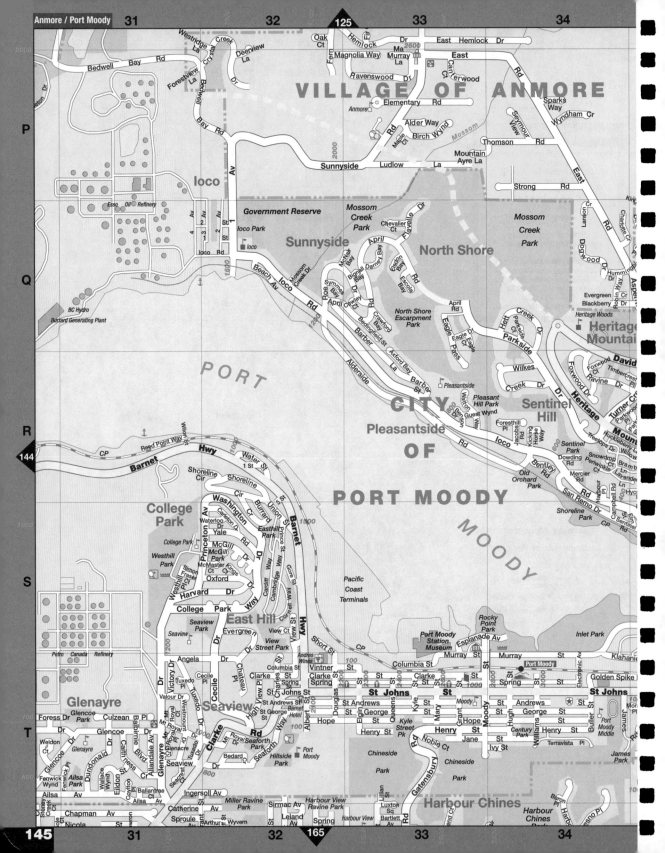

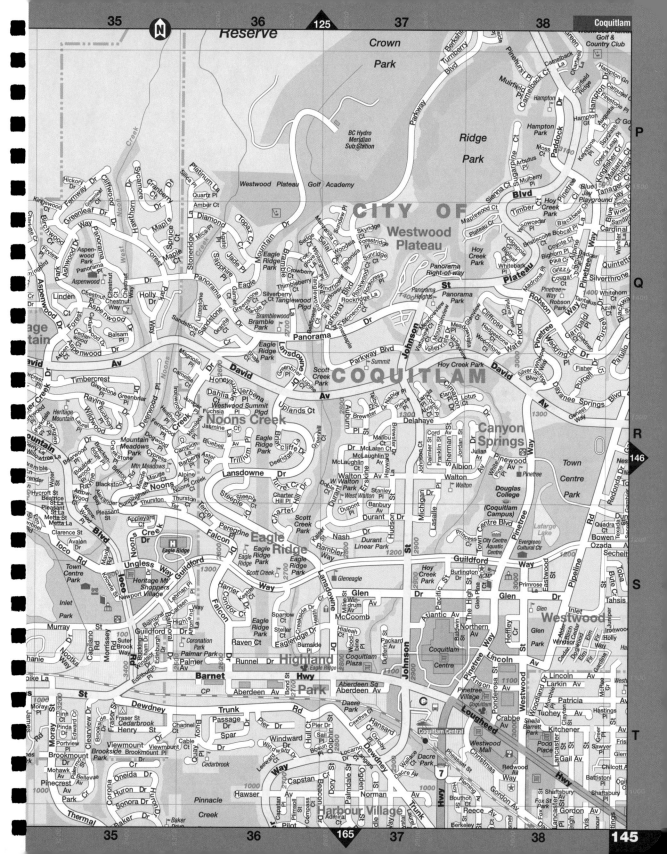

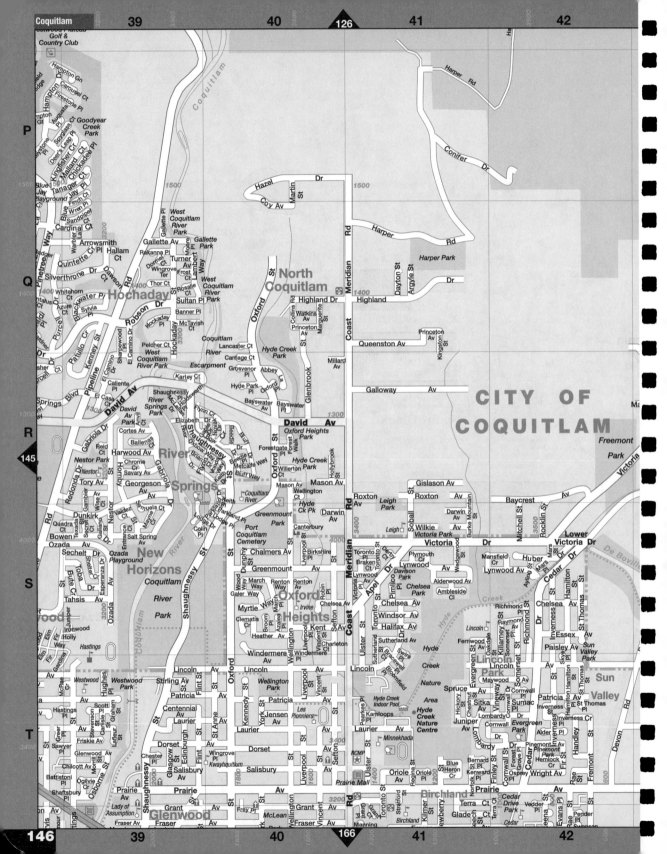

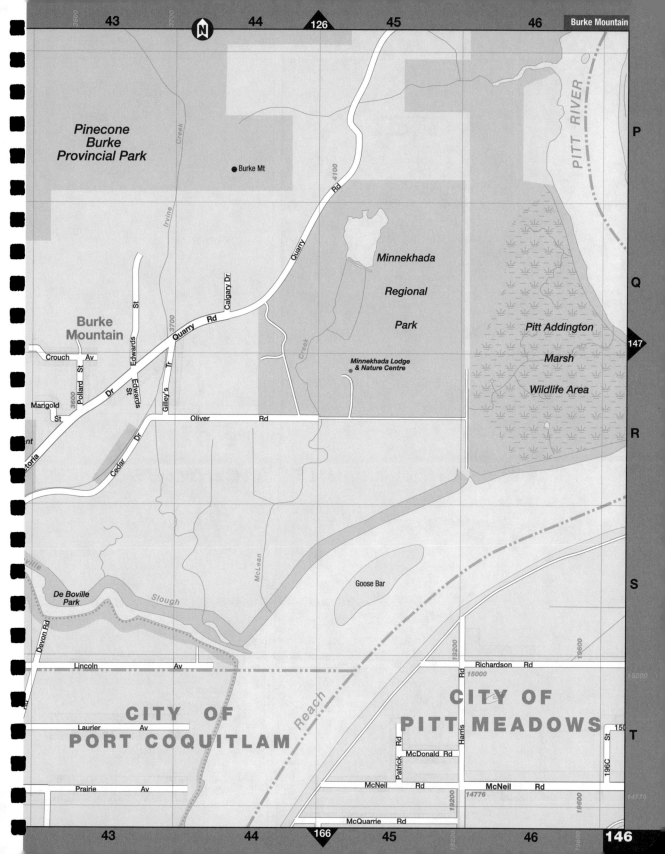

N

P

Pinecone Burke Provincial Park

PITT RIVER

● Burke Mt

Creek

Irvine

Quarry Rd

4100

Minnekhada

Regional

Park

Q

147

Pitt Addington

Marsh

Wildlife Area

Burke Mountain

Edwards St

3700

Quarry Tr

Calgary Dr

Gilley's Tr

Rd

Crouch Av

Pollard St

3600

Edwards Dr

Edwards St

Marigold St

Creek

Minnekhada Lodge
& Nature Centre

ent

toria

Cedar Dr

Oliver Rd

R

McLean

De Boville Park

Boville

Slough

Goose Bar

S

Devon Rd

Lincoln Av

19200

Richardson Rd

15000

19600

5000

Reach

CITY OF PITT MEADOWS

Harris Rd

CITY OF PORT COQUITLAM

Laurier Av

Patrick Rd

McDonald Rd

196C St

150

T

Prairie Av

McNeil Rd

McNeil Rd

19200

14776

19600

14776

McQuarrie Rd

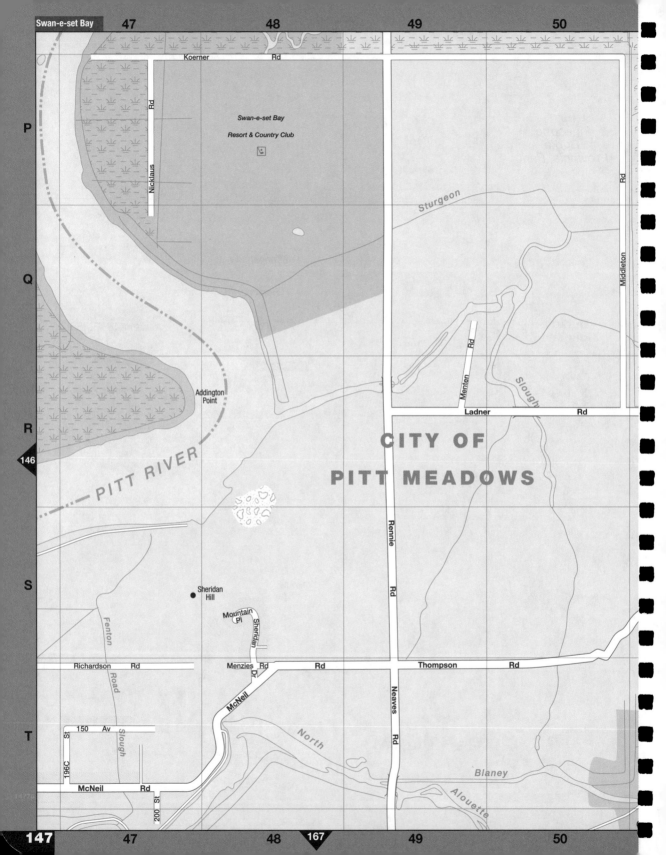

47   48   49   50

Koerner   Rd

P

Rd

Swan-e-set Bay

Resort & Country Club

Nicklaus

Sturgeon

Rd

Q

Middleton

Menten   Rd

Slough

Addington
Point

Ladner   Rd

R

146

PITT RIVER

CITY OF

PITT MEADOWS

Rennie

Rd

S

Sheridan
Hill

Fenton

Mountain
Pl

Sheridan Dr

Richardson   Rd

Road

Menzies   Rd   Rd

Thompson   Rd

Neaves

Rd

McNeil

150   Av

St

Slough

North

T

196C St

McNeil   Rd

200 St

Blaney

Alouette

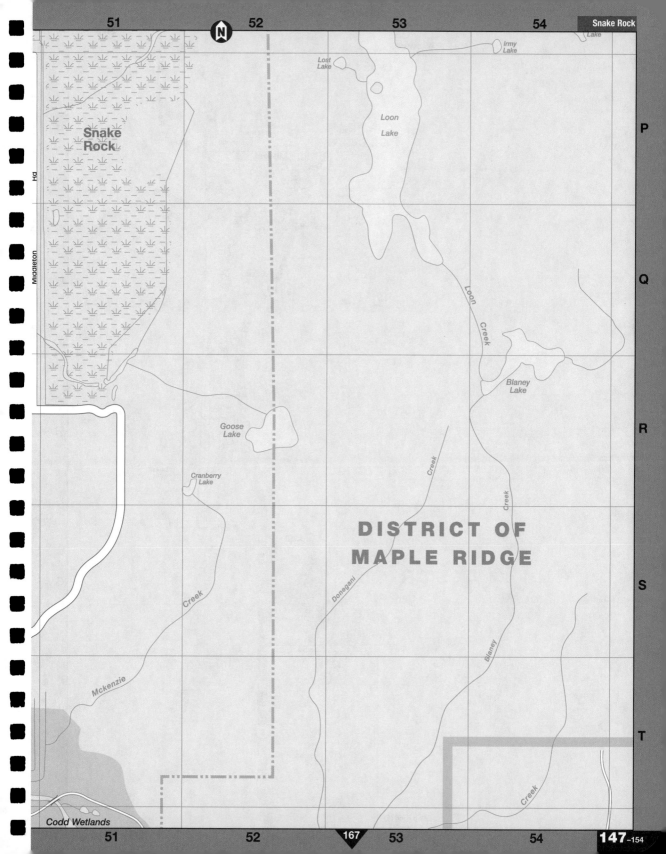

51 52 53 54

P

Q

R

S

T

Snake Rock

Lost Lake

Irmy Lake

Lake

Loon Lake

Loon Creek

Blaney Lake

Goose Lake

Creek

Creek

Cranberry Lake

DISTRICT OF MAPLE RIDGE

Donegeni

Blaney

Creek

Mckenzie

Creek

Codd Wetlands

Ha

Middleton

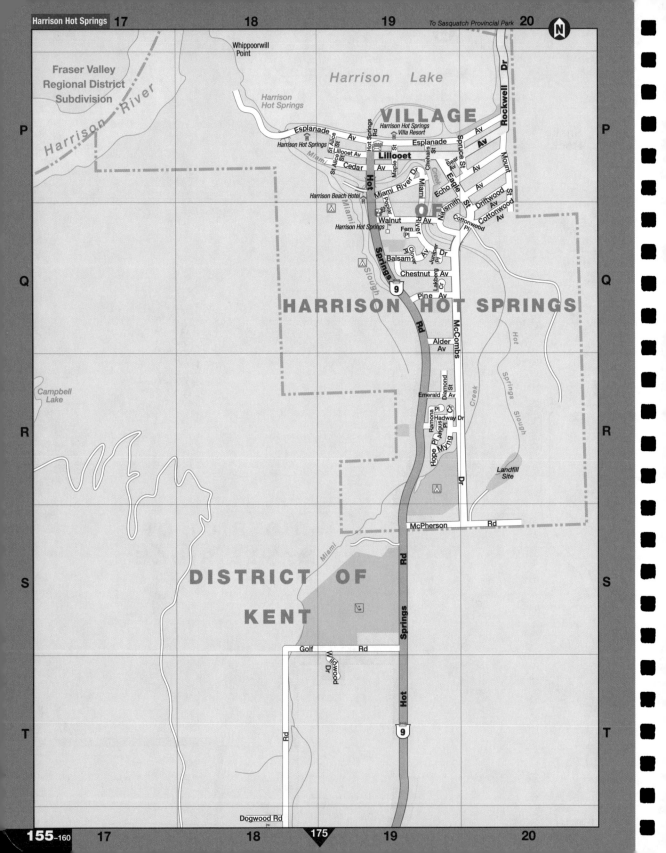

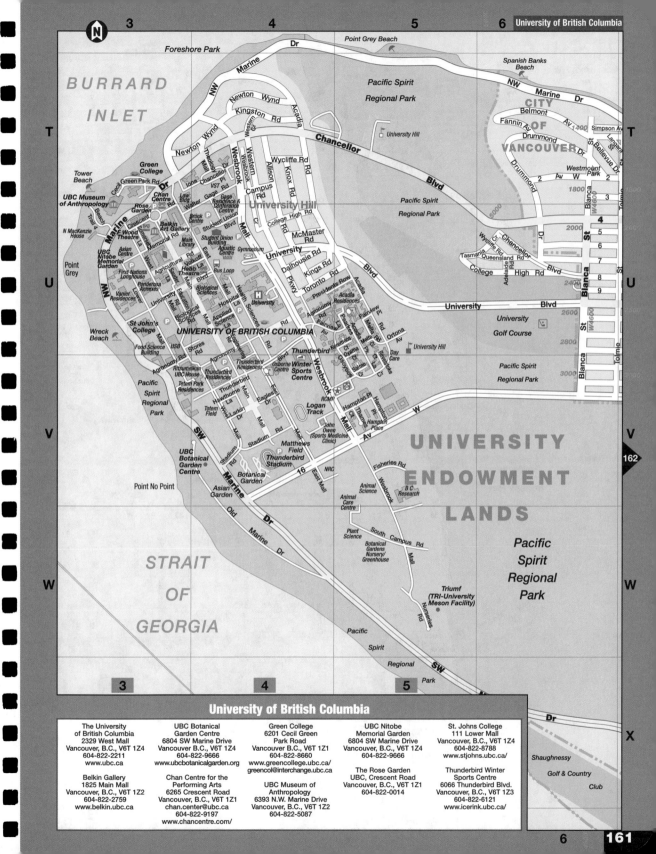

BURRARD INLET

STRAIT OF GEORGIA

UNIVERSITY ENDOWMENT LANDS

Pacific Spirit Regional Park

Pacific Spirit Regional Park

Point Grey Beach

Spanish Banks Beach

CITY OF VANCOUVER

Foreshore Park

University Hill

Tower Beach

Green College

UBC Museum of Anthropology

N MacKenzie House

Point Grey

Wreck Beach

Point No Point

University Golf Course

UNIVERSITY OF BRITISH COLUMBIA

UBC Botanical Garden Centre

Botanical Garden

Asian Garden

Thunderbird Stadium

Matthews Field

Logan Track

John Owen (Sports Medicine Clinic)

Triumf (TRI-University Meson Facility)

Animal Care Centre

Animal Science

B C Research

Plant Science

Botanical Gardens Nursery/ Greenhouse

Fisheries Rd

Shaughnessy Golf & Country Club

162

161

University of British Columbia

The University of British Columbia
2329 West Mall
Vancouver, B.C., V6T 1Z4
604-822-2211
www.ubc.ca

UBC Botanical Garden Centre
6804 SW Marine Drive
Vancouver B.C., V6T 1Z4
604-822-9666
www.ubcbotanicalgarden.org

Green College
6201 Cecil Green Park Road
Vancouver B.C., V6T 1Z1
604-822-8660
www.greencollege.ubc.ca/
greencol@interchange.ubc.ca

UBC Nitobe Memorial Garden
6804 SW Marine Drive
Vancouver, B.C., V6T 1Z4
604-822-9666

St. Johns College
111 Lower Mall
Vancouver, B.C., V6T 1Z4
www.stjohns.ubc.ca/

Belkin Gallery
1825 Main Mall
Vancouver, B.C., V6T 1Z2
604-822-2759
www.belkin.ubc.ca

Chan Centre for the Performing Arts
6265 Crescent Road
Vancouver, B.C., V6T 1Z1
chan.center@ubc.ca
604-822-9197
www.chancentre.com/

UBC Museum of Anthropology
6393 N.W. Marine Drive
Vancouver, B.C., V6T 1Z2
604-822-5087

The Rose Garden
UBC, Crescent Road
Vancouver, B.C., V6T 1Z1
604-822-0014

Thunderbird Winter Sports Centre
6066 Thunderbird Blvd.
Vancouver, B.C., V6T 1Z3
604-822-6121
www.icerink.ubc.ca/

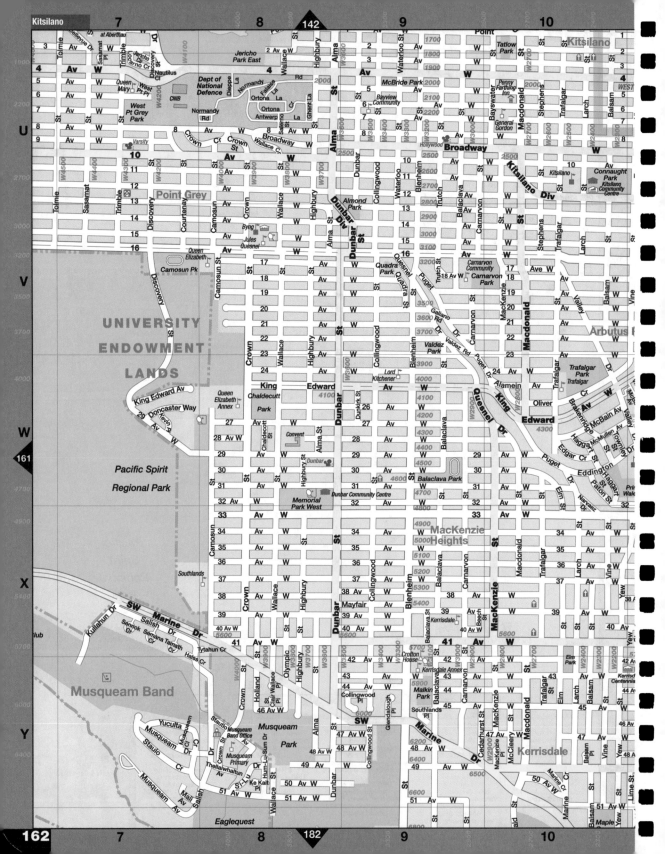

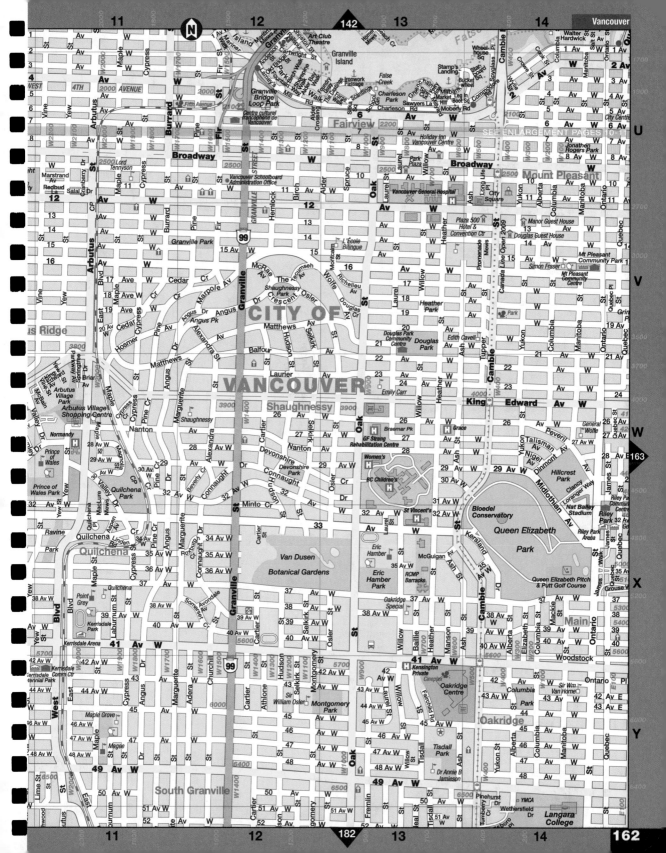

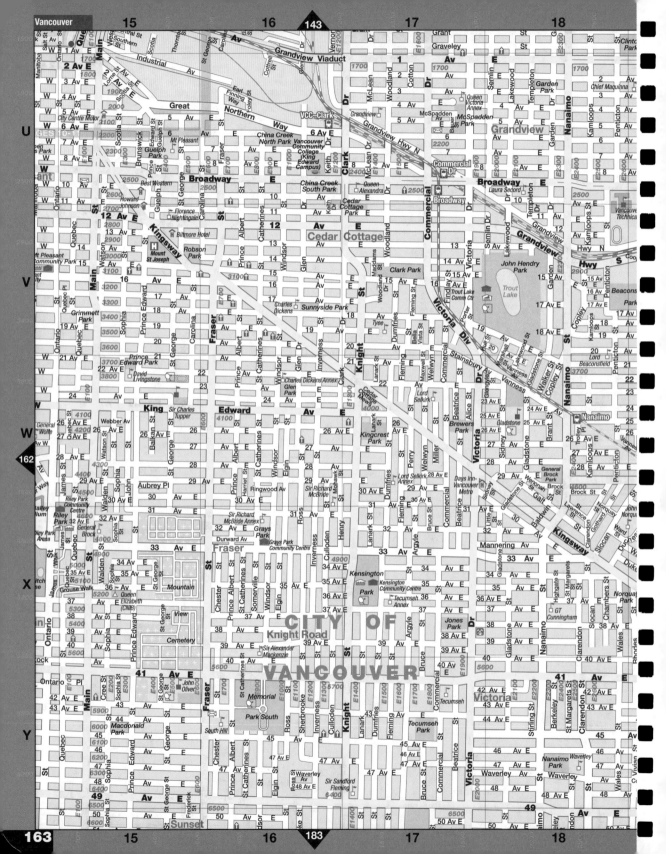

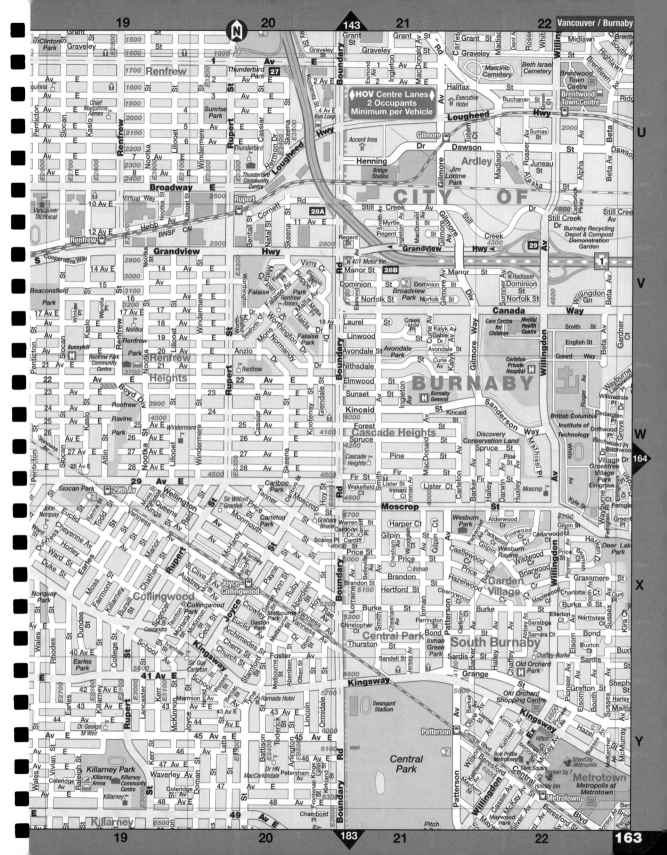

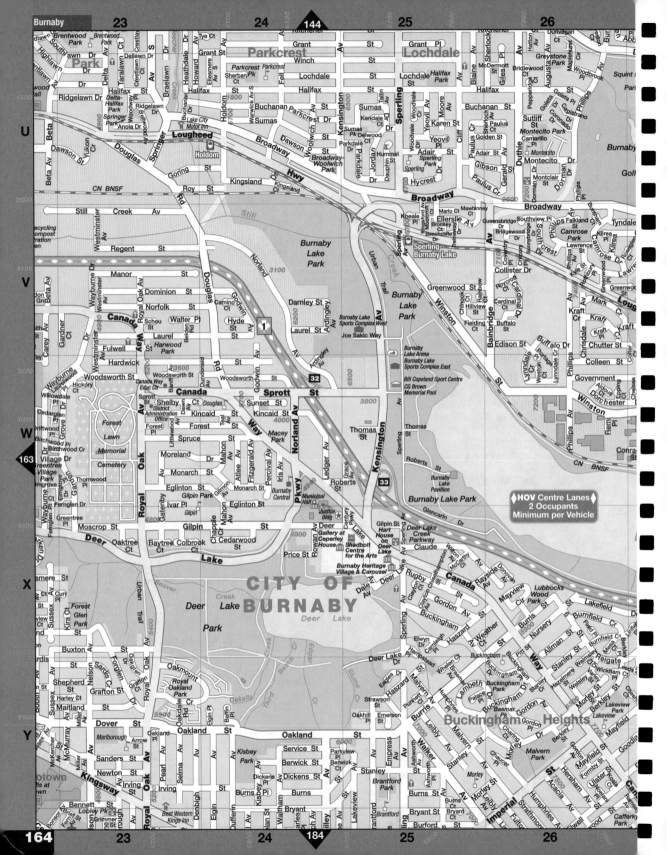

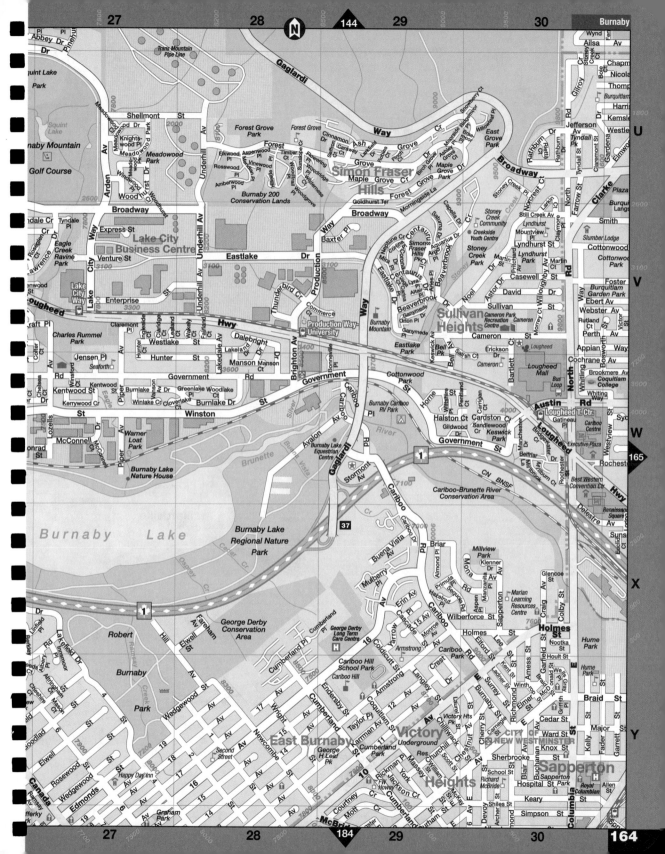

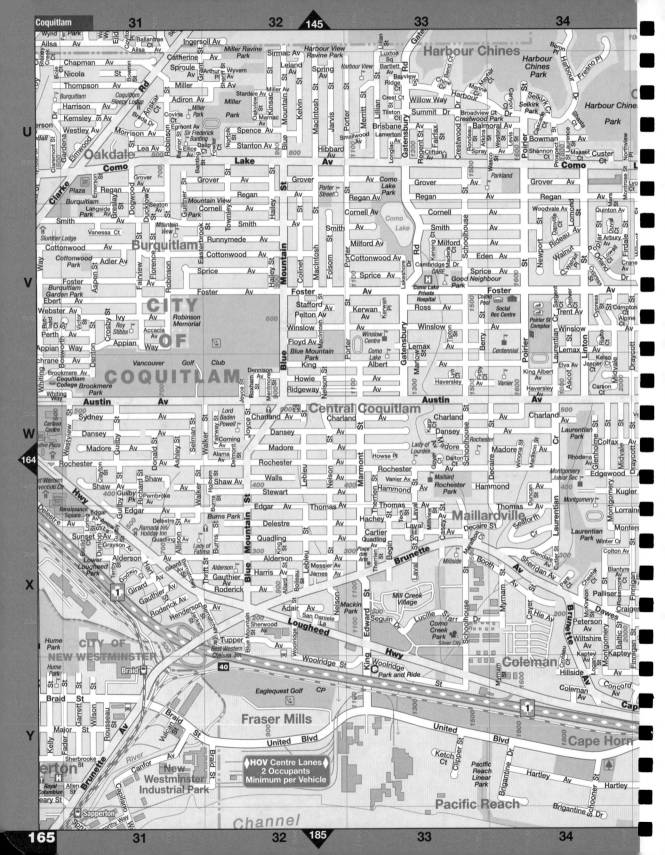

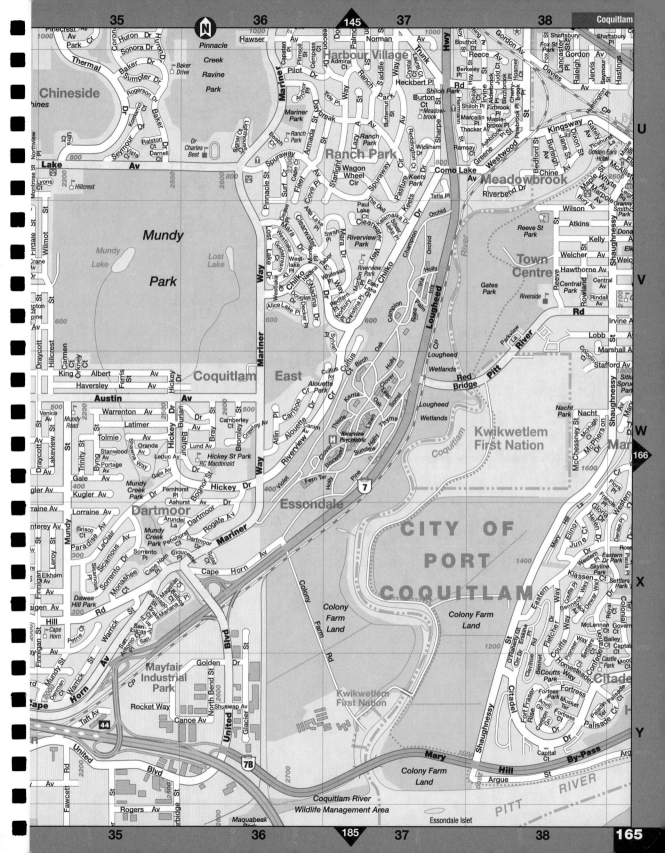

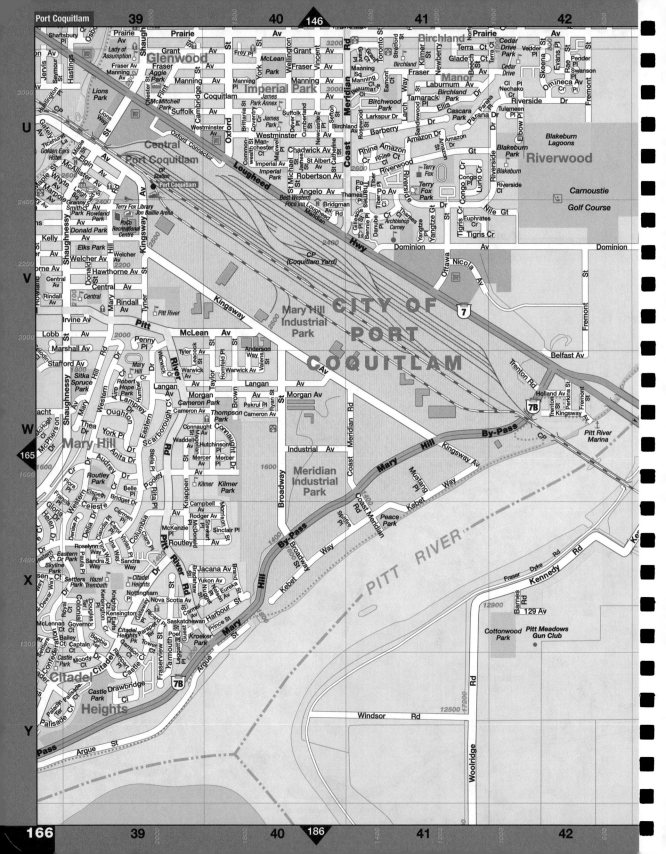

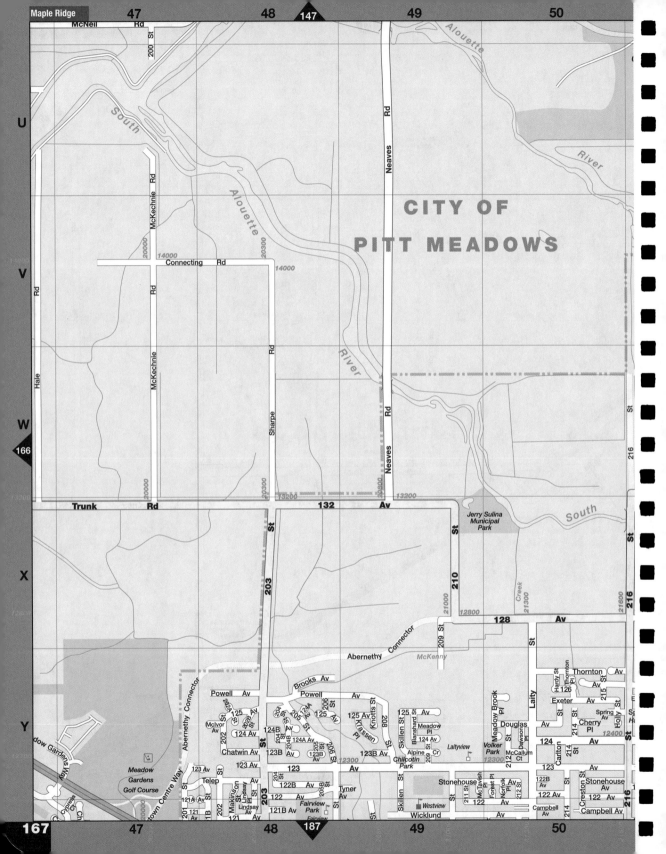

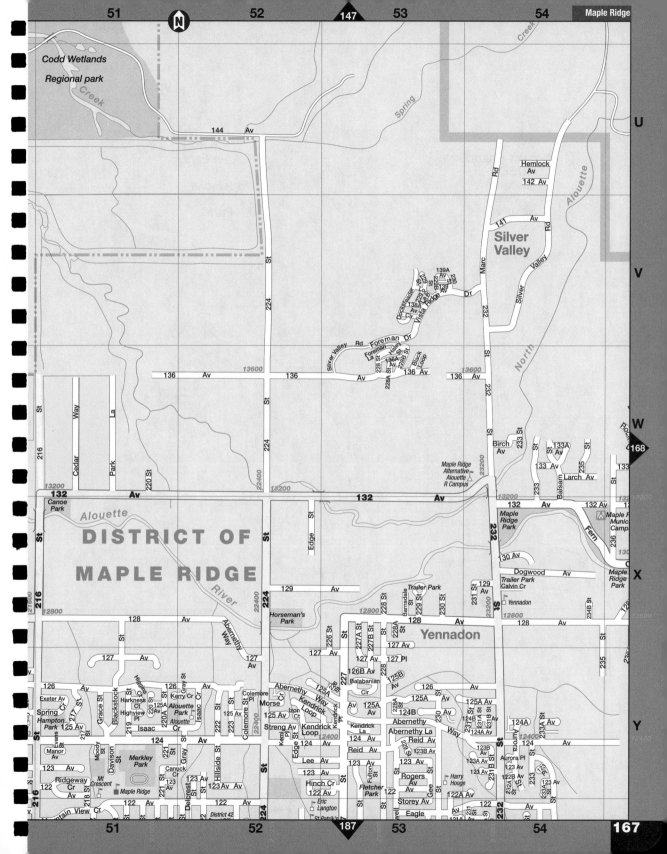

Codd Wetlands
Regional park

Creek

Spring

Creek

N

144 Av

Alouette

U

Hemlock Av

142 Av

141 Av

Rd

Marc

Silver Valley

V

139A Av

139

St

Docksteader Cr

138A Av

Vista Ridge

232

Silver Valley Rd

Foreman Dr

Foreman

Haley St

Black Loop

228B St

228 St

136A Av

136 Av

136 Av

136 Av

228A Av

13600

232

North

13600

W

168

216

St

Cedar

Way

Park La

220 St

224 St

22400

Birch Av

233 St

133A Av

Larch Av

133 Av

235

233

Balsam

133

13200

13200

Maple Ridge Alternative Alouette R Campus

23200

13200

132 Av

132 Av

132 Av

132 Av

Canoe Park

Alouette

DISTRICT OF MAPLE RIDGE

St

Edge St

River

22400

232

St

Maple Ridge Park

130 Av

Fern

Maple Ridge Municipal Camp

236

130

Maple Ridge Park

X

Dogwood Av

Trailer Park

Calvin Cr

129 St

231 St

23200

129 Av

230 St

234B St

Yennadon

216 St

27800

12800

12800

129 Av

129

Av

Trailer Park

Barnsdale

228 St

229 St

12800

128 Av

12800

128 Av

235 St

128 Av

128 Av

Abernethy Way

Horseman's Park

226 St

227 St

227A St

227B St

127 Av

Yennadon

127 Av

127 Av

127 Pl

228 St

127 Av

127 Av

126B Av

Balabanian Cir

125B Av

126 Av

126 Av

227

125A Way

Kendrick Loop

Kendrick St

228A St

124B Av

Abernethy

125A Av

125A Av

124A St

126

Exeter Av

217 St

Grace St

Harkness Ct

Highview Pl

125A Ct

Kerry Cr

Isaac Cr

Colemore Pl

Colemore St

Morse Cr

Abernethy Way

125A

Av

124B Av

231A St

230 St

124A Av

Spring Hampton Park

125 Av

219 St

220A St

Alouette Cr

Alouette

222

Colemore St

22400

125 Av

Streng Av

Kendrick Loop

Kendrick La

Abernethy La

Way

Aurora

124A St

124A

124

124 Av

126

127 Av

127 Av

124 Av

Reid Av

124 Av

Reid Av

123B Av

233A Av

233A St

Manor Cr

221 St

Davison

Gray St

Merkley Park

Canuck Cr

123 St

Hillside St

Edge St

Lee Av

Fulton St

123 Av

123B Av

123 Av

Rogers Av

Harry Hooge

Aurora Pl

122B Av

123 Av

123

122

Ridgeway Cr

Mt Crescent

123 Av

123 Av

Hinch Cr

122 Av

Gee St

Storey Av

122A Av

124

233 St

233A St

122 Av

122

Mountain View Cr

122 Av

District 42

St Patrick's St

Eric Langton

224 St

232 St

Fletcher Park

Eagle Av

Maple Ridge

216 St

Y

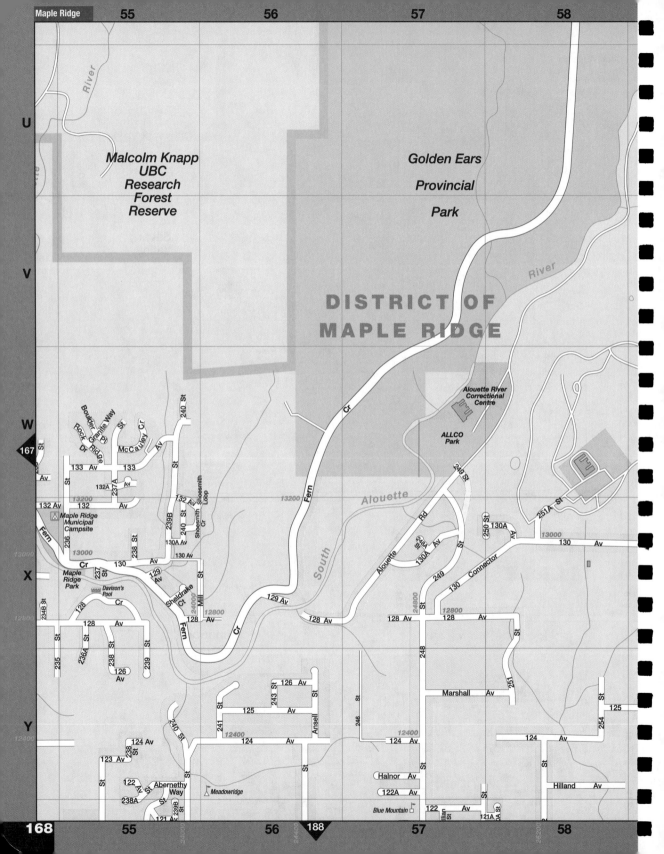

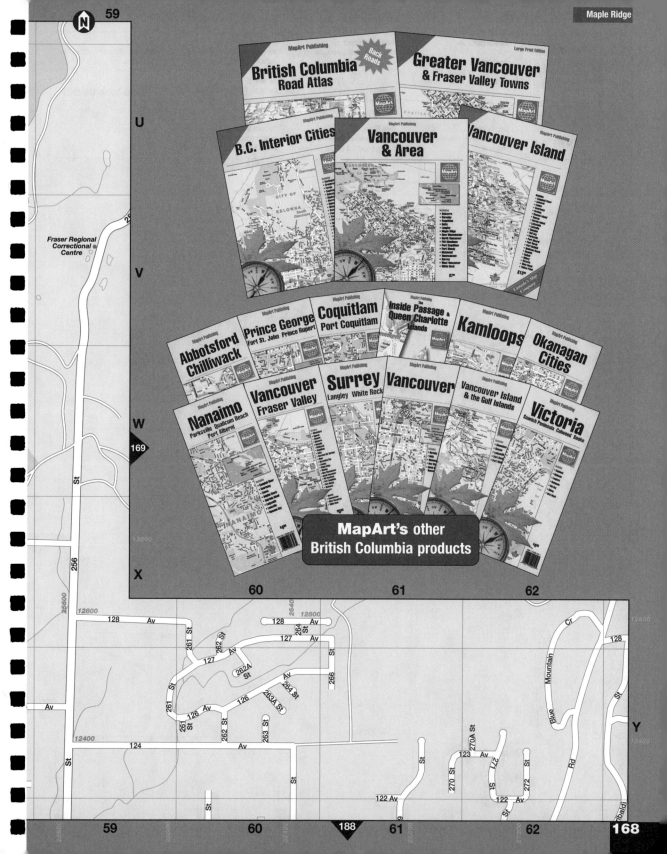

Fraser Regional Correctional Centre

63 64 65 66

U

V

W

168

X

Y

DISTRICT

OF

MAPLE RIDGE

McNutt Rd

GREATER VANCOUVER REGIONAL DISTRICT

FRASER VALLEY REGIONAL DISTRICT

128 Av

Willow Pl

Arbutus Pl

Laurel Pl

Aspen Pl

Sayers

Kathryn St

St

Garibaldi

Kanaka Creek

Regional Park

Creek

123 Av

St

Creek

Powell St

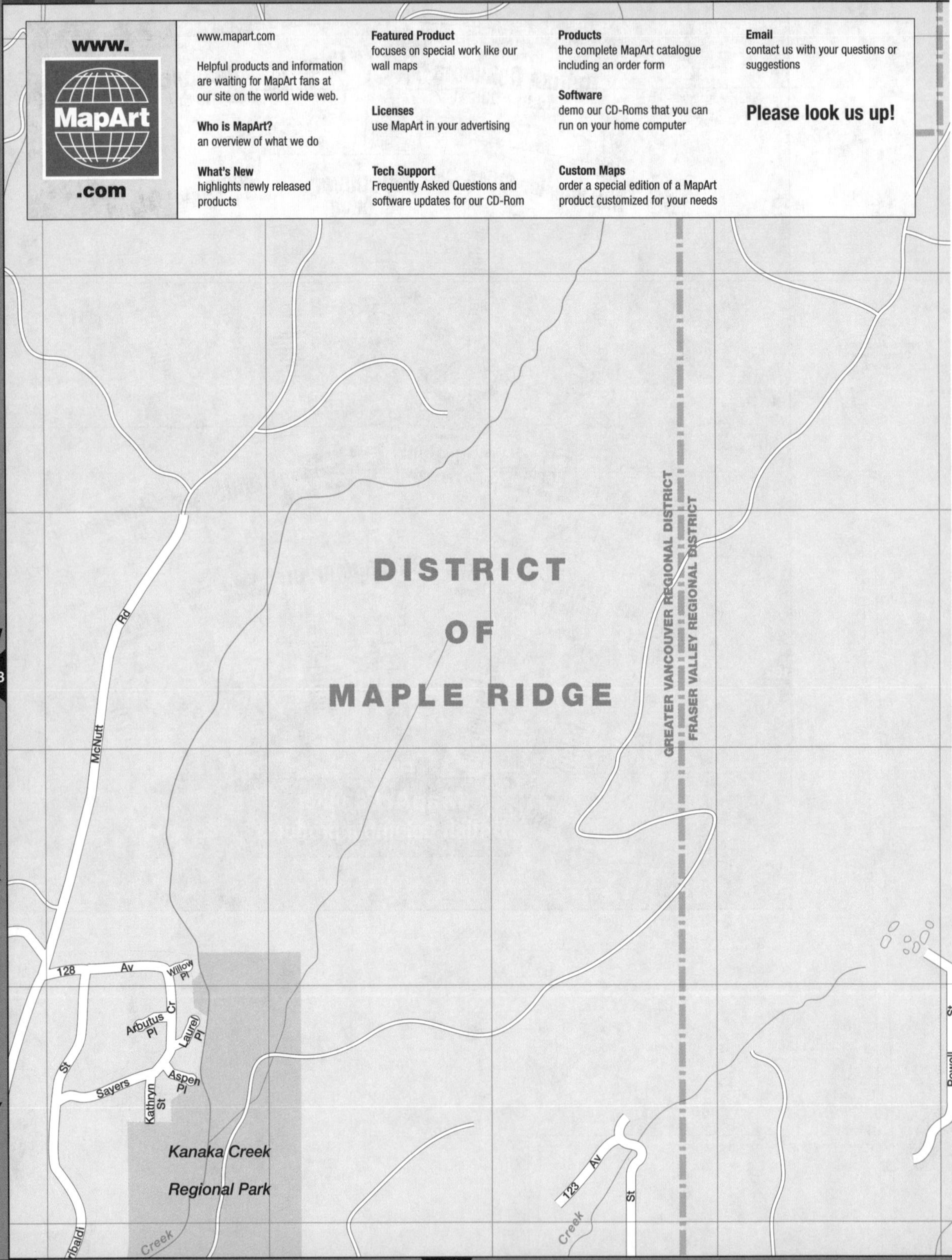

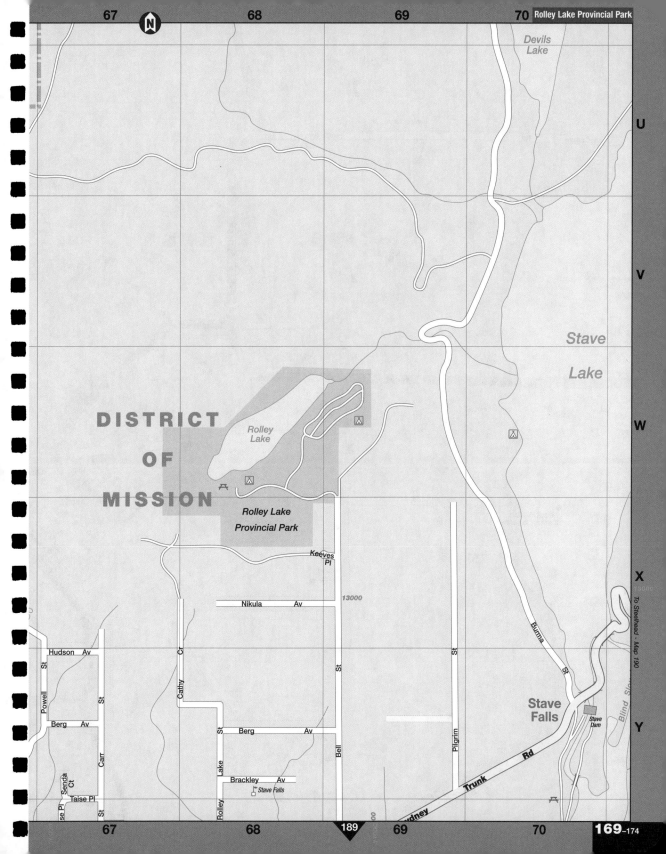

N

U

V

W

X

Y

Devils Lake

Stave

Lake

DISTRICT

OF

MISSION

Rolley Lake

Rolley Lake Provincial Park

Keeves Pl

13000

Nikula Av

Hudson Av

Powell St

Berg Av

Carr St

se Pl

Senda Ct

Taise Pl

St

Cathy Ct

Lake St

Berg Av

Brackley Av

Stave Falls

Rolley

Bell St

St

Pilgrim St

Burma St

To Steelhead - Map 190

Blind Slo

Stave Falls

Stave Dam

udney Trunk Rd

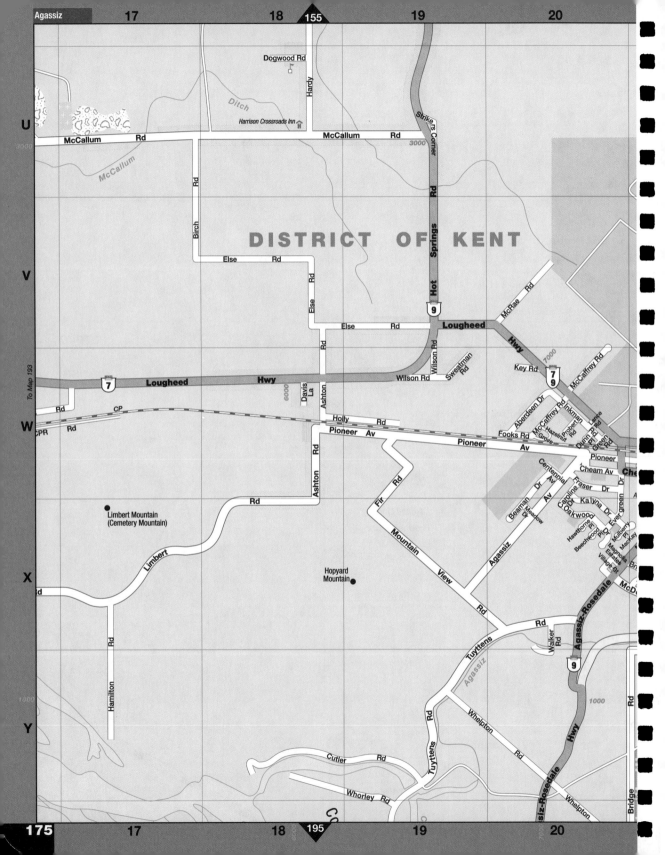

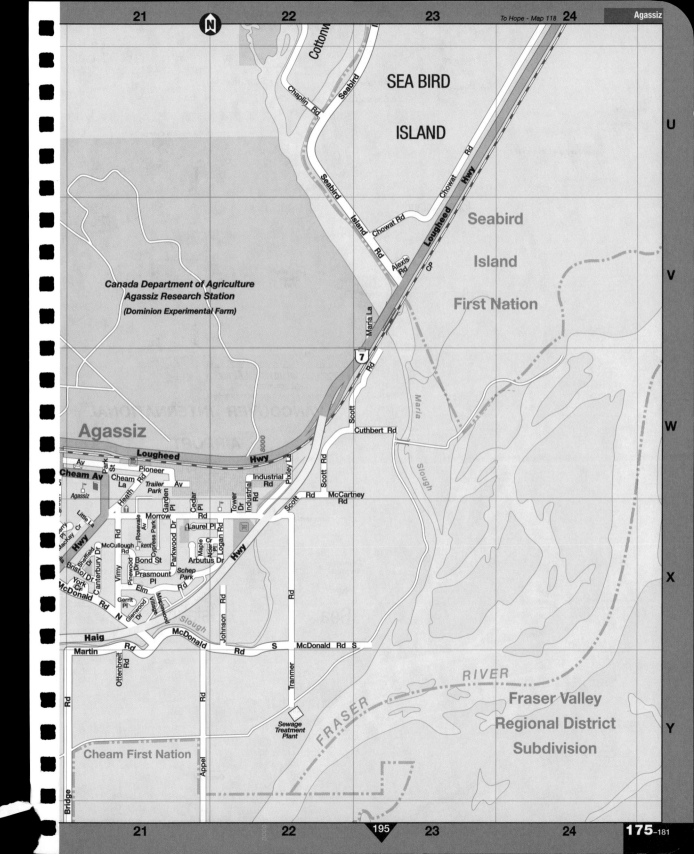

N

To Hope - Map 118

SEA BIRD

ISLAND

Cottonw

Chaplin Rd

Seabird

Seabird

Island

Rd

Chowat Rd

Chowat Rd

Lougheed Hwy

Seabird

Island

First Nation

Alexis Rd

CP

Canada Department of Agriculture
Agassiz Research Station
(Dominion Experimental Farm)

Maria La

7

Maria

Slough

Agassiz

Scott Rd

Cuthbert Rd

Lougheed Hwy

Cheam Av

Av

Park St

Pioneer

Cheam La

Av

Heath Rd

Trailer Park

Agassiz

Industrial Rd

Pixley La

Scott Rd

Little La

Garden Pl

Cedar Pl

Industrial Rd

Tower Dr

Scott Rd

McCartney Rd

Cr

MacKay

Morrow Av

Rosevale Av

Cypress Park

Laurel Pl

Rd

kent

McCullough Rd

Parkwood Dr

Logan Rd

Hwy

Sheffield Dr

Bristol Dr

Canterbury Dr

Pinewood Dr

Bond St

Maple Cr

Alder Cr

Vimy

Prasmount Pl

Arbutus Dr

Schep Park

York Cr

Elm

Maplewood Village

McDonald Rd N

Gerrit Pl

Glenwood Dr

Rd

Johnson Rd

Rd

Haig

Slough

McDonald

Rd

McDonald Rd S

Martin

Ottenbreit Rd

Rd

S

McDonald Rd S

Tranmer

Rd

RIVER

Fraser Valley

Regional District

Subdivision

FRASER

Sewage Treatment Plant

Appel

Cheam First Nation

Bridge

U

V

W

X

Y

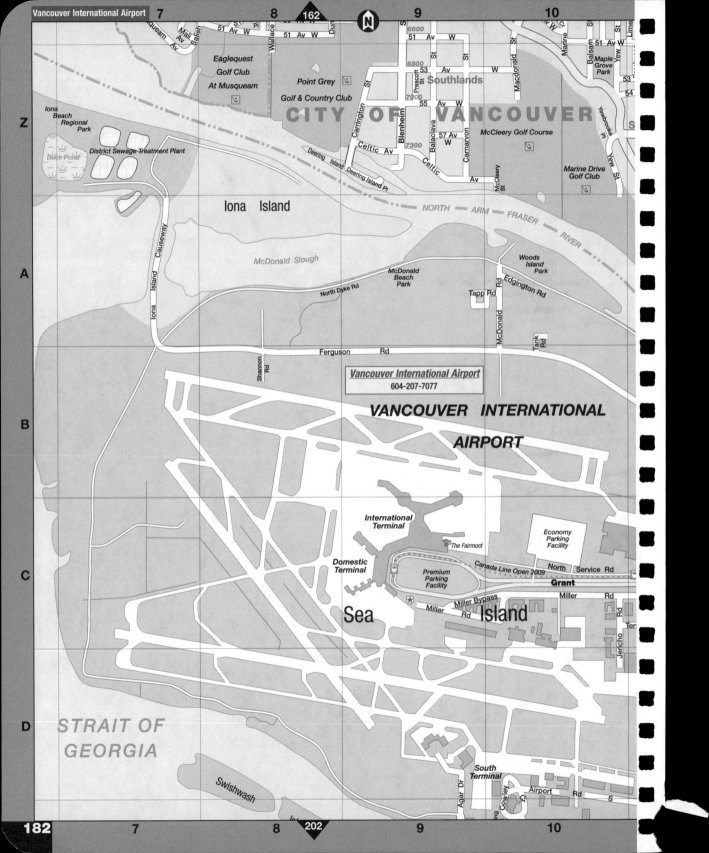

7   8   162   N   9   10

Z

Iona
Beach
Regional
Park

Duck Pond

District Sewage Treatment Plant

Eaglequest
Golf Club
At Musqueam

Point Grey
Golf & Country Club

Southlands

CITY OF VANCOUVER

Mali
Av

Salish

51 Av W

Wallace

51 Av W

Dunb

51 Av   W

6600

Prescott St

51 Av   W

Marine

Balsam

51 Av W

53 Av

6800

St
St
St

53
Av   W

Maple
Grove
Park

Macdonald
St

Yew St
Carrington St
Blenheim St
Balaclava
Celtic Av

7000
7300

55
Av   W

57 Av
W

McCleery Golf Course

Yewbrooke
Pl

Yew St

53
54

Carnarvon
Av

Celtic

Marine Drive
Golf Club

McCleery St

Iona Island

NORTH ARM FRASER RIVER

Deering Island Deering Island Pl

A

McDonald Slough

North Dyke Rd

McDonald
Beach
Park

Tapp Rd

McDonald Rd

Woods
Island
Park

Edgington Rd

Iona Island Causeway

Ferguson   Rd

Shannon Rd

Tank Rd

B

Vancouver International Airport
604-207-7077

VANCOUVER INTERNATIONAL

AIRPORT

International
Terminal

The Fairmont

Economy
Parking
Facility

C

Domestic
Terminal

Premium
Parking
Facility

Canada Line Open 2009

North   Service Rd

Grant

Miller   Rd

Sea   Island

Miller

Miller Bypass
Rd

Jericho Rd

Ten

D

STRAIT OF
GEORGIA

Swishwash

South
Terminal

Agar Dr

Cowley

Airport   Rd

S

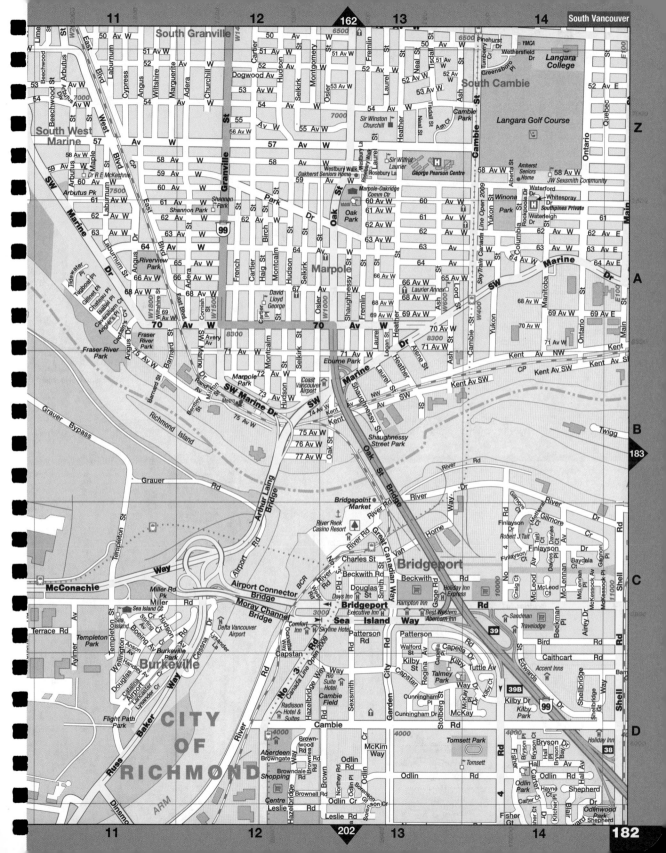

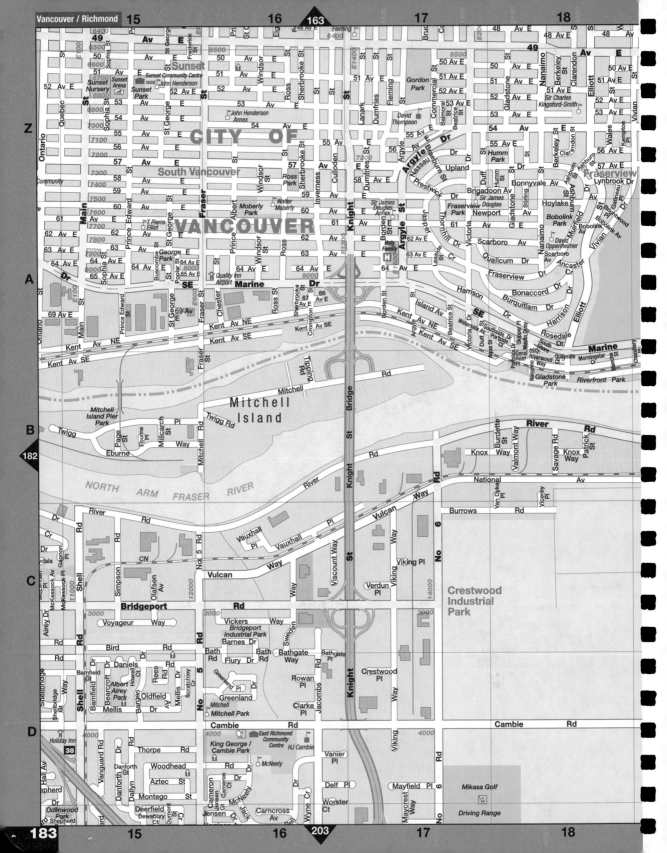

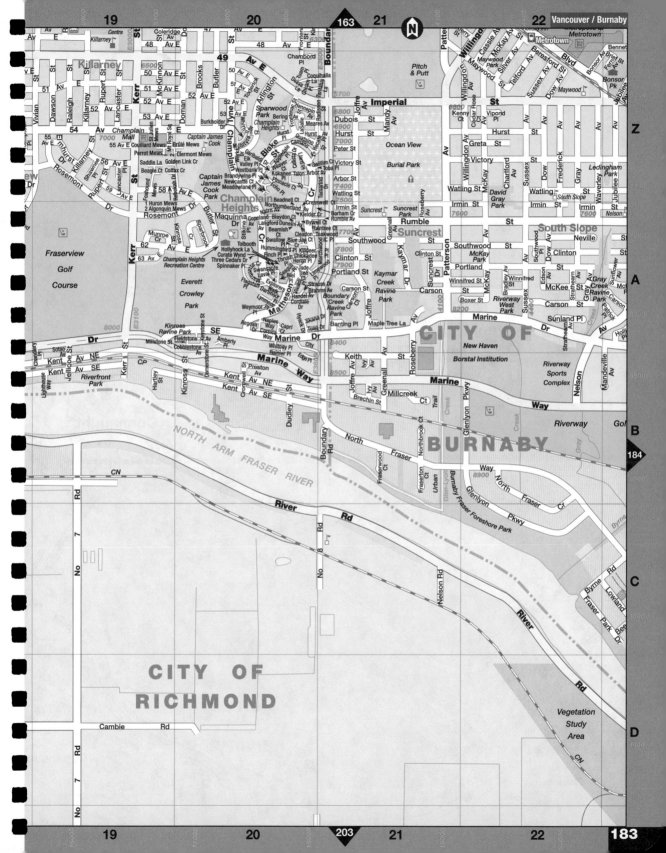

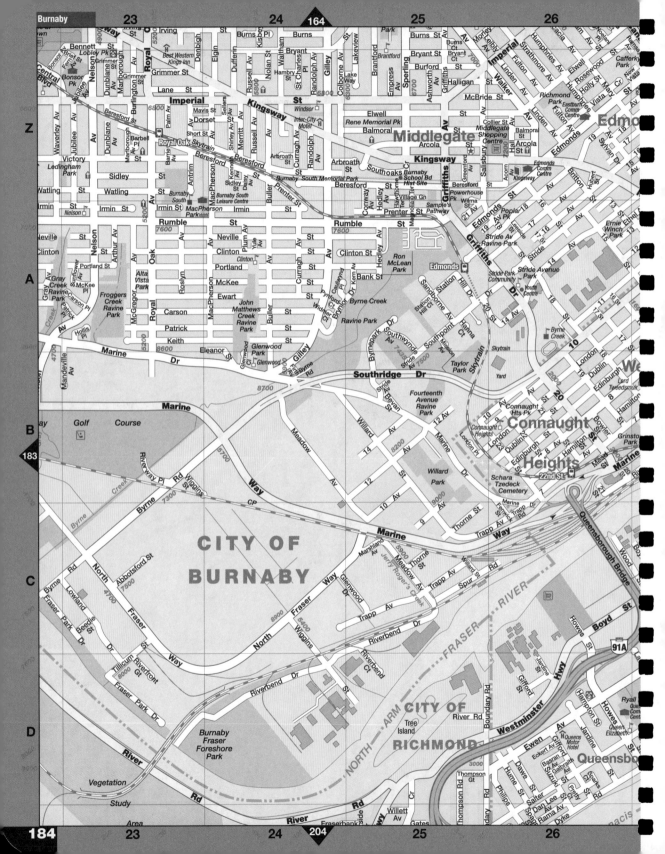

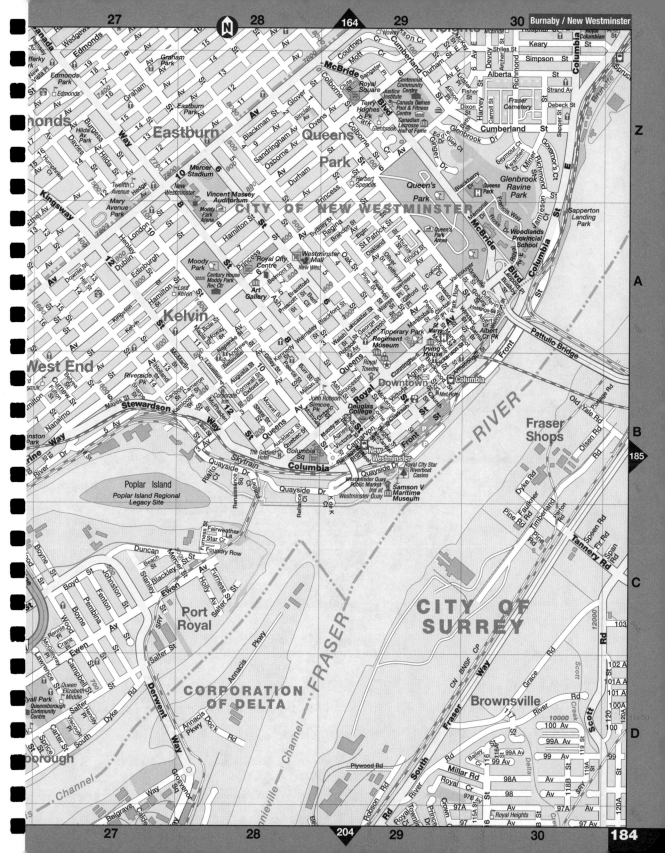

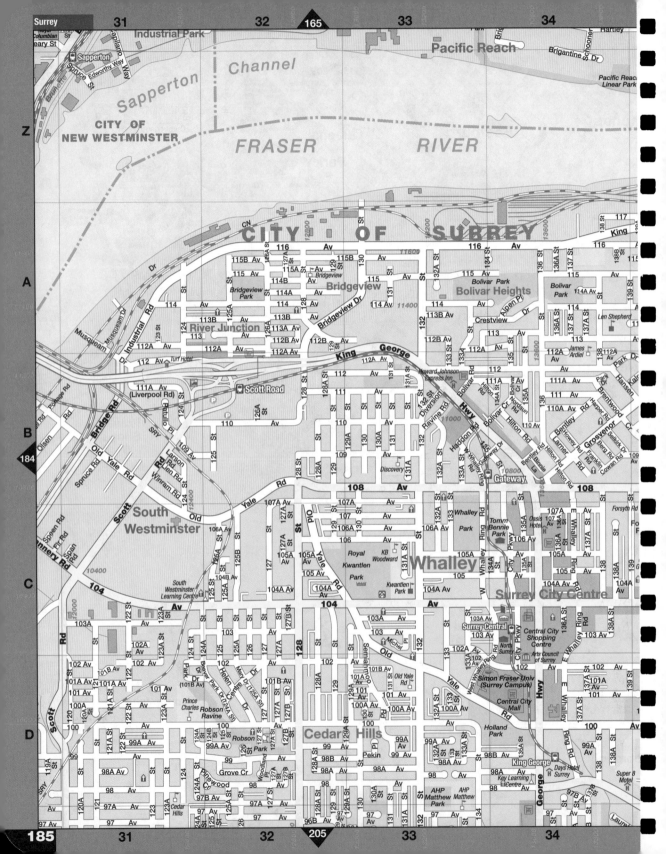

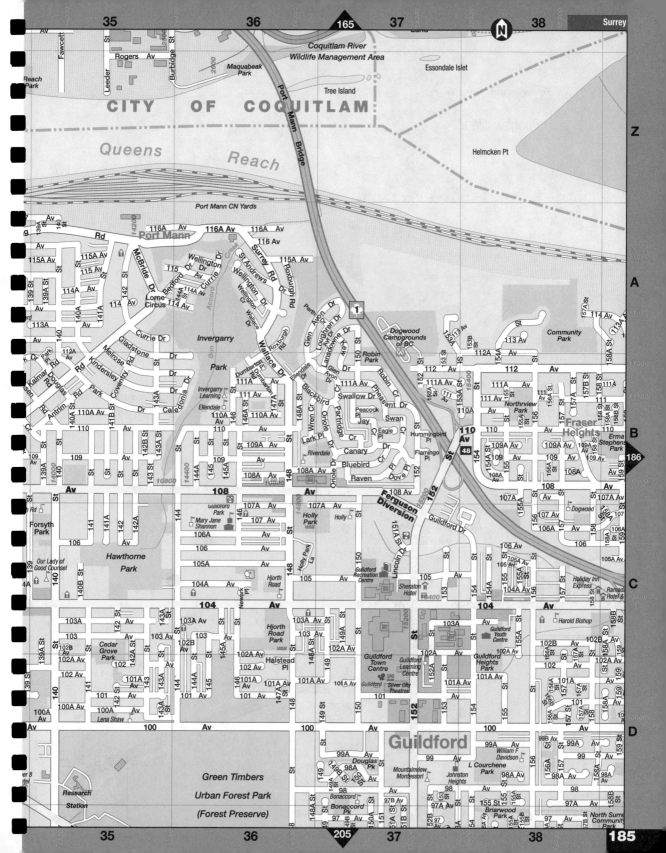

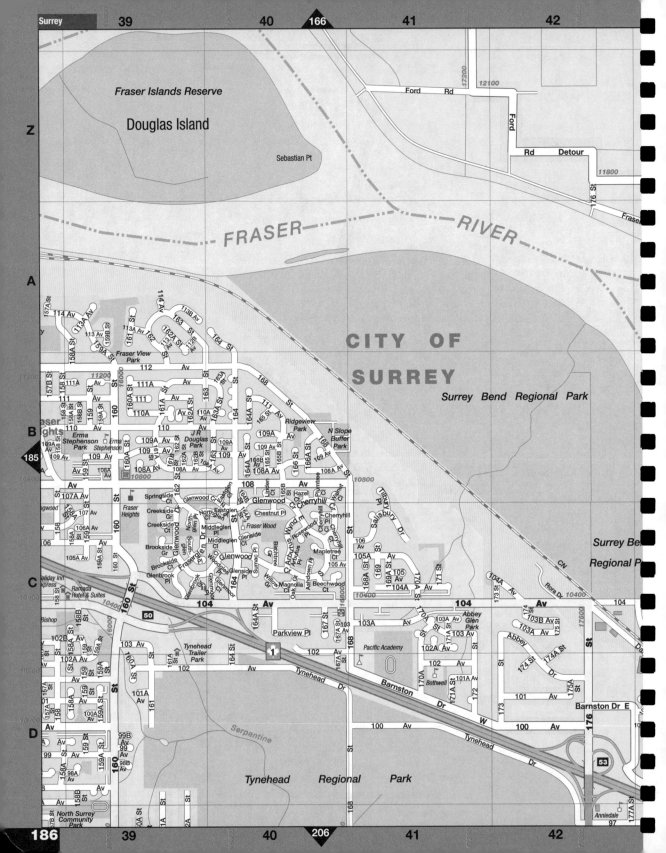

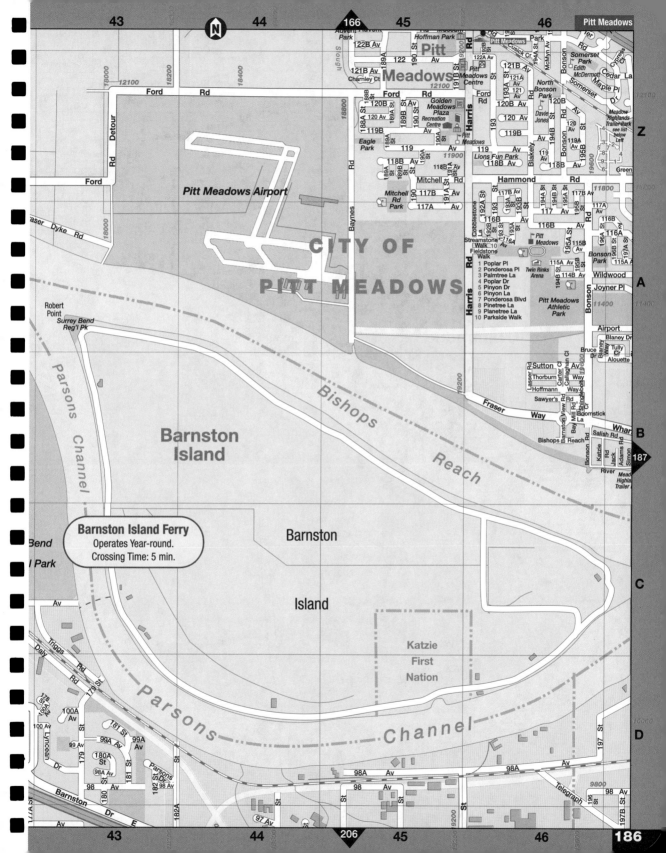

Pitt Meadows

Advent Park

122B Av
121B Av
Charnley Ct
120B St
120 Av
119B

Pitt Meadows Centre

Hoffman Park
Cusick Cr

121B Av
121 Av
121 Av
120B Av
120 Av
119B

North Bonson Park

Somerset Park
Edith McDermott
Somerset
Cedar
Maple Pl

Golden Meadows Plaza
Recreation Centre
Pitt Meadows

Eagle Park

119 Av

118B Av
118B
117B Av
117A

Mitchell Rd Park

Mitchell Rd Park

117B Av
117A

Lions Fun Park
118B Av

Hammond Rd

116B
116B

Cobblestone La

Streamstone Walk
Fieldstone Walk

Pitt Meadows

115B Av
115A

Meadow Highlands Trailer Park see list below left

Davie Jones

194B Av
119A

120B Av
120 Av
119B

118B Av

Bonson Park

116B
116A
115A

Wildwood
Joyner Pl

Bonson

Airport
Blaney Dr
Blaney Way
Tully Cr
Alouette

1 Poplar Pl
2 Ponderosa Pl
3 Palmtree La
4 Poplar Dr
5 Pinyon Dr
6 Pinyon La
7 Ponderosa Blvd
8 Pinetree La
9 Planetree La
10 Parkside Walk

Twin Rinks Arena

Pitt Meadows Athletic Park

CITY OF PITT MEADOWS

Robert Point
Surrey Bend Reg'l Pk

Parsons Channel

Bishops Reach

Fraser

Sutton
Thorburn
Hoffmann
Sawyer's
Barnston View Rd
Bay Mill Rd

Laser Rd
Case Ct
Callaghan Ct

Way
Way
Way La
Bloomstick

Bishops Reach Rd

Bonson Rd

Salish Rd

Katzie
Wharf
Jack Adams Simon

River

Meadow Highland Trailer Park

187

Barnston Island

Barnston Island Ferry
Operates Year-round.
Crossing Time: 5 min.

Bend
l Park

Barnston

Island

Katzie
First
Nation

Triggs Rd
Daly Rd
Lyncean Dr

100A Av
100 Av
99A Av
99A Av

178 St
179
180A St
181 St
182A
180

99A Av
99A Av
98A Av
98

Parsons Dr
98 Av

182 St

Parsons

Channel

98A Av

98 Av

Telegraph

98 Av

Barnston Dr E

97 Av

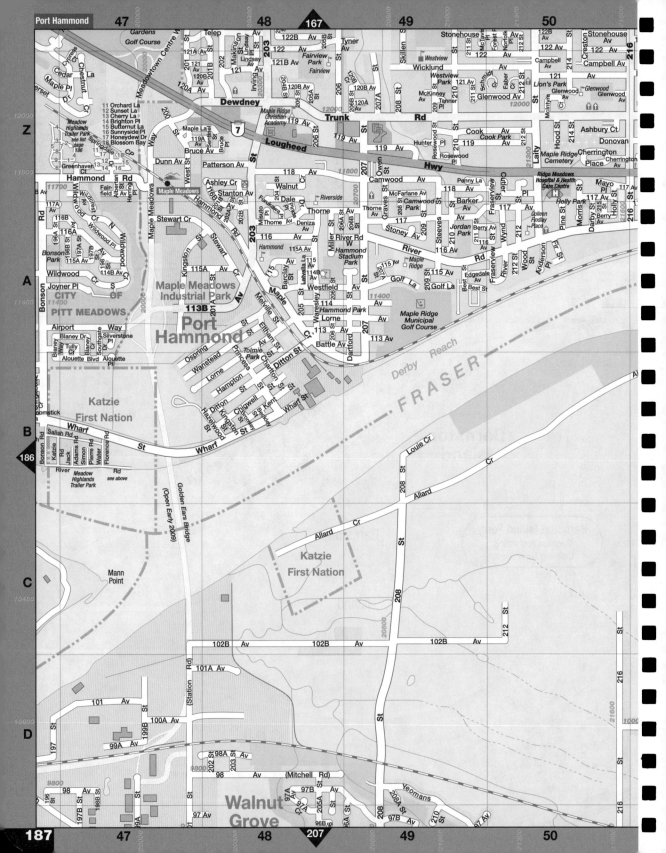

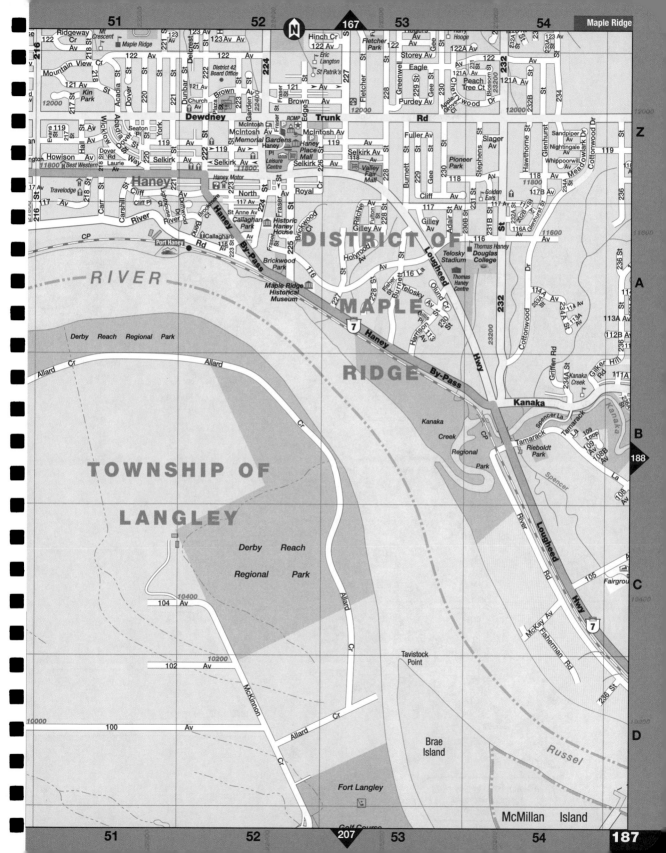

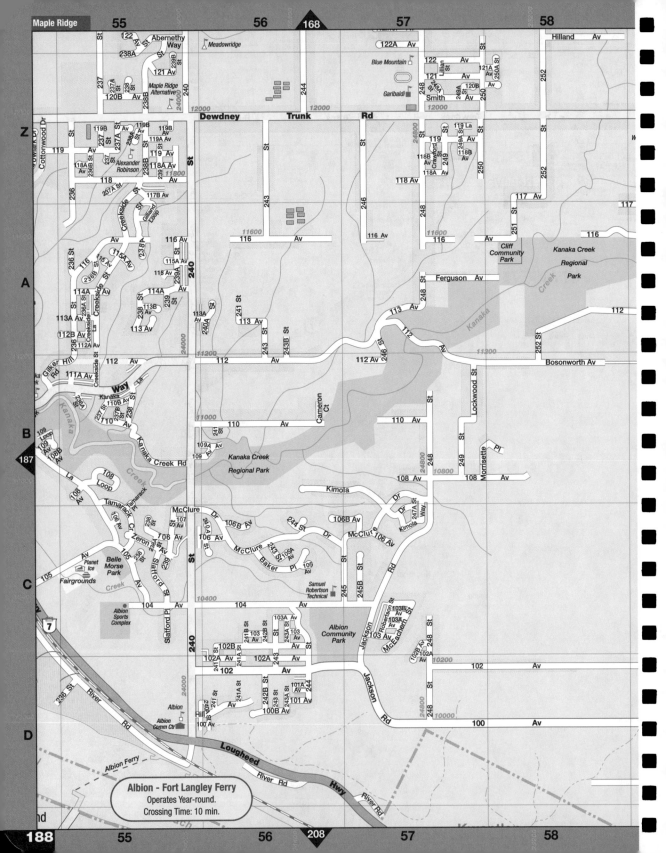

Albion - Fort Langley Ferry
Operates Year-round.
Crossing Time: 10 min.

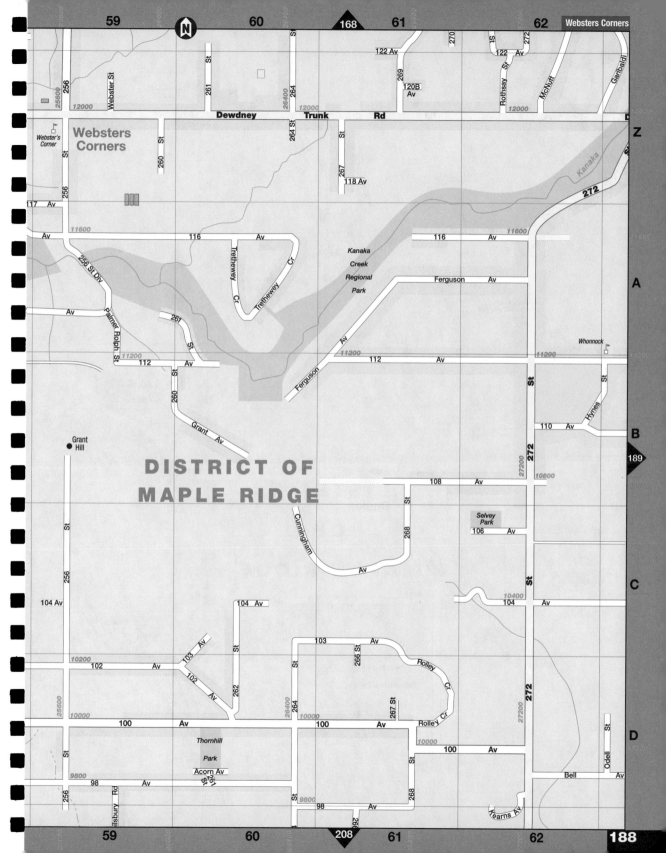

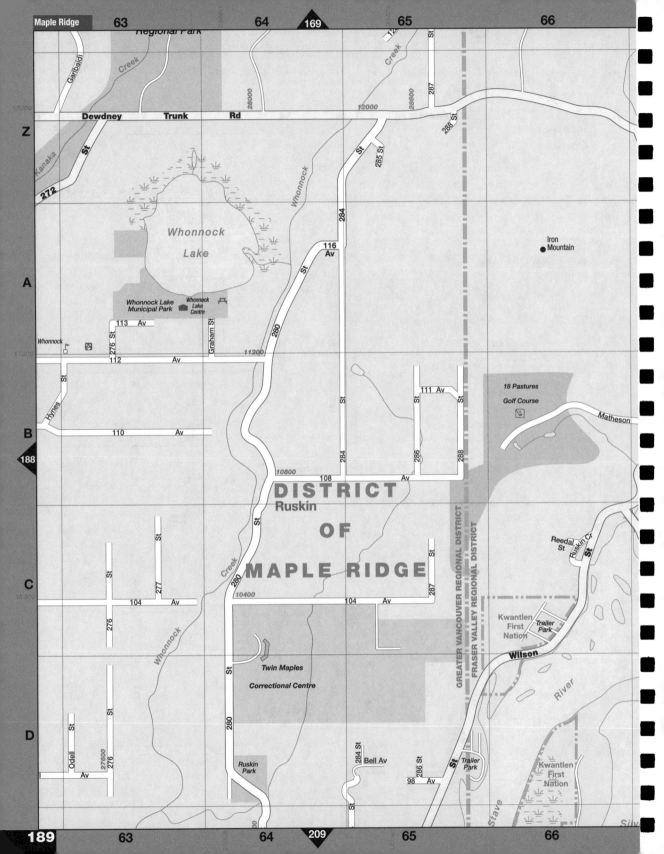

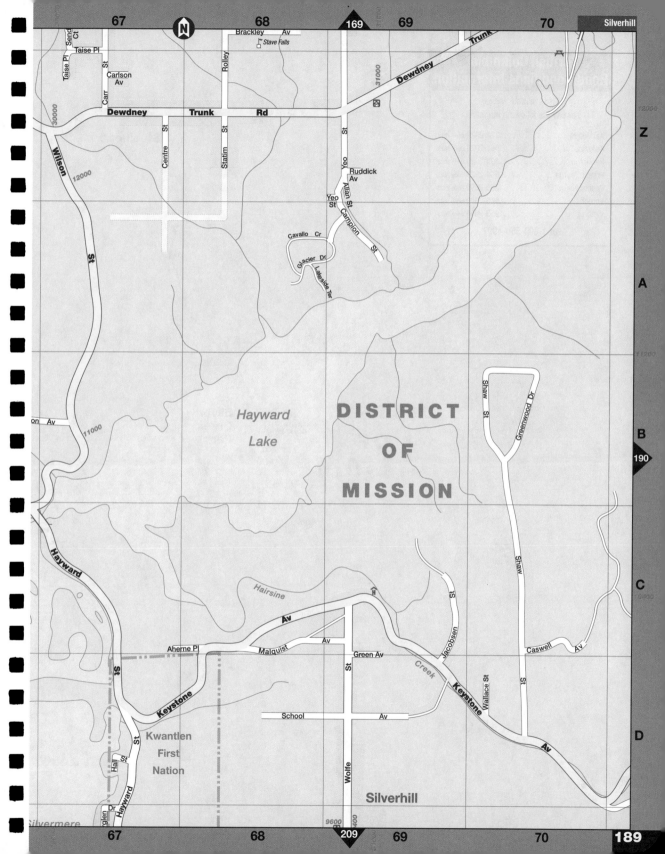

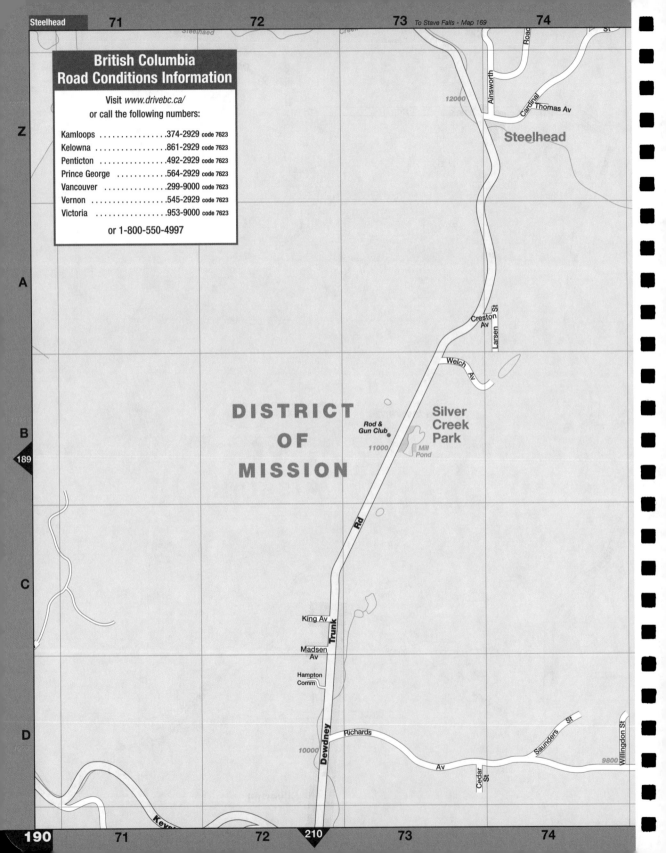

**British Columbia
Road Conditions Information**

Visit *www.drivebc.ca/*
or call the following numbers:

Kamloops . . . . .374-2929 code 7623
Kelowna . . . . .861-2929 code 7623
Penticton . . . . .492-2929 code 7623
Prince George . . . . .564-2929 code 7623
Vancouver . . . . .299-9000 code 7623
Vernon . . . . .545-2929 code 7623
Victoria . . . . .953-9000 code 7623

or 1-800-550-4997

Z

A

B

189

C

D

Steelhead

12000

Ainsworth Road

Cardinal

Thomas Av

Creston Av

Larsen St

Welch Av

DISTRICT OF MISSION

Rod & Gun Club

11000

Mill Pond

Silver Creek Park

Rd

King Av

Trunk

Madsen Av

Hampton Comm

Dewdney

10000

Richards

Saunders St

Willingdon St

9800

Av

Cedar St

Keyne

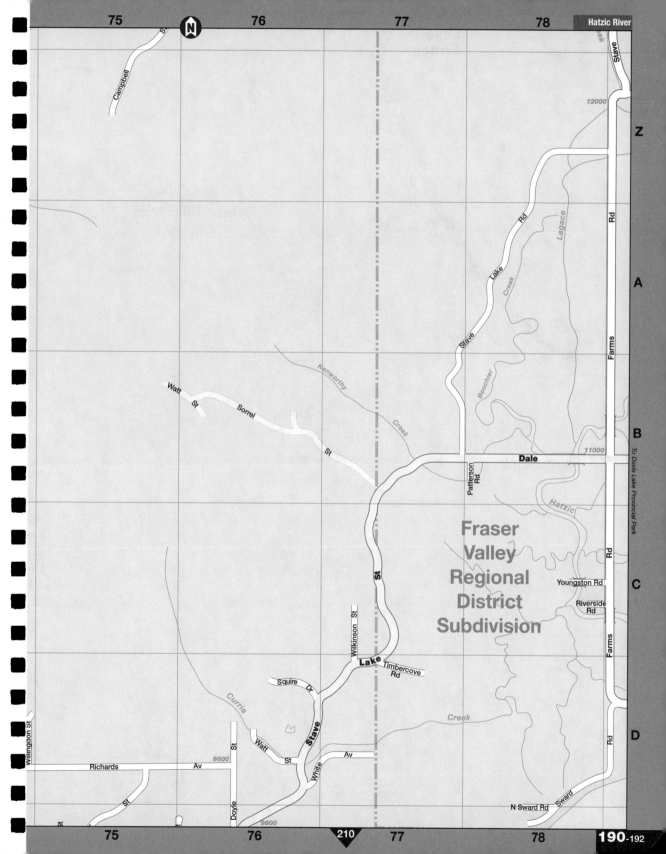

75 76 77 78

N

Campbell St

Z

Stave

12000

Lagace

Lake Rd

Stave

Creek

Rd

A

Bouchier

Farms

Watt St

Sorrel

Kenworthy

St

Creek

B

Dale

11000

Patterson Rd

To Davis Lake Provincial Park

Hatzic

Fraser Valley Regional District Subdivision

Youngston Rd

Rd

C

Riverside Rd

Stave St

Farms

Wilkinson St

Lake

Timbercove Rd

Squire Dr

Currie

Creek

Rd

D

Willingdon St

Watt St

Stave

White

9800

Av

St

Richards Av

Doyle

9600

N Sward Rd

Sward

St

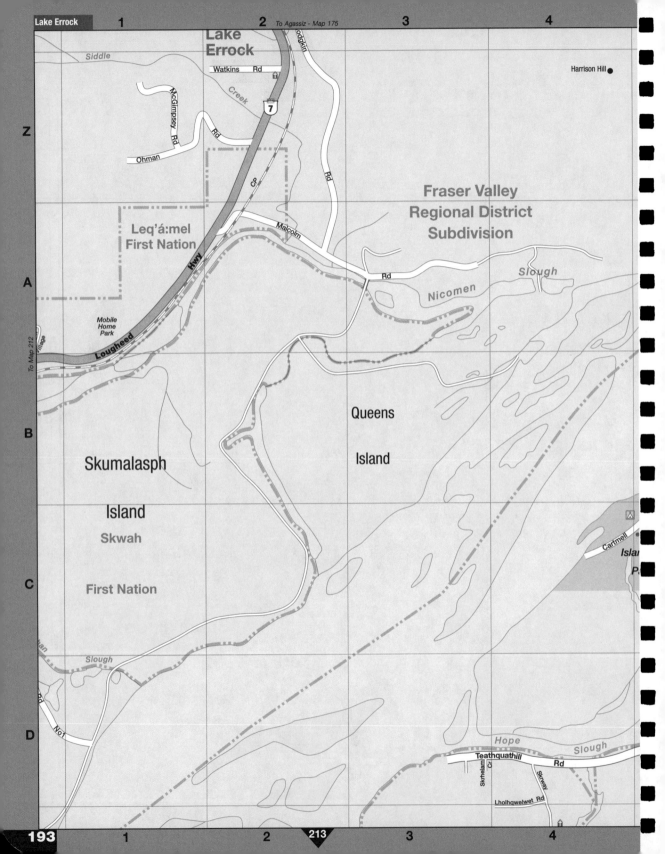

1 2 3 4

Lake
Errock

To Agassiz - Map 175

Siddle

Watkins Rd

McGimpsey Rd

Creek

Rd

7

Ohman

Z

CP

Harrison Hill ●

Fraser Valley
Regional District
Subdivision

Hwy

Malcolm

Leq'á:mel
First Nation

Rd

Slough

A

Nicomen

To Map 212

Mobile
Home
Park

Village

Lougheed

Queens

B

Skumalasph

Island

Island

Skwah

First Nation

☐

Cartmell

Islar

P

C

Slough

Rd

Not

Hope

Slough

D

Teathquathill Rd

Skrelamh Cr

Skrway

Lholhqwelwet Rd

⛺

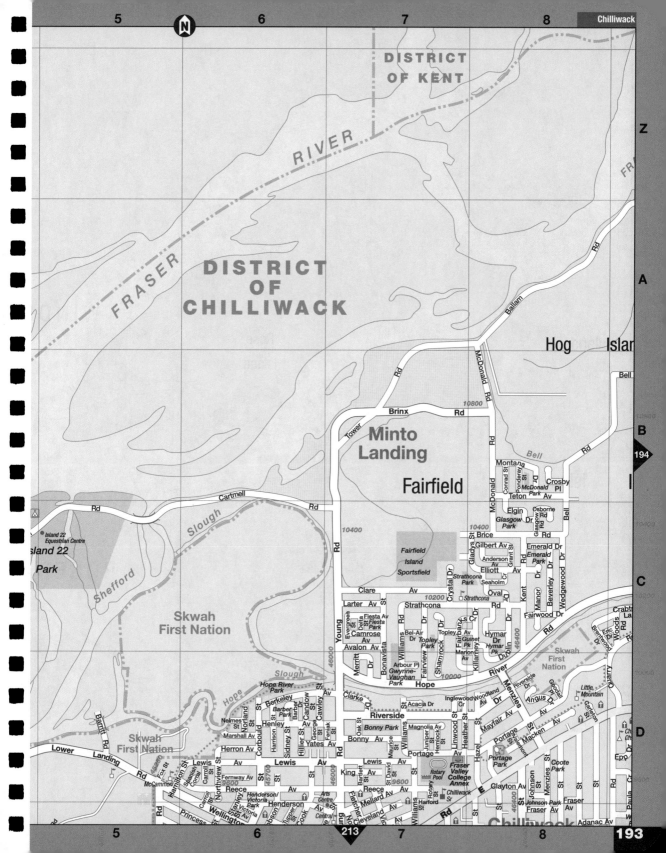

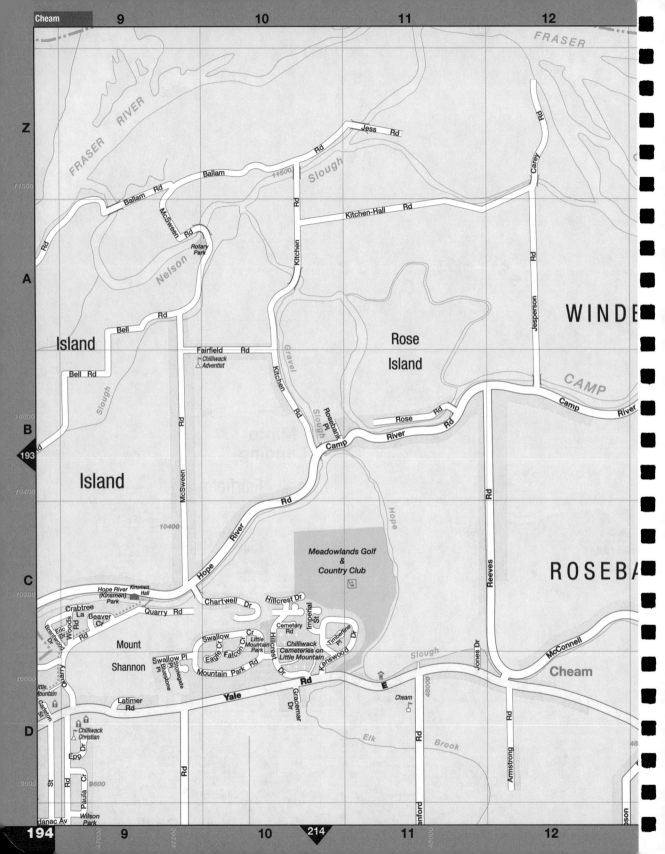

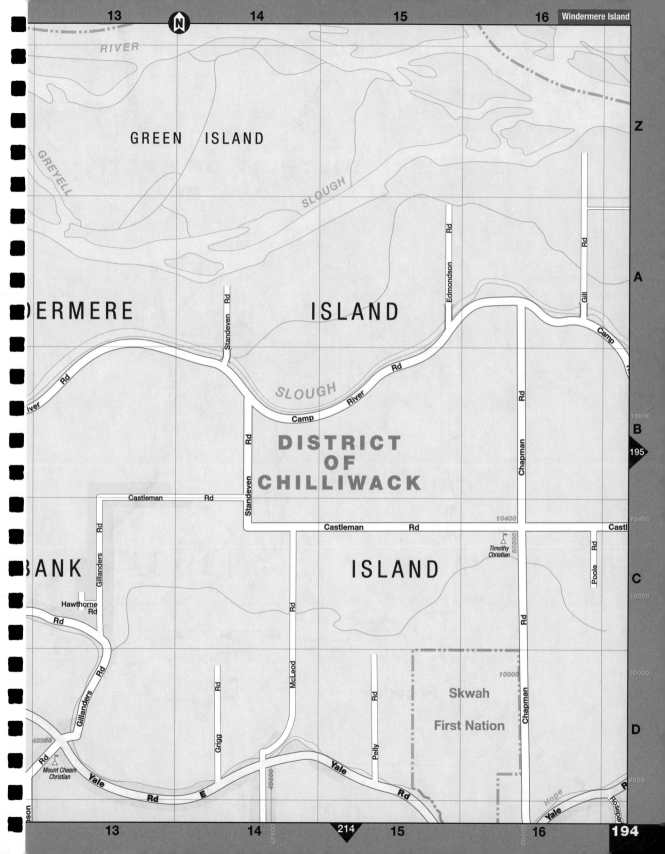

N

RIVER

GREYELL

GREEN ISLAND

SLOUGH

Z

DERMERE

ISLAND

Standeven Rd

Edmondson Rd

Gill Rd

A

Camp

River Rd

SLOUGH

River Rd

Camp

Rd

Rd

Chapman Rd

B

195

DISTRICT
OF
CHILLIWACK

Standeven

Castleman Rd

Rd

Castleman Rd

Castl

10400

10400

Timothy
Christian

50500

Castl

10200

Gillanders Rd

BANK

ISLAND

Rd

Poole Rd

C

Hawthorne Rd

Rd

Rd

10000

Gillanders Rd

Grigg Rd

McLeod Rd

Pelly Rd

Skwah

First Nation

Chapman Rd

D

48988

Mount Cheam
Christian

Rd

Yale Rd E

49690

Yale Rd

Hope

9600

son

Yale R

Rosedar

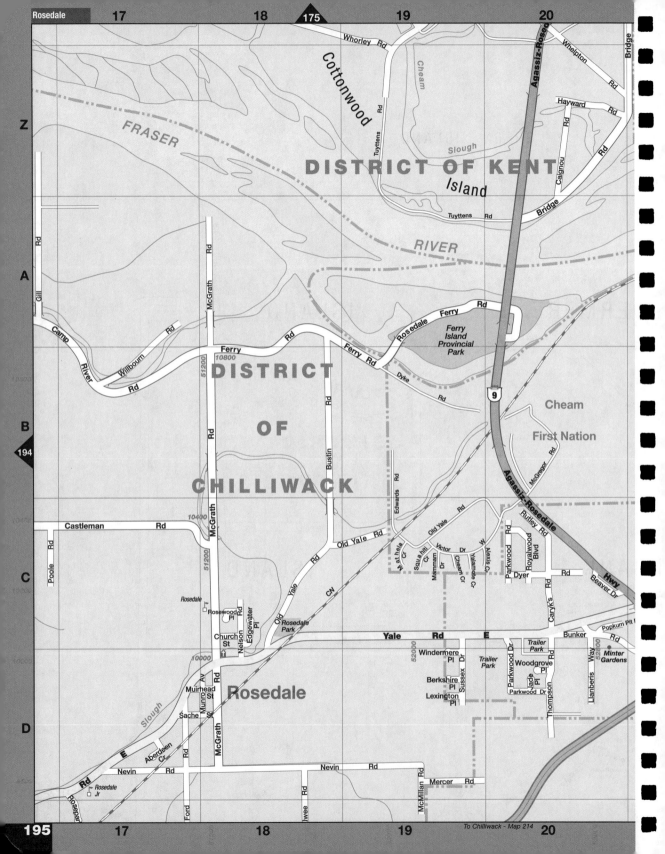

DISTRICT OF KENT

Cottonwood

FRASER

Slough

Island

RIVER

DISTRICT

OF

CHILLIWACK

Whorley Rd

Cheam

Tuyttens Rd

Agassiz-Rosedale

Whelpton

Bridge

Hayward Rd

Caignou Rd

Rd

Tuyttens Rd

Bridge

Rosedale Ferry Rd

Ferry
Island
Provincial
Park

Camp

River

Willbourn Rd

Gill Rd

McGrath Rd

Rd

Rd

Ferry

10800

51200

Rd

Bustin Rd

Ferry Rd

Dyke

Rd

9

Cheam

First Nation

Agassiz-Rosedale

McGregor Rd

Castleman Rd

Poole Rd

McGrath Rd

51200

10400

Edwards Rd

Old Yale Rd

Old Yale Rd

Yale Rd

CN

Rd

Mathela Ct

Squahill Cr

Marmam Dr

Victor Dr

Cheam Cr

Yelamute Cr

W

Alexis Cr

W

Rutley Rd

Parkwood

Royalwood Blvd

Dyer

Rd

Caryk's

Hwy

Beaver Dr

Rosedale

Rosewood Pl

Nelson Rd

Edgewater Pl

Church St

Rosedale Park

Yale Rd E

Popkum Pit Rd

10000

Windermere Pl

Trailer
Park

Bunker Rd

Trailer
Park

Minter
Gardens

52800

Berkshire Pl

Lexington Pl

Sussex Dr

Woodgrove Pl

Parkwood Dr

Jade Pl

Parkwood Dr

Thompson Rd

Llanberis Way

Muirhead St

Munro Av

Rd

Rosedale

Slough

Sache St

Aberdeen Ct

Rd

E

Nevin Rd

Nevin Rd

McGrath Rd

Ford Rd

Iwee Rd

McMillan Rd

Mercer Rd

Rosedale Jr

Rospear Rd

194

175

17   18   19   20

Z

A

B

C

D

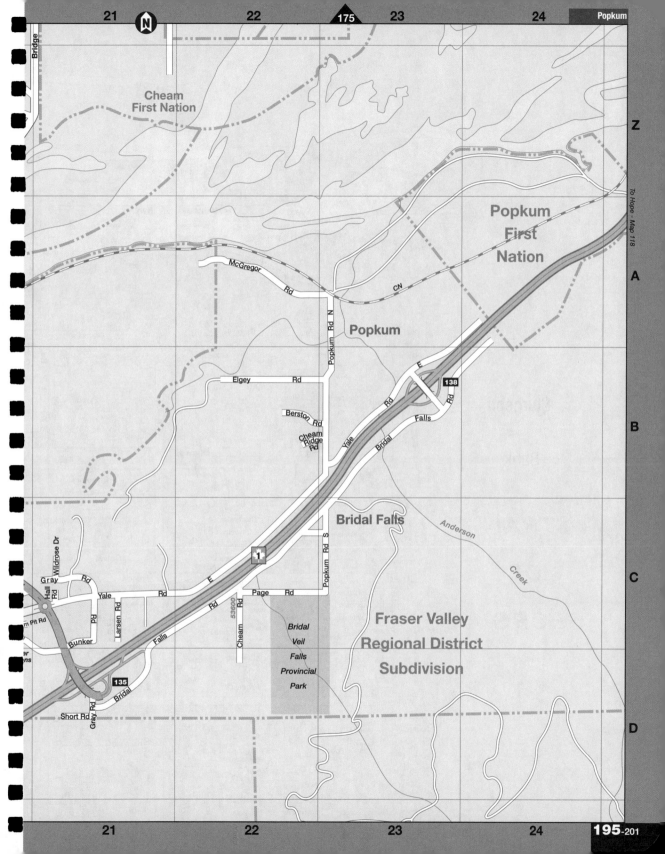

21 22 **175** 23 24

N

Cheam
First Nation

Popkum
First
Nation

To Hope - Map 118

Z

McGregor Rd

CN

A

Popkum Rd N

Popkum

Elgey Rd

F Rd

138

Berston Rd

Falls Rd

Cheam
Ridge Rd

Yale

Bridal

B

Bridal Falls

Anderson

Creek

Popkum Rd S

Wildrose Dr

1

Gray Rd

C

Page Rd

Fraser Valley

Yale Rd

E Rd

53600 Rd

Regional District

Hall Rd

Larsen Rd

Cheam Rd

Bridal

Subdivision

Pit Rd

Bunker

Falls Rd

Veil

Falls

Provincial

Park

135

Bridal

D

Short Rd

Gray Rd

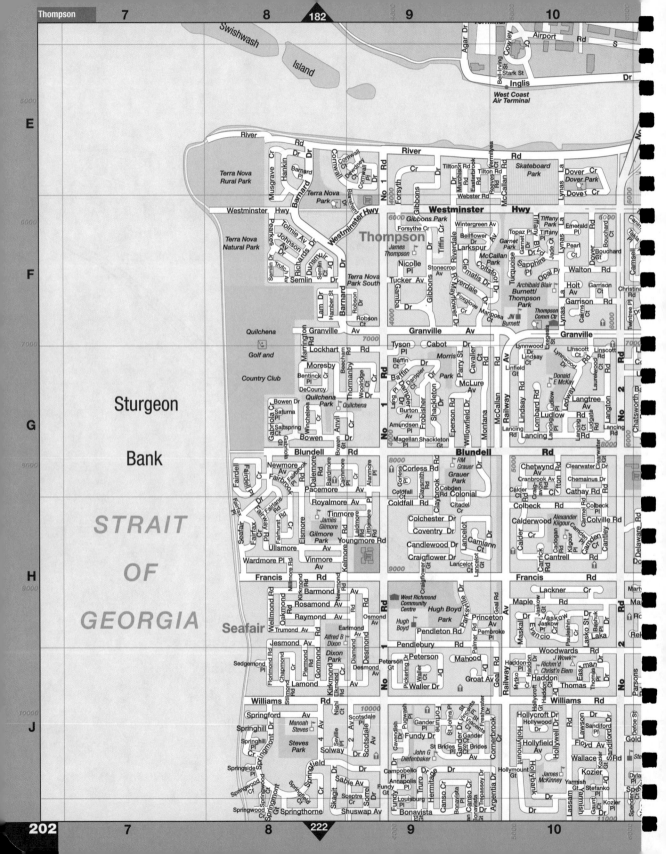

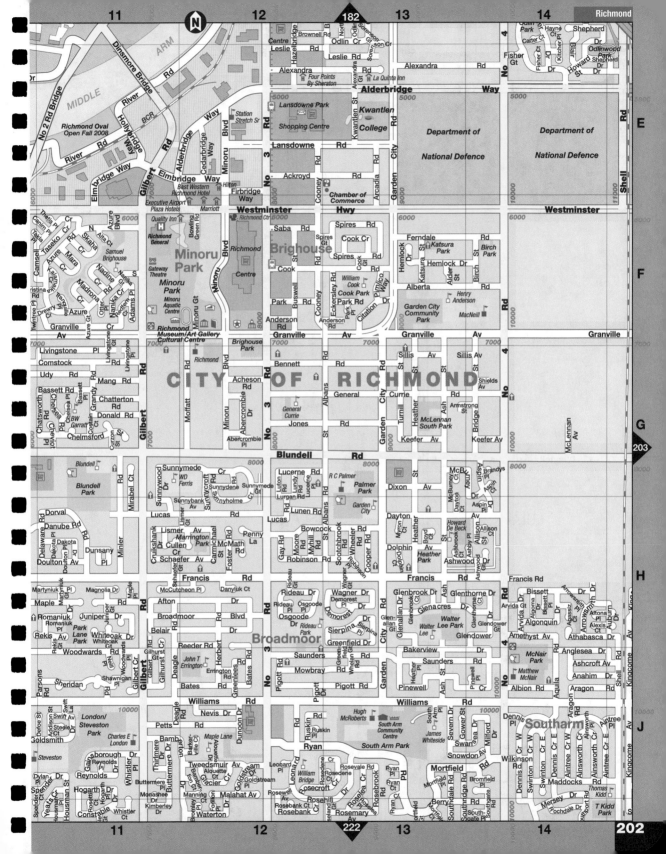

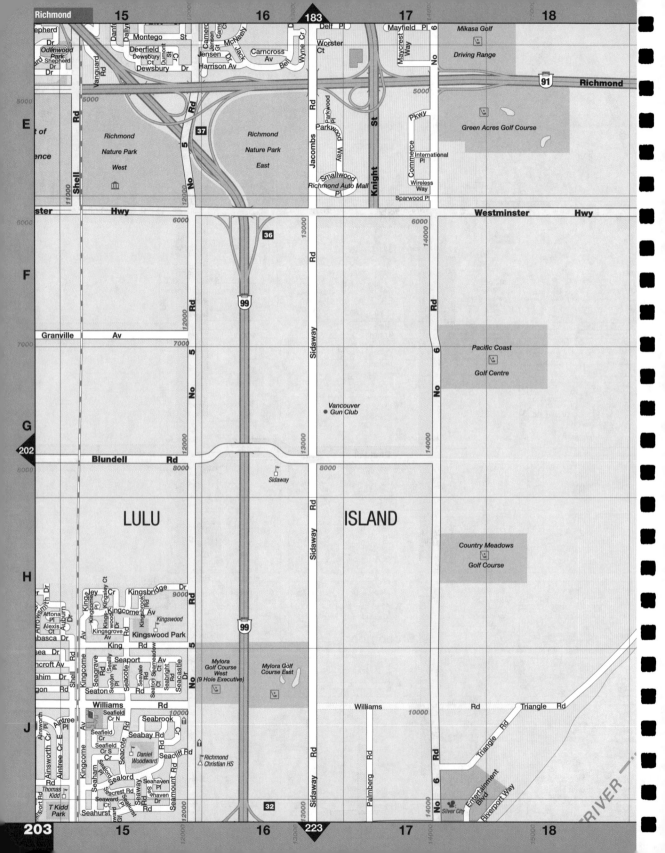

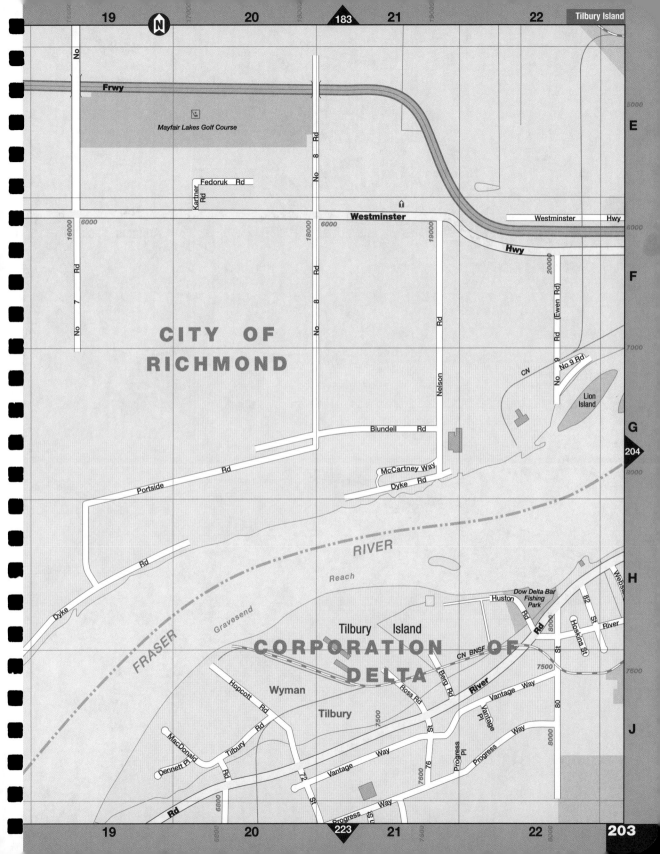

N

Frwy

Mayfair Lakes Golf Course

Fedoruk Rd

Kartner Rd

No

No 8 Rd

Westminster

Westminster Hwy

Hwy

No 7 Rd

16000

6000

6000

18000

6000

19000

20000

No 9 Rd (Ewen Rd)

CITY OF
RICHMOND

Nelson Rd

CN

Lion Island

Blundell Rd

McCartney Way

Dyke Rd

Portside Rd

RIVER

Reach

Dyke Rd

Dow Delta Bar Fishing Park

Huston

Webb

82 St

Hoskins St

FRASER

Gravesend

Tilbury Island

CORPORATION OF
DELTA

CN BNSF

Berg Rd

Ross Rd

River

River

Rd

St

Wyman

Hopcott Rd

Tilbury Rd

7500

8000

7500

7500

Vantage Way

80

Tilbury

76 St

Vantage Pl

Progress Pl

Progress Way

8000

MacDonald Rd

Dennett Pl

Tilbury Rd

Vantage Way

72 St

7600

Progress Way

Rd

6800

6800

7600

E

F

G

204

H

J

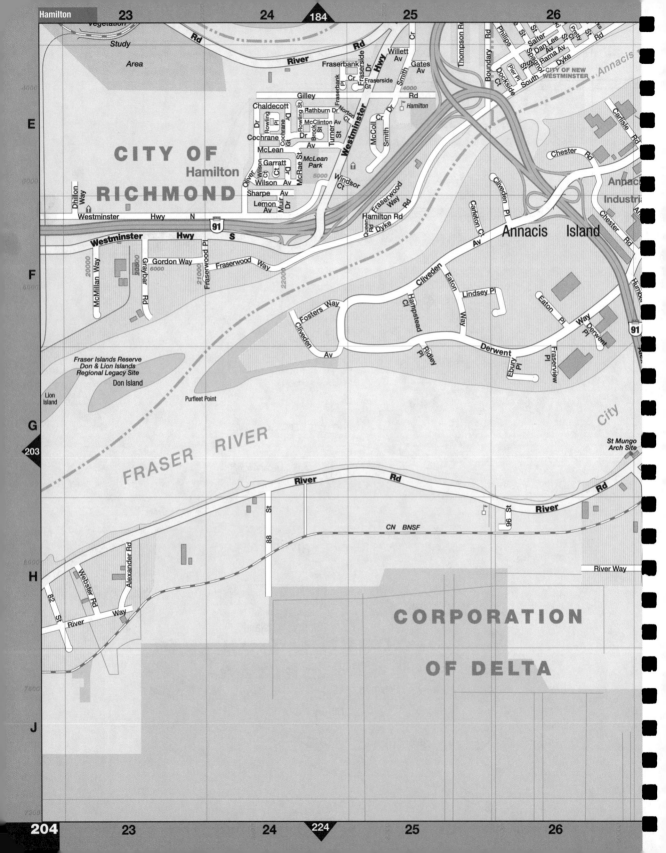

Vegetation
Study
Area

River

Fraserbank
Cr
Fraserside
Gt

Willett
Av

Gates
Av

Hwy

Smith
Ct

CITY OF NEW
WESTMINSTER

Annacis

Gilley

Rd

Hamilton

Dock Rd

Chaldecott
Dr

Rathburn Dr

McClinton Av

Cochrane
Dr

McLean

Garratt

Westminster Hwy

McColl
Cr

Smith
Dr

Chester   Rd

CITY OF
Hamilton
RICHMOND

McLean
Park

Windsor
Ct

Fraserwood
Way

Rd

Annacis

Industri

Sharpe   Av

Lemon
Av

Dhillon
Way

Westminster   Hwy   N

91

Hamilton Rd

Queen Rd

Dyke

Carleton Cr

Cliveden   Av

Annacis   Island

Chester   Rd

Westminster   Hwy   S

Graybar
Rd

Gordon Way

Fraserwood Pl

Fraserwood   Way

McMillan Way

Cliveden
Ct

Eaton
Av

Lindsey Pl

Eaton
Pl

Way

91

Fosters Way

Hampstead
Av

Derwent
Pl

Fraserview Pl

Cliveden

Ridley
Pl

Derwent

Ebury Pl

Fraser Islands Reserve
Don & Lion Islands
Regional Legacy Site
Don Island

Cliveden
Av

Lion
Island

Purfleet Point

City

St Mungo
Arch Site

203

FRASER   RIVER

River   Rd

River   Rd

St

88 St

CN   BNSF

96 St

River

River Way

H

Webster Rd

Alexander Rd

CORPORATION

82 St

River

Way

OF DELTA

J

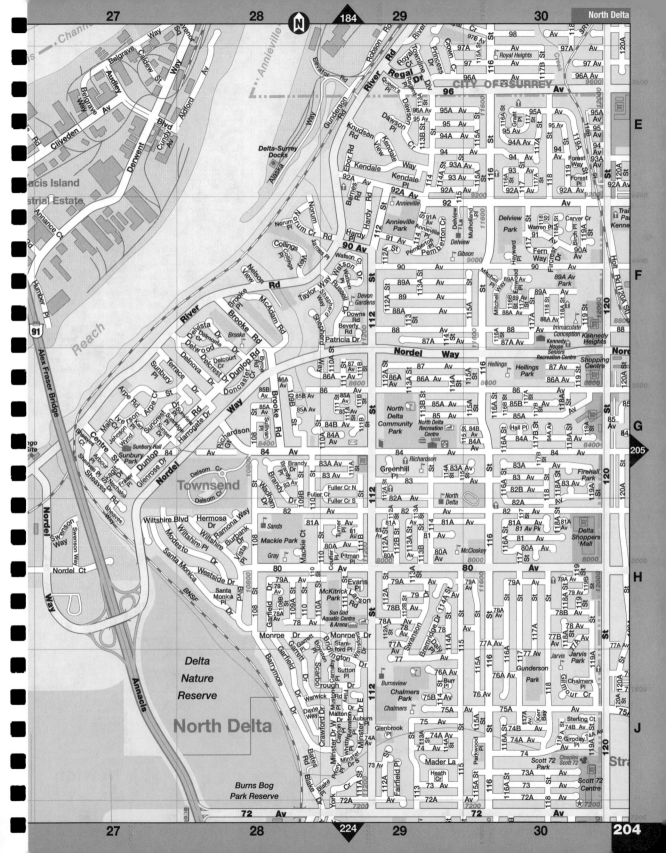

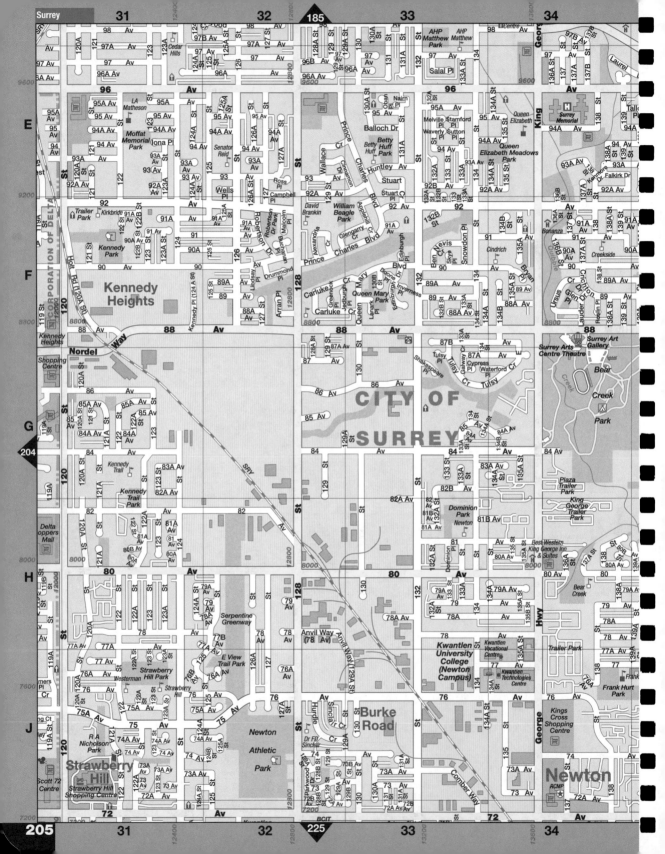

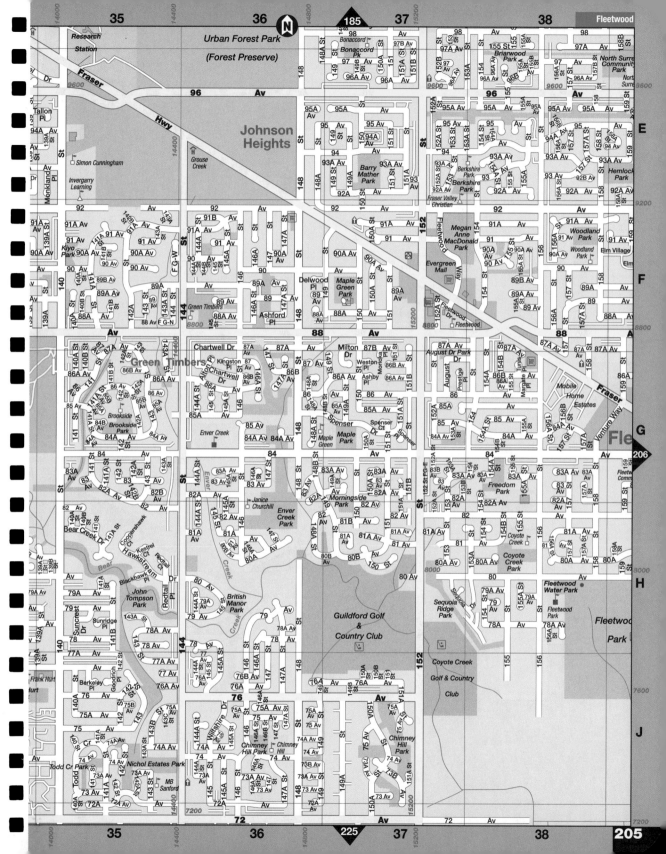

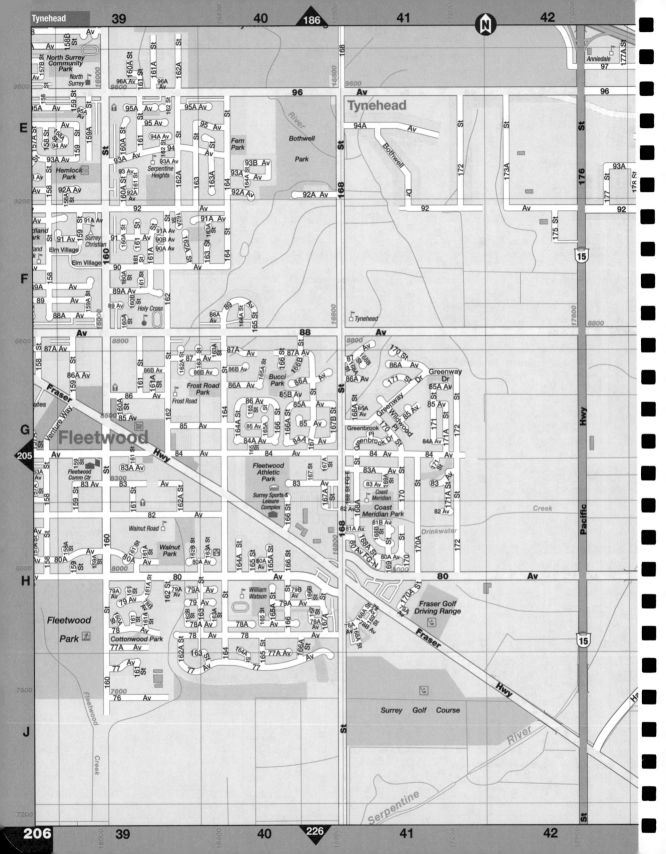

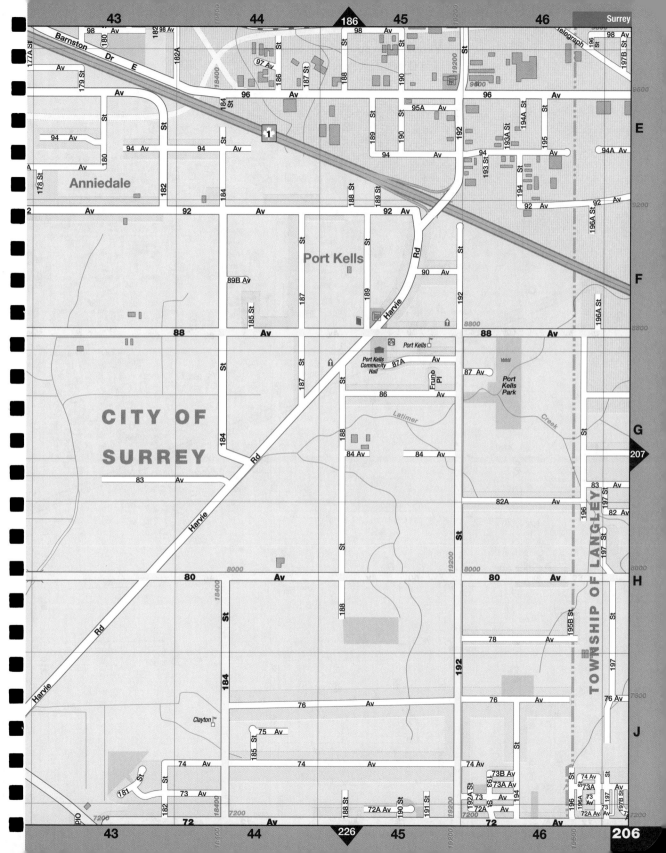

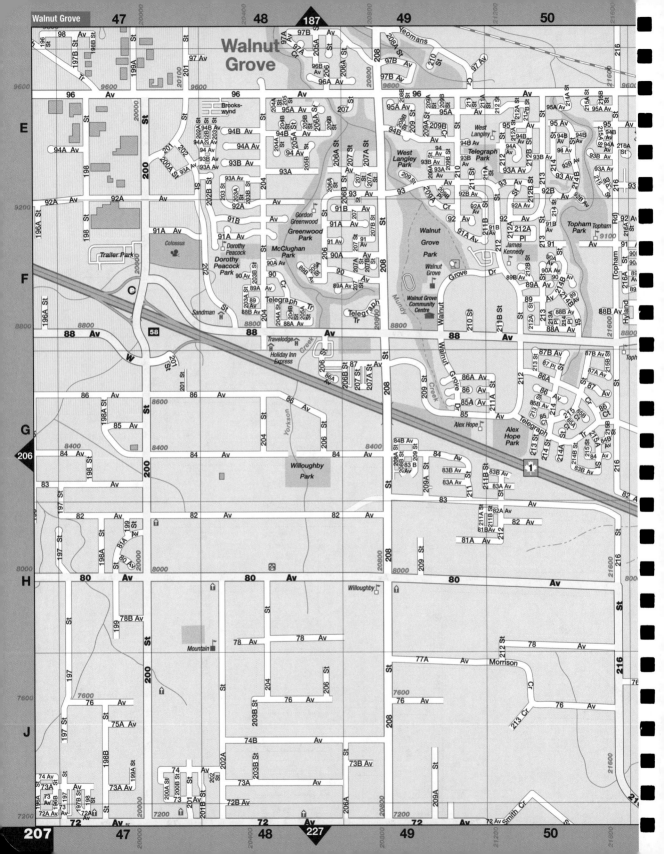

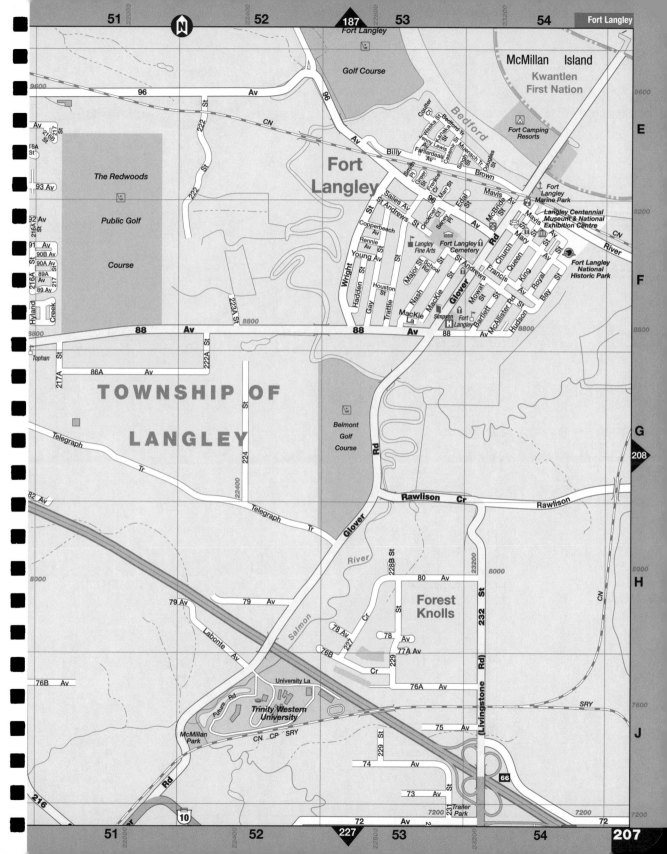

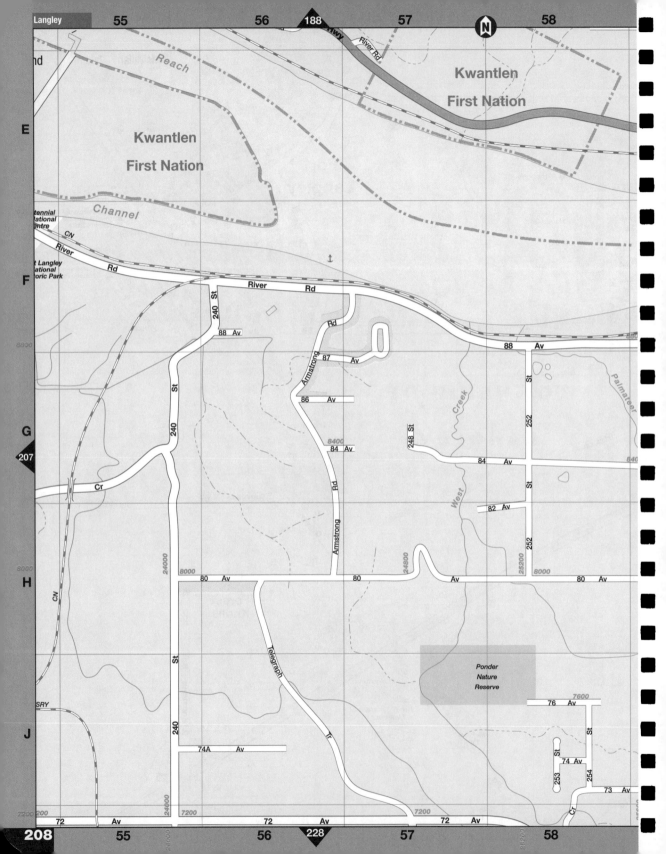

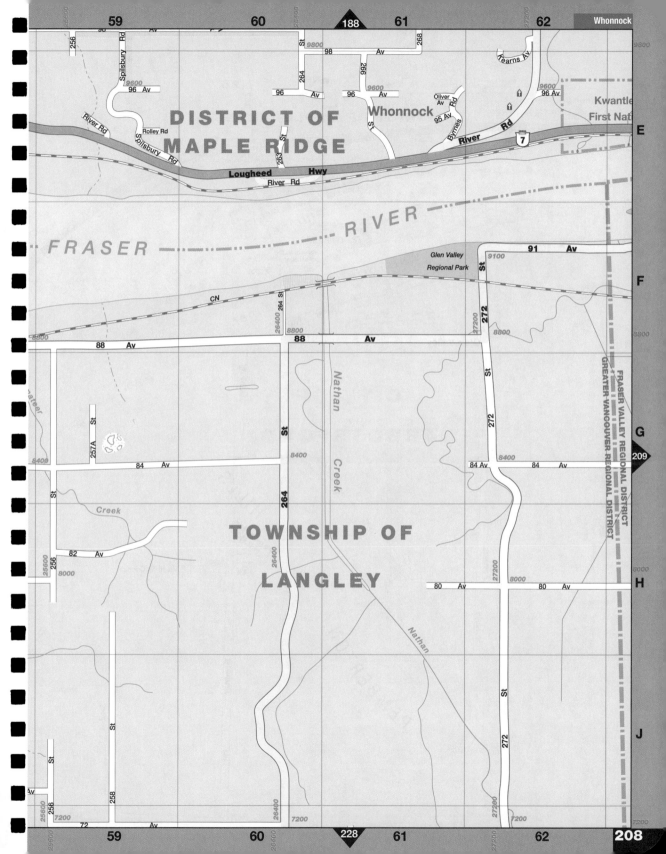

256

Spilsbury Rd

98 Av

9800

264

266

268

96 Av

9600

96

96

9600

Oliver Av

95 Av

Byrnes Rd

Kearns Av

96 Av

9600

9800

Kwantle
First Nati

River Rd

Rolley Rd

Spilsbury Rd

DISTRICT OF
MAPLE RIDGE

Whonnock

263

River Rd

7

E

Lougheed Hwy

River Rd

FRASER
RIVER

Glen Valley
Regional Park

91 Av

9100

272 St

F

CN

264 St

26400

8800

8800

88 Av

8800

27200

272 St

8800

88 Av

88 Av

257A St

Nathan

Creek

St

8400

84 Av

272 St

84 Av

8400

84 Av

G

209

St

Creek

264 St

26400

TOWNSHIP OF

256

25600

82 Av

8000

272

27200

8000

LANGLEY

80 Av

8000

80 Av

H

Nathan

St

258

St

256

25600

272 St

J

St

256

25600

7200

72 Av

26400

27200

7200

7200

FRASER VALLEY REGIONAL DISTRICT

GREATER VANCOUVER REGIONAL DISTRICT

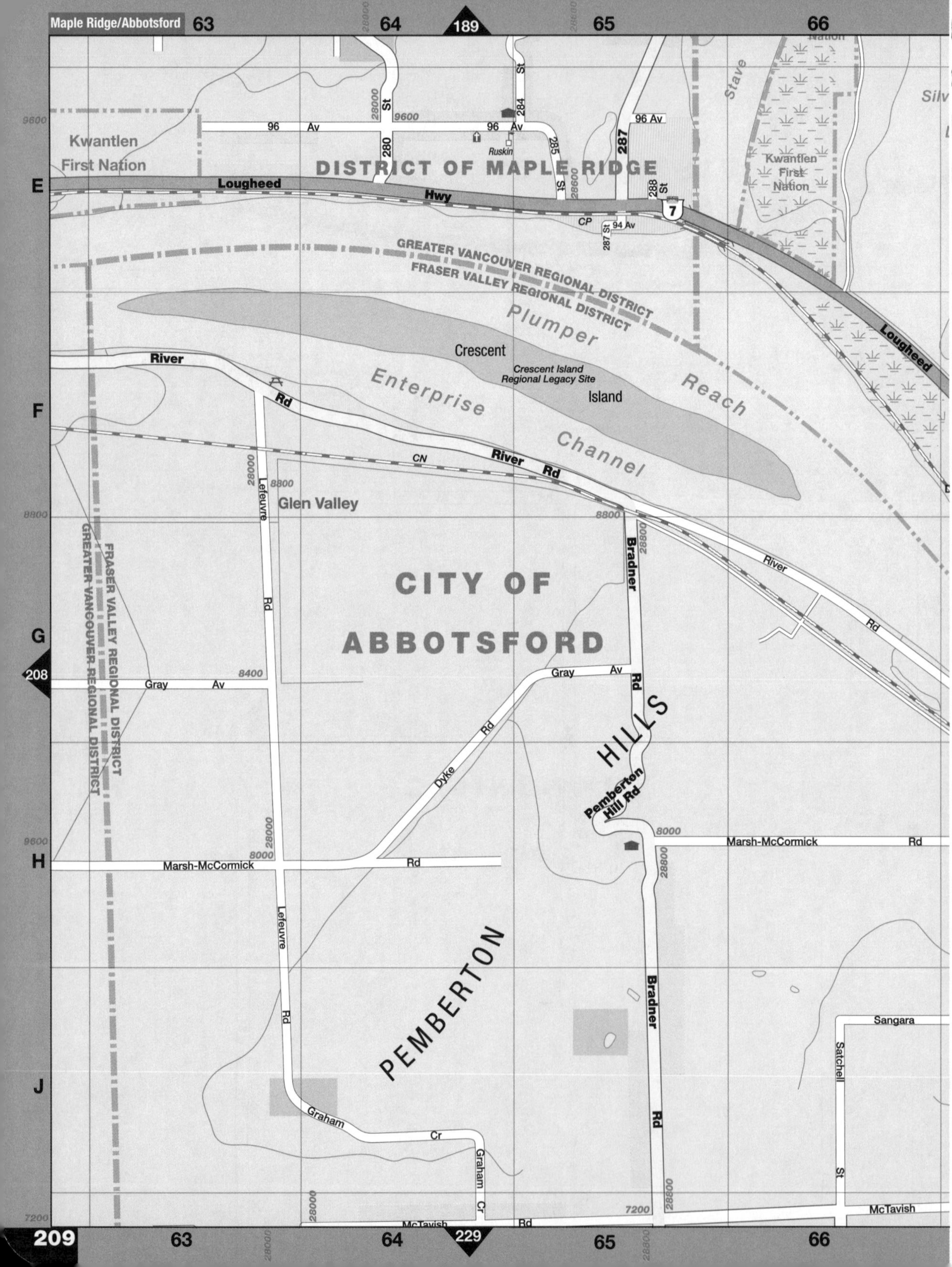

96 Av

96 Av

96 Av

Ruskin

DISTRICT OF MAPLE RIDGE

Kwantlen
First Nation

Kwantlen
First
Nation

Silv

Stave

E Lougheed Hwy

CP

94 Av

7

Lougheed

GREATER VANCOUVER REGIONAL DISTRICT

FRASER VALLEY REGIONAL DISTRICT

Plumper

Crescent

Crescent Island
Regional Legacy Site

Island

Reach

River

Enterprise

Channel

Rd

F

CN

River

Rd

Glen Valley

8800

CITY OF

Bradner

River

ABBOTSFORD

Rd

Rd

G

Gray

Av

208

Gray

Av

Rd

Rd

HILLS

Dyke

Pemberton
Hill Rd

Marsh-McCormick

Rd

H

Marsh-McCormick

Rd

Rd

Lefeuvre

Rd

PEMBERTON

Bradner

Rd

Sangara

Satchell

St

J

Graham

Cr

Graham

Cr

McTavish

Rd

McTavish

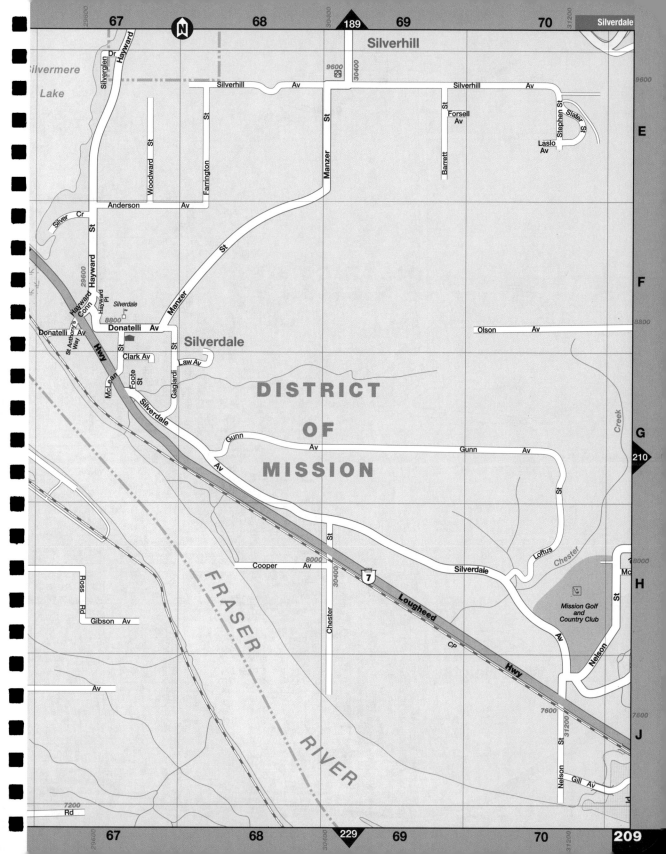

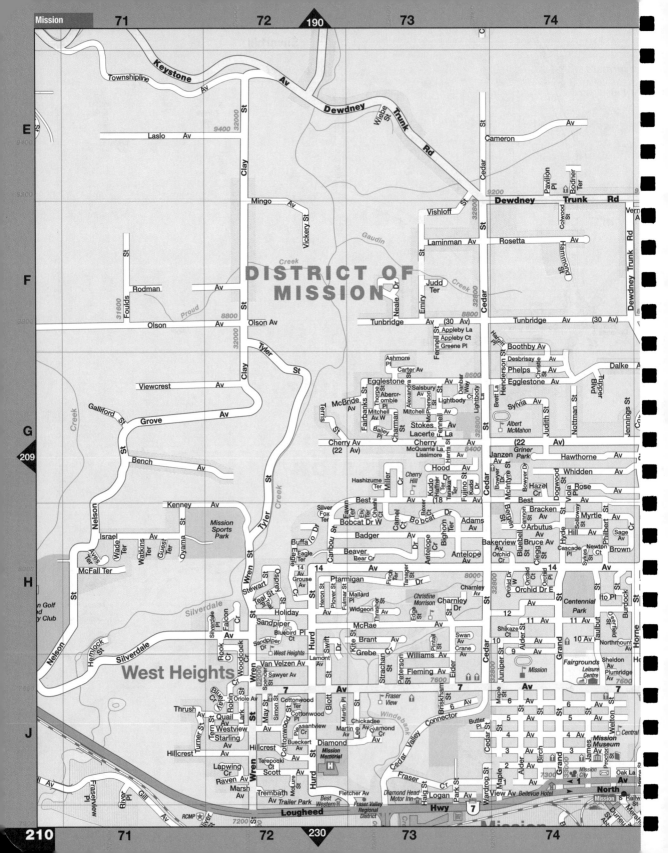

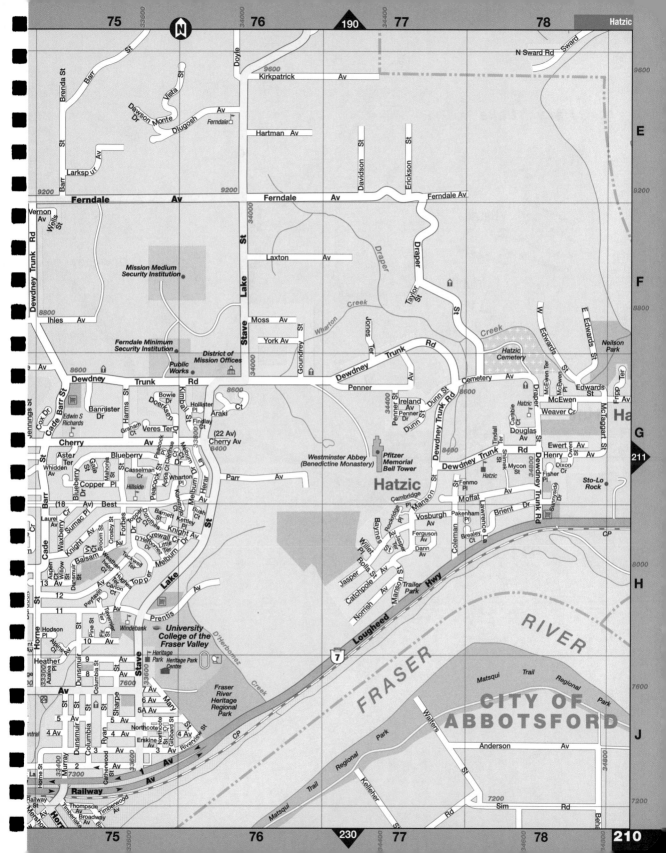

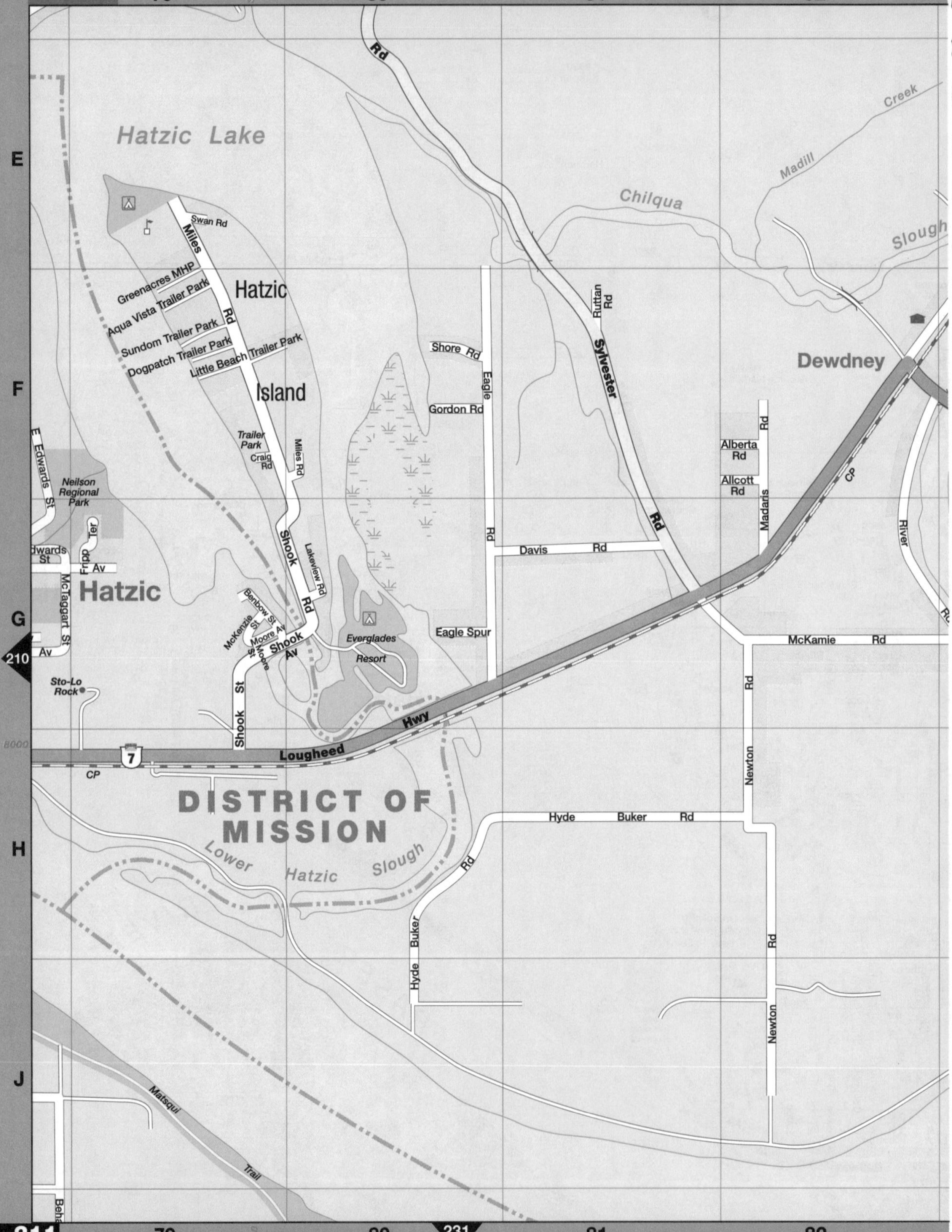

79　　　　　80　　　　　81　　　　　82

E

Hatzic Lake

Swan Rd

Miles

Greenacres MHP

Aqua Vista Trailer Park

Sundom Trailer Park

Dogpatch Trailer Park

Little Beach Trailer Park

Hatzic

F

Island

Trailer Park

Craig Rd

Miles Rd

Shook Rd

Lakeview Rd

E Edwards St

Neilson Regional Park

Poplar Ter

Edwards St

McTaggart St

Poplar Av

Hatzic

Av

Benbow St

McKenzie St

Moore Av

Moore St

Shook St

Shook Av

Everglades Resort

Eagle Spur

Shore Rd

Gordon Rd

Eagle

Rd

Rd

Davis　　Rd

Ruttan Rd

Sylvester Rd

Chilqua

Slough

Madill Creek

Dewdney

Alberta Rd

Allcott Rd

Madaris Rd

CP

River

McKamie　Rd

Newton Rd

G

210

Sto-Lo Rock

8000

7

CP

Lougheed

Hwy

DISTRICT OF MISSION

Lower　Hatzic　Slough

Rd

H

Hyde　Buker　Rd

Hyde

Buker Rd

Newton Rd

J

Matsqui

Trail

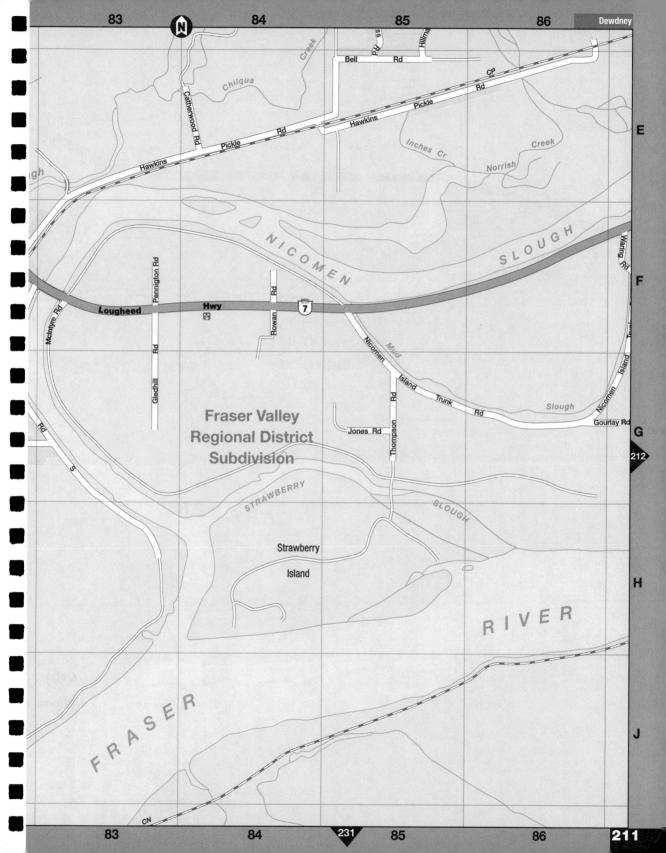

N

E

F

G

212

H

J

Creek

Chilqua

Bell Rd

Rd

Hillma

CP

Rd

Catherwood Rd

Pickle

Rd

Hawkins

Pickle

Rd

Inches Cr

Norrish

Creek

Hawkins

ugh

N I C O M E N

S L O U G H

Waring Rd

Pennington Rd

Rd

Lougheed   Hwy

7

Rowan

McIntyre Rd

Gledhill   Rd

Nicomen

Mud

Island

Trunk

Rd

Slough

Nicomen   Island

Fraser Valley Regional District Subdivision

Rd

S

Jones Rd

Thompson   Rd

Gourlay Rd

STRAWBERRY

SLOUGH

Strawberry

Island

R I V E R

F R A S E R

CN

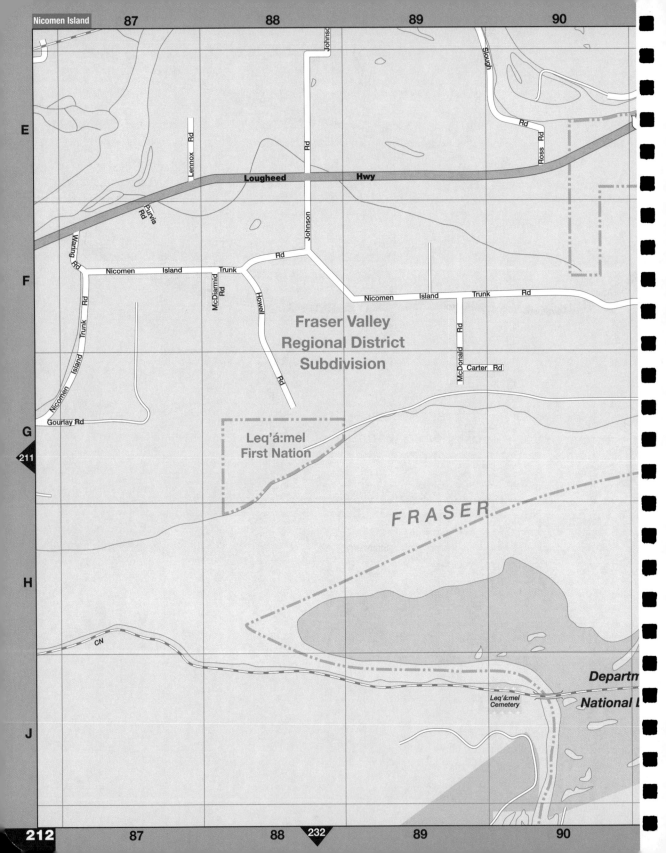

87 88 89 90

Johnson

Slough

Rd

Ross Rd

E

Lennox Rd

Rd

Lougheed Hwy

Purvis Rd

Johnson

Waring Rd

Rd

F

Nicomen Island Trunk

McDiarmid Rd

Howell

Nicomen Island Trunk Rd

Trunk Rd

Rd

**Fraser Valley
Regional District
Subdivision**

McDonald Rd

Rd

Nicomen Island

Carter Rd

McDonald

Gourlay Rd

G

**Leq'á:mel
First Nation**

F R A S E R

H

CN

Departm

Leq'á:mel
Cemetery

National

J

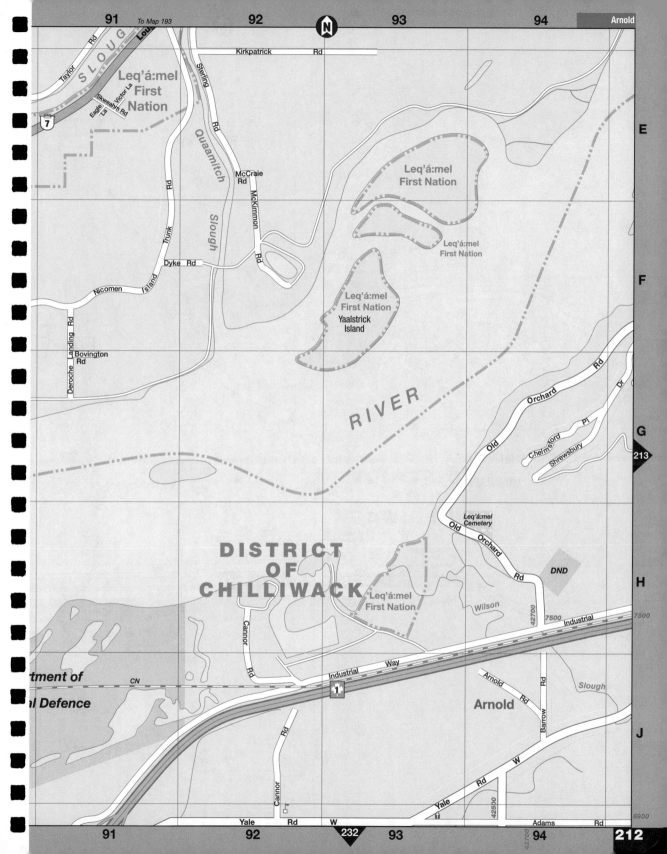

SLOUG

Taylor Rd

7

Leq'á:mel First Nation

Skweahm Rd
Eagle Ln
Victor La

Kirkpatrick Rd

N

E

Sterling Rd

Quaamitch

Trunk Rd

McCraie Rd

McKinnon Rd

Leq'á:mel First Nation

Leq'á:mel First Nation

Slough

Dyke Rd

Nicomen Island

F

Leq'á:mel First Nation
Yaalstrick Island

Deroche Landing Rd

Bovington Rd

RIVER

Orchard Rd

Old

Chelmsford Pl

Dr

Shrewsbury

G
213

Old

Leq'á:mel Cemetery

Orchard

DISTRICT OF CHILLIWACK

Leq'á:mel First Nation

Rd

DND

H

Wilson

42700

7500

Industrial

7500

Cannor Rd

Industrial Way

1

rtment of

CN

Arnold Rd

Rd

Slough

al Defence

Arnold

Barrow

J

Cannor Rd

Yale Rd W

42500

Adams Rd

6900

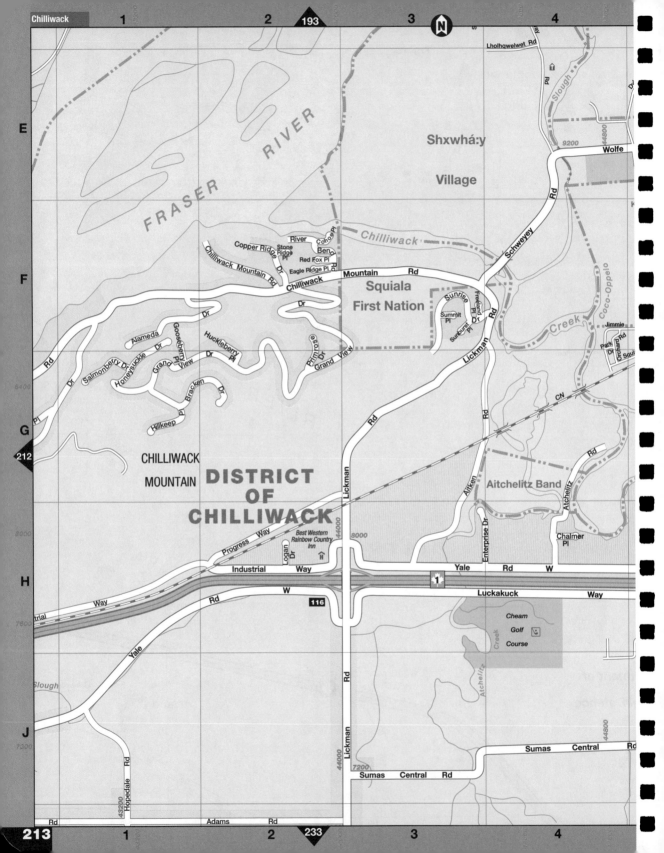

FRASER RIVER

Shxwhá:y

Village

Wolfe

Chilliwack

Schweyey Rd

Coco-Oppelo

Creek

Jimmie

River Cohoe Pl
Copper Ridge Stone Ben
Chilliwack Mountain Rd Ridge Pl Red Fox Pl
Eagle Ridge Pl
Chilliwack Mountain Rd

Squiala
First Nation

Sunrise
Summit Pl Freeland Dr
Pl
Sunburst Pl

Lickman

Park Orchard Rd
Dr

CN

Nameda
Gooseberry Pl
Alameda
Salmonberry Dr Huckleberry Pl
Honeysuckle Dr Grand View Dr Primrose Dr
Bracken Dr
Hillkeep

Rd

Pl

CHILLIWACK
MOUNTAIN

DISTRICT
OF
CHILLIWACK

Lickman Rd

Aitken

Enterprise Dr

Aitchelitz Band

Aitchelitz

Chalmer Pl

Rd

Progress Way
Logan Best Western
Dr Rainbow Country
Inn

Industrial Way

Yale Rd W

Way W

1

116

Luckakuck Way

Way

Yale

Rd

Cheam
Golf
Course

Creek

Aitchelitz

Lickman Rd

Slough

Hopedale Rd

Sumas Central Rd

Sumas Central Rd

Sumas Central Rd

Rd

Adams Rd

213

193

212

233

N

1 2 3 4

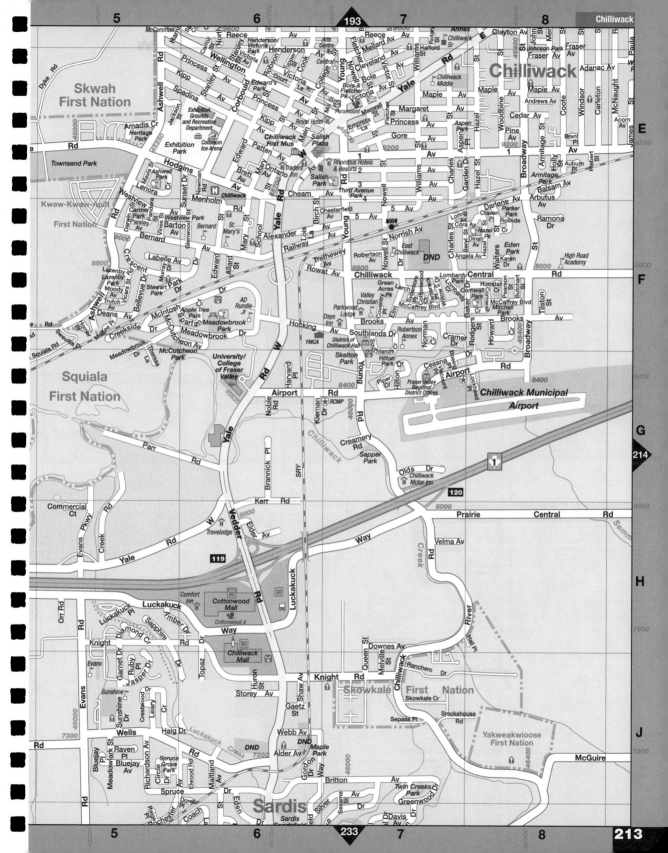

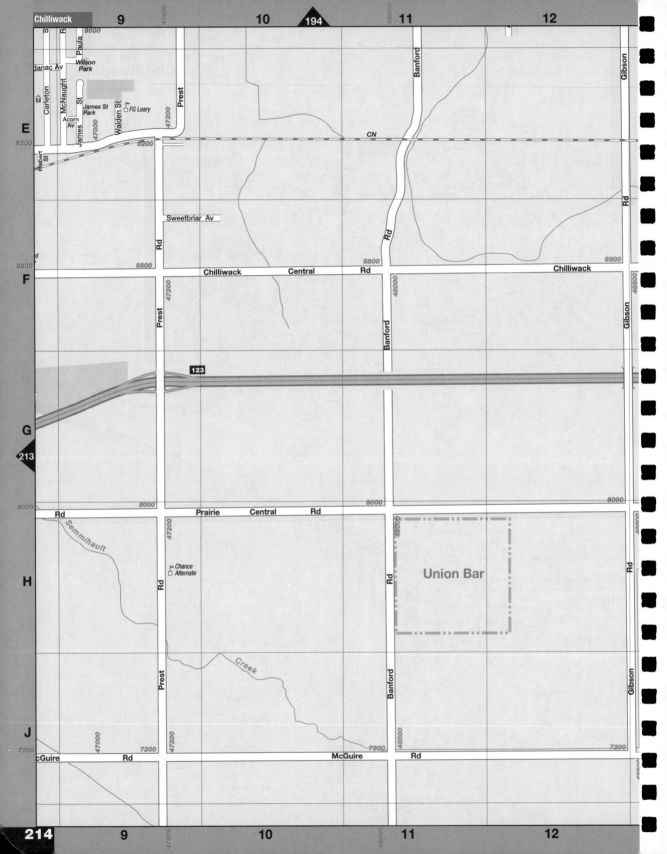

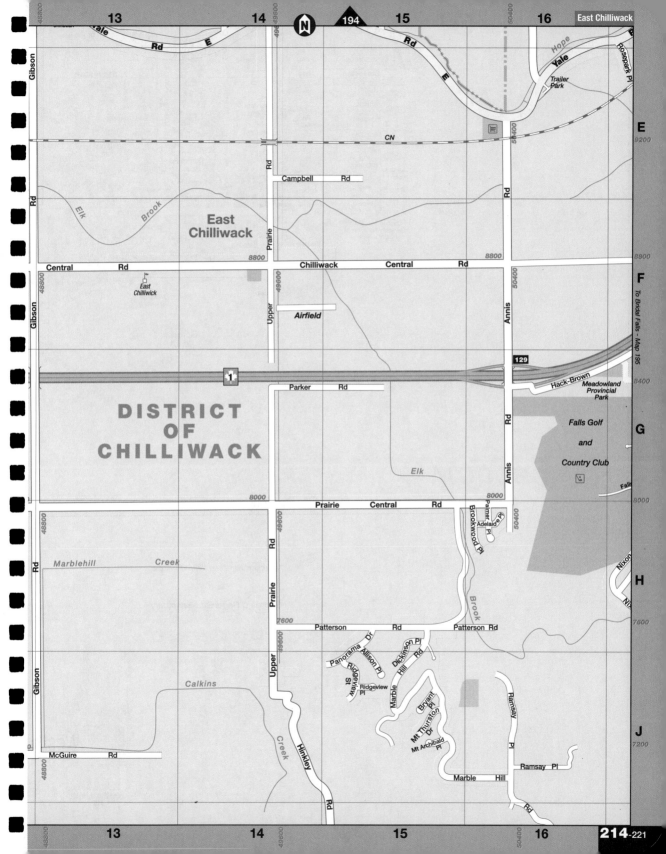

13 14 15 16

N

194

District Yale Rd E
Hope
Yale

Rosepark Pl

Trailer Park

E
9200

Gibson Rd

CN

Elk Brook

Campbell Rd

East Chilliwack

Rd

8800

Central Rd

Chilliwack Central Rd

8800

Gibson Rd

East Chilliwick

Prairie Rd

Upper Prairie Rd

Airfield

Annis Rd

F

129

To Bridal Falls - Map 195

8400

1

Parker Rd

Hack-Brown

Meadowland Provincial Park

G

DISTRICT
OF
CHILLIWACK

Elk

Annis Rd

Falls Golf
and
Country Club

Falls

8000

8000

Prairie Central Rd

Brookwood Pl

Palmer Pl

Adelaid

Nixon

Rd Marblehill Creek

Prairie Rd

Brook

H
7600

Gibson Rd

Rd

7600

Patterson Rd

Patterson Rd

Calkins

Upper Prairie Rd

Panorama Dr

Allison Pl

Ridgeview St

Dickinson Pl

Marble Hill Rd

Ridgeview Pl

Bryant Pl

Mt Thurston Dr

Mt Archibald Pl

Ramsay Pl

J
7200

McGuire Rd

Hinkley Creek

Rd

Marble Hill

Ramsay Pl

Rd

13 14 15 16

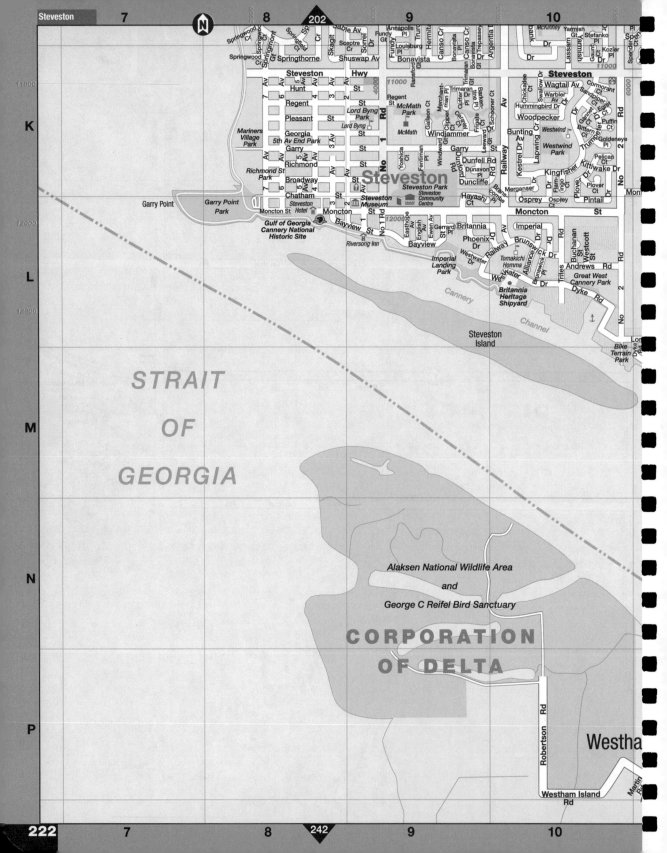

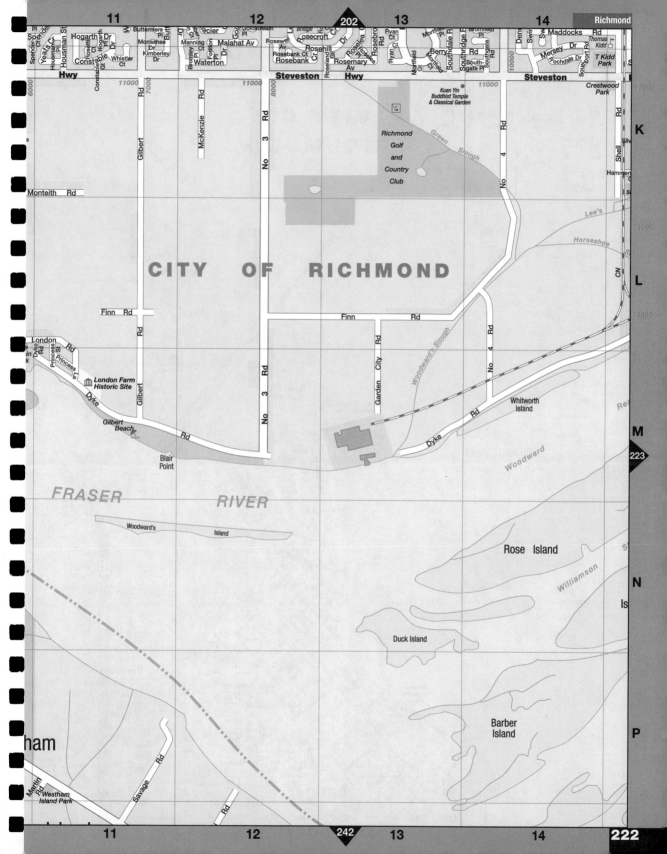

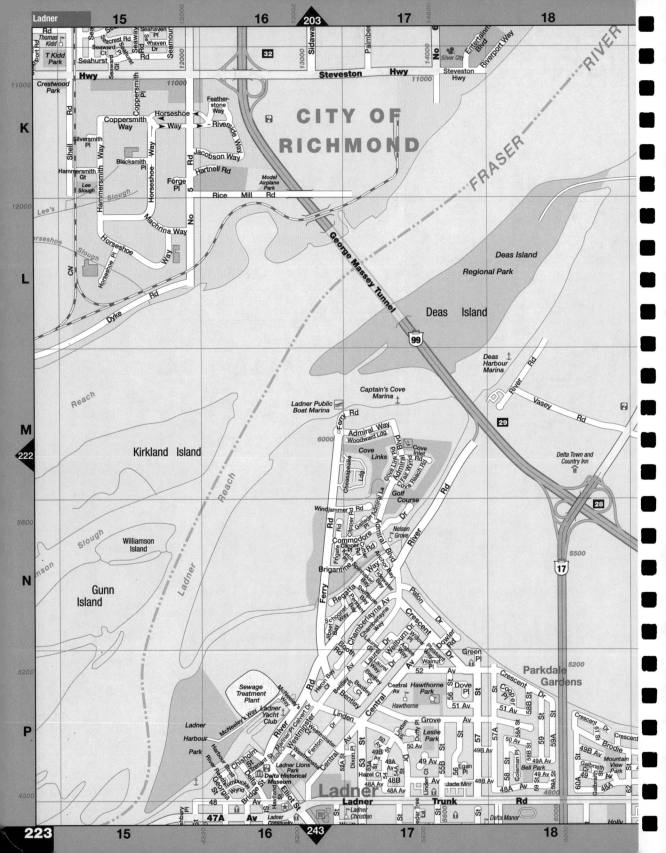

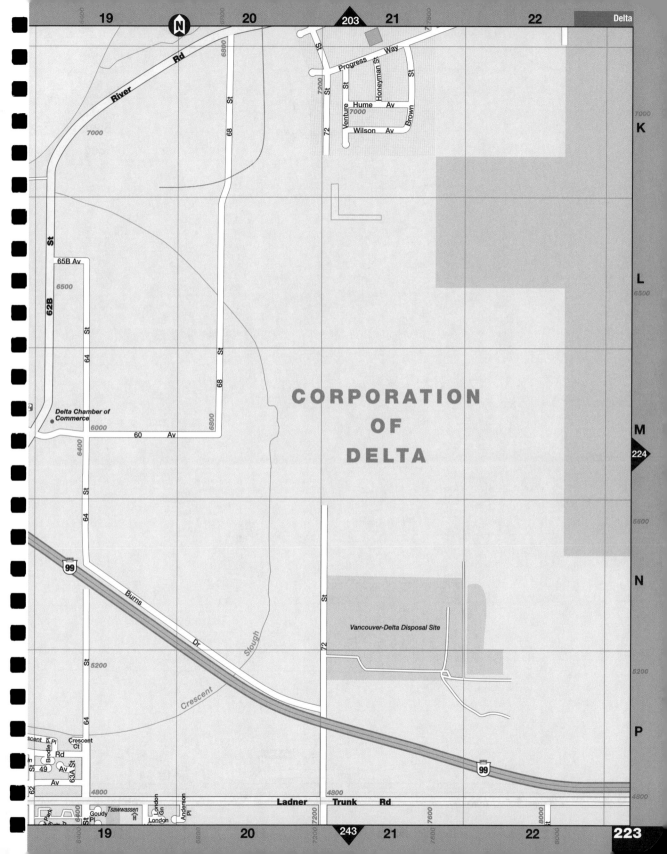

N

K

L

M

224

N

P

7000

6500

5600

5200

4800

7000

6500

River   Rd

6800

St   68

St

7200

Progress   Way

Venture   St

St   72

7000

Honeyman St

Hume   Av

Brown   St

Wilson   Av

St   62B

65B Av

6500

St   64

6000

St   68

6800

Delta Chamber of
Commerce

60   Av

St   6400

St   64

CORPORATION

OF

DELTA

99

Burns   Dr

St   64

St   5200

Crescent

Slough

St   72

Vancouver-Delta Disposal Site

scent Pl   Crescent
Ct

Brodie   Rd

In   St   49   Av

63A St

St   62

Av

4800

London
Gn

Tsawwassen

Goudy
Pl

London

Anderson
Pl

Ladner   Trunk   Rd

4800

7600

8000

St

99

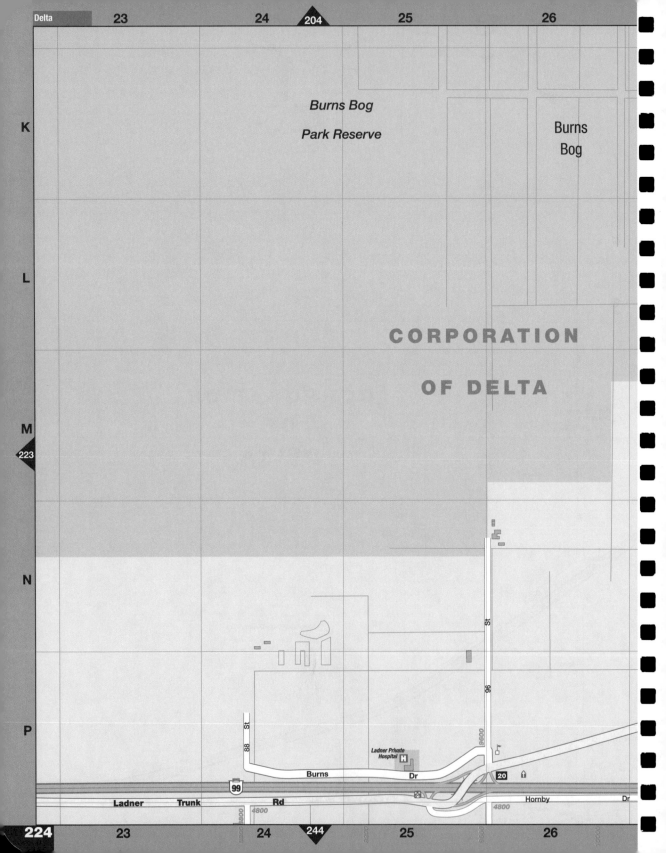

K

Burns Bog

Park Reserve

Burns
Bog

L

CORPORATION

OF DELTA

M

223

N

St

96

St

P

88 St

9600

Ladner Private
Hospital H

Burns   Dr

20

99

Hornby Dr

Ladner Trunk Rd

5800

4800

4800

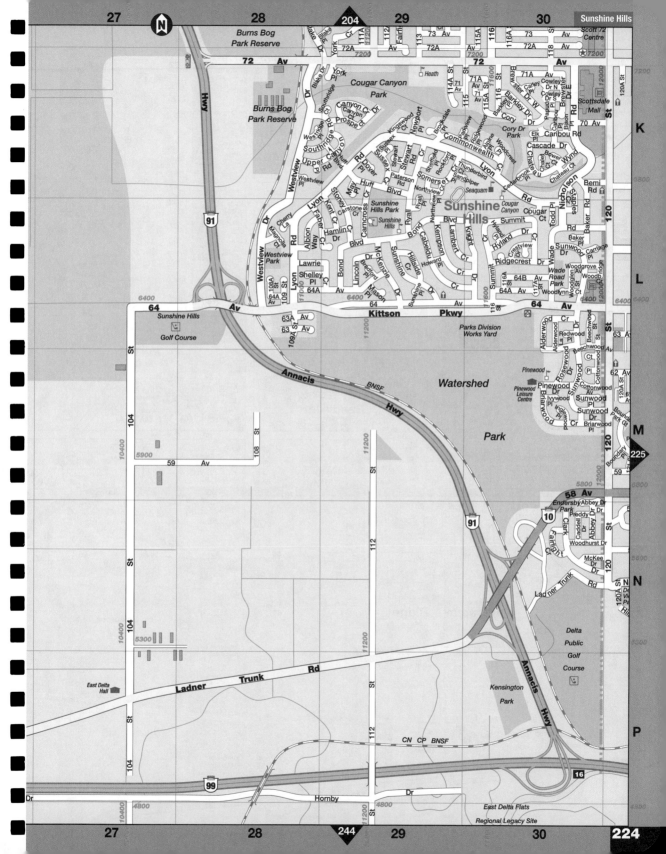

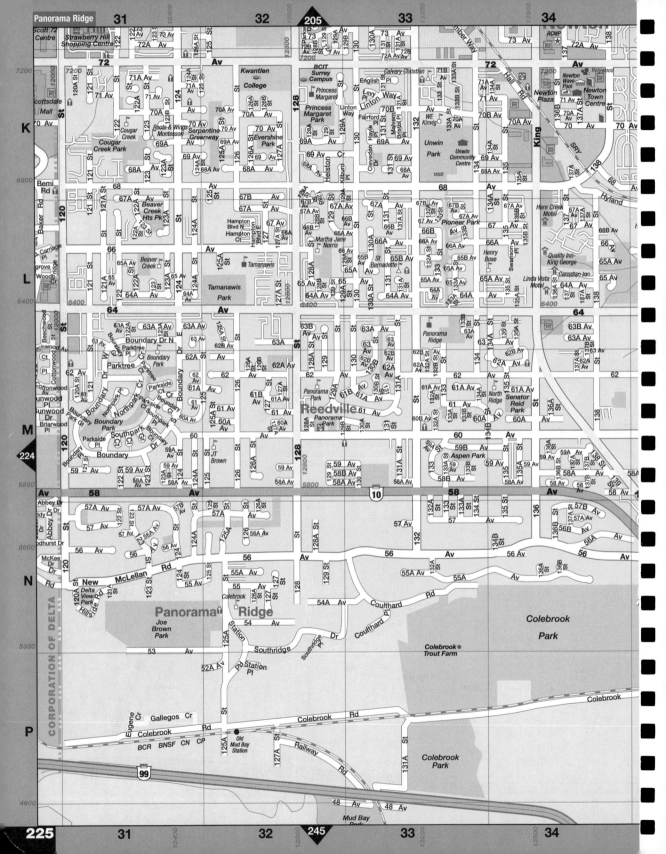

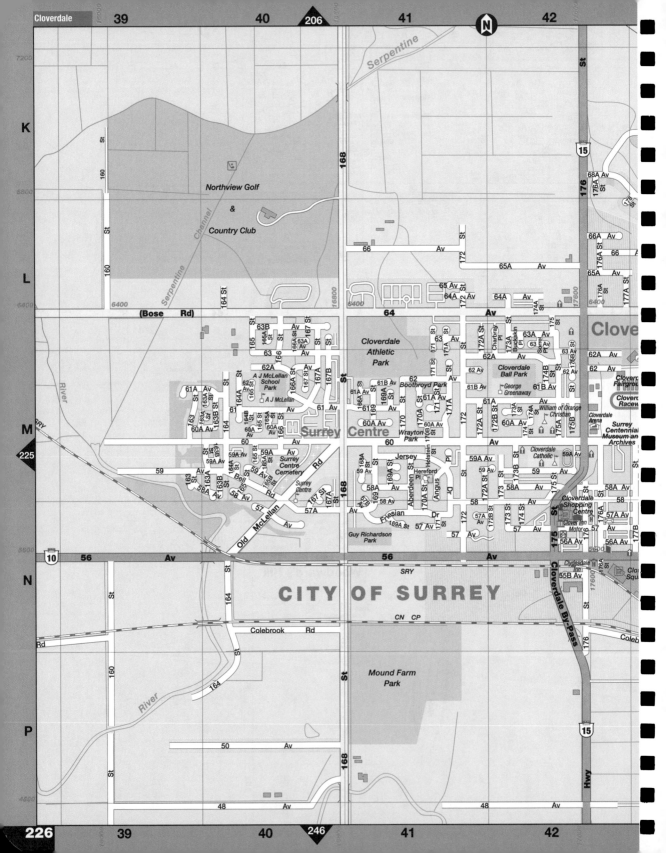

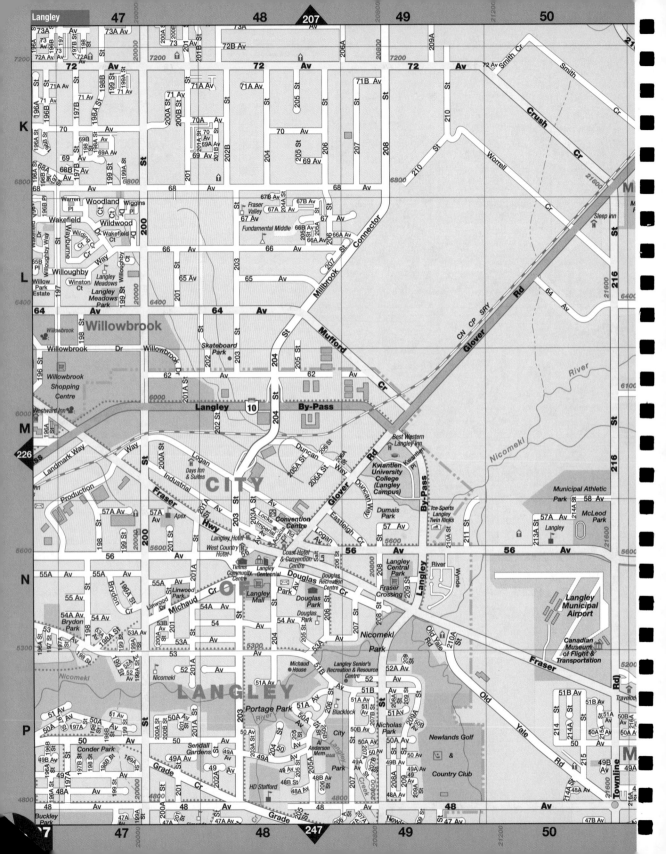

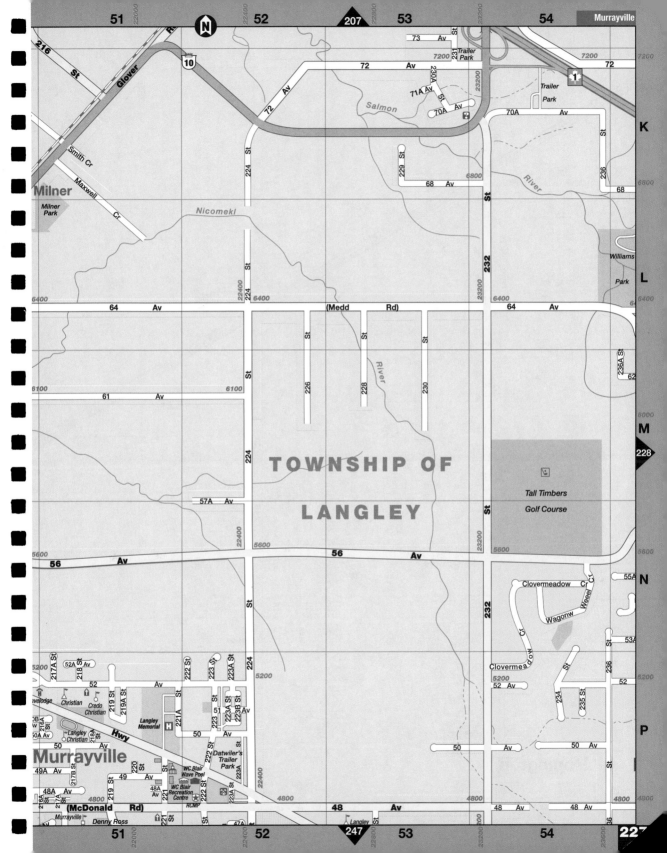

TOWNSHIP OF

LANGLEY

Milner

Milner Park

Murrayville

Salmon

River

Nicomekl

River

Tall Timbers
Golf Course

Clovermeadow Cr

Wagonw

Clovermea

Williams
Park

Trailer Park

Trailer
Park

Langley
Memorial

WC Blair
Wave Pool

WC Blair
Recreation
Centre

Datwiler's
Trailer Park

Credo
Christian

Langley
Christian

Christian

RCMP

Langley

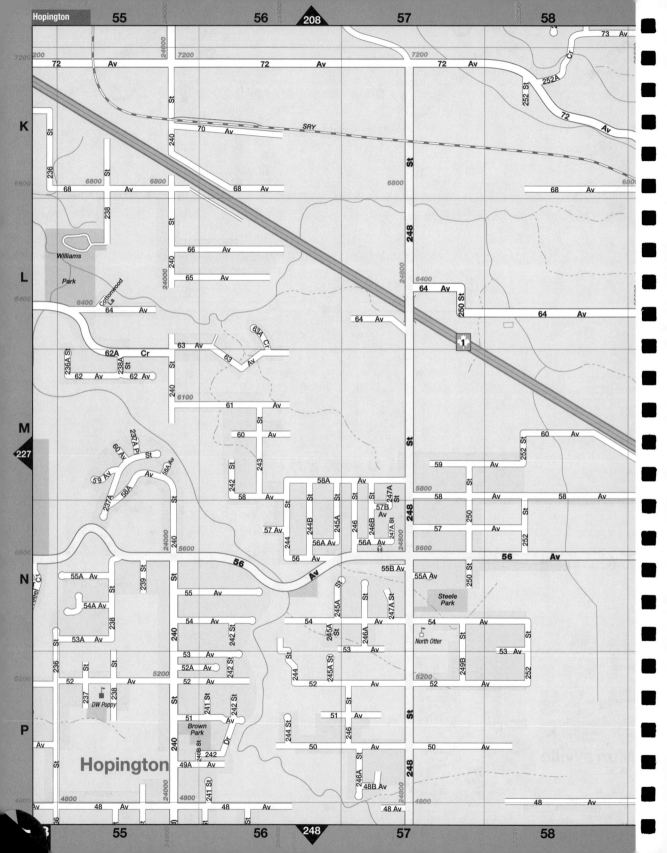

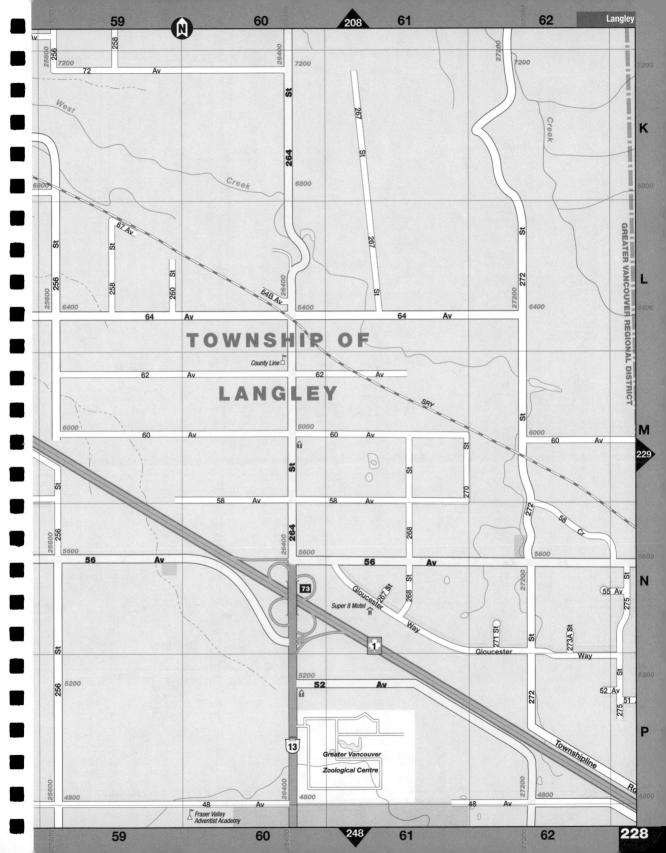

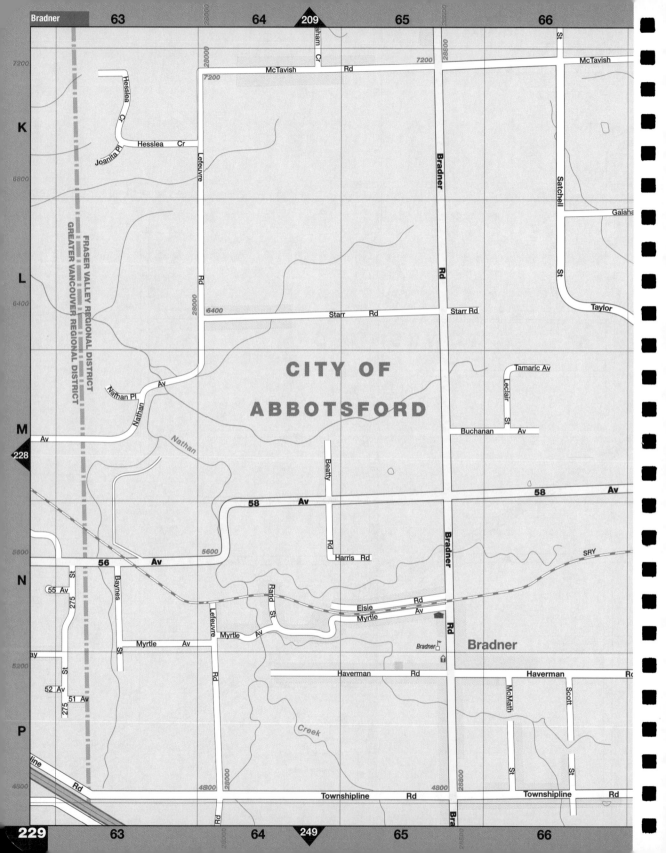

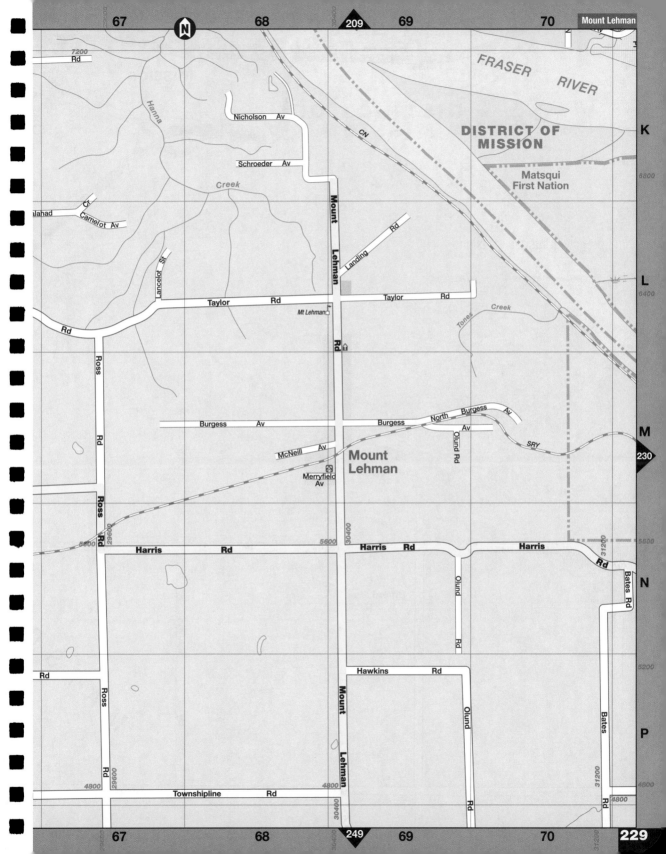

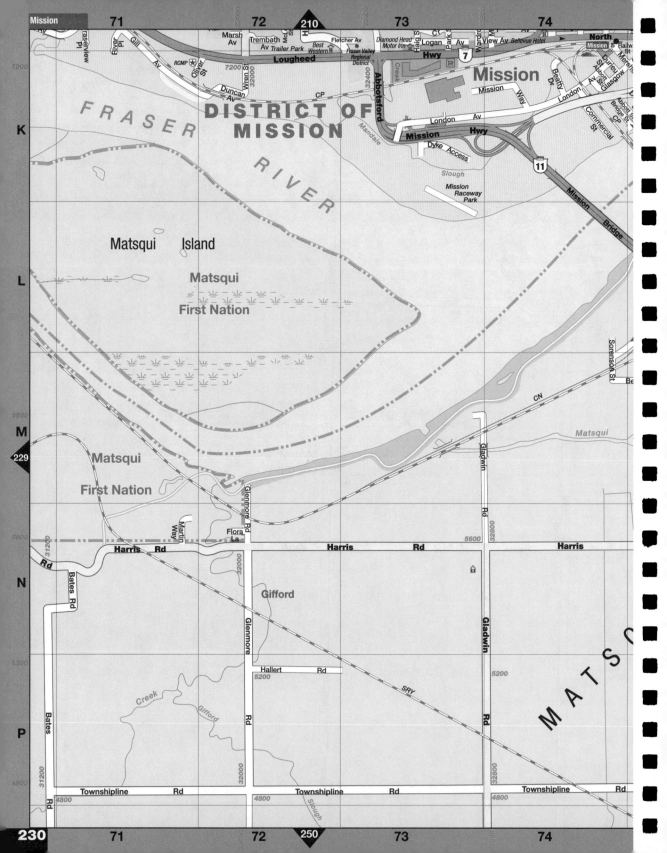

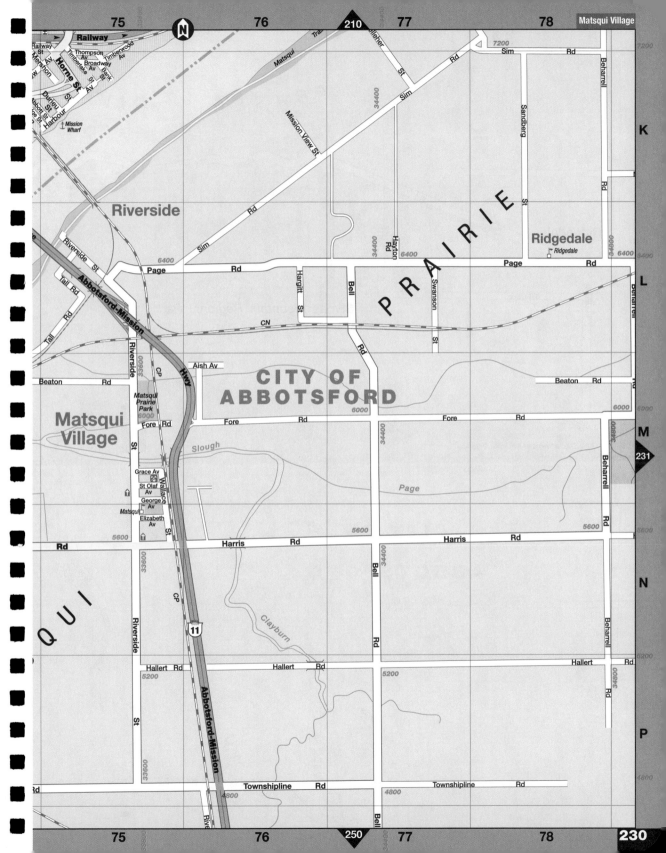

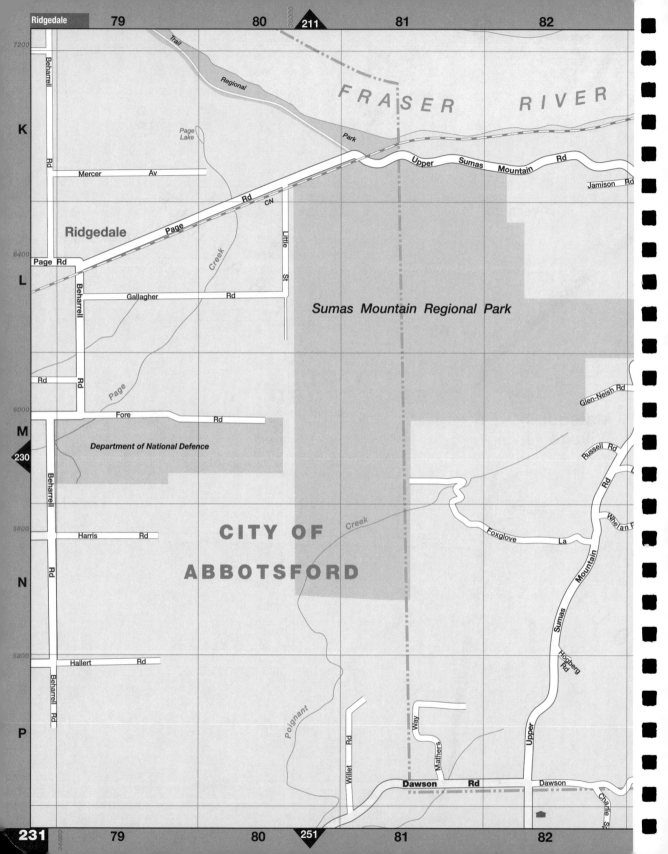

K

7200

Trail

Regional

Page
Lake

F R A S E R   R I V E R

Park

Beharrell

Rd

Mercer   Av

Rd

CN

Upper   Sumas   Mountain   Rd

Jamison   Rd

Ridgedale

Page

6400

Page Rd

L

Beharrell

Gallagher   Rd

Creek

Little

St

Sumas Mountain Regional Park

Rd

Rd

Page

6000

Fore   Rd

M

230

Department of National Defence

Glen-Neish Rd

Russell Rd

Rd

Beharrell

Whelan

5600

Harris   Rd

Creek

Foxglove   La

CITY OF

Rd

N

ABBOTSFORD

Sumas

Mountain

5200

Hallert   Rd

Hogberg

Rd

Beharrell

Rd

Poignant

P

Willet

Rd

Way

Mathers

Upper

Dawson

Dawson   Rd

Charlie St

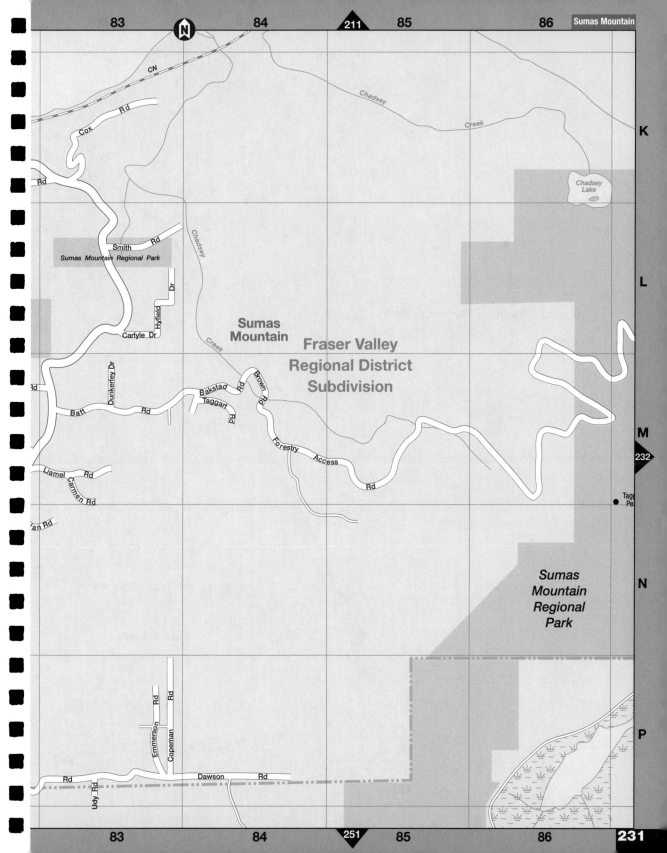

N

CN

Cox Rd

Chadsey

Creek

K

Rd

Chadsey Lake

Chadsey

Smith Rd

Sumas Mountain Regional Park

Hyfield Dr

L

Carlyle Dr

Sumas Mountain

Creek

Fraser Valley Regional District Subdivision

Dunkerley Dr

Bakstad Rd

Brown Rd

Taggart Rd

Rd

Batt Rd

Forestry Access Rd

M

232

Llamel Rd

Carmen Rd

Tagg Pe

an Rd

Sumas Mountain Regional Park

N

Emmerson Rd

Copeman Rd

P

Rd

Udy Rd

Dawson Rd

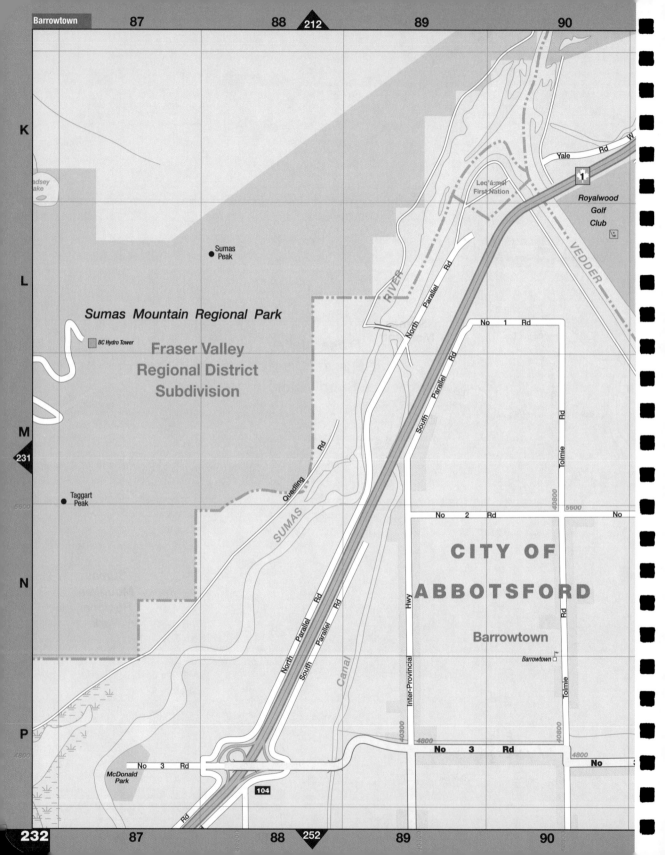

K

adsey
ake

1

Yale Rd W

Leq'á:mel
First Nation

Royalwood
Golf
Club

L

● Sumas
Peak

RIVER

VEDDER

Sumas Mountain Regional Park

■ BC Hydro Tower

**Fraser Valley
Regional District
Subdivision**

North Parallel Rd

No 1 Rd

M

◆ 231

5600

● Taggart
Peak

South Parallel Rd

Quedling

Rd

SUMAS

Tolmie Rd

40800

5600

No

No 2 Rd

CITY OF

N

North Parallel Rd

South Parallel Rd

Canal

Inter-Provincial Hwy

ABBOTSFORD

Rd

Barrowtown

Barrowtown □

Tolmie Rd

P

McDonald
Park

4800

No 3 Rd

40300

4800

No 3 Rd

40800

4800

No

Rd

104

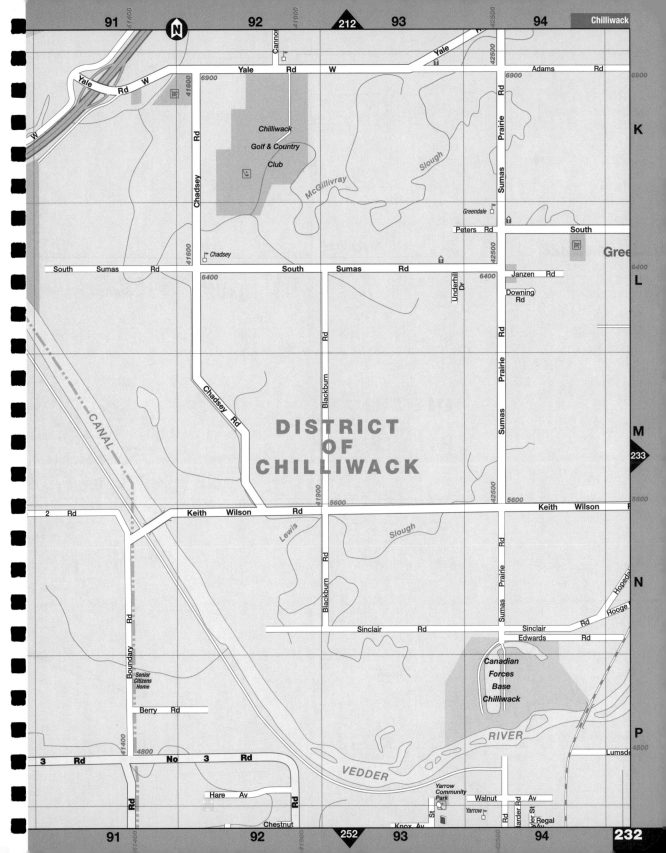

N

91   92   93   94

K

L

M

233

N

P

Yale   Rd   W
Cannor
Yale
Yale   Rd   W
Adams   Rd
6900
6900
6900
Chadsey   Rd
41600
6900
Chilliwack
Golf & Country
Club
McGillivray
Slough
Prairie   Rd
Sumas
Greendale
Peters   Rd
South
41600
42500
6400
Chadsey
South   Sumas   Rd
Janzen   Rd
Gree
South   Sumas   Rd
South   Sumas   Rd
6400
6400
6400
Downing
Rd
Underhill
Dr
L
Blackburn   Rd
Rd
Prairie   Rd
Sumas
DISTRICT
OF
CHILLIWACK
Chadsey   Rd
CANAL
41900
5600
5600
5600
2   Rd
Keith   Wilson   Rd
Keith   Wilson
Lewis
Slough
Blackburn   Rd
Prairie   Rd
Sumas
Rd
N
Sinclair   Rd
Sinclair   Rd
Hooge
Edwards   Rd
Hooge
Boundary   Rd
Canadian
Forces
Base
Chilliwack
Senior
Citizens
Home
Berry   Rd
RIVER
41400
4800
4800
3   Rd
No   3   Rd
Lumsde
VEDDER
Hare   Av
Yarrow
Community
Park
Walnut   Av
Harder Rd
Regal
Chestnut
Knox   Av
Yarrow
St
41400
41300
42500

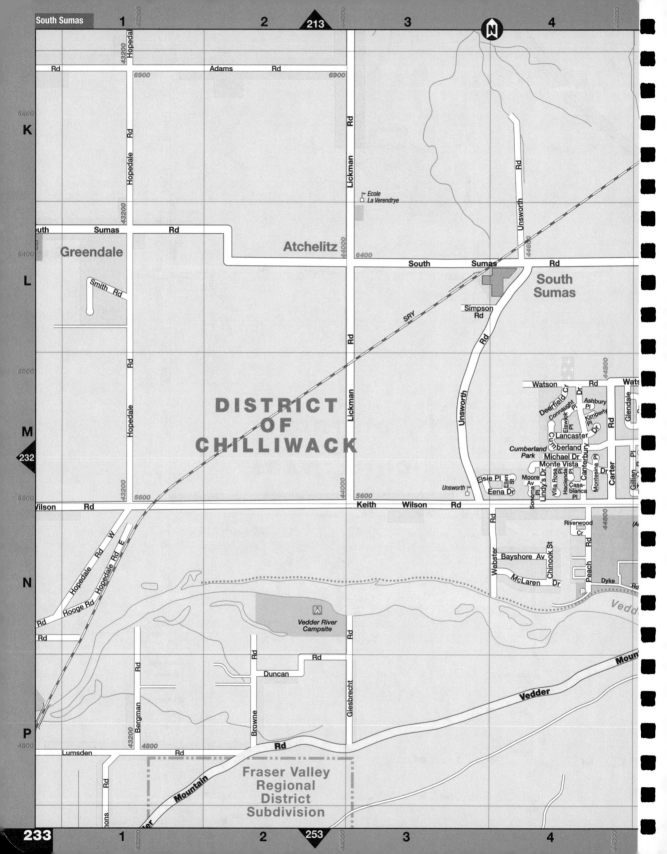

1   2   **213**   3   N   4

K

Greendale

Smith Rd

L

Atchelitz

South Sumas

Simpson Rd

Ecole La Verendrye

Hopedale Rd
Hopedale Rd
Hopedale Rd

Adams Rd

South Sumas Rd

Lickman Rd

Unsworth Rd

South Sumas Rd

SRY

Watson Rd   Wats

Deerfield Cr   Dr   Ashbury Pl   Rd   Glendale

Connaught   Elswick Pl   Kimberly Pl

Lancaster

Cumberland Park

Cumberland   Carter   Dr

Michael Dr

Monte Vista

Villa Rosa Pl   Montesina Pl   Carter

Moore Av

Hacienda Pl   Gillen Pl

Lindy's Dr

Casa-blanca Pl

Elsie Pl   Ellen St

Eena Dr

Unsworth

M   **232**

**DISTRICT
OF
CHILLIWACK**

Wilson Rd   Keith   Wilson   Rd

Riverwood Cr   Rd

Webster   Bayshore Av   Chinook St

McLaren   Dr

Peach   Dyke

N

Hopedale Rd W
Hopedale Rd E

Hooge Rd

Rd

Rd

Vedder River Campsite

Vedder

Vedd

Rd   Rd

Duncan   Rd

Bergman Rd

Browne   Rd

Giesbrecht Rd

Mountain

Vedder

Moun

P

Lumsden   Rd

Mountain

**Fraser Valley
Regional
District
Subdivision**

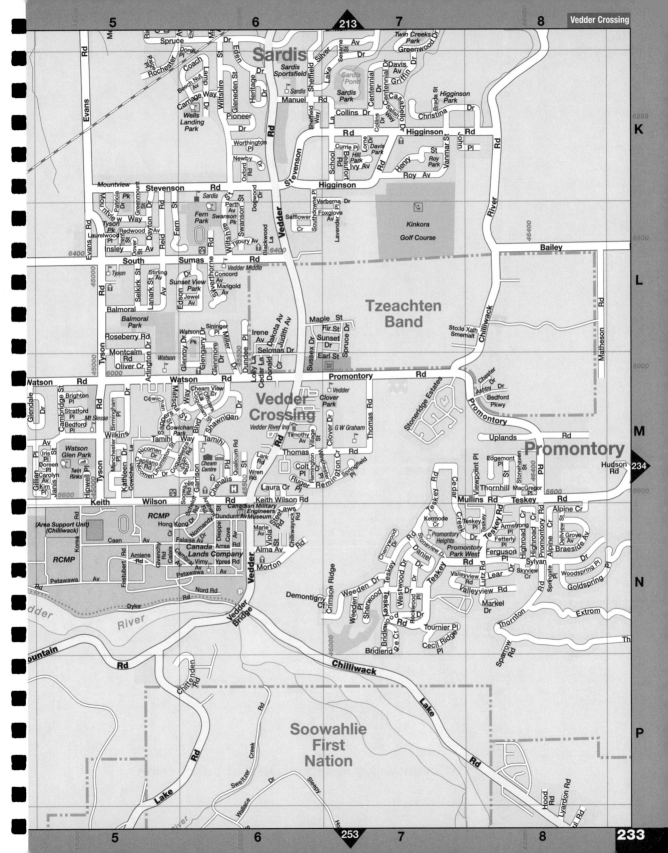

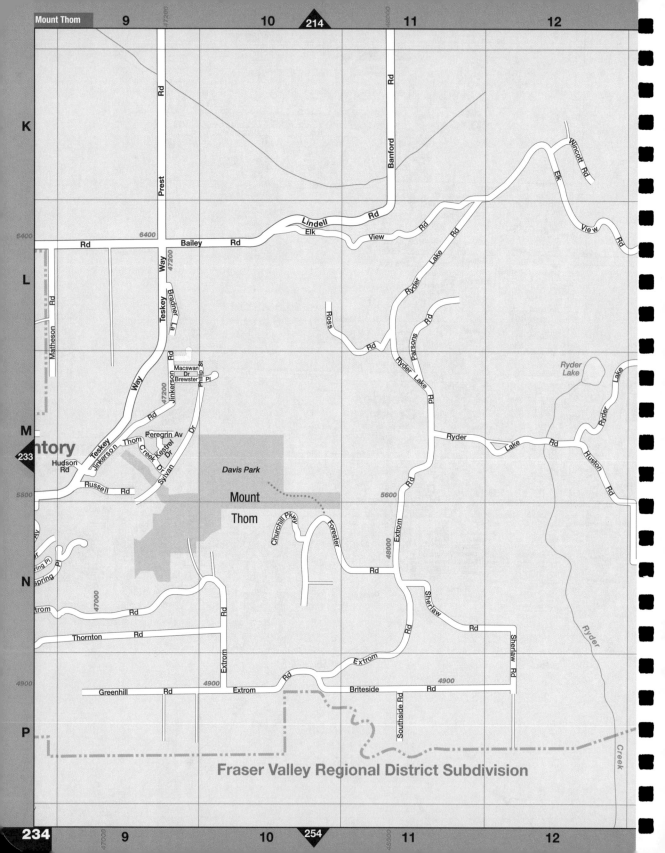

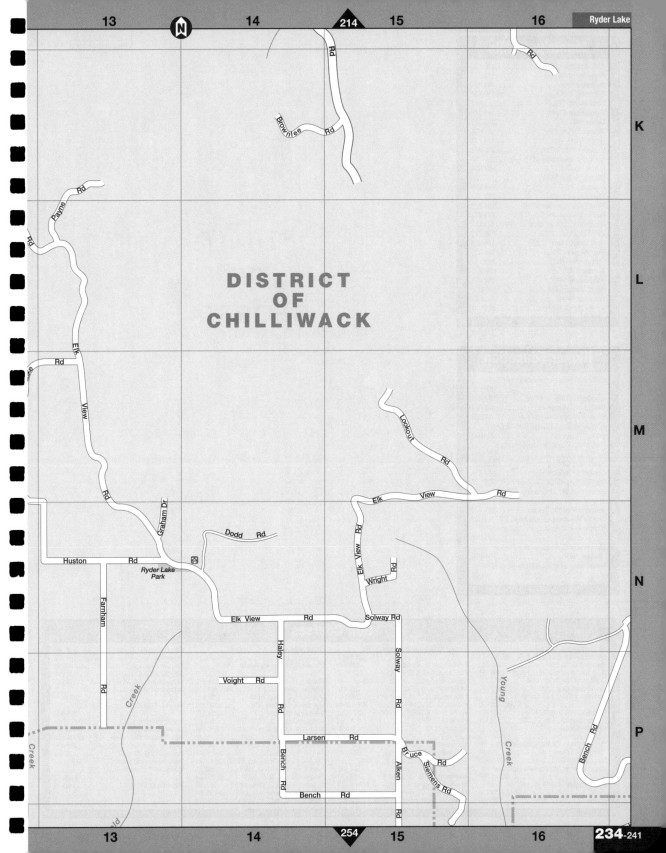

K

L

**DISTRICT
OF
CHILLIWACK**

M

Payne Rd

Rd

Elk

View

Rd

Graham Dr

Lookout Rd

Elk View Rd

N

Rd

Dodd Rd

Elk View Rd

Huston Rd

Ryder Lake
Park

Wright Rd

Farnham Rd

Elk View Rd

Solway Rd

Haley Rd

Solway Rd

Voight Rd

Creek

Young Creek

Larsen Rd

Bench Rd

Aiken Rd

Bruce Rd

Siemens Rd

Bench Rd

Bench Rd

P

Creek

Rd

Municipal Halls

Abbotsford ABT	.250 U73
Anmore ANM	.145 P33
Belcarra BEL	.144 P29
Burnaby BUR	.164 W-X24
Chilliwack CHL	.213 F7
Coquitlam CQT	.145 S38
Delta DEL	.243 Q18
Fraser Valley FRA	.213 G7
Hope HOP	.118 E44
Langley City LGC	.227 N48
Langley Township LGT	.227 P51
Lions Bay LIO	.101 B24
Maple Ridge MAP	.187 Z52
Matsqui ABT	.250 U73
Mission MIS	.210 G76
New Westminster NEW	.184 B29
North Vancouver City CNV	.123 N17
North Vancouver District DNV	123 L17
Pitt Meadows PTM	.186 Z45
Port Coquitlam PCQ	.166 U39
Port Moody PMD	.145 S35
Richmond RMD	.202 F12
Surrey SUR	.225 M35
Vancouver VAN	.162 U14
West Vancouver WVA	.122 M10
Whistler WHS	.401 A1
White Rock WRK	.265 X37

Higher Education

B.C. Institute of Technology BUR 163 W22
Capilano College DNV 123 N21
Douglas College MAP 187 A54
Fraser Valley College CHL 213 G6
Fraser Valley College Annex CHL 193 D7-8
Kwantlen College (Langley) LGC 227 M49
Kwantlen College SUR 225 K32
Langara College VAN 182 Z14
Pacific Life Bible College SUR 225 L37
Simon Fraser University BUR 144 T28-29
Summit Pacific College ABT .251 Q79
Trinity Western University LGT 207 J52
Vancouver Community College VAN 163 U16
University College of the Fraser Valley ABT 270 W76
University of British Columbia UEL 161 U4

STRAIT

OF

GEORGIA

Westham Island Rd

Frew ... Rd

Golf Courses

18 Pastures G. C. MIS	.189 B66
Beach Grove Golf Club DEL	263 W17-18
Belmont G. C. LGT	.207 G53
Burnaby Mountain G. C. BUR	.164 U27
Capilano G. & C. C. WVA	.122 J-K13
Carnousite Golf Club PCQ	.166 U-V42
Chateau Whistler G. C. WHS	.401 A3, D-E5
Chilliwack G. & C. C. CHL	.232 K92
Coast Meridian Par 3 SUR	.266 X41
Country Meadows G. C. RMD	.203 H17-18
Coyote Creek Golf Club SUR	.205 H-J37
Cultus Golf Park FRA	.253 R6
Delta Public G. C. DEL	.224 N-P30
Eaglequest at Musqueam Golf Club DEL	.224 N-P30
Fort Langley G. & C. C. LGT	.187 D53 207 E53
Fraser Glen G. C. ABT	.271 W80
Fraser Golf Driving Range SUR	.206 H41
Fraserview G. C. BUR	.183 A19
Gleneagles Golf Club WVA	.101 H1-2
Green Acres G. C. RMD	.203 E17-18
Guildford G. & C. C. SUR	.205 H37
Hazelmere G. & C. C. SUR	.266 Y43
Hollies G. C. SUR	.226 L-M46
Hollyburn Country Club WVA	.122 K12
Hope G. C. HOP	.118 D45
Kinkora G. C. CHL	.233 L7
Langara G. C. VAN	.182 Z14
Langley Golf Centre LGT	.247 R50
Ledgeview G. C. ABT	.251 R80
Maple Ridge Municipal G. C. MAP	.187 A49
Marine Drive G. C. VAN	.182 Z10
Mayfair Lakes G. C. RMD	.203 E19-20
McCleery G. C. VAN	.182 Z9-10
Meadow Gardens G. C. PTM	.167 Y47
Meadowlands G. & C. C. CHL	.194 C10-11
Mikasa Golf Driving Range RMD	.183 D17-18
Mission G. & C. C. MIS	.209 H70
Morgan Creek G. & C. C. SUR	.246 S39
Mylora G. C. East RMD	.203 J16
Mylora G. C. West RMD	.203 J16
Newlands G. & C. C. LGC	.227 P49
Nicklaus North G. C. WHS	.401 C3
Nico Wynd Golf Club SUR	.245 R-S35
Northview G. & C. C. SUR	.226 K-L40
Peace Arch Golf Centre SUR	.266 Y41
Peace Portal G. C. SUR	.266 Y-Z41
Pitt Meadows Golf Club PTM	166 V-W45
Point Grey G. & C. C. VAN	.182 Z8
Poppy Estates G. C. LGT	.248 S57-58
Quilchena G. & C. Club RMD	.202 F-G8
Redwoods Public G.C. LGT	.207 E-F51
Richmond G. & C. C. RMD	.222 K13
Riverside Golf Centre SUR	.245 S36
Riverway G. C. BUR	.183 B22 184 B23
Royalwood Golf Club CHL	.232 L90-91
Seymour G. & C. C. DNV	.144 P25
Shaughnessy G. & C. C. VAN	.161 X6
Squamish Valley G. & C. C. SQM	.301 D3-4
Sunrise Golf & Racquet Club SUR	.226 N45
Sunshine Hills G. C. DEL	.224 L27-28
Surrey G. C. SUR	.206 J41
Tall Timbers Golf Club LGT	.227 M-N54
Tsawwassen Golf Club DEL	.263 W16
University G. C. UEL	.161 U6
Vancouver Golf Club CQT	.165 W31-32
Westwood Plateau G. A. CQT	.145 P36-37
Whistler G. C. WHS	.401 F3

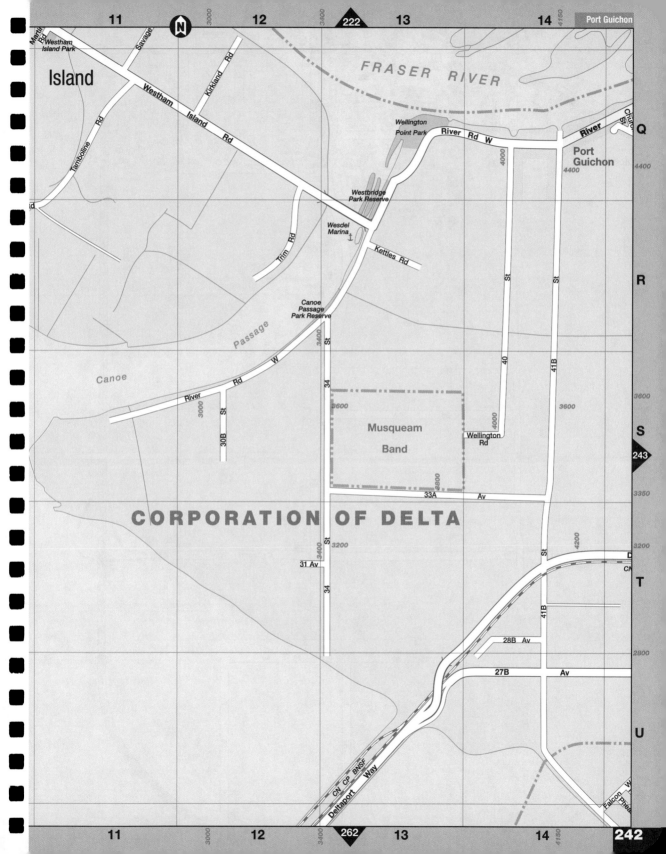

11 12 222 13 14

N

Westham Island Park

Island

Martin Rd

Westham Island Rd

Savage

Tamboline Rd

Kirkland Rd

FRASER RIVER

Wellington Point Park

River Rd W

4000

River

Port Guichon

Chilton St

Q

4400

Westbridge Park Reserve

Wesdel Marina

Kettles Rd

Trim Rd

St

St

R

3000

Canoe Passage Park Reserve

Canoe

Passage

River Rd W

3000

3400

St

St

40

41B

3600

3600

St

30B

34

3600

Musqueam Band

4000

Wellington Rd

S

243

3350

3800

33A

Av

3350

CORPORATION OF DELTA

3400

St

3200

31 Av

34

St

4200

3200

D

CN

T

41B

28B Av

2800

27B

Av

2800

U

CN CP BNSF

Deltaport Way

Falcon Rd

Phea

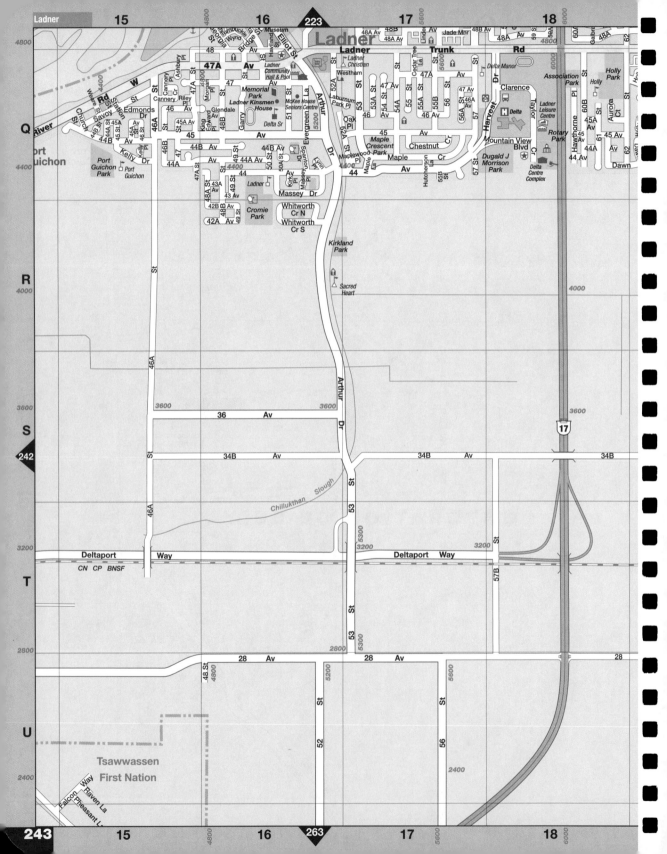

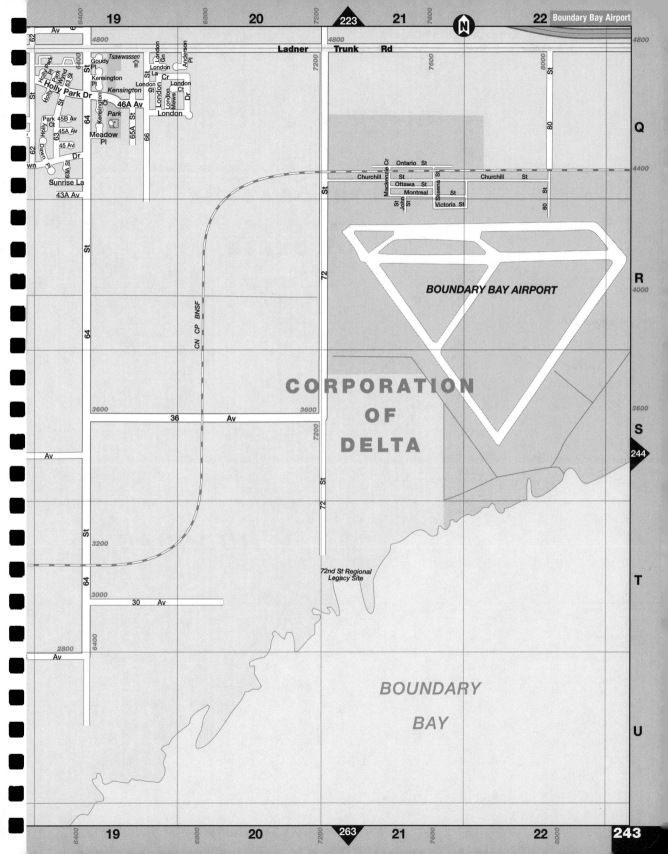

19   20   223   21   22

N

62
Av
4800
4800

6400
6800
7200
7600
8000

St
Ladner   Trunk   Rd
4800

Tsawwassen
Goudy
London
Gn
London
La
London
Cr
Anderson
Pl
H

Holly Park
Kensington
Pl
63 St
London
Gt
London
Ct
London
Mews
St

80
St

Holly Park Dr
Kensington
46A Av
London Ct
London Mews
Dr

Q

Park 45B Av
45A Av
45A Av
45 Av
Kensington Pl
Meadow
Pl
Park
65A St
66

62
Holly
Dr
63A St
wn
Sunrise La
43A Av

St
72

80
St

Ontario   St
Churchill   St
Ottawa   St
Montreal
St John
St
Skeena   St
Victoria St
Mackenzie Cr
Churchill   St

4400
4400

64
St
BOUNDARY BAY AIRPORT

R
4000

CN CP BNSF

3600
36   Av
3600

7200
St

CORPORATION
OF
DELTA

S
3600

244

Av
St
3200

St
72

72nd St Regional
Legacy Site

T

64
St
3000
30   Av

2800
Av
6400

BOUNDARY

BAY

U

19   20   263   21   22   243

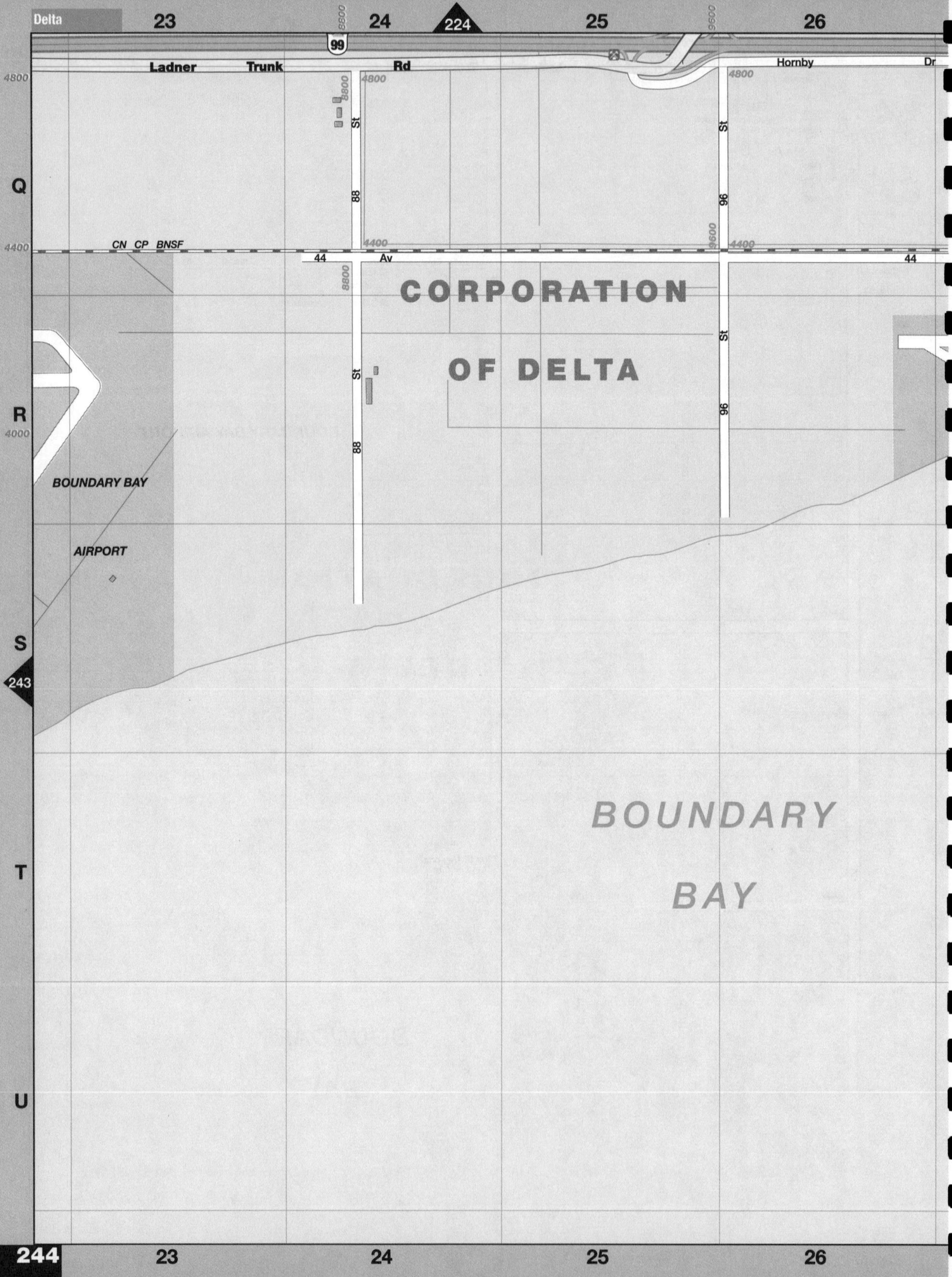

23　　**24**　△ **224**　　**25**　　**26**

99

Ladner　　Trunk　　Rd　　　　　　　Hornby　　　Dr

4800　　　　　　　　　　　　4800　　　　4800

Q

8800 St

88 St

96 St

4400　　　CN CP BNSF　　　　　　　4400　　　9600　　4400

44　　Av　　　　　　　　　　　　44

8800 St

CORPORATION

OF DELTA

96 St

R

4000

BOUNDARY BAY

88 St

St

AIRPORT

96 St

S

△ **243**

BOUNDARY

T

BAY

U

27　28　224　29　30

99

Dr
Hornby　Dr
4800　4800
East Delta Flats
Regional Legacy Site

St
112

St
44　Av　Rd
Av
104

Irwin

Delta Air Park
Regional Legacy Site

Delta Air Park

Q

R

S　245

T

U

Accommodations

401 Motor Inn Ltd *BUR* 163 V21	Days Inn *CHL* 213 F7	Oasis Hotel *SUR* 185 C35
Accent Inns *RMD* 182 D14	Days Inn & Suites *LGC* 227 M47	Ocean Promenade Hotel *WRK* 265 X-Y38
Accent Inns *BUR* 163 U21	Days Inn Vancouver Airport *RMD* ..182 C13	Ocean View Lodging *DEL* 263 Z19
Alpine Motel *HOP* 118 F45	Days Inn-Vancouver Metro *VAN* ...163 W17	Pakwood Lodge *CHL* 213 F7
Alpine Motor Inn *ABT* 270 V72	Delta Vancouver Airport *RMD* 182 C12	Park Plaza Hotel *VAN* 162 U13
Aston Pacific Inn Resort & Conference	Diamond Head Motor Inn *MIS* ...210 J-K73	Parkland Motor *SUR* 266 Y39-40
Centre *SUR* 266 X40	Douglas Guest House *VAN* 162 V14	Penny Farthing Inn *VAN* 162 U10
Astoria Hotel *VAN* 143 S16	Executive Hotel *BUR* 163 U21-22	Plaza 500 Hotel & Convention Centre *VAN*
Barnet Hotel *PMD* 145 T32	Executive Airport Plaza Hotels & Conference	...........................162 V13-14
Beach Grove Motel *DEL* 263 X18	Centre *RMD* 202 F12	Quality Inn *HOP* 118 F45
Bellevue Hotel Ltd. *MIS* 210 J74	Executive Inn Express Hotel *RMD* ..182 C13	Quality Inn Airport *VAN* 183 A16
Best Continental Motel *HOP* 118 E44	Executive Plaza *CQT* 164 W30	Quality Inn Airport South *RMD* ..202 F11-12
Best Value Westward Inn *LGC* ...226 M46	Flamingo Motor Hotel *SUR* 185 B34	Queens Motor Hotel *NE* 184 D26
Best Western *CQT* 164 W30	Four Points By Sheraton Vancouver Airport	Radisson Hotel *BUR* 163 V22
Best Western *VAN* 163 U15	*RMD* 202 E12-13	Radisson President Hotel & Suites *RMD*
Best Western Abercorn Inn *RMD* ..182 C13	Fraser Valley Inn *RMD* 250 U75	...........................182 D12
Best Western Bakerview *ABT* ...270 V77	Golden Ears Hotel *PCQ* 166 U39	Radisson Suites *RMD* 182 D12
Best Western Capilano Inn & Suites *DNV* ...	Grouse Creek Motel *SUR* 205 E34	Rainbow Motor Inn *CH* 213 G6
...........................122 M13	Grouse Inn *DNV* 122 M13	Ramada Hotel & Suites *SUR* 185 C38-39
Best Western Chelsea Inn *CQT* ..165 X32	Hampton Inn & Suites *LGC* 226 M46	Ramada Inn *ABT* 271 V80-81
Best Western Convention Ctr *CQT* ..165 W30	Hampton Inn-Vancouver Airport *RMD*	Ramada Inn *CQT* 165 X31
Best Western Country Meadows *LGT*	...........................182 C13	Ramada Inn Hotel *PTM* 166 Y46
...........................248 T60	Haney Motor Hotel Ltd *MAP* 187 Z52	Ramada Inn *SUR* 226 N46
Best Western Exhibition Park *VAN* ..143 S20	Happy Day Inn *BUR* 164 Y27	Ramada Limited *RMD* 202 F12
Best Western Heritage Inn *HOP* ...118 F45	Hare Creek Motel *SUR* 225 L34	Red Roof Inn *HOP* 118 E44
Best Western Heritage Inn *HOP* ...118 F45	Harrison Beach Hotel *HHS* 155 P18-19	Rhombus Hotels & Resorts *CHL* ..213 E7
Best Western King George Inn & Suites *SUR*	Harrison Crossroads Inn *KNT* ...175 U18	Rio Suite Hotel *RMD* 182 D13
...........................205 H34	Harrison Hot Spring Villa Resort *HHS*	River Rock Casino Resort Hotel *RMD*
Best Western Kings Inn & Conference Centre	...........................155 P18-19	...........................182 C12-13
BUR 184 Y-Z23	Hilton Vancouver Airport *RMD* ...202 E12	Riversong Inn Ltd *RMD* 222 L9
Best Western Langley Inn *LGC* ...227 M49	Hilton Vancouver Metrotown *BUR* ..163 Y22	Royal Hotel *CHL* 213 E6-7
Best Western Maple Ridge *MAP* ..187 Z51	Holiday Inn Express *VAN* 143 S19	Royal Lodge Motel *HOP* 118 F45
Best Western Mission City Lodge *MIS*	Holiday Inn Express *ABT* 270 V72	Royal Towers *NEW* 184 B28
...........................230 J-K72	Holiday Inn Express Hotel & Suites *LGT*	Sandman Hotel Vancouver Airport *RMD*
Best Western Peace Arch Inn *SUR* ...	...........................207 F-G48	...........................182 C14
...........................265 U-V38	Holiday Inn Express Metrotown *BUR*	Sandman Hotels Inns & Suites *LGT* 207 F47-48
Best Western Poco Inn & Suites *PCQ* ...	...........................163 Y22	Shamrock Hotel *VAN* 143 S16
...........................166 U-V40	Holiday Inn Express Vancouver Airport *RMD*	Shaughnessy Village *VAN* 162 U-V13
Best Western Rainbow Country Inn *CHL*	...........................182 C13-14	Sheraton Vancouver Guildford Hotel *SUR* ...
...........................233 H2	Holiday Inn Hotel & Suites *DNV* ..143 P20	...........................185 C37
Best Western Regency Inn *ABT* ...270 V72	Holiday Inn Vancouver Airport *RMD*	Skyline Airport Hotel *RMD* 182 C12-13
Best Western Richmond Hotel &	...........................182 D14-15	Sleep Inn *LGT* 227 L50
Convention Centre *RMD* 202 E-F12	Holiday Inn Vancouver Centre *VAN* ..162 U13	Slumber Lodge *HOP* 118 E44
Biltmore Hotel *VAN* 163 V15	Hope Windsor Motel *HOP* 118 E44	Steveston Hotel *RMD* 222 L8
Bonanza Motel *SUR* 205 F34	Horseshoe Bay Motel *WVA* 101 G2	Sunset Inn *WRK* 265 W-X35
Break Away Motel *SUR* 266 V24	Hostelling International *VAN* 142 T7	Super 8 *ABT* 270 V77
Canadian Inn *SUR* 225 L34	Howard Johnson Express Inn *SUR* ..185 B33	Super 8 Motel *LGT* 228 N61
Canyon Court Inn & Suites *DNV* ..122 M13	Howard Johnson Plaza Hotel *VAN* .163 U-V15	Super 8 Motel *SUR* 185 D34-35
Carlson Hotel & Resorts *DNV* ...122 M14	Inn at King's Crossing *SUR* 270 V77	The Coast Hotel & Suites *ABT* ...270 V77
Cassandra Hotel *VAN* 163 X19	Inn at Westminster Quay *NEW* ...184 B29	The Coast Tsawwassen Inn *DEL* ..263 W17
Cedar Lane Motel *SUR* 266 X39	Inn at Westminster Quay *NEW* ...184 B29	The Fairmont Vancouver Airport *RMD* ...
Chilliwack Motor Inn *CH* 213 G7	Inn Corporate *NEW* 184 B28	...........................182 B9
City Center Motor Hotel *VAN* ...163 U15	Inter-City Motel *BUR* 184 Z24	The Garfield Hotel *NEW* 184 B28
Clover Inn Motor *SUR* 226 N42	La Quinta Inn Vancouver Airport *RMD*	The Run Inn *DEL* 263 X17
Clydesdale Inn *SUR* 226 N42	...........................202 E13	Timberland Motel & Campground *SUR*
Coast Hotel & Suites *ABT* 270 V77	Lake City Motor Inn *BUR* 164 U23-24	...........................245 S37
Coast-Vancouver Airport *VAN* ...182 B12-13	Langley Hotel *LGC* 227 N48	Traders Inn *CHL* 213 E6
Colonial 900 Motel *HOP* 118 F46	Linda Vista Motel *SUR* 225 L34	Travelodge Chilliwack *CHL* 213 H6
Comfort Inn *CHL* 213 H6	Lonsdale Quay *VAN* 143 P16-17	Travelodge Hotel *RMD* 182 C14
Comfort Inn & Suites *DNV* 122 M13	Lucky Strike Motel *HOP* 118 F45	Travelodge *LGT* 227 P50-51
Comfort Inn Airport *RMD* 182 C12	Manor Guest House *VAN* 162 V14	Travelodge *LGT* 207 F48
Comfort Inn Airport *RMD* 182 C12	Marriott Hotels Resorts Suites *RMD* ...	Travelodge Lions Gate *VAN* 122 M13
Coquitlam Sleepy Lodge *CQT* ...165 U31	...........................202 F12	Travelodge Maple Ridge *MAP* ...187 Z51
Days Hotel *SUR* 185 D34	Met Hotel *NEW* 184 B29	Turf Hotel *SUR* 185 B31
	North Vancouver Hotel *DNV* 122 M13	Vedder River Inn *CHL* 233 M6

27　28　29　30

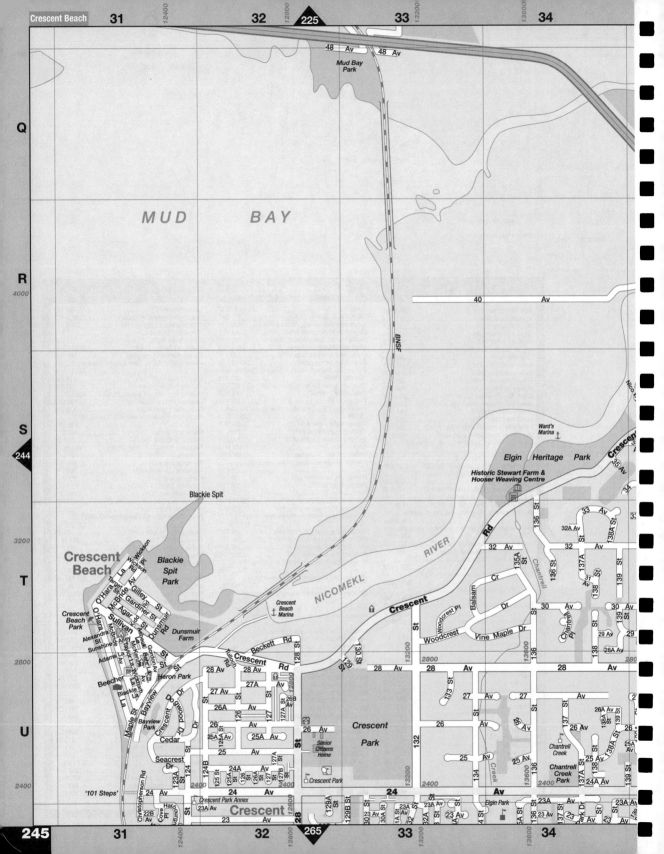

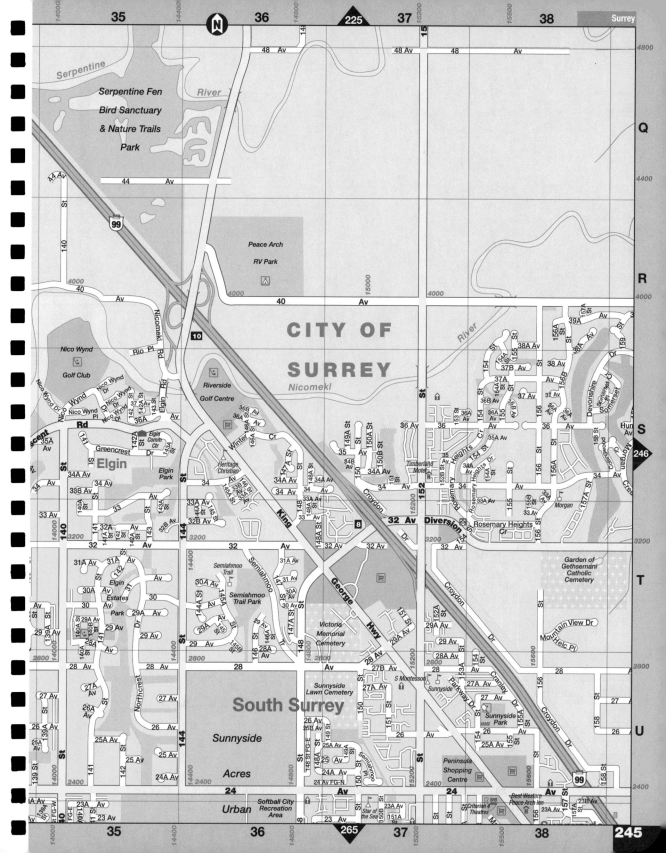

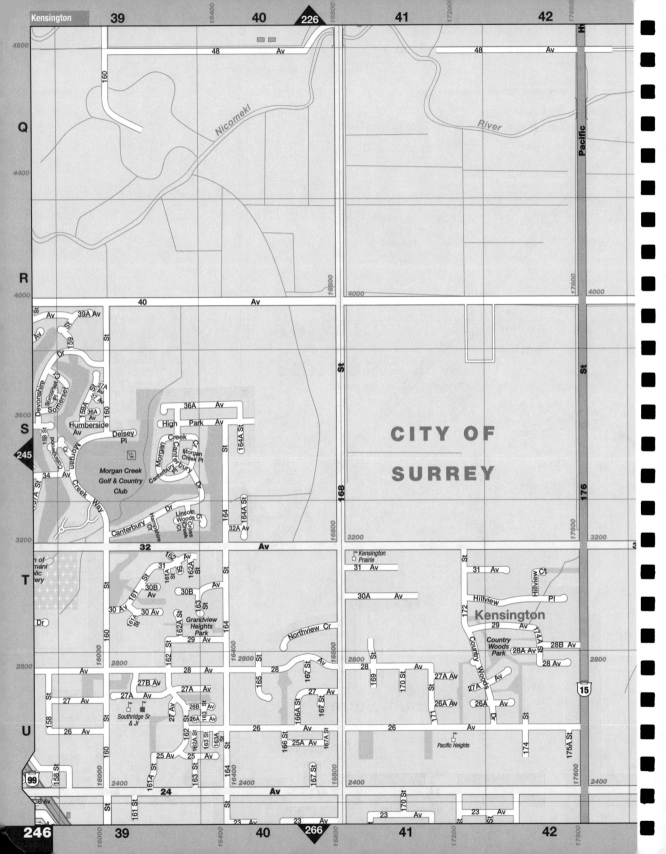

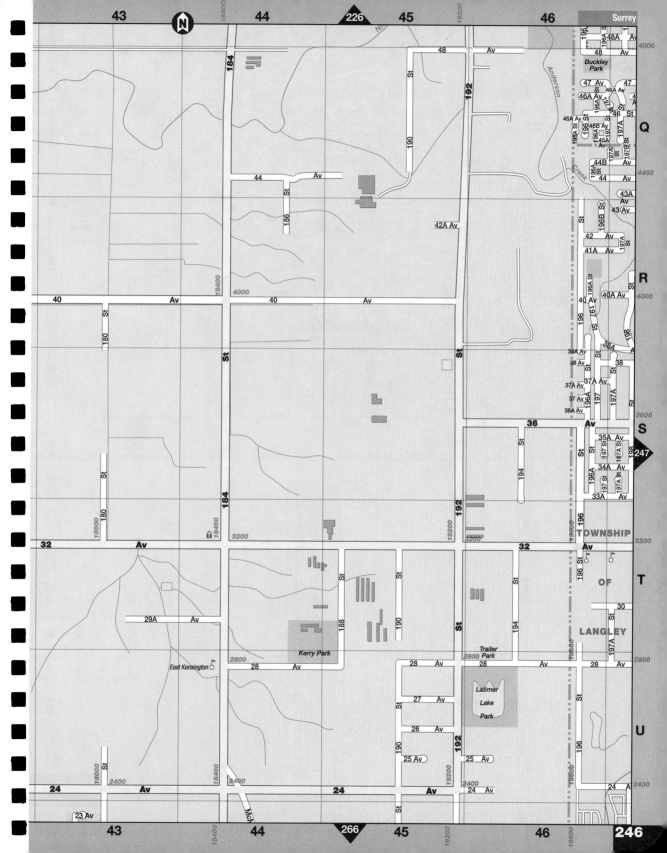

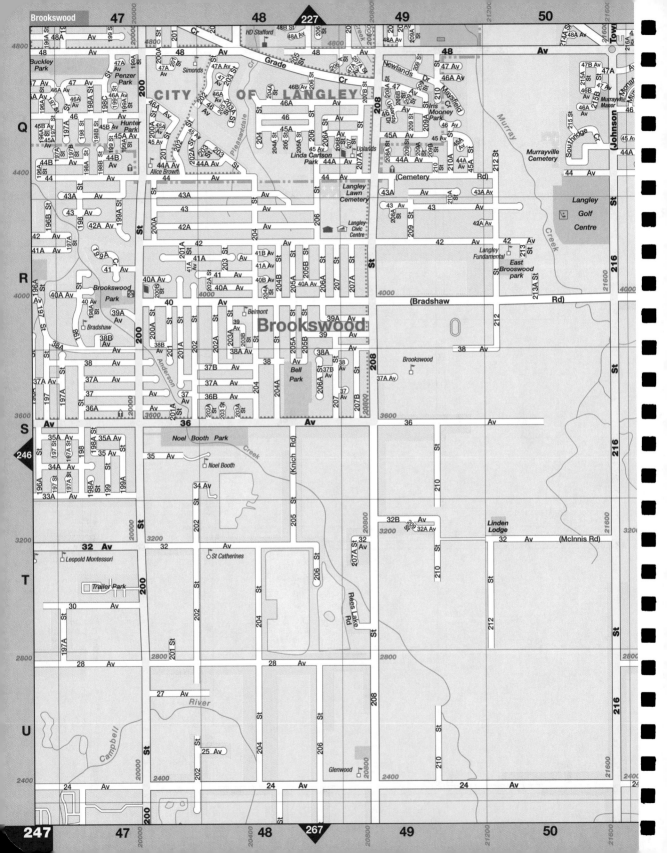

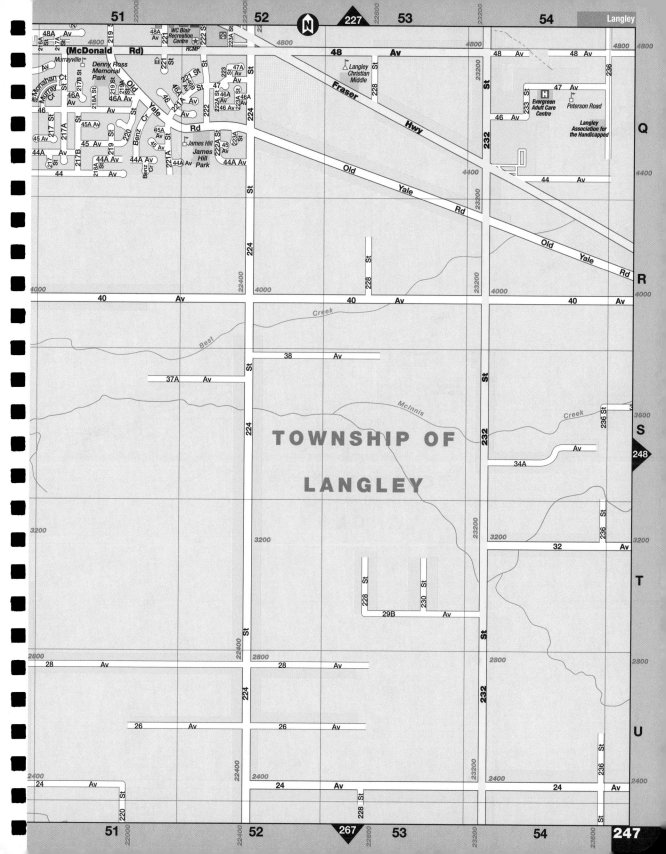

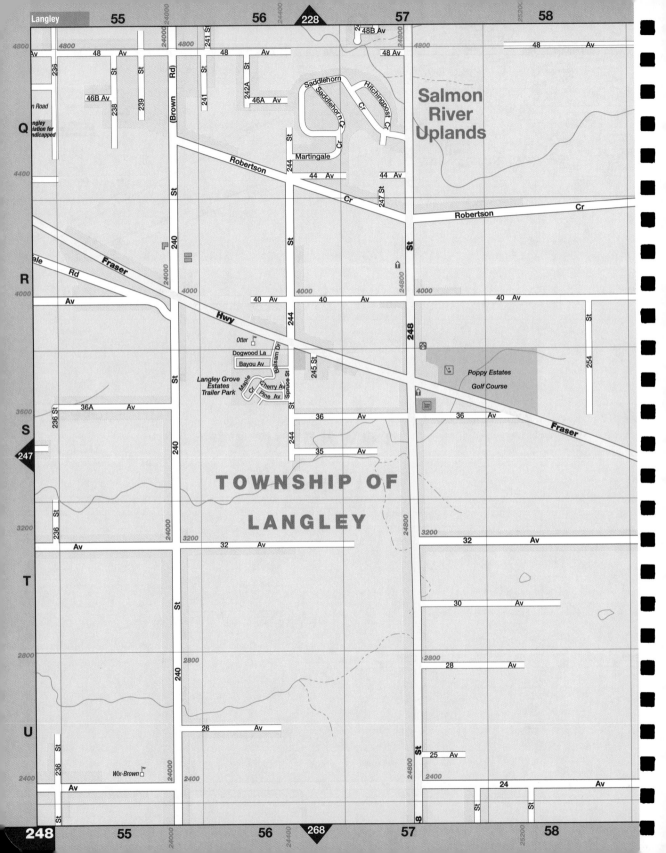

Q

Salmon River Uplands

48 Av

4800   4800   48   Av   48   Av   48 Av   4800   48   Av

235   46B Av   238   239

46A Av   241   242A   46A Av

Saddlehorn Cr   Saddlehorn Cr   Hitchingpost Cr

(Brown Rd)   St

Martingale   244

44 Av   44 Av

Robertson   247 St   Robertson   Cr

R

240   24000   St   244   St   248   St   254 St

4400   4000   4000   4000   4000

ale Rd   Fraser   Hwy

Av   40 Av   40 Av   40 Av

Otter

Dogwood La   Balsam Dr   245 St

Bayou Av

Langley Grove Estates Trailer Park   Maple Cr   Cherry Av   Spruce St   Pine Av

Poppy Estates Golf Course

36A   Av   36 Av   36 Av

236 St   St   240 St   244 St

S

247

3600   3600

35 Av

TOWNSHIP OF LANGLEY

3200   236 St   3200   3200   24800   3200

32   Av   32 Av

T

30 Av

2800   240 St   2800   2800   28 Av

U

26 Av

236 St   25 Av

Wix-Brown   24000   2400   2400

Av   24 Av

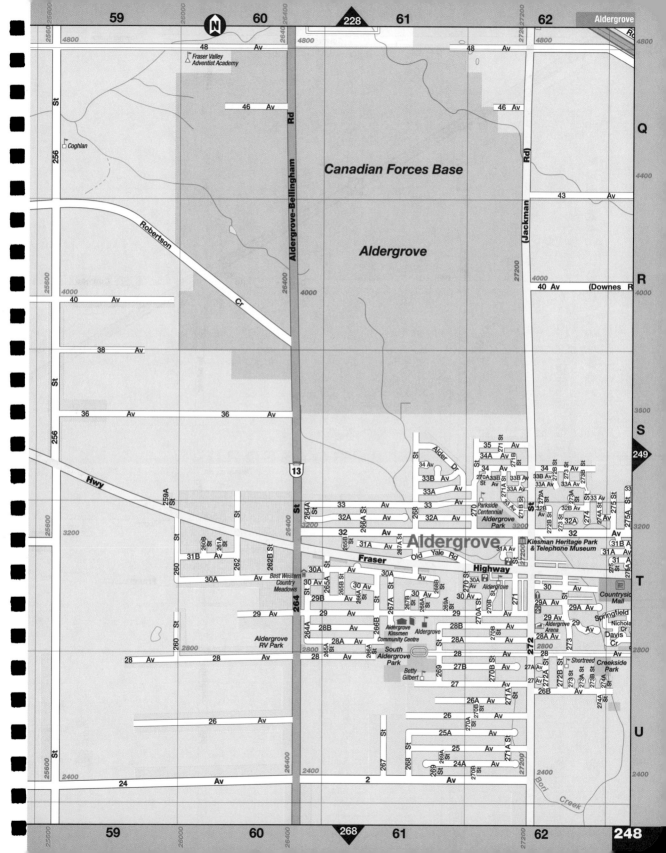

N

4800   48   Av   4800   48   Av   4800

Fraser Valley
Adventist Academy

46   Av   46   Av

Q

Coghlan

256

Canadian Forces Base

Jackman Rd

43   Av   4400

Robertson   Cr

Aldergrove-Bellingham Rd

Aldergrove

R

4000   40 Av   (Downes R

25600   4000   40   Av   26400   4000   27200   4000   4000

38   Av

St

36   Av   36   Av   3600

256

13

Hwy

259A St

35   271 St   S

34A   249

34 Av   34   271B St

Alder Dr   270A 33B B Av

33B   St   33B Av   273 St   Av

33A   271A St   33A Av   33A Av   273A Av

33   Av   33   Av   27PA   33

264A St   33   268   270   271B St   274A   275 St

32A   266A St   32A   Av   32B St   32B Av   275A

3200   3200   Parkside Centennial Aldergrove Park   272B St   32A   274   32   Av

32   Av   3200

265B St   31   Av   267 St   **Aldergrove**   Kinsman Heritage Park & Telephone Museum   31B A   31A Av

31A Av   31   275

Fraser   Old   Yale Rd   **Highway**   31   A   275A

260B St   261A St   262   262B St

31B   30A   30A   Aldergrove   30   Av   T

260   30A   Av   Best Western Country Meadows   30 Av   265A St   30A   270 St   270B   271   30   Countrysid Mall

30A   Av   30   266A St   30   268B St   29A   Av   29A   Springfield

29B   267A St   29A   Aldergrove Arena   29   Nichola Cr

29   Av   29   Av   267B St   268A St   269A St   9   Av   273   272   Davis Cr

264A   28B   Aldergrove Kinsmen Community Centre   Aldergrove   28B   270B   28A   Av

260 St   28A   Av   265A St   266A St   28A   270A St   28A   272   2800

2800   Aldergrove RV Park   2800   South Aldergrove Park   269   28   27B   270B St   27A Av   Shortreed   Creekside Park

28   Av   28   Betty Gilbert   27   27   272B   273 St   273B St   274A   St   26B   274A St

260 St   271A St

26A   Av

26   Av   26   270A St   270B St   Av

25A   Av

25   St   25   Av   271A St   U

25600 St   267   288   269 St   269A St   24A   Av   270B St   27200

2400   24   Av   2400   2   Av   2400   2400

Bon Creek

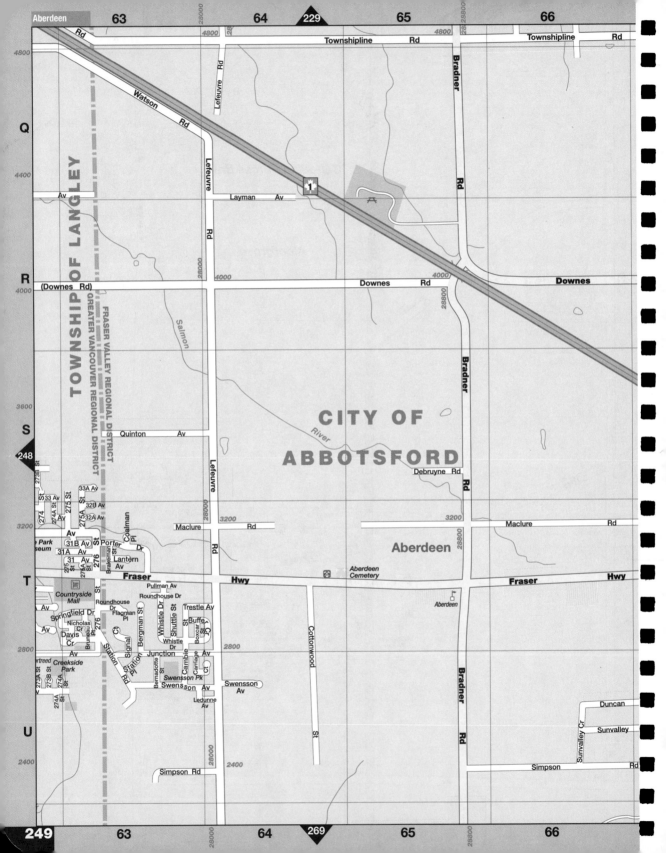

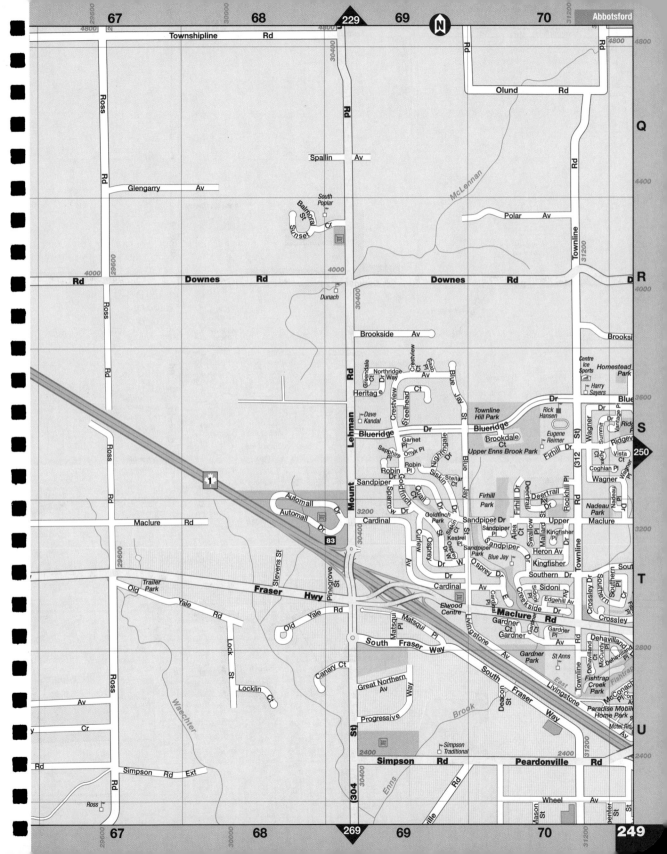

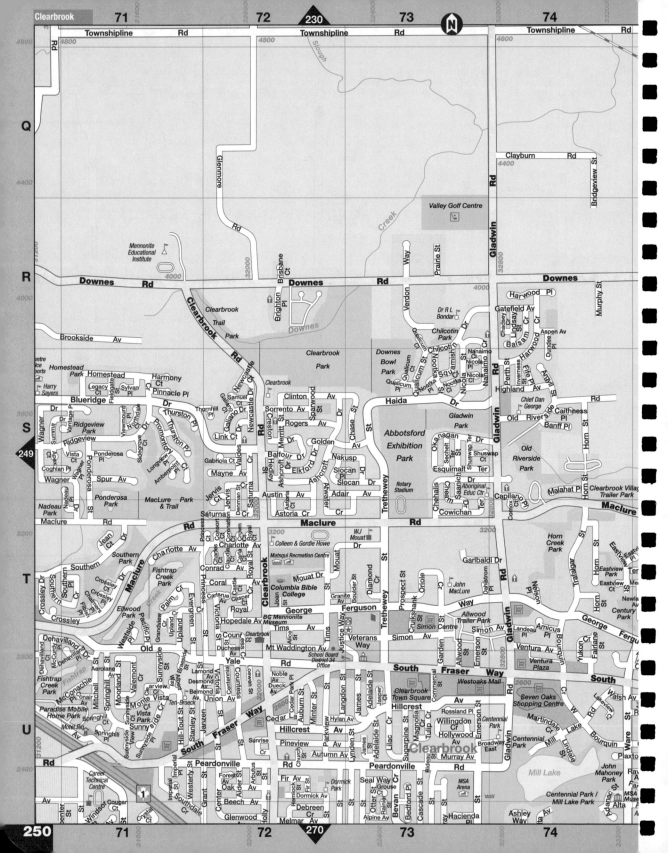

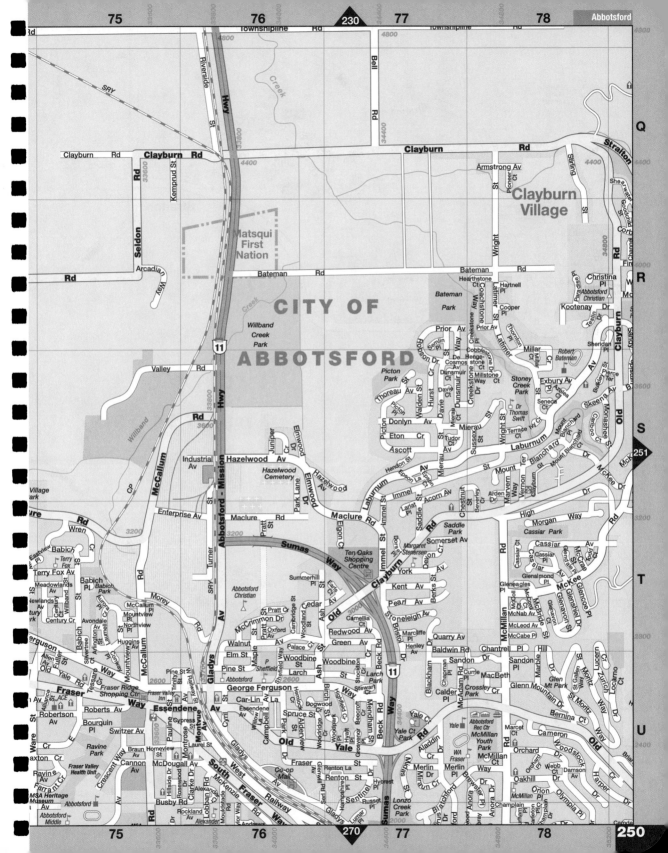

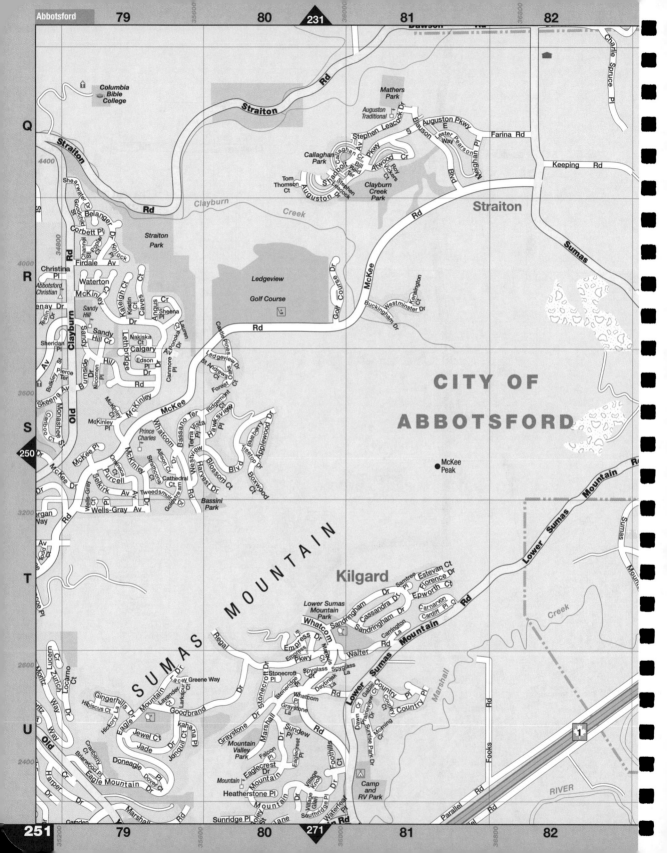

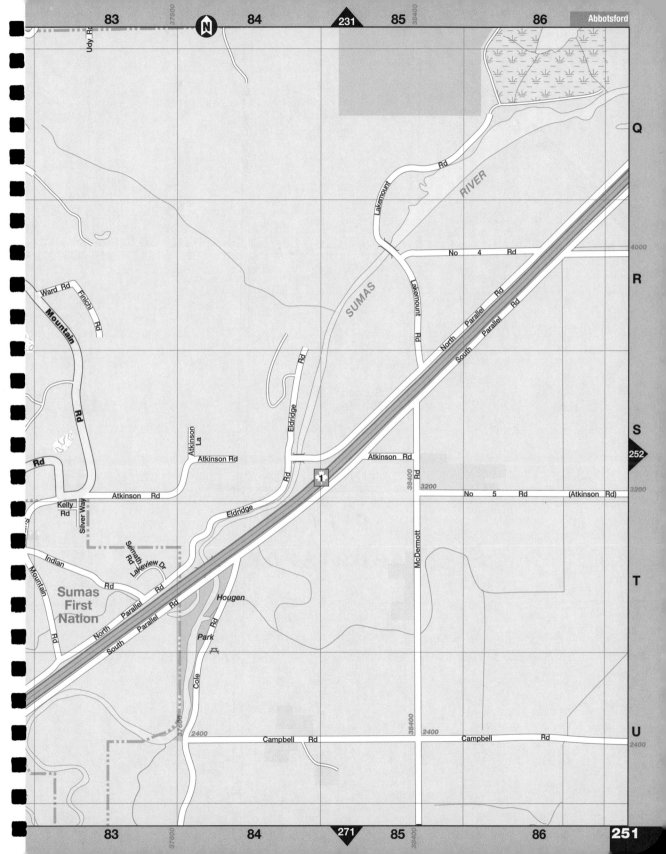

N

Q

4000

R

Udy Rd

Ward Rd

Finich Rd

Mountain

Rd

Rd

Lakemount

SUMAS

RIVER

Rd

Lakemount Rd

No 4 Rd

North Parallel Rd

South Parallel Rd

S

252

Rd

Atkinson La

Eldridge Rd

Atkinson Rd

Atkinson Rd

Rd

Atkinson Rd

1

3200

No 5 Rd (Atkinson Rd)

3200

Kelly Rd

Silver Way

Eldridge

McDermott Rd

Indian

Semath Rd

Lakeview Dr

Sumas First Nation

Rd

Rd

North Parallel Rd

South Parallel Rd

Mountain Rd

Hougen

T

Park Rd

Cole

37600

2400

Campbell Rd

38400

2400

Campbell Rd

U

2400

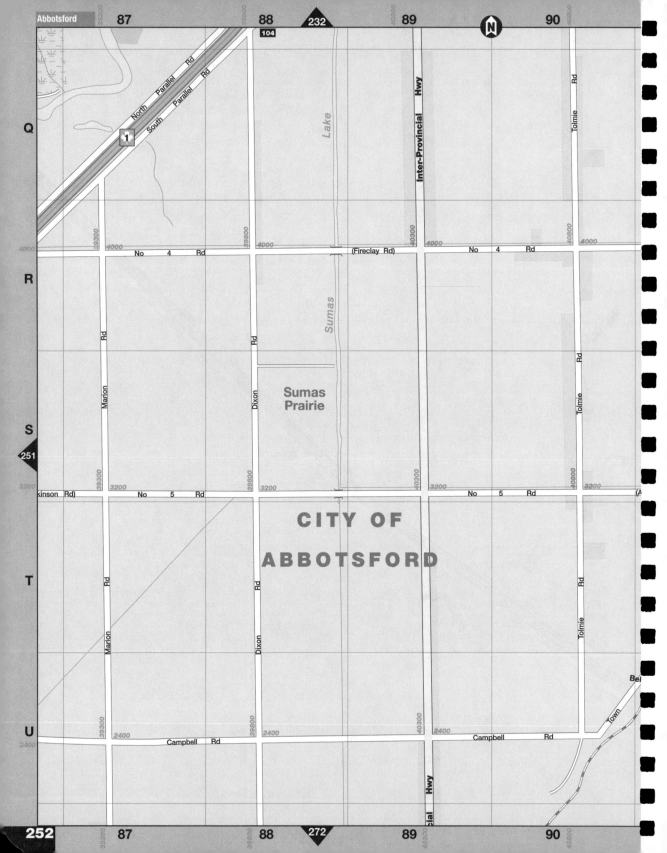

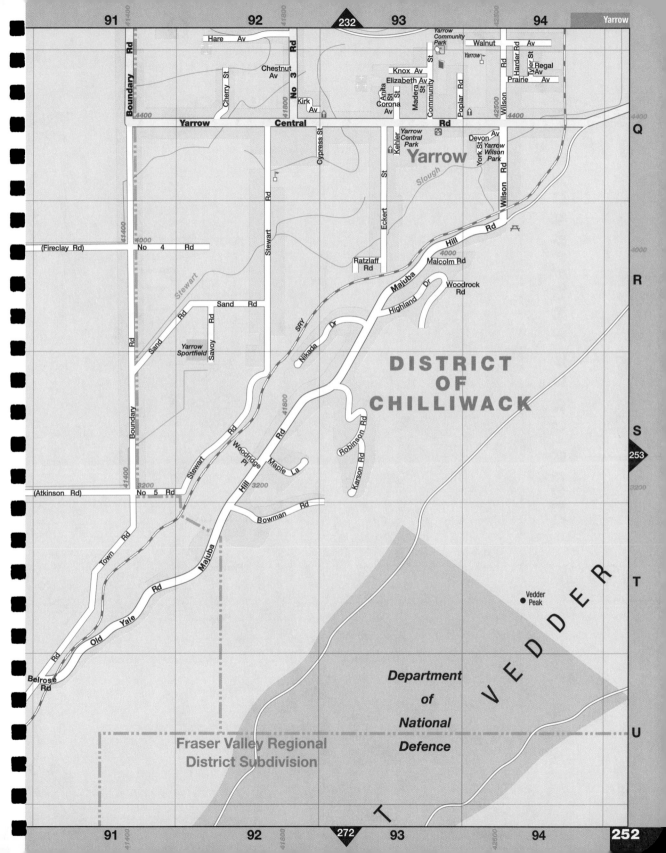

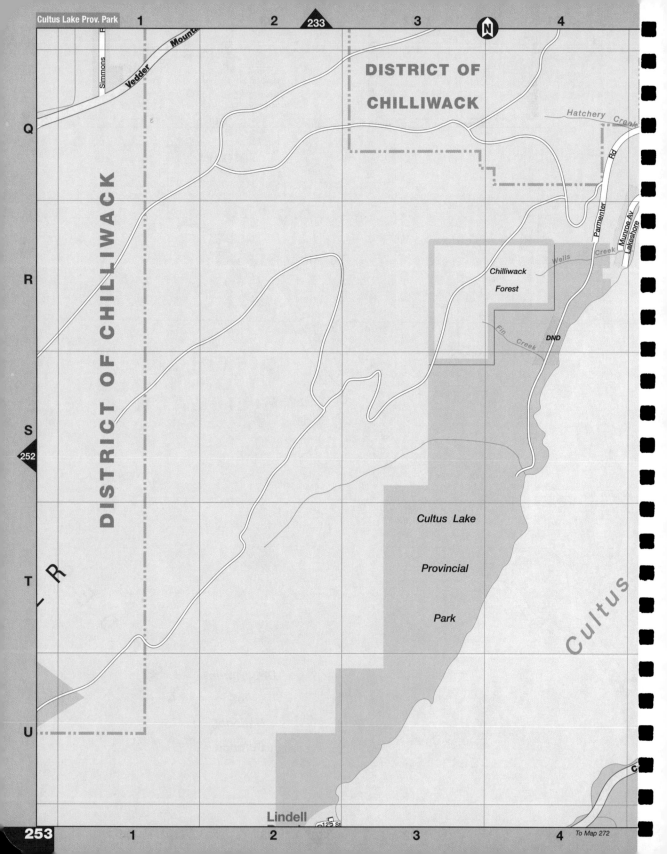

233

N

DISTRICT OF
CHILLIWACK

Hatchery Creek

Q

Vedder Mountain

Simmons

Rd

Parmenter

Munroe Av

Lakeshore

R

Chilliwack

Forest

Wells Creek

Fin Creek

DND

DISTRICT OF CHILLIWACK

S

252

Cultus Lake

Provincial

Park

Cultus

T   R

U

Lindell

123 St

1   2   3   4

To Map 272

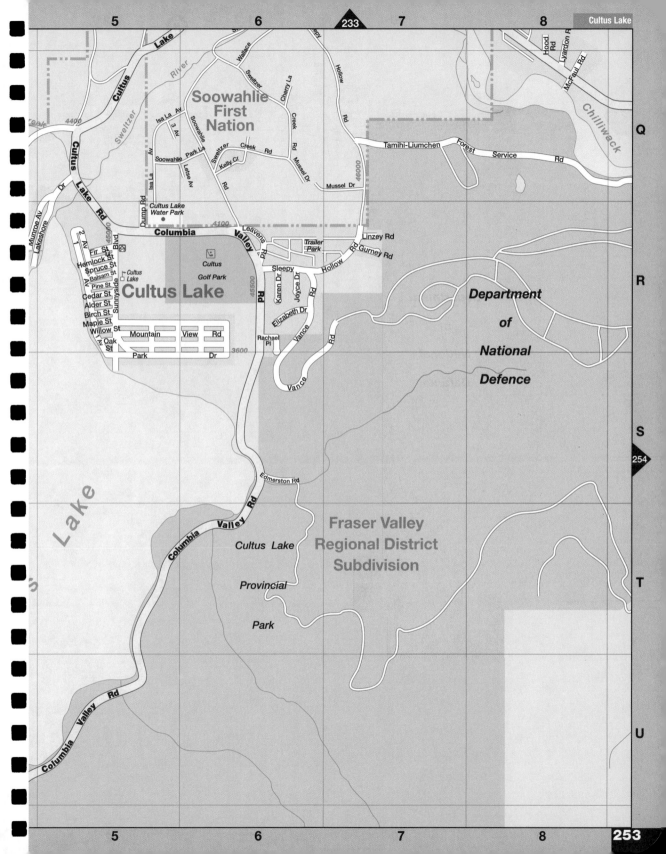

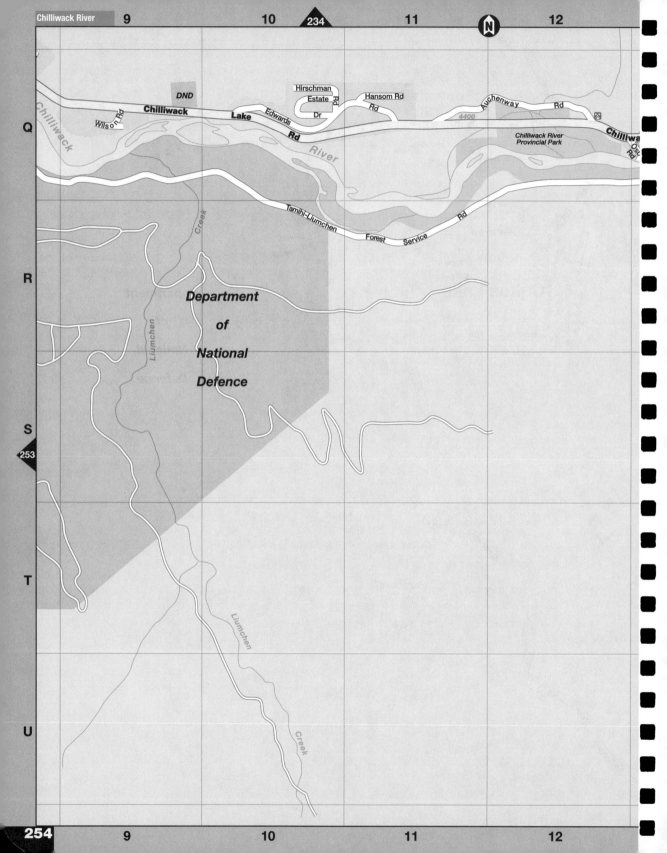

Q

Chilliwack

Wilson Rd

Chilliwack Lake Rd

Edwards

River

DND

Hirschman
Estate
Dr

Hansom Rd
Rd

Auchenway Rd

4400

Chilliwa
Chilliwack River
Provincial Park

Lk
Rd

Creek

Tamihi-Liumchen Forest Service Rd

R

Department

of

National

Defence

Liumchen

S

253

Liumchen

T

Creek

U

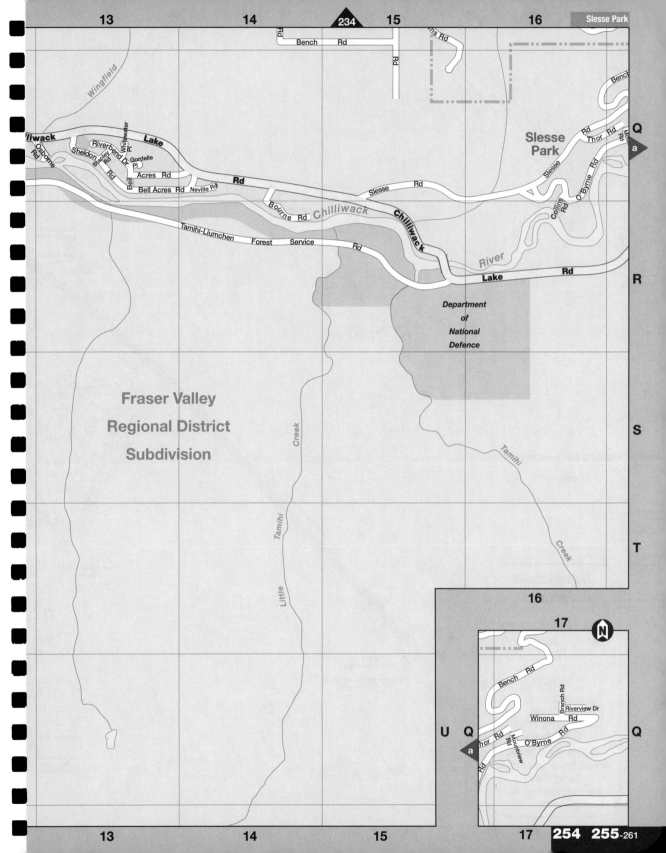

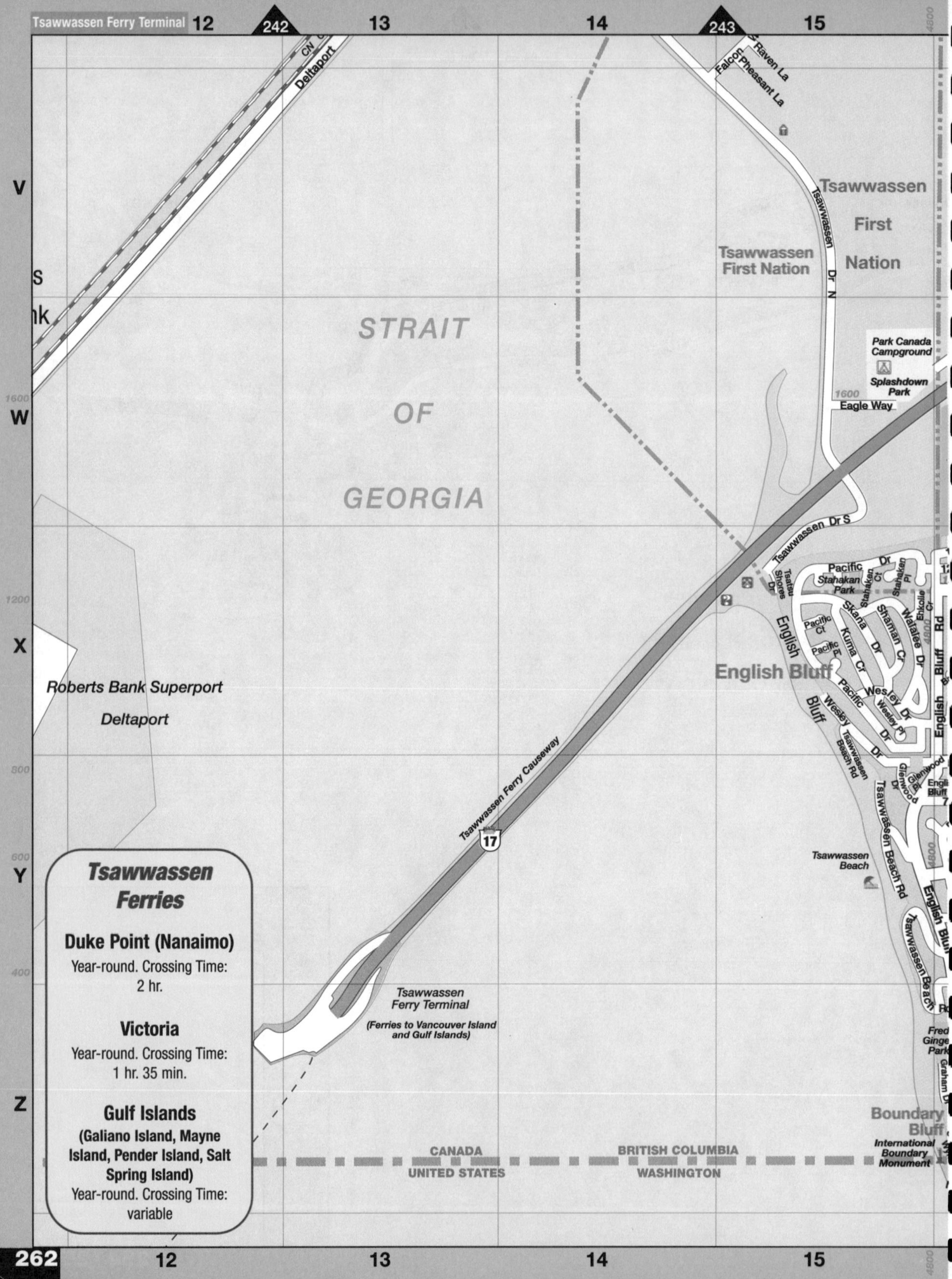
12
242
13
14
243
15
V
W
X
Y
Z
STRAIT
OF
GEORGIA
CN
Deltaport
Falcon
Raven La
Pheasant La
Tsawwassen Dr N
Tsawwassen
First
Nation
Tsawwassen
First Nation
Park Canada
Campground
Splashdown
Park
1600
Eagle Way
Tsawwassen Dr S
Pacific Dr
Stahakan Park
Stahakan Ct
Stahakan Pl
Tsatsu Shores Dr
Skana
Pacific Ct
Pacific Pl
Kuma Cr
Shaman Cr
Ehkolie Cr
Walatee Dr
English Bluff Rd
English Bluff
English Bluff
Pacific
Wesley Dr
Wesley Pl
Wesley
Tsawwassen Beach Rd
Glenwood Dr
Glenwood Pl
Tsawwassen Beach Rd
Tsawwassen Beach
English Bluff
Tsawwassen Beach
Fred Ginger Park
Graham Dr
Boundary Bluff
International Boundary Monument
Roberts Bank Superport
Deltaport
Tsawwassen Ferry Causeway
17
Tsawwassen
Ferry Terminal
(Ferries to Vancouver Island
and Gulf Islands)
CANADA
UNITED STATES
BRITISH COLUMBIA
WASHINGTON
1600
1200
800
600
400
4800
Tsawwassen
Ferries
Duke Point (Nanaimo)
Year-round. Crossing Time:
2 hr.
Victoria
Year-round. Crossing Time:
1 hr. 35 min.
Gulf Islands
(Galiano Island, Mayne
Island, Pender Island, Salt
Spring Island)
Year-round. Crossing Time:
variable

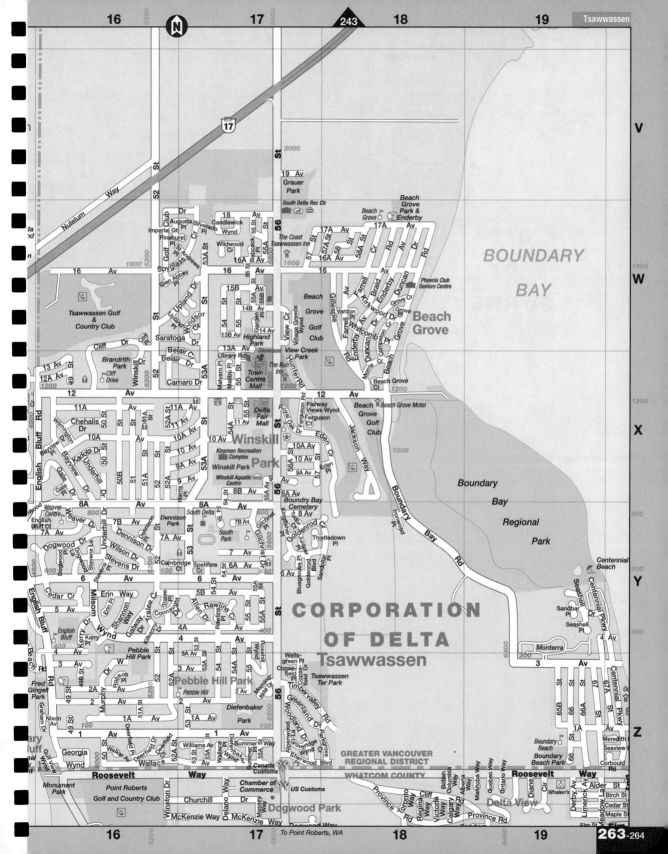

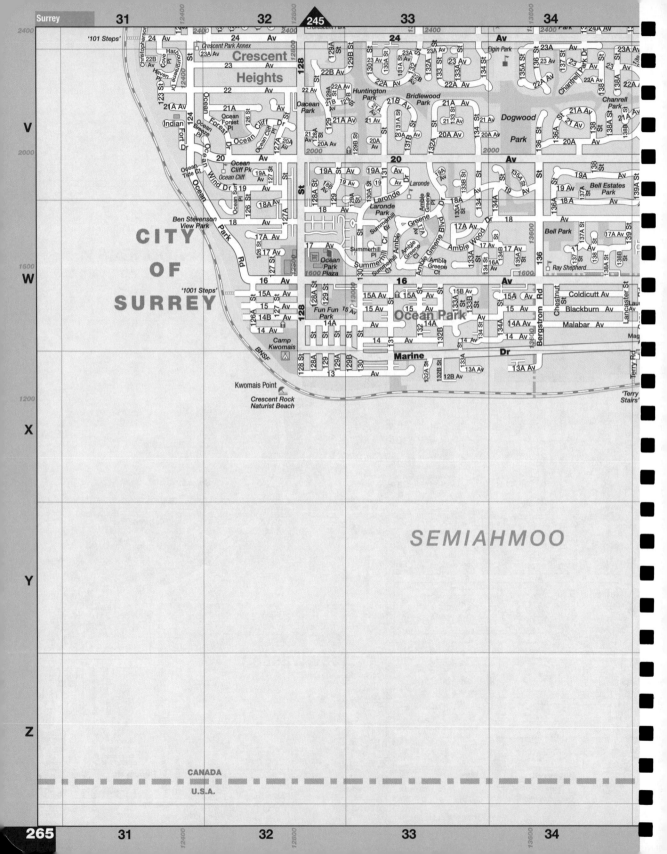

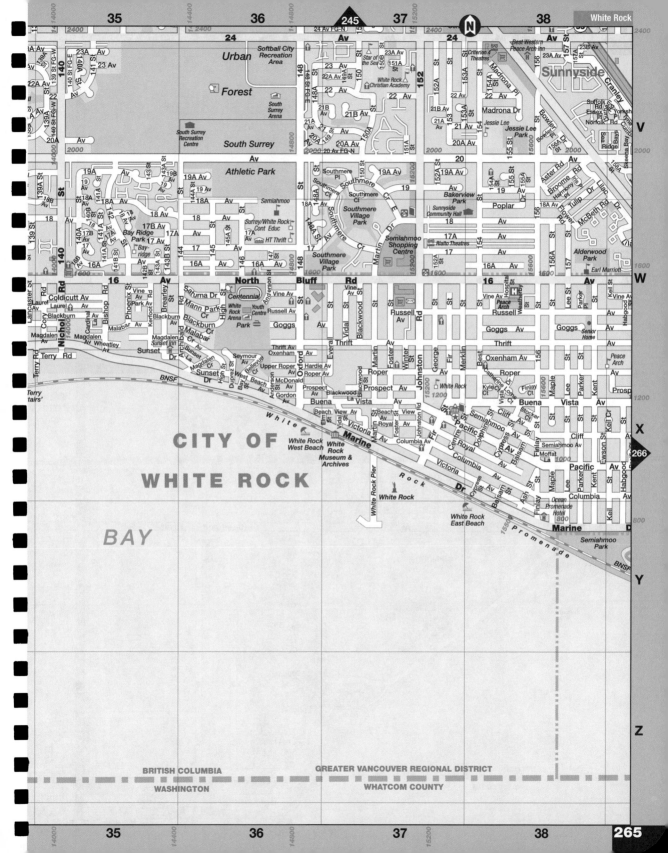

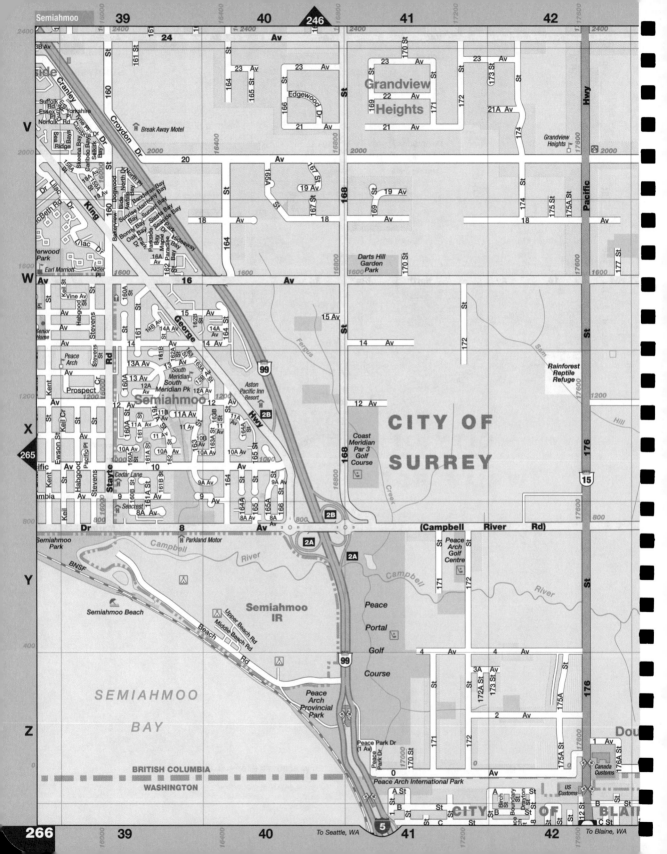

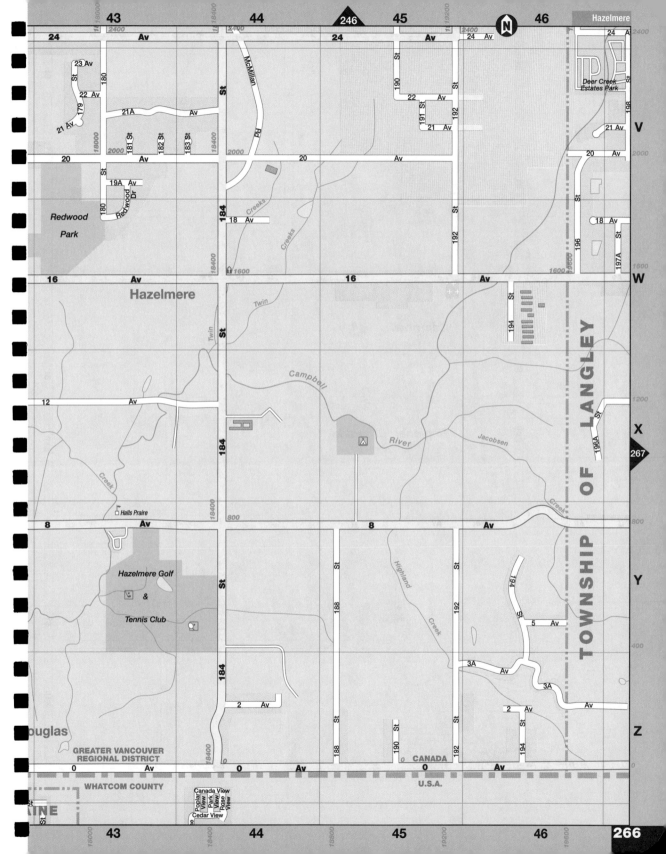

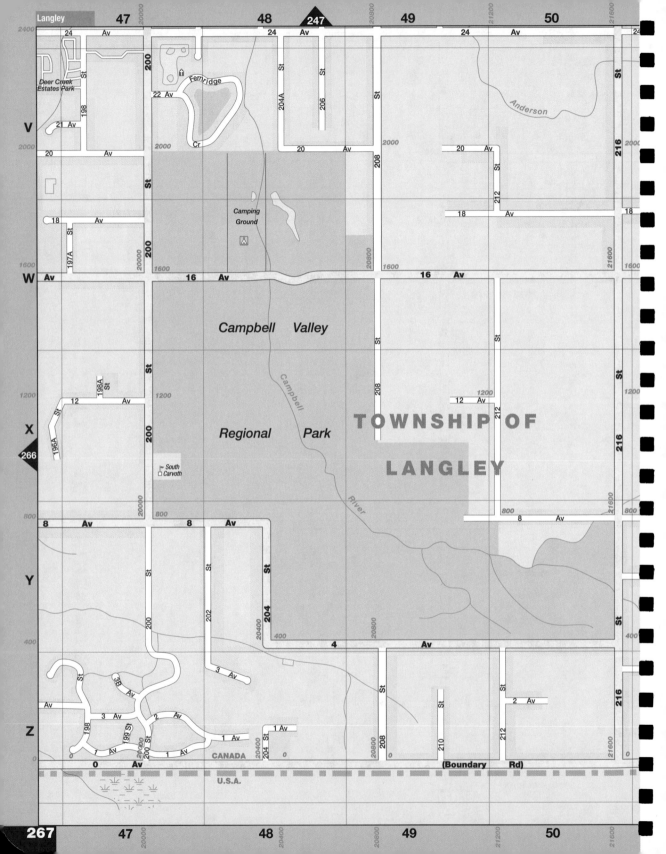

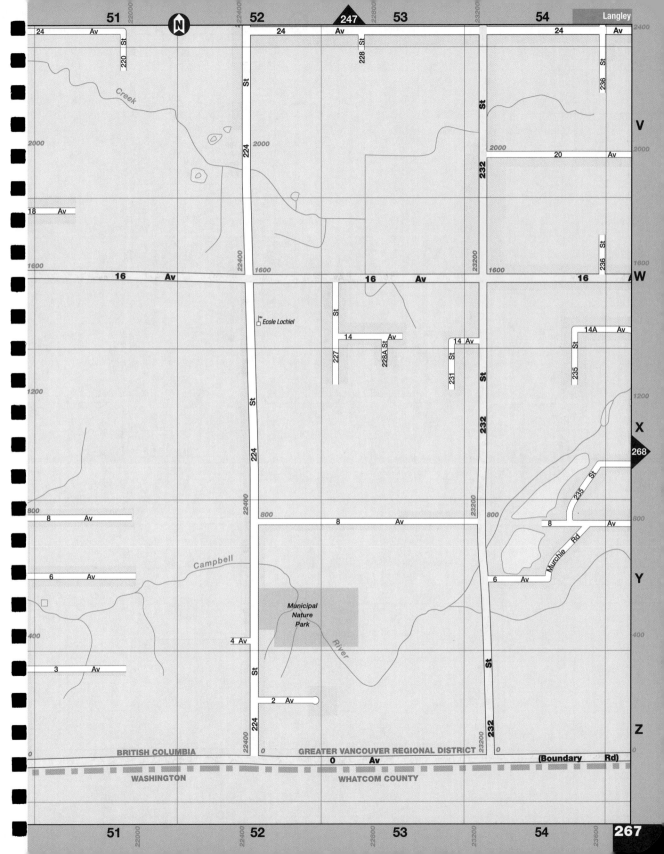

24 Av
24 Av
24 Av
220 St
228 St
236 St
224 St
232 St
V
Creek
2000
2000
2000
20 Av
18 Av
236 St
1600
1600
1600
16 Av
16 Av
16 Av
W
Ecole Lochiel
227 St
14 Av
14 Av
14A Av
228A St
231 St
235 St
232 St
224 St
X
268
1200
1200
235 St
800
800
800
8 Av
8 Av
8 Av
22400
23200
Murchie Rd
Campbell
6 Av
6 Av
6 Av
Y
Municipal
Nature
Park
400
River
400
4 Av
3 Av
224 St
232 St
2 Av
224 St
Z
0
0
0
BRITISH COLUMBIA
GREATER VANCOUVER REGIONAL DISTRICT
0 Av
(Boundary Rd)
WASHINGTON
WHATCOM COUNTY

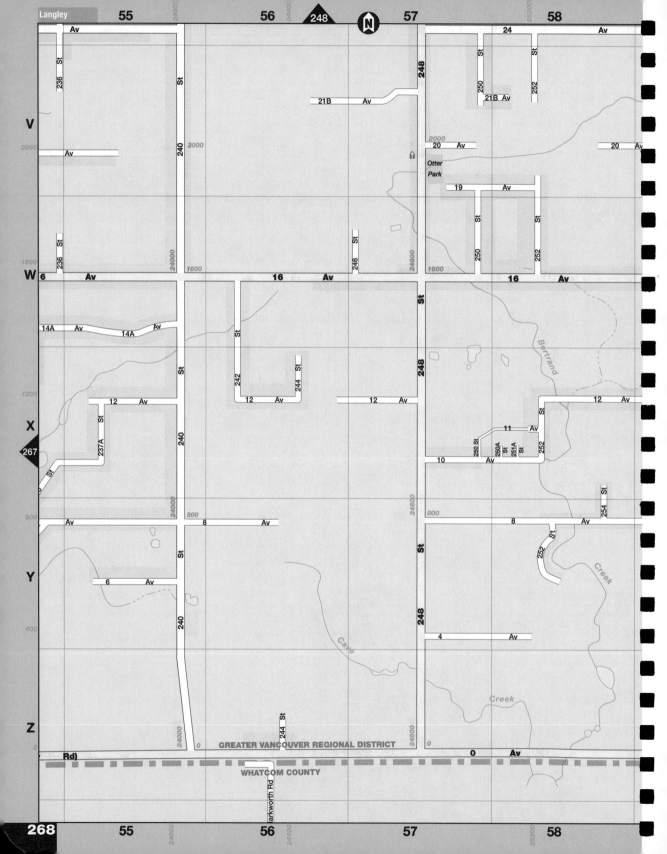

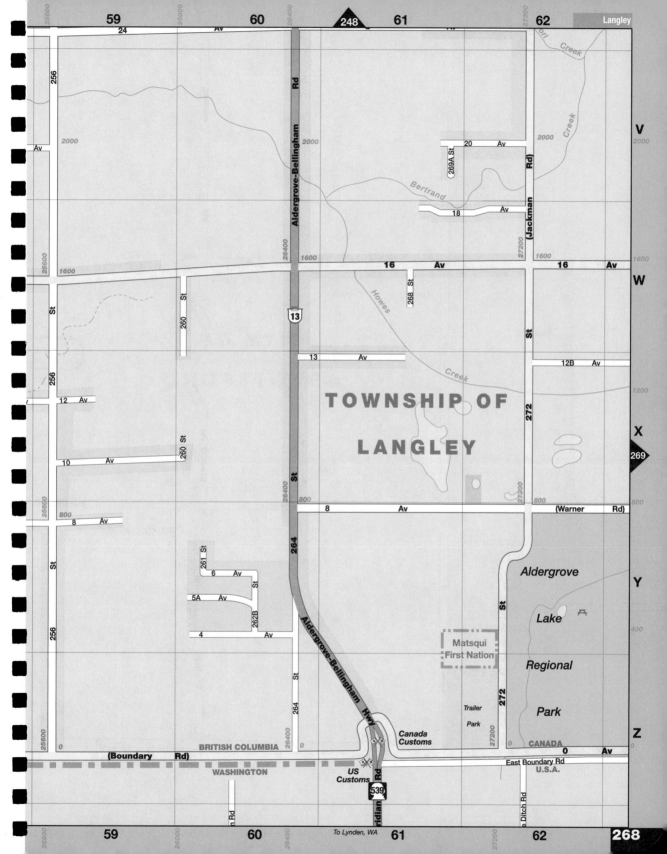

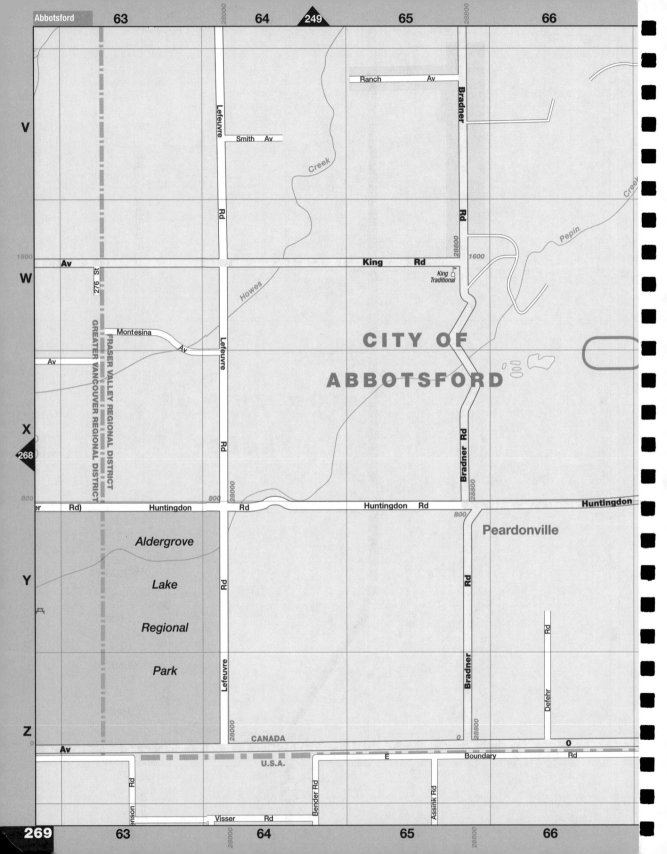

63   64   249   65   66

V

Ranch   Av

Bradner

Lefeuvre

Smith   Av

Creek

Rd

Pepin   Creek

1600

Av   King   Rd   1600

W   King
Traditional

276 St

GREATER VANCOUVER REGIONAL DISTRICT

FRASER VALLEY REGIONAL DISTRICT

Montesina

Av   Av

Lefeuvre

Howes

CITY OF

ABBOTSFORD

X

268

Rd

Bradner Rd

28800

800   800

er   Rd)   Huntingdon   Rd   Huntingdon   Rd   Huntingdon

Peardonville

Aldergrove

Lake

Y

Regional

Rd

Bradner

Rd

Park

Rd

Lefeuvre

Defehr

Z

0   0   0

Av   CANADA

U.S.A.   E   Boundary   Rd

Rd

Visser   Rd   Bender Rd

Assink Rd

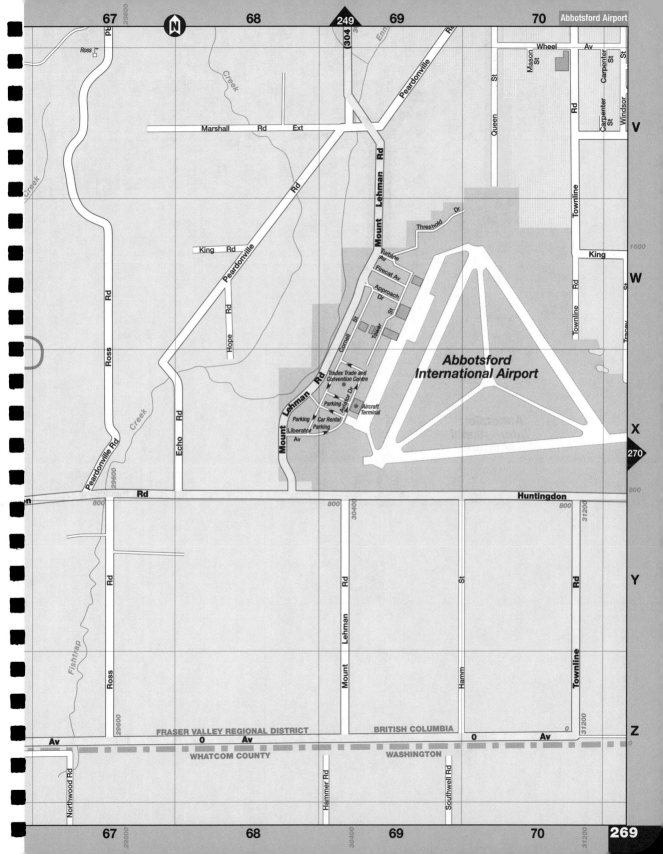

Abbotsford
International Airport

Tradex Trade and
Convention Centre

Aircraft
Terminal

Car Rental

Parking

Parking

Parking

Liberator
Av

Aviator Dr

Cornell St

Tower St

Approach
Dr

Firecat Av

Turbine
Av

Threshold Dr

Mount Lehman Rd

Peardonville Rd

Peardonville Rd

Marshall Rd Ext

King Rd

Hope Rd

Ross Rd

Echo Rd

Creek

Creek

Creek

Fishtrap

Ross Rd

Mount Lehman Rd

Hamm St

Townline Rd

Queen St

Townline Rd

King St

Tracey Av

Mason St

Wheel Av

Carpenter St

Carpenter St

Windsor St

Huntingdon

Northwood Rd

Hammer Rd

Southwell Rd

FRASER VALLEY REGIONAL DISTRICT

BRITISH COLUMBIA

Av

Av

Av

WHATCOM COUNTY

WASHINGTON

Rd

800

800

800

800

29600

30400

31200

31200

0

0

0

Ross

N

249

304

270

V

W

X

Y

Z

67

68

69

70

1600

800

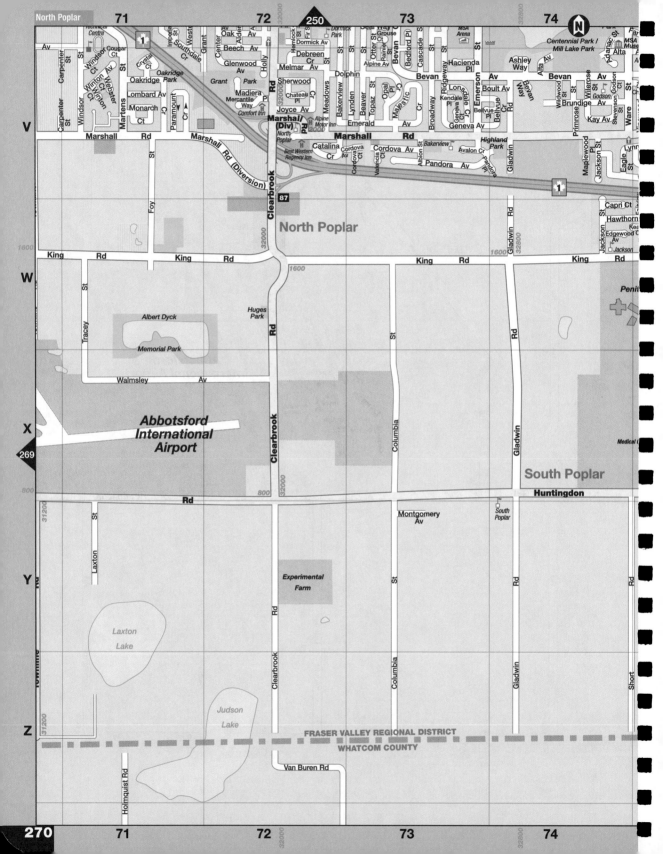

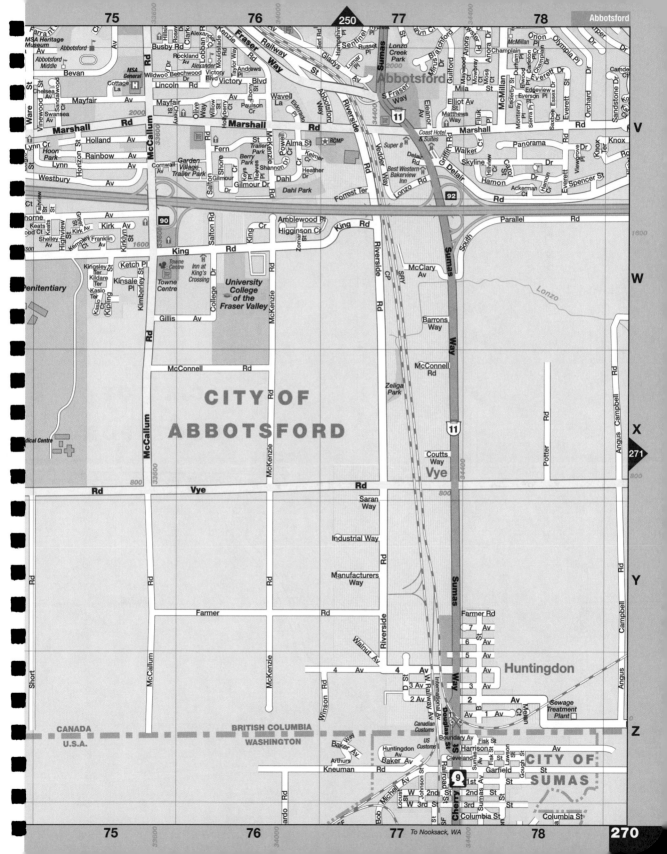

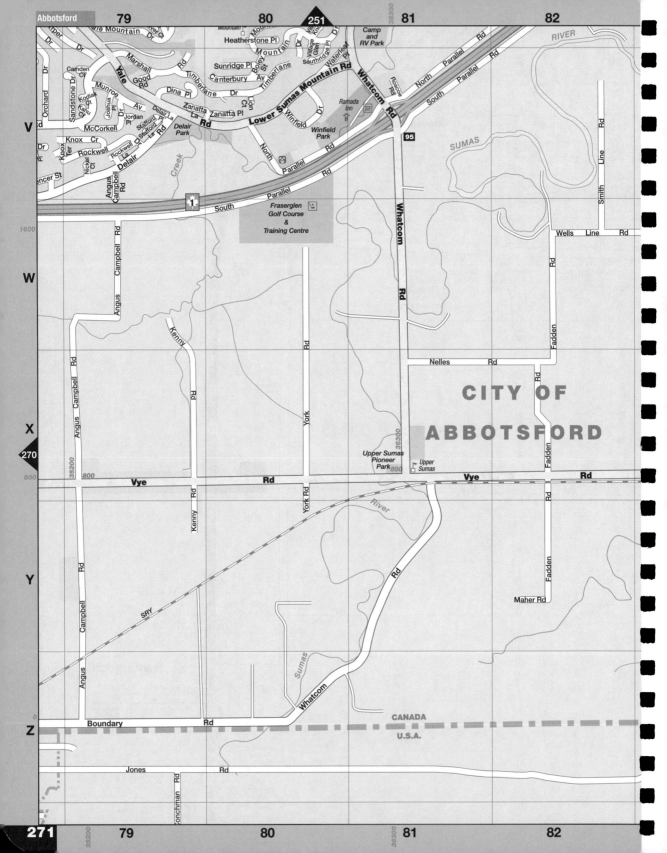

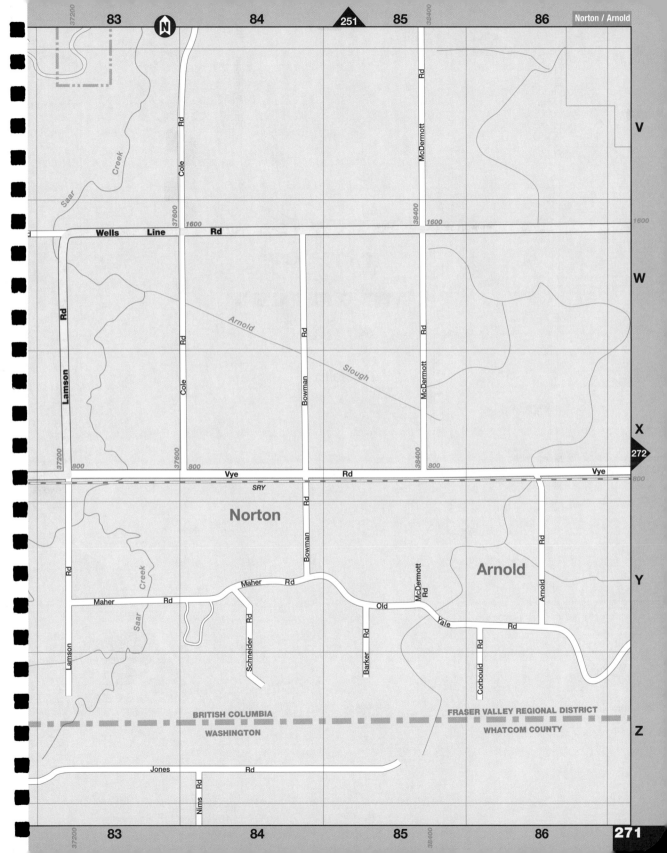

83   84   251   85   86

N

V

W

X

272

Y

Z

Cole Rd

McDermott Rd

Lamson Rd

Wells Line Rd

Saar Creek

Arnold Slough

Cole Rd

Bowman Rd

McDermott Rd

Vye Rd

Vye Rd

SRY

Norton

Bowman Rd

Lamson Rd

Maher Rd

Maher Rd

Schneider Rd

Saar Creek

McDermott Rd

Arnold

Arnold Rd

Old Yale Rd

Barker Rd

Corbould Rd

BRITISH COLUMBIA

WASHINGTON

FRASER VALLEY REGIONAL DISTRICT

WHATCOM COUNTY

Jones Rd

Nims Rd

37200

37600

38400

1600

1600

800

800

800

37200

38400

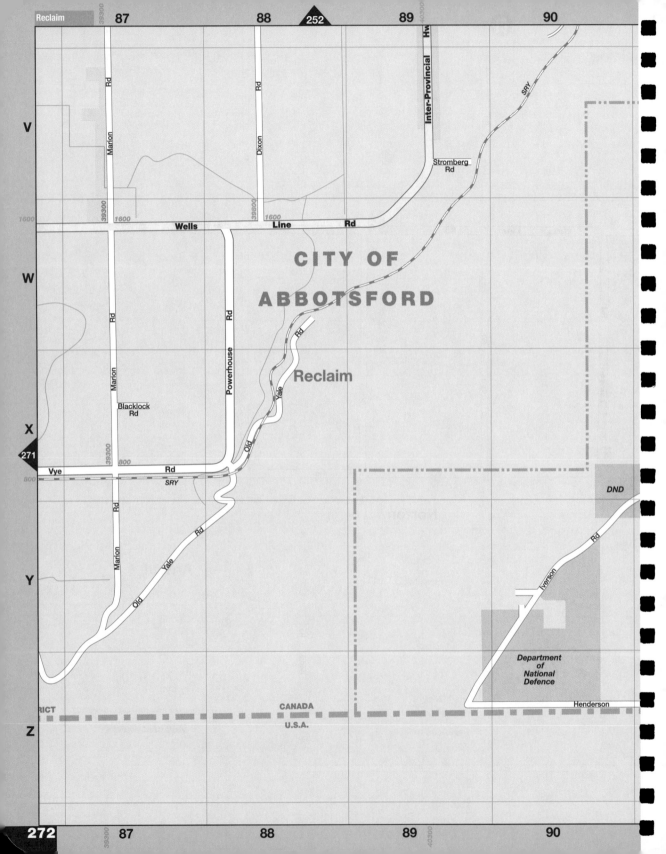

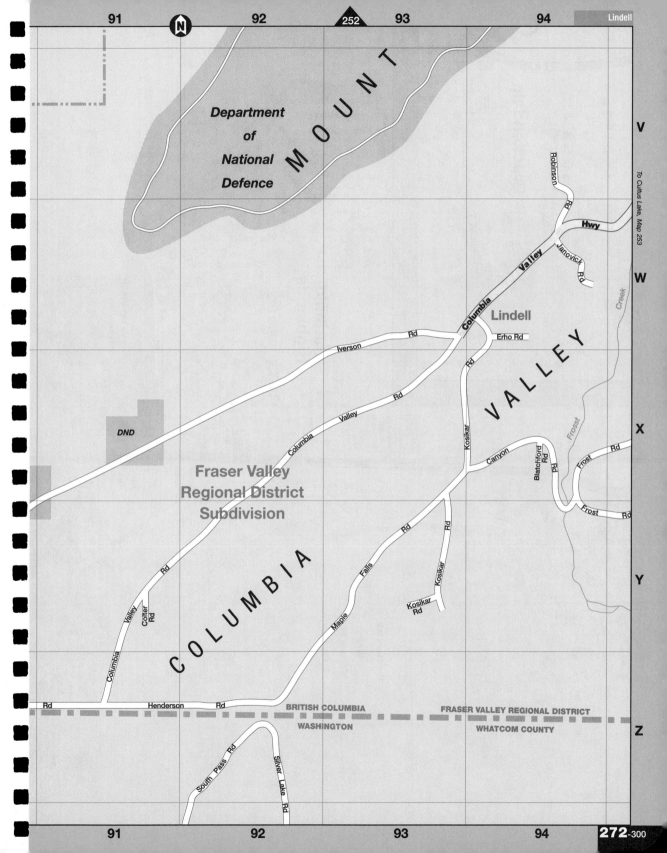

N

Department
of
National
Defence

M O U N T

V

W

To Cultus Lake, Map 253

Robinson Rd

Hwy

Valley

Janovick Rd

Columbia

Creek

Lindell

Iverson Rd

Erho Rd

V A L L E Y

Rd

Kosikar Rd

DND

Valley

Columbia

Rd

Frost

Frost Rd

Canyon

Blatchford Rd

Frost Rd

Fraser Valley
Regional District
Subdivision

C O L U M B I A

Rd

Falls

Kosikar Rd

Colter Rd

Valley

Columbia

Maple

Kosikar Rd

Rd

X

Y

Rd

Henderson Rd

BRITISH COLUMBIA
WASHINGTON

FRASER VALLEY REGIONAL DISTRICT
WHATCOM COUNTY

Z

South Pass Rd

Silver Lake Rd

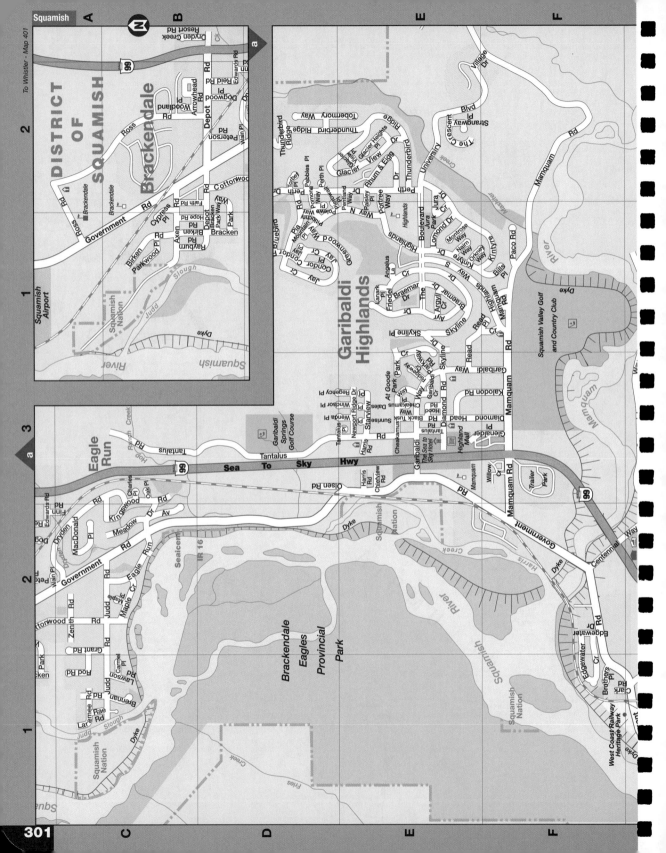

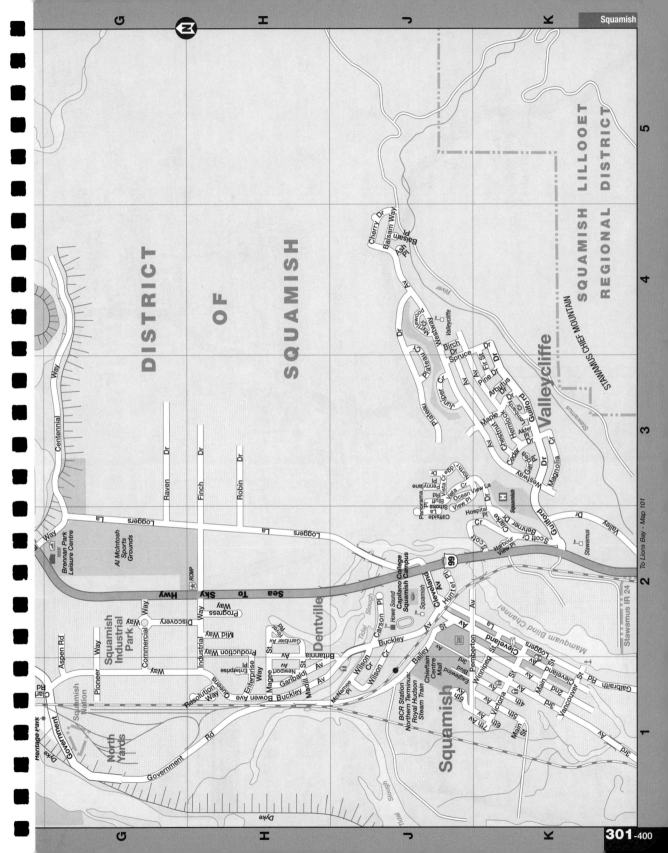

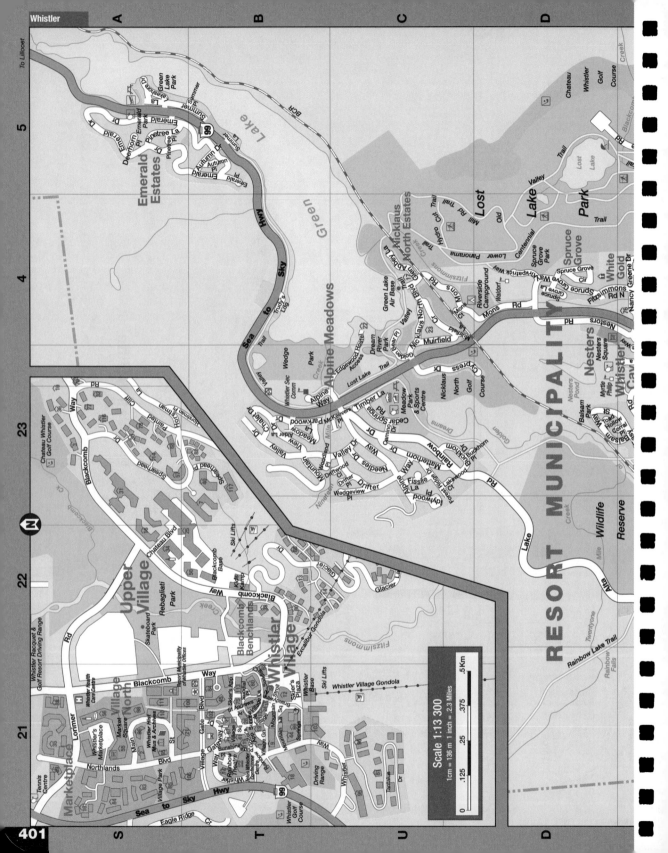

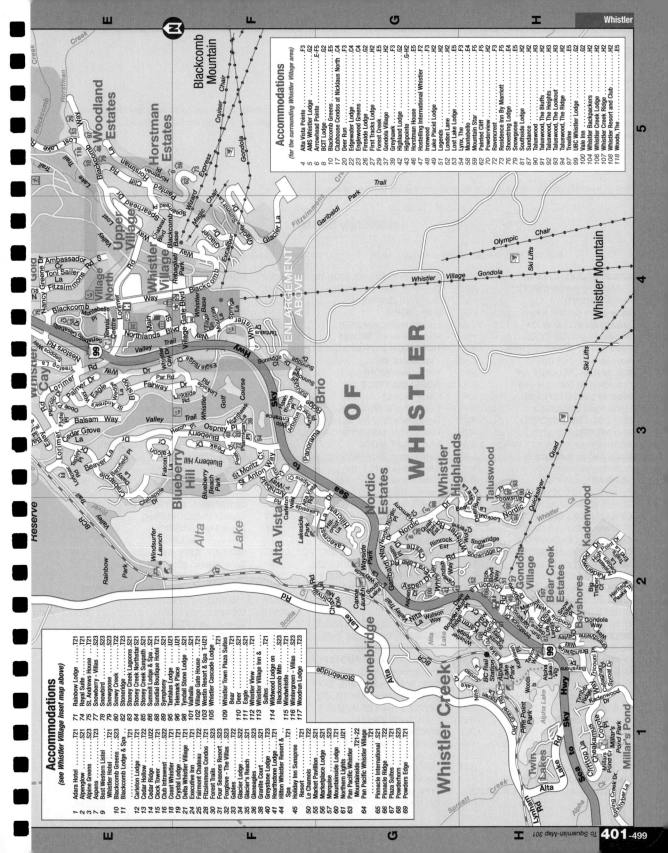

Street Index

How to use the index

To find a street, search through the alphabetically arranged columns. A three letter code beside the street name indicates which municipality the street is located in. Note the page number and the reference square to the right of the street name. For example, to find the location of Sidney Street in Chilliwack:

Sidney St *CHL* **193** D6

Turn to map **193** and locate the square D6. Scan the square to find the street.

Community Codes

BOLD TYPE indicates an official municipal name.   Blue type indicates a local community name.

ABBOTSFORD, CITY OF . . . .*ABT*	Garibaldi Highlands (SQUAMISH) .*SQU*	**POINT ROBERTS, WASHINGTON,**
Abbotsford (ABBOTSFORD) . . . . . .*ABT*	Gastown (VANCOUVER) . . . .*VAN*	**U.S.A.** . . . .*PRB*
Agassiz (KENT) . . . .*KNT*	Guildford (SURREY) . . . .*SUR*	Popkum (F.V.R.D.S.) . . . .*FRA*
Aldergrove (LANGLEY) . . . .*LGT*	Haig (HOPE) . . . .*HOP*	**PORT COQUITLAM, CITY OF** . . . .*PCQ*
ANMORE, VILLAGE OF . . . .*ANM*	Hamilton (RICHMOND) . . . .*RMD*	Port Guichon (DELTA) . . . .*DEL*
Anniedale (SURREY) . . . .*SUR*	Haney (MAPLE RIDGE) . . . .*MAP*	Port Hammond (MAPLE RIDGE) . .*MAP*
Barrowtown (ABBOTSFORD) . . . . . .*ABT*	**HARRISON HOT SPRINGS,**	Port Kells (SURREY) . . . .*SUR*
Bayshores (WHISTLER) . . . .*WHS*	**VILLAGE OF** . . . .*HHS*	**PORT MOODY, CITY OF** . . . .*PMD*
BELCARRA, VILLAGE OF . . . .*BEL*	Hatzic (MISSION) . . . .*MIS*	Promontory (CHILLIWACK) . . . .*CHL*
Brackendale (SQUAMISH) . . . .*SQU*	**HOPE, DISTRICT OF** . . . .*HOP*	**RICHMOND, CITY OF** . . . .*RMD*
Bradner (ABBOTSFORD) . . . .*ABT*	Hope (HOPE) . . . .*HOP*	Rosedale (CHILLIWACK) . . . .*CHL*
Bridal Falls (F.V.R.D.S.) . . . .*FRA*	Hopington (LANGLEY) . . . .*LGT*	Ruskin (MAPLE RIDGE) . . . .*MAP*
Bridgeport (RICHMOND) . . . .*RMD*	Horseshoe Bay (W. VANCOUVER) .*WVA*	Queensborough (NEW WESTMINSTER)
Brio (WHISTLER) . . . .*WHS*	Huntingdon (ABBOTSFORD) . . . . . .*ABT*	. . . .*NEW*
British Properties (WEST VAN.) . . . .*WVA*	Ioco (PORT MOODY) . . . .*PMD*	Sapperton (NEW WESTMINSTER) .*NEW*
Brookswood (LANGLEY) . . . .*LGT*	Kensington (SURREY) . . . .*SUR*	Sardis (CHILLIWACK) . . . .*CHL*
Burkville (RICHMOND) . . . .*RMD*	**KENT, DISTRICT OF** . . . .*KNT*	Semiahmoo (SURREY) . . . .*SUR*
BURNABY, CITY OF . . . .*BUR*	Kitsilano (VANCOUVER) . . . .*VAN*	Silverdale (MISSION) . . . .*MIS*
Burquitlam (COQUITLAM) . . . .*CQT*	Ladner (DELTA) . . . .*DEL*	South Burnaby (BURNABY) . . . .*BUR*
Cheam (CHILLIWACK) . . . .*CHL*	Lake Errock (F.V.R.D.S.) . . . .*FRA*	**SQUAMISH, DISTRICT OF** . . . .*SQU*
CHILLIWACK, DISTRICT OF . . . .*CHL*	**LANGLEY, CITY OF** . . . .*LGC*	Squamish (SQUAMISH) . . . .*SQU*
Chilliwack (CHILLIWACK) . . . .*CHL*	**LANGLEY, TOWNSHIP OF** . . . .*LGT*	Stave Falls (MISSION) . . . .*MIS*
Chinatown (VANCOUVER) . . . .*VAN*	Lindell (F.V.R.D.S.) . . . .*FRA*	Steelhead (MISSION) . . . .*MIS*
Clayburn Village (ABBOTSFORD) . .*ABT*	**LIONS BAY, VILLAGE OF** . . . .*LIO*	**SURREY, CITY OF** . . . .*SUR*
Clearbrook(F.V.R.D.S.) . . . .*FRA*	Lynn Valley (N. VANCOUVER) . . . . .*DNV*	Tsawwassen (DELTA) . . . .*DEL*
Cloverdale (SURREY) . . . .*SUR*	**MAPLE RIDGE, DISTRICT OF** . .*MAP*	Tynehead (SURREY) . . . .*SUR*
COQUITLAM, CITY OF . . . .*CQT*	Matsqui Village (ABBOTSFORD) . .*ABT*	**UNIVERSITY ENDOWMENT LANDS**
Crescent Beach (SURREY) . . . .*SUR*	Middlegate (BURNABY) . . . .*BUR*	**(U.E.L.)** . . . .*UEL*
Cultus Lake Park Board (F.V.R.D.S.)*FRA*	Minoru Park (RICHMOND) . . . .*RMD*	University Hill (U.E.L.) . . . .*UEL*
Deep Cove (N. VANCOUVER) . . . . . .*DNV*	Minto Landing (CHILLIWACK) . . . . .*CHL*	Valleycliffe (SQUAMISH) . . . .*SQU*
DELTA, CORPORATION OF . . . . .*DEL*	**MISSION, DISTRICT OF** . . . .*MIS*	**VANCOUVER, CITY OF** . . . .*VAN*
Dollarton (BURNABY) . . . .*BUR*	Mission (MISSION) . . . .*MIS*	Vedder Crossing (CHILLIWACK) . . .*CHL*
Douglas (SURREY) . . . .*SUR*	Mount Lehman (ABBOTSFORD) . .*ABT*	Walnut Grove (LANGLEY) . . . .*LGT*
Downtown (VANCOUVER) . . . .*VAN*	Murrayville (LANGLEY) . . . .*LGT*	Websters Corners (MAPLE RIDGE) . .
East Burnaby (BURNABY) . . . .*BUR*	**NEW WESTMINSTER, CITY OF** .*NEW*	. . . .*MAP*
East Chilliwack (CHILLIWACK) . . . .*CHL*	Nordic Estates (WHISTLER) . . . . . .*WHS*	West Heights (MISSION) . . . .*MIS*
Elgin (SURREY) . . . .*SUR*	North Burnaby (BURNABY) . . . .*BUR*	**WEST VANCOUVER, DISTRICT OF** . . .
Emerald Estaes (WHISTLER) . . . . .*WHS*	North Delta (DELTA) . . . .*DEL*	. . . .*WVA*
English Bluff (DELTA) . . . .*DEL*	**NORTH VANCOUVER, CITY OF** .*CNV*	**WHISTLER, RESORT MUN. OF** . .*WHS*
Fishermans Cove (WEST VAN.) . . . .*WVA*	**NORTH VANCOUVER, DISTRICT OF**	Whistler Creek (WHISTLER) . . . .*WHS*
Forest Knolls (LANGLEY) . . . .*LGT*	. . . .*DNV*	Whistler Highlands (WHISTLER) . . .*WHS*
Fort Langley (LANGLEY) . . . .*LGT*	Panorama Ridge (SURREY) . . . . . .*SUR*	Whistler Village (WHISTLER) . . . . . .*WHS*
FRASER VALLEY REGIONAL	Peardonville (ABBOTSFORD) . . . . .*ABT*	**WHITE ROCK, CITY OF** . . . .*WRK*
DISTRICT SUBDIVISION (F.V.R.D.S.)	**PITT MEADOWS, CITY OF** . . . . . .*PTM*	Whonnock (MAPLE RIDGE) . . . . . .*MAP*
. . . .*FRA*	Pitt Meadows (PITT MEADOWS) .*PTM*	Yarrow (CHILLIWACK) . . . .*CHL*

Street Generics and Abbreviations

Av . . . . .Avenue	Cv . . . . .Cove	Heath . . . . . . .Heath	Mnr . . . . .Manor	Sq . . . . .Square
Bay . . . . .Bay	Dr . . . . .Drive	Hill . . . . .Hill	Path . . . . .Path	St . . . . .Street
Blvd . . . .Boulevard	Expwy . .Expressway	Hts . . . . . . .Heights	Pk . . . . .Park	Ter . . . . .Terrace
Cir . . . . .Circle	Frwy . . . . . .Freeway	Hwy . . . . . . .Highway	Pkwy . . . . .Parkway	Tr . . . . .Trail
Cl . . . . .Close	Gdns . . . . .Gardens	La . . . . .Lane	Pl . . . . .Place	View . . . . .View
Cr . . . . . . .Crescent	Gn . . . . . . .Green	Ldg . . . . . .Landing	Pt . . . . .Point	Vill . . . . .Villas
Crct . . . . . . .Circuit	Gr . . . . .Grove	Ln . . . . .Line	Rd . . . . .Road	Walk . . . . .Walk
Ct . . . . .Court	Gt . . . . .Gate	Mews . . . . . .Mews	Rise . . . . .Rise	Way . . . . .Way

Duplicated Street Names

When two or more streets in a municipality share the same name, an area name in brackets following the street name indicates in which part of the municipality the street is located.

Highways

1	ABT	**.249** Q64 S68 **270** V74	**3**	HOP	**.118** F45	**10**	DEL	**.224** N30
		271 V-W79 V-W80					LGT	**.227** K52
	BUR	**.163** V22 **164** V24 W29 X27	**5**	HOP	**.118** F46		SUR	**.225** M32 N38 **226** N46
	CHL	**.212** J93 **213** G8 H3						
		214 G14 **232** K90	**7**	CQT	**.145** T37 **165** W37 Y33	**11**	ABT	**.230** N76 **250** R-S76 T-U77
	CNV	**.123** M18		FRA	**.193** Z2 **211** F84 **212** E91			**270** V77 X77
	CQT	**.165** X31 Y34		HOP	**.118** D43		MIS	**.230** K74
	DNV	**.143** Q20		KNT	**.175** W17 W20 W23			
	FRA	**.195** C22		MAP	**.187** Z48 Z53 **188** C-D55	**13**	LGT	**.228** P60 **248** S60 **268** W60
	HOP	**.118** C43 E44 H43			**208** E62 **209** E65			
	LGT	**.207** G50 **228** L-M57 N61		MIS	**.209** H69 **210** H-J77 J73	**15**	SUR	**206** F42 H42 **226** K42 M42 P42
	SUR	**.185** A37 C38			**211** H79 **230** K73			**246** U42 **266** X42
		186 C-D40 **206** E44		PCQ	**.166** V41			
	WVA	**.101** G2 **121** K6 **122** K10 L13		PTM	**.166** X-Y45	**17**	DEL	**.223** N18 **243** S18 **262** Y13
								263 V17
1A	ABT	**.249** T64 T67	**7B**	PCQ	**.166** W42 Y39			
	BUR	**163** Y21 **164** Y23 **184** Z23 Z26-27				**91**	DEL	**.204** F26-27 **224** L28 N30
	NEW	**.184** Z28 Z29					RMD	**.203** E18 **204** F24
	VAN	**.142** Q12	**9**	CHL	**.195** B20			
	WVA	**.122** M12		KNT	**.175** X21			

91A	NEW	**.184** C26-27 C-D27
99	DEL	**.223** L17 N19 P22
		224 P24 P28
	LIO	**.101** B23
	RMD	**.182** D14 **203** F16 H16
	SQM	**.301** B2 C-D3 F3 J2
	SUR	**.225** P31 **245** R35 U38
		266 X40 Z40-41
	VAN	**.142** Q12 S-T13 T13
		162 V12 Y12 **182** A12
	WHS	**.401** B5 E3-4 H1 T21
	WVA	**.101** D4 G2 **121** K6
		122 K10 M12
99A	BUR	**.163** Y21 **164** Y23
		184 Z23 Z26-27
	NEW	**.184** Z28 Z29

Numbered Streets

0 Av SUR **266** Z41-42 Z43-46
0 Av (Boundary Rd) LGT . . . .
. . . .**267** Z47 Z49-50 Z53-54
. . . .**268** Z55 Z57-60 Z62 **269** Z63

1 Av LGT **267** Z47 Z48
1 Av MIS **210** J74-76
1 Av PMD **145** P-Q32
1 Av RMD **222** K-L9
1 Av SUR **266** Z42
1 Av VAN **11** K-L41
1 Av E BUR **163** U21
1 Av E VAN . . . .
. . .**11** K40 K-L41 **143** T15 **163** U15 U17-20
1 Av W VAN **10** K32-34 **11** K39-40
. . . .**142** T10-12 T14 T7 T9
1 St BUR **164** Y28
1 St NEW **184** A29-30 Z28-29
1 St PMD **145** Q32
1 St E CNV **143** P17-18
1 St W CNV **123** N15 N16 **143** P16
1 St W DNV **122** N14
1A Av DEL **263** Z16 Z17 Z19-20

2 Av DEL **263** Z16-17
2 Av LGT **267** Z47 Z50 Z52
2 Av MIS **210** J74-75
2 Av PMD **145** Q32
2 Av RMD **222** K8-9 L8-9
2 Av SUR **266** Z42 Z44 Z46
2 Av VAN **11** L41
2 Av E BUR **163** U21
2 Av E VAN . .**11** K40 L41 **163** U15 U17-20

2 Av W VAN **10** K32-33 **11** K39-40
. .**142** T10 T7 T8 T9 **161** T6 **162** U10 U11 U14
2 St BUR **164** Y28 **184** Z28
2 St NEW **184** A29 Z28
2 St PMD **145** Q32
2 St E CNV **143** P17-18
2 St W CNV . . .**123** N15-16 N16 **143** P16
2A Av DEL **263** Z16
2nd Av SQM **301** K1

3 Av DEL **263** Z16 Z17 Z19
3 Av LGT **267** Z47 Z48 Z51
3 Av MIS **210** J74-75
3 Av NEW **184** A28-29 B28
3 Av PMD **145** Q32
3 Av RMD **222** K8-L8
3 Av E VAN . . .**11** L40 **163** U15 U17-20
3 Av W VAN . . .**10** K32 K-L33 **11** L39-40
. . . .**142** T7 **161** T6 **162** U14 U9-11
3 St NEW **184** A29
3 St E CNV **143** P17-18 P19
3 St W CNV . . .**123** N15 N16 **143** P16
3 St W DNV **122** N14 **123** N15
3A Av DEL **263** Y-Z17
3A Av SUR **266** Z41-42 Z46
3B Av LGT **267** Z47
3rd Av SQM **301** K1

4 Av DEL **263** Y17 Y19-20 Y-Z16
4 Av LGT .**267** Y48-49 Y52 **268** Y57-58 Y60
4 Av MIS **210** J74 J75
4 Av NEW **184** A28-29 B29
4 Av PMD **145** Q31

4 Av RMD **222** K8
4 Av SUR **266** Y-Z42
4 Av E VAN . . . .
. . . . .**11** L40 **163** U15 U17 U18-19 U20
4 Av W VAN **10** L32-33 **11** L39-40
. . . .**161** U6 **162** U14 U7-12
4 St BUR **164** Y27 **184** Z28
4 St NEW **184** A28-29 B29 Z28
4 St E CNV **143** P17-18 P19
4 St W CNV **123** N16
4A Av DEL **263** Y17
4th Av SQM **301** K1

5 Av DEL **263** Y16
5 Av MIS **210** J74 J75
5 Av NEW **184** A28-29 B27-28
5 Av RMD **222** K8
5 Av SUR **266** Y46
5 Av VAN **11** L41
5 Av E VAN . . . .
. . . .**11** L40 **163** U15 U15-16 U17 U18-20
5 Av W VAN **10** L32-33 **11** L39-40
. .**161** U6 **162** U7 **163** U15-16 U17 U18-20
5 St NEW **184** A28-29 Z28
5 St E CNV **143** P17-18 P19
5 St W CNV **123** N16-17
5A Av LGT **268** Y60
5A Av MIS **210** J75
5B Av DEL **263** Y17
5th Av SQM **301** K1

6 Av DEL **263** Y16-17
6 Av LGT **267** Y51 Y54 **268** Y55
6 Av MIS **210** J73-74 J75

6 Av NEW **184** A28-29 B27
6 Av RMD **222** K8
6 Av (Ferguson Rd) LGT **268** Y60
6 Av E NEW **164** Y30 **184** Z30
6 Av E VAN .**163** U15 U15-16 U16 U17-20
6 Av W VAN **10** L32-36 **11** L37-40
. . . . . .**161** U6 **162** U12-14 U14 U7 U9-12
6 St BUR **164** X26 Y27 **184** Z27
6 St NEW **184** A28-29 B29 Z28
6 St W VAN **122** M12-13 M13
6 St E CNV **143** P17-18
6 St W CNV . . .**123** N16 N16-17
6A Av DEL **263** Y17
6th Av SQM **301** K1

7 Av DEL **263** Y17
7 Av MIS **210** J72-75 J75
7 Av NEW **184** A28 B26-27 Z28-29
7 Av RMD **222** K8
7 Av E NEW **184** Z29-30
7 Av E VAN .**163** U15 U16 U17-18 U18-20
7 Av W VAN . . . .
. . . . .**10** L32-33 **161** U6 **162** U14 U7 U9-13
7 St BUR **164** Y26 **184** Z27
7 St NEW **184** A28 A-B29
7 St E CNV **143** P18
7A Av DEL **263** Y16 Y16-17
7B Av DEL **263** Y16 Y17
7th Av SQM **301** K1

8 Av DEL **263** Y17
8 Av LGT . . . .
. .**267** Y50-51 Y53 Y54 **268** Y55-56 Y58-59
8 Av MIS **210** J75

28 St W / 54A St

28 St W CNV 123 L16-17
28A Av LGT 248 T61 T61-62 T62
28A Av SUR 245 T34-35 T-U35 T-U36 U37 246 T42
28B Av DEL 242 T14
28B Av LGT 248 T60-61 T61-62
28B Av SUR 246 T42

29 Av LGT 248 T60 T60-61 T61-62 T62
29 Av SUR 245 T34 T35 T36 T37 246 T39-40 T42
29 Av E VAN 163 W15-16 W16-17 W17 W18 W18-20
29 Av W VAN 162 W11 W11-12 W12-13 W13-14 W7-10
29 St WVA 122 K-L8 L8
29 St E CNV 123 L17-18
29 St E DNV 123 L20
29 St W CNV 123 L16 L17
29A Av LGT 248 T62
29A Av SUR 245 T35 T36 T37 246 T43
29B Av LGT 247 T53 248 T60-61

30 Av DEL 243 T19
30 Av LGT 246 T46 247 T47 248 T57 T60 T61 T61-62 T62
30 Av SUR 245 T34 T34-35 T35 T36 246 T39
30 Av (Reid Rd) LGT 248 T57-58
30 Av E VAN 163 W15 W15-16 W16 W17 X18
30 Av W VAN 162 W11 W13 W13-14 W8-9 W9-10
30 St WVA 122 K-L8
30A Av LGT 248 T60 T60-61 T61 T62
30A Av SUR 245 T35 T36 246 T41
30B Av SUR 246 T39 T39-40
30B St DEL 242 S12

31 Av DEL 242 T12-13
31 Av LGT 248 T62 249 T63
31 Av SUR 245 T34 T35 T36 246 T41 T41-42
31 Av E VAN 163 W-X17 X15-16 X17-18
31 Av W VAN 162 W13-14 W8-10
31 St WVA 122 L7
31A Av LGT 248 T61 T62 249 T63
31A Av SUR 245 T35 T36
31B Av LGT 248 T60 249 T63

32 Av LGT 247 T47-48 T49 T50 T54 248 T55 T56 T57-58 T61 T62 249 T63
32 Av SUR 245 T34-36 246 T39-46
32 Av (McInnis Rd) LGT 246 T46 247 T47
32 Av Diversion SUR 245 T37
32 Av E VAN 163 X15 X16 X17-18
32 Av W VAN 162 W11-12 W8 W9-10 W-X10 W-X11 X12-13 X13
32A Av LGT 247 T49 248 T61 T62 249 T63
32A Av SUR 245 T34
32B Av LGT 247 T49 248 T62 249 T63
32B Av SUR 245 T35 T36

33 Av LGT 248 S62 S-T62 T61 249 S63
33 Av SUR 245 T34 T35 T36-37 T38
33 Av E VAN 163 X15-18
33 Av W VAN 162 X8-13
33A Av DEL 242 S13-14
33A Av LGT 246 S-T46 T46 247 T47 248 S61 S62 249 S63
33A Av SUR 245 S-T36 S-T38 T36
33B Av LGT 248 S61 S62
33B Av SUR 245 S35 S36

34 Av LGT 247 S47-48 248 S61 S62
34 Av SUR 245 S34-35 S36 S36-37 S37 S37-38 246 S39-40
34 Av E VAN 163 X15 X16-17 X17 X18
34 Av W VAN 162 X8-12
34 St DEL 242 R-T13
34A Av LGT 246 S46 247 S47 S54 248 S62
34A Av SUR 245 S35 S36-37 S37-38
34B Av DEL 243 S16 S17-19
34B Av SUR 245 S37

35 Av LGT 247 S47 248 S56-57 S62
35 Av SUR 245 S34-35 S37
35 Av E VAN 163 X15 X16 X16-17 X17 X18
35 Av W VAN 162 X11-12 X12 X13 X14 X8-10
35A Av LGT 246 S46 247 S47
35A Av SUR 245 S35 S38

36 Av DEL 243 S16 S19-20
36 Av LGT 247 S47 S49 248 S56-57 S57-58 S59
36 Av SUR 245 S37 S38 246 S46
36 Av E VAN 163 X15 X16-17 X17-18
36 Av W VAN 162 X11-12 X12 X8-10
36A Av LGT 246 S46 247 S47 248 S55
36A Av SUR 245 S35 S36 S37-38 S38 246 S39 S39-40
36B Av LGT 247 S48
36B Av SUR 245 S36 S38

37 Av LGT 246 S46 247 S47 S48-49
37 Av SUR 245 S35 S38
37 Av E VAN 163 X15 X16 X16-17 X18
37 Av W VAN 162 X8-14
37A Av LGT 246 S46 247 S47 S48 S49 S51-52
37A Av SUR 245 S38
37B Av LGT 247 S48

38 Av LGT 246 S46 247 S47 S48 S48-49 S49-50 S52 248 R-S59
38 Av SUR 245 S38
38 Av E VAN 163 X15 X16 X17 X18-19
38 Av W VAN 162 X10-11 X11 X12-13 X13 X14 X8 X9 X9-10
38A Av LGT 246 R-S46 247 R-S47 R-S48 S48
38A Av SUR 245 R-S38
38B Av LGT 247 R47 R-S47

39 Av LGT 247 R48
39 Av E VAN 163 X15 X16-17 X17 X18
39 Av W VAN 162 X11 X12 X12-13 X13-14 X8-9 X9-10
39A Av LGT 247 R47 R48-49
39A Av SUR 245 R38 246 R39

40 Av LGT 246 R46 247 R47 R51 R54 248 R55 R56-57 R59 R62
40 Av SUR 245 R33-35 R35-38 246 R39-45
40 Av (Bradshaw Rd) LGT 247 R47-50 R51-53 248 R56-58
40 Av (Downes Rd) LGT 248 R62 249 R63
40 Av E VAN 163 X15 X19 X-Y17 X-Y18 Y16 Y17
40 Av W VAN 162 X10-11 X11-12 X12 X12-13 X14 X8 X9
40 St DEL 242 R-S14
40A Av LGT 246 R46 247 R47 R48
40B Av LGT 247 R48

41 Av LGT 247 R47 R48
41 Av E VAN 163 Y15-19
41 Av W VAN 162 X8 X9-11 X-Y12 X-Y13
41A Av LGT 246 R46 247 R47 R47-48
41B Av LGT 247 R48
41B St DEL 242 R-T14

42 Av LGT 246 R46 247 R47 R47-48 R49
42 Av E VAN 162 Y14 163 Y15 Y17-18 Y18 Y19
42 Av W VAN 162 Y10-11 Y11 Y12-13 Y13 Y14 Y9 Y9-10
42A Av DEL 243 R16
42A Av LGT 247 R47 R49-50
42A Av SUR 246 R45
42B Av DEL 243 R16

43 Av DEL 243 Q-R16
43 Av LGT 247 R47 R49 248 Q62 249 Q63
43 Av E VAN 162 Y14 163 Y15 Y15 Y17 Y17-18 Y18 Y19-20 Y20
43 Av W VAN 162 Y11-13 Y14 Y9 Y9-10
43A Av DEL 243 Q16 Q19
43A Av LGT 246 Q-R46 247 Q49 Q49-50 Q-R47

44 Av DEL 243 Q16-17 Q18 244 Q28
44 Av LGC 247 Q47-48 Q48-49
44 Av LGT 246 Q46 247 Q50 Q51-52 Q54 248 Q56 Q57
44 Av SUR 245 Q35 246 Q44
44 Av (Cemetery Rd) LGT 247 Q48-50
44 Av E VAN 163 Y15 Y17-18 Y19 Y20
44 Av W VAN 162 Y10-11 Y11 Y13 Y14 Y9 Y9-10
44A Av DEL 243 Q15-16 Q18
44A Av LGC 247 Q47 Q47-48 Q48-49
44A Av LGT 247 Q49 Q50-51 Q51 Q51-52 Q52
44A St DEL 243 Q15
44B Av DEL 243 Q15 Q15-16 Q16
44B Av LGT 246 Q46 247 Q47
44B St DEL 243 Q15

45 Av DEL 243 Q15-16 Q17 Q18 Q19
45 Av LGC 247 Q47 Q47-48 Q48 Q49
45 Av LGT 247 Q49 Q50 Q50-51 Q51 Q52
45 Av E VAN 163 Y15-17 Y18-20
45 Av W VAN 162 Y13 Y13-14 Y9-13
45 St DEL 243 Q15
45A Av DEL 243 Q15 Q18 Q19
45A Av LGC 246 Q46 247 Q47 Q48 Q48-49 Q49
45A Av LGT 247 Q49 Q51
45A St DEL 243 Q15
45B Av DEL 243 Q19
45B Av LGC 246 Q46 247 Q47

46 Av DEL 243 Q15 Q17
46 Av LGC 246 Q46 247 Q47 Q48 Q48-49 Q49
46 Av LGT 247 Q49 Q50-51 Q51 Q52 Q54 248 Q60 Q62
46 Av E VAN 163 Y15 Y17 Y18-19 Y19-20 Y20
46 Av W VAN 162 Y10-11 Y11 Y12-13 Y14 Y8
46 St DEL 243 Q15
46A Av DEL 243 Q17 Q19
46A Av LGC 246 Q46 247 Q47 Q48 Q48-49
46A Av LGT 247 Q49 Q50 Q51 Q52 248 Q56
46A St DEL 243 Q-T15
46B Av LGC 247 Q48
46B Av LGT 247 Q50 Q52 248 Q55
46B St DEL 243 Q15

47 Av DEL 243 Q16 Q17
47 Av LGC 246 Q46 247 Q47 Q48 Q49
47 Av LGT 247 Q49 Q50 Q52 Q54
47 Av E VAN 163 Y15-16 Y16-17 Y17 Y17-18 Y18-19 Y19-20 Y20
47 Av W VAN 162 Y10 Y10-11 Y11 Y11-13 Y13 Y14 Y8-9
47 St DEL 243 Q15
47A Av DEL 243 Q16 Q17
47A Av LGC 247 Q47 Q48 Q49
47A Av LGT 247 Q50 Q52
47A St DEL 243 Q15
47B Av LGT 247 Q50

48 Av DEL 223 P16 243 Q16
48 Av LGC 226 P46 246 Q46 Q46 247 Q47-48 Q48-49
48 Av LGT 228 P58 P62 247 Q53 Q54 248 Q55 Q57 Q58 Q62
48 Av SUR 225 P33 P36-37 245 Q33 Q36 Q37-38 246 Q39-40 Q41-42 Q45-46
48 Av (McDonald Rd) LGT 228 P58 P59 247 Q49-51 248 Q55-56 Q58 Q59
48 Av E VAN 163 Y15 Y16 Y18 Y18-19 Y19-20 Y20
48 Av W VAN 162 Y10-11 Y11 Y12-13 Y13 Y14 Y8-9 Y9
48 St DEL 243 U16
48A Av DEL 223 P17 P18 P19
48A Av LGC 226 P46 227 P47 P48 P49
48A Av LGT 227 P50 P51
48A St DEL 243 Q-R16
48B Av DEL 223 P17 P17-18
48B Av LGC 227 P48
48B Av LGT 228 P57
48B St DEL 243 Q16 Q-R16

49 Av DEL 223 P17 P18 P19
49 Av LGC 226 P46 227 P47 P48 P49
49 Av LGT 227 P51
49 Av E VAN 163 Y15-17 Y18 183 Z18 Z18-20
49 Av W VAN 162 Y10-14 Y8-9 Y9
49 St DEL 243 Q16 R16 263 X16 Z16
49A Av DEL 223 P17 P18
49A Av LGC 227 P47 P48 P49
49A Av LGT 227 P50-51 228 P55-56
49B Av DEL 223 P17 P17-18 P18
49B Av LGC 226 P46 227 P47 P49
49B Av LGT 227 P50
49B St DEL 263 Z16

50 Av DEL 223 P17 P18
50 Av LGC 226 P46 227 P47-48 P48 P49
50 Av LGT 227 P50 P51 P52 P53-54 P54 228 P56-57 P57-58
50 Av SUR 226 P40
50 Av E VAN 183 Z15-16 Z17 Z17-18 Z18-19 Z19-20 Z20
50 Av W VAN 162 Y10 Y11 Y12 Y13 Y8
50 St DEL 243 Q16 263 X16 Z16
50A Av LGC 226 P46 227 P47 P48 P49
50A Av LGT 227 P50 P50-51
50A St DEL 243 Q16
50B Av LGC 227 P49
50B Av LGT 227 P50
50B St DEL 263 X16

51 Av DEL 223 P17 P18
51 Av LGC 226 P46 227 P47 P49
51 Av LGT 227 P52 228 P55 P56-57 P62 229 P63
51 Av E VAN 183 Z15-17 Z17 Z18 Z19 Z19-20 Z20
51 Av W VAN 162 Y10 Y11 Y12 Y8 Y9 182 Z10 Z11 Z12 Z13
51 St DEL 243 Q16 263 X16
51A Av LGC 227 P48 P49
51A Av LGT 227 P50
51A St DEL 263 X16 Z16
51B Av LGC 227 P48-49
51B Av LGT 227 P50
51B Av SUR 226 P45

52 Av DEL 223 P17
52 Av LGC 227 P47 P49
52 Av LGT 227 P51 P54 228 P55 P55-56 P56-57 P57-58 P60-61 P62 229 P63
52 Av SUR 226 P45
52 Av E VAN 182 Z14 183 Z15-17 Z17 Z18 Z19 Z19-20 Z20
52 Av W VAN 182 Z11-13 Z13
52 St DEL 243 U16 263 V-X16 X-Y16 Y-Z16
52A Av LGC 227 P47 P49
52A Av LGT 227 P51 228 P55-56
52A Av SUR 225 P31-32
52A St DEL 223 P16 243 Q16-17 263 X16 Y-Z16 Z16

53 Av LGC 226 N46 227 N47 P47-48
53 Av LGT 228 N-P57 P55-56 P58
53 Av SUR 225 N-P31 226 N44
53 Av E VAN 183 Z15-17 Z18 Z19-20 Z20
53 Av W VAN 182 Z10-11 Z12 Z13 Z9
53 St DEL 223 P17 243 Q17 S-T17 263 Y17 Y-Z17 Z17
53A Av LGC 227 N47 N47-48 N-P48
53A Av LGT 228 N55
53A Av SUR 226 N45
53A St DEL 223 P17 243 Q17 263 W-X17 Y-Z17 Z17
53B Av LGC 227 N47
53B Av SUR 226 N45

54 Av LGC 226 N46 227 N47 N48
54 Av LGT 228 N55-56 N56-57 N57-58
54 Av SUR 225 N32 N36 226 N44 N44-45 N46
54 Av E VAN 183 Z15 Z16 Z18-20
54 Av W VAN 182 Z10-11 Z11-13
54 St DEL 223 P17 243 Q17 263 W17 X-Y17 Y17 Y-Z17
54A Av LGC 227 N47 N47-48
54A Av LGT 228 N55
54A Av SUR 225 N32-33 N37 226 N44-45 N45
54A St DEL 223 P17 243 Q17 263 X17 Y-Z17

107 Av / 134B St

107 Av SUR .185 C32-33 C34 C36 C38 186 C39
107A Av SUR .185 B38 B38 B-C32 B-C33 B-C36 B-C37 C34 C38 C38 186 B39 C39

108 Av MAP 188 B55 B57-58 B61-62 189 B64-65
108 Av SUR 185 B33 B34-35 B36-37 B37 B38 186 B39 B40
108 Loop MAP 188 B55
108 St DEL 204 G-H28
108A Av SUR .185 B36 B36-37 B38 186 B39 B39-40 B40
108A St DEL 224 L28 M28
108B Av MAP 187 B54 188 B55
108B Av SUR 186 B40
108B St DEL 204 H28

109 Av MAP 187 B54 188 B55-56
109 Av SUR 185 B31 B32-33 B34-35 B35 B36 B38 186 B39 B40
109 St DEL 224 L28
109A Av MAP 188 B55-56
109A Av SUR .185 B36 B38 186 B39 B40
109A St DEL 204 H28 224 L28
109B St DEL 204 G28 G-H28

110 Av MAP 188 B55 B56 B57 B62 189 B63 B63
110 Av SUR .185 B32 B32-33 B34 B35 B36 B37-38 B38 186 B39 B39-40
110 St DEL 204 H28 H28-29
110A Av SUR .185 B34 B35 B36 B37-38 186 B39 B39-40
110A St DEL 204 F-G29 G28-29 H28 H28-29
110B Av MAP 188 B55

111 Av MAP 189 B65
111 Av SUR 185 B32-33 B34 B36 B37 B38 B38 186 B39 B39 B40
111 St DEL 204 G29 H29
111A Av MAP 188 B55
111A Av SUR 185 B31 B33-34 B34 B36 B37 B38 186 B39
111A St DEL 204 G29 J29
111B St DEL 204 G29 G-H29

112 Av MAP 188 A58-59 A-B57 B56 B59-60 B61-62 189 B63 B63
112 Av SUR .185 B31 B32-33 B34 B37-38 B38 186 B39
112 St DEL .204 F-J29 224 N-P29 244 Q29
112A Av SUR 185 A31 A-B31 A-B32 A-B33 A-B34 A-B35 A-B38 B33
112A St DEL .204 F29 G29 G-H29 H29 J29
112B Av MAP 188 A55
112B Av SUR 185 A32 A33 186 A-B39
112B St DEL 204 H29

113 Av MAP .187 A48-49 A53 188 A55 A56 A57 189 A63
113 Av SUR 185 A31 A33-34 A34-35 A37-38 186 A39
113 St DEL 204 F29 J29
113A Av MAP 187 A54 188 A55-56
113A Av SUR 185 A32 A35 186 A39
113A St DEL 204 E29 F29 G29 H29 J29
113B Av MAP 187 A47-48 188 A55
113B Av SUR 185 A31-32 A32 A33 186 A39
113B St DEL 204 E29 G29 H29

114 Av MAP 187 A48-49 A54
114 Av SUR 185 A31-32 A32 A33 A34-35 A35 A38 186 A39
114 St DEL 204 E-F29 G-H29 J29
114A Av MAP 187 A54 188 A55
114A Av SUR 185 A32 A34 A35 A36
114A St DEL .204 E29 F29 G29 H29 H-J29 J29 224 K29
114B Av MAP 187 A48
114B Av PTM 186 A46
114B Av SUR 185 A32

115 Av MAP 187 A48 A49 188 A55
115 Av SUR 185 A32 A34 A35 A35-36
115 St DEL .204 E29 E-F29 G29-30 H-J29 224 K29-30
115A Av MAP 187 A47-48 A48 188 A55
115A Av PTM 186 A46
115A Av SUR 185 A32 A33 A34-35 A35 A36
115A St DEL 204 E30 F30 G30 H-J30 J30 224 K30
115A St SUR 184 D30 204 E30
115B Av PTM 186 A46
115B Av SUR 185 A32 A32-33

116 Av MAP187 A48 A49 A49-50 A52 A52-54 188 A55 A56 A57 A57-58 A58-60 A61-62 189 A64
116 Av SUR .185 A32 A33-34 A34-35 A36
116 St DEL 204 H-J30 224 K30 L30
116 St SUR 184 D30 204 E30
116A Av MAP 187 A54
116A Av PTM 186 A46 A46 187 A47
116A Av SUR 185 A36
116A St DEL .204 E30 F30 G30 H30 H-J30 J30 224 L30
116A St SUR 184 D30
116B Av MAP 187 A48 Z48
116B Av PTM 186 A46 A46 187 A47
116B St DEL 204 F30 G30

117 Av MAP 187 A49-50 A51 A52 A53 A54 Z50 Z51 Z52 Z54 188 A58-59 Z58
117 Av PTM 186 A46
117 Av SUR 185 A34-35
117 St DEL .204 E30 E-F30 F30 H30 H-J30
117 St SUR 184 D30
117A Av PTM 186 A45 A46
117A St DEL 204 E30 F30 G30 H30 J30 224 L30
117B Av MAP 187 Z54 188 Z55
117B Av PTM 186 Z45 Z46
117B St DEL 204 G30
117B St SUR 204 E30

118 Av MAP 187 Z48 Z49 Z53-54 Z54 188 Z55 Z61
118 Av MAP 188 Z57
118 St DEL 204 E30 F30 G-H30 H-J30 J30 224 K30
118A Av MAP 188 Z55 Z57
118A St DEL 204 F30 G30 H30 J30
118B Av MAP 188 Z57
118B Av PTM 186 Z45 Z46
118B St DEL 204 E30
118B St SUR 184 D30

119 Av MAP .187 Z48 Z48-49 Z49 Z49-50 .Z51 Z51-52 Z52 Z53 Z54 188 Z55 Z57
119 Av PTM 186 Z45 Z46
119 La MAP 188 Z57
119 St DEL 204 E30 F30 G30 H30
119 St SUR 184 D30
119A Av MAP 187 Z47-48 188 Z55
119A Av PTM 186 Z46
119A St DEL 204 E30 F30 G30 G-H30 H-J30 J30
119A St SUR 184 D30
119B Av MAP 188 Z55
119B Av PTM 186 Z45 Z46
119B St DEL 204 H30

120 Av PTM 186 Z45 Z46
120 St SUR 185 D31 204 H30 J30 205 E-G31 H31 J31 225 K-N31
120A Av MAP 187 Z47-48 Z49
120A St SUR 185 D31 205 E31 E31 G31 G-H31 H31 J31 225 K31 M31 N31
120B Av MAP 187 Z47-48 Z48 Z49 188 Z55 Z57 Z61
120B Av PTM 186 Z45 Z46

121 Av MAP 187 Z47-48 Z48 Z49 Z50 Z51 Z52 Z52-53 188 Z55 Z57
121 Av PTM 186 Z46
121 St SUR 185 C-D31 D31 205 E31 E31 E-F31 F31 G31 225 K31 L-M31 M31
121A Av MAP 167 Y47-48 187 Z47-48 Z53 Z54 188 Z57-58
121A Av PTM 186 Z46
121A St SUR 185 D31 205 G31 H31 J31 225 K-L31 L31 N31
121B Av MAP 187 Z48
121B Av PTM 186 Z45 Z46

122 Av MAP .167 Y48 Y50 Y50 Y52-53 Y53 168 Y61 Y62 187 Z48 Z49-50 Z50 Z51-52 Z54 188 Z57 Z61 Z62
122 Av PTM 186 Z45
122 St SUR 185 C31 C-D31 D31 205 E31 F31 G31 H-J31 J31 225 K31 L31 M31 N31
122A Av MAP 167 Y53-54 168 Y57
122A Av PTM 186 Z46
122A St SUR 205 G31 H31 J31 225 K31 L31
122B Av MAP 167 Y48 Y50 Y54
122B Av PTM 166 Y45 186 Z45
122B St SUR 205 F31

123 Av MAP 167 Y47-48 Y48-51 Y51 Y52 Y52-53 Y53 Y54 168 Y55 Y61-62 169 Y65
123 Av PTM 166 Y46
123 Pl MAP 167 Y54
123 St SUR 185 A31 D31 205 E31 F31 F-G31 G31 H31 H-J31 J31 225 K31 L31 M31 N31 265 V31
123A Av MAP 167 Y54
123A Av PTM 166 Y45
123A St SUR 185 C31 C-D31 D31 D31 205 E31 F31 H31 H-J31 J31 225 K31 K-L31 L31 M31 245 U31
123B Av MAP 167 Y48 Y49 Y53 Y54
123B Av PTM 166 Y45
123B St SUR 225 K31

124 Av MAP .167 Y48 Y49 Y50-53 Y53 Y54 168 Y55 Y56 Y57 Y58 Y59-60
124 Av PTM 166 Y45
124 St SUR185 A31 B31 B-C31 C-D31 D31 205 E-F31 F-G31 G-J31 225 K-L31 M31 N31 245 U31 265 V31
124A Av MAP 167 Y48 Y54
124A Av PTM 166 Y45
124A St SUR 185 C-D31 D31-32 205 E31 E-F31 H31 J31 225 K31 L31 M31 N31
124B Av MAP 167 Y48 Y53 Y53-54
124B St SUR 185 D32 205 J32 245 U32

125 Av MAP 167 Y48 Y49 Y51 Y52 168 Y56 Y58-59
125 St SUR 185 B32 C-D32 D32 205 E32 F32 H32 J31-32 J32 225 K-L32 M31-32 M32 M-N32 N32 245 U32
125A Av MAP 167 Y51 Y52-53 Y53 Y54
125A St SUR 185 A32 C32 C-D32 D32 205 E32 E32 F32 J32 225 K32 L32 M32 N32 P32 245 U32
125B Av MAP 167 Y53
125B St SUR 185 C32

126 Av MAP 167 Y50 Y50-52 Y53-54 168 Y56 Y60
126 St SUR 185 C-D32 D32 D32 205 E-F32 225 K32 L-M32 M-N32
126 St (Crescent Heights) SUR 245 U32 265 V32 V-W32 W32
126A St SUR 185 A32 B32 205 E32 E-F32 J32 225 K32 M32 M-N32 N32 245 U32 265 W32
126B Av MAP 167 Y53
126B St SUR 225 K32 M32

127 Av MAP 167 X53 Y51 Y52 Y52-53 168 X61 X-Y60
127 Pl MAP 167 Y53
127 St SUR 185 C32 C-D32 D32 205 E32 E-F32 F32 H-J32 225 L32 M32 N32
127 St (Crescent Heights) SUR 245 U32 265 V32 W32
127A St SUR 185 A32 C32 C-D32 D32 205 E32 J32 225 K32 L32 M32 P32 245 U32 265 V32 W32
127B St SUR 185 C32 D32 245 U32

128 Av MAP 167 X50 X51-52 X53-54 .168 X55 X55-56 X56 X57-58 X59 X60-61 169 X63
128 Cr MAP 168 X55
128 St SUR 185 A32 B32 C-D32 205 E-J32 225 K-M32 M-N32
128 St (Crescent Heights) SUR 245 U32 265 V-W32 X32
128A St SUR 185 B32 C-D32 D32 D32 205 E32 F-G32 J32 225 K32 K-L32 L32 L-M32 M32 N32 265 V32 V-W32 W32 X32
128B St SUR .205 J32 225 K32 K-L32 L32

129 Av MAP 167 X52-53 X54 168 X55 X56
129 Av PTM 166 X42
129 St SUR 185 A32-33 B32 C32 C-D32 D32 205 E32 E-F32 F-G32 G32 J32 225 K32 K-L32 L32 L-M32 N32
129 St (Crescent Heights) SUR 265 V32 V-W32 W32 X32
129A St SUR 185 B32-33 C-D33 D32 D32-33 D33 205 E32 E33 G32-33 J32 J32-33 225 K32-33 L32-33 M32 245 U32 265 V32 V-W32 X32
129B St SUR 205 J33 225 K33 M32-33 245 U33 265 V32-33 V33 X32-33

130 Av MAP 167 X54 168 X55 X58
130 Connector MAP 168 X57-58
130 St SUR 185 A33 B33 C33 D33 205 E33 F-G33 H33 J33 225 K-L33 L-M33
130 St (Crescent Heights) SUR 245 T-U33 U33 265 V33 W-X33
130A Av MAP 168 X55 X57 X58
130A St SUR 185 B33 D33 205 E33 J33 225 L33 M33 245 U33 265 V33 V-W33
130B St SUR 205 F33 225 M33

131 St SUR 185 A33 B33 D33 205 E33 J33 225 K33 K-L33 L33 M33
131 St (Crescent Heights) SUR 265 V33 W-X33
131A St SUR 185 B33 C33 D33 205 E33 J33 225 K33 L33 L-M33 M33 P33 265 V33
131B St SUR 265 V33

132 Av MAP 167 W-X51 W-X53 X48-49 X54 X54 168 W-X55 X55
132 St SUR .185 A33 B33 C-D33 205 E-J33 225 K-N33
132 St (Crescent Heights) SUR 245 T-U33 265 V33 W33
132 St Diversion SUR 185 B33
132A Av MAP 168 W55
132A St SUR 185 A33 B33 B-C33 C33 D33 205 E33 E-F33 H33 225 L33 M33 M-N33 N33 265 V33 X33
132B St SUR 205 E-F33 F33 265 W33 X33

133 Av MAP 168 W55
133 St SUR 185 A33 A-B33 B-C33 C-D33 D33 205 E33 E-F33 H33 225 K33 L33 M33 M-N33
133 St (Crescent Heights) SUR 245 U33 265 V33
133A Av MAP 167 W54
133A St SUR 185 A33 B33 C-D33 D33 205 E33 E-F33 F33 G33 H33 225 K33 L33 M33 M-N33 265 V33 W33 X33
133B St SUR 225 K33 L33 M33 265 V33 W33

134 St SUR 185 A34 D33 205 E-F33 F-G33 G33 H33 H-J33 225 K-M33 M-N33
134 St (Crescent Heights) SUR 245 U33 265 V33 V-W33 W33
134A St SUR 185 B34 C33-34 205 E33-34 E34 F33-34 G33-34 G34 H33-34 J33-34 J34 225 K34 K-L34 L-M34 M33 265 V-W34 W34
134B St SUR 205 F34 G34 225 M33-34 N34 265 W34

135 St SUR 185 A-B34 C-D34
205 E34 H34 J34 225 K-L34 L34 M34 M-N34
135A St SUR 205 F34 G34 H34 H-J34
. .225 K34 L34 M34 245 T34 265 V34 W34
135B St SUR 205 H34 225 L34

136 Av MAP 167 W52 W53-54
136 St SUR ...185 A34 A-B34 225 M-N34
......245 S-T34 T-U34 265 V34 V-W34
136A Av MAP 167 V53
136A St SUR 185 A34 C34
.....205 E34 F34 H34 225 L34 M34 N34
.................265 V34 V-W34
136B St SUR ....
......205 E-F34 F34 225 K34 M34 N34

137 St SUR 185 A34 D34 205 E34 F34 J34
...225 K34 K-L34 245 U34 265 V34 W34
137A St SUR 185 A34 C34 D34
.....205 E-F34 F34 H34
.....225 K34 L34 M34 N34 245 T34 U34
.................265 V-W34 W34
137B St SUR ...205 E34 225 L-M34 M34

138 St SUR ...185 A34 A-B34 B-C34 D34
.....205 E34 E-F34 F34 H34 H-J34 J34
........225 K34 L34 L-M34 M34 J34
.....245 T34 T-U34 U34 265 V34 W34
138A Av MAP 167 V53
138A St SUR 185 C34 D34
.....205 E34 F34 H34 225 T34U34
.................265 V34 W34
138B St SUR 185 A34 265 V34 W34

139 Av MAP 167 V53
139 St SUR ....
.....185 A34-35 B34-35 C34-35 D34
...........205 E34 F34 225 M34
.....245 T34 U34 U34-35 265 W34-35
139 St FG-W SUR 265 V35
139A Av MAP 167 V53
139A St SUR 185 A35 B35 C-D35
.205 E35 F35 H35 H-J35 245 T35 U35
.................265 V34-35 V35
139B St SUR 205 H35

140 St SUR ...185 A35 B-D35 205 E-J35
.........225 K35 K35 L35 M35 N35
.........245 R35 S-U35 265 V-W35
140 St FG-E SUR 265 V35
140 St FG-W SUR ...245 U35 265 V35
140A St SUR 185 A35 B35
.....205 F35 F-G35 H35 J35 J35
.....225 K35 K35 L35 245 T35 T-U35
.................265 V35 W35
140B St SUR 185 C35
. . .205 F35 F-G35 H35 245 T35 265 W35

141 Av MAP 167 V54
141 Av PTM 166 V44
141 St SUR 185 B-C35 C35 C-D35
.....205 G35 H35 J35 225 K35 L35
.....245 S35 T-U35 265 V35
141A St SUR 185 A35 C35
.205 F35 G35 H35 225 K35 L35 M35
.................245 T35 265 V-W35 W35
141B St SUR 185 B35
.....205 F35 G35 H35 225 L35 265 W35

142 Av MAP 167 U54
142 St MAP 168 U59-60
142 St SUR 185 A35 B-C35 C35 D35
.....205 G35 H-J35 J35 225 K35 L-N35
.................245 S35 T35 U35 265 V35
142A St SUR 185 C35 C-D35
205 F35 G35 J35 225 K35 L35 245 S35 T35
142B St SUR ....
...............185 B35 205 F35 G35 265 W35

143 St SUR 185 B35 C-D35
...........205 F35 G35 H-J35 J35
.....225 K35 245 S35 265 V35
143A St SUR 185 B35 C35 C-D35 D35
.....205 F35 F-G35 G35 H35 J35
.....225 K35 L35 245 S35 265 W35
143B St SUR 205 J35 265 W35
143C St SUR 205 J35

144 Av MAP 167 U52

144 St SUR ..185 B-C36 C-D36 205 F-J36
.225 K-N36 245 S-U36 265 V35-36 W35-36
144 St FG-W SUR 205 F35
144A St SUR 185 A36 B36 C-D36
.....205 F36 G36 G-H36 225 K36 N36
.................245 T36 265 V-W36

145 St SUR 185 B36 C-D36
...........205 F36 G36 H36 J36 225 L36
.................245 T36 265 W36
145A St SUR 185 B36 C-D36
.....205 F36 G36 H36 H-J36 J36
.....225 N36 245 S-T36 T36 265 W36
145B St SUR ....
.....225 K-L36 M36 245 T36 T-U36

146 St SUR 185 B36 B-C36 C-D36
...........205 F-G36 G-H36 H-J36 J36
225 L36 M-N36 N36 245 S36 T36 265 W36
146A St SUR 185 B36
.....205 F36 G36 H36 225 K36
.....225 M36 M-N36 245 S36 T36
146B St SUR 205 J36 225 K-L36

147 St SUR ..205 F36 F-G36 H-J36 J36
.....225 K36 M36 245 T36 265 W36
147A St SUR 185 B36 B36
.....205 F36 G36 J36 225 K-L36 M-N36
...................245 S36 T36

148 St SUR 185 B36 C-D36
.....205 E36 E-G36 H-J36 225 K-N36 P36
.....245 S-T36 T-U36 U36 265 V-W36
148 St FG-E SUR ...245 U36 265 V36
148A St SUR 185 B36 C-D36
...........205 E36 G36 H36
.....225 K36 L36-37 M36 N36
.....245 S36 T36 T36-37 U36
.................265 V36 V-W36 W36
148B St SUR ....
. . .205 G36 G36-37 225 K36-37 N36-37

149 St SUR 185 C-D37 D37
.....205 E37 F36-37 G37 G-H37 H37
. . .225 K37 M-N37 N37 245 U37 265 V37
149A St SUR 185 C37 D37
.....205 E37 G37 J37 225 K37 M37 N37
...................245 S37 U37 N37
149B St SUR ...185 D37 205 E37 J37

150 Av PTM 147 T47
150 St SUR 185 B-C37 C-D37 D37
.....205 E37 E-F37 F-G37 G-H37 H37
. . .225 K37 L37 L-M37 M37 245 S37 U37
...........................265 V37
150A St SUR 185 D37
. . .205 E37 F37 G37 J37 225 K37 L37 M37
.................245 S37 U37
150B St SUR ....
.....205 J37 225 K37 L37 M37 265 V37
151 St SUR 185 D37
...........205 E37 F37 M-F37 J37
.....225 K37 K-L37 M37 245 S37 T37 U37
151A St SUR 185 C37 D37
.....205 E37 F37 G37 J37 225 K37 M37 265 V37
151B St SUR ...185 D37 205 E37 F-G37

152 St SUR 185 B37 C-D37
205 E-J37 225 K-P37 245 Q-U37 265 V-W37
152 St FG-E SUR 205 G37
152A St SUR 185 B37 C-D37
.....205 E37 F37 G37 H37
...........225 T37 245 T37 265 V37 W37
152B St SUR ..185 D37 205 E37 245 S37

153 St SUR 185 A-B37 C37 D37
.....205 E37 G-H37 H37 265 V37
153A St SUR ..185 A37 B37-38 D37 D38
...........205 E37 E37-38 E38 G37 H38
.................245 T-U37 265 V37-38
153B St SUR 185 A38 205 G37-38

154 St SUR 185 B38 C-D38 D38
.....205 E38 E-F38 G38 G-H38 H38
.................245 S38 U38 265 V-W38
154A St SUR 185 A-B38 B38 C38
.....205 E38 G38 225 M38 245 S-U38
154B St SUR ...205 F-G38 G38 H38

155 St SUR 185 B38 C38 D38
...........205 E38 F38 G38 H38 H-J38
.....245 R-S38 S-T38 U38 265 V38
155A St SUR 185 B38 B-C38 C38 D38
. .205 E38 F38 G38 H38 245 U38 265 V38
155B St SUR 205 E38 245 S-T38

156 St SUR 185 B38 B-C38 C-D38
...........205 E-J38 225 M-N38
.....245 S-T38 T-U38 265 V-W38
156A St SUR 185 C-D38 D38
.....205 E38 E-F38 F38 G38 H38
.....245 R38 265 V38 266 W39
156B St SUR ....
.....185 D38 205 E38 G38 245 R-S38

157 St SUR185 B38 B-C38 C38 C-D38 D38
.....205 E38 F38 F-G38 G38 G-H38 H38
.....225 P38 245 U38 265 V38 W38
157A St SUR 185 A37 B38 C-D38 D38
.....205 E38 F38 G38 H38 245 R38
157B St SUR 185 B38 205 E38

158 St SUR 185 B38 B-C38 C38 C-D38
205 E38 E-F38 F-G38 G38 H38 245 S38 U38
158A St SUR 185 D38
.186 A-B39 B39 C39 C-D39 D39 205 E38
.....206 E39 E-F39 H39 265 V38 266 V39
158B St SUR 186 B39 C39 D39

159 St SUR 186 B39 B-C39 C39 D39
.206 E39 E-F39 G39 G-H39 H39 246 R39
159A St SUR186 A-B39 B39 C39 C-D39 D39
...........206 E39 F39 H39 266 V39
159B St SUR 186 A39

160 St SUR 186 B39 B-C39 C-D39
.....206 E-F39 G-J39 226 L39 N-P39
.....246 Q39 R-S39 T-U39 266 V39 V-W39
160A St SUR 186 B39 C-D39
.206 E39 E-F39 F39 G39 H39 266 W39 X39
160B St SUR 206 F39 266 X-Y39

161 St SUR 186 A39 C-D39
.....206 E39 F39 G-H39 H39 J39
.....246 T39 U39 266 V39 W39 X39
161A St SUR 186 B39 D39
.................206 E39 F39 G39 H39
.....246 T39 U39 266 X39 X-Y39
161B St SUR ....
.....186 B39 266 W-X39 X39

162 St SUR 186 A-B39 B39
206 E39 F-G39 H39 246 T-U39 266 W39 X39
162A St SUR 186 A39 B39 D39
.....206 E39 F39 G39 H39 H-J39
.....246 U40 266 W-X39
162B St SUR ....
.............186 B39 206 H39 266 W39-40

163 St SUR 186 A-B39 B39-40 B40
.206 E39 F40 G39-40 H39-40 H-J39 H-J40
.....226 M39 246 T39-40 U39 U40 U41
..........................266 W-X39 X39
163A St SUR 186 B39-40
.....206 E40 F40 F-G40 H40
. . .226 M39-40 246 U41 266 X39-40 X40
163B St SUR 226 M40 266 X40
164 St SUR 186 A-C40 C-D40
.206 E40 F40 G-J40 226 M40 N-P40
.....246 S-U40 266 V40 W40 X40 Y40
164A St SUR 186 B40 C40
.....206 E40 F40 G40 H40 H-J40
. . .226 M40 246 S40 266 X40 X-Y40
164B St SUR 226 M40

165 St SUR 186 B40
.....206 F40 G40 H40 H-J40
.226 M40 246 U40 266 V40 X40 Y40
165A St SUR ....
.....206 G40 H40 226 M40 266 V40 Y40
165B St SUR 186 B40 C40 226 M40

166 St SUR 186 B40
206 F-G40 G40 H40 246 U40 266 V40 X-Y40
166A St SUR ....
. .186 B40 206 G40 H-J40 226 M40 246 U40
166B St SUR 206 F-G40 H40

167 St SUR 186 C40 206 G40 H40
. .226 M40 M-N40 246 U40 266 V40 W40

167A St SUR 186 C40 D40
. .206 G-H40 H40 226 M40 M-N40 246 U40
167B St SUR 206 G40 226 L-M40

168 St SUR 186 B40 C40-41 D40-41
...........206 E40-41 J40-41
...................226 K40-41 M40-41 P40-41
.246 S40-41 266 V40-41 W40-41 X40-41
168 St FG-E SUR 206 G41
168A St SUR ....
......186 C41 206 G41 H41 226 M41 N44
168B St SUR 206 G41 H41

169 St SUR 186 C41 206 H41
226 M41 M-N41 246 T-U41 266 V41 V-W41
169A St SUR ....
..........186 C41 206 G41 226 M41 N41

170 St SUR ...206 G41 226 M41 246 U41
...................266 V41 W41 Z41
170A St SUR ....
. .186 C41 C-D41 206 H41 226 M41 M-N41
170B St SUR 226 M41

171 St SUR 186 C41 206 G41
.....226 L-M41 M41 N41 246 U41
...................266 V41 W41 Z41
171A St SUR ....
. .186 C41 D41 206 G-H41 226 L-M41 M41

172 St SUR 186 C-D41 206 E41 G41
226 L41 L-N41 246 T41 266 V41 W41 Y-Z41
172A St SUR ....
............226 L-M41 M41 M41-42 266 Z41
172B St SUR 226 M42 N41-42

173 St SUR ....
.186 C42 D42 226 M42 N42 266 V42 Z42
173A St SUR ...206 E42 226 L-M42 M42
173B St SUR 226 M42

174 St SUR 186 C42 C-D42
.....226 M42 N42 246 U42 266 V42
174A St SUR ....
......186 C-D42 226 L42 M42 246 T-U42
174B St SUR 226 M42

175 St SUR 186 C42 206 F42
........226 L42 M42 N42 266 V-W42
175A St SUR ....
.186 D42 226 M42 246 U42 266 V-W42 Z42
175B St SUR 226 M42

176 St PTM 186 A42 Z42
176 St SUR 186 C-D42 206 E-J42
........226 K-P42 246 Q-U42 266 V-Z42
176A St SUR ...226 K42 L42 N42 266 Z42

177 St SUR 206 E-F42 266 W42
177A St SUR ..186 D42 206 E42 226 L42
177B St SUR 226 N43

178 St SUR ....
......186 D43 206 E43 226 L42-43 N43
178A St SUR 226 K43 L43
178B St SUR 226 L43

179 St SUR ....
186 D43 206 E43 226 K43 L43 M43 V43
179A St SUR ...226 K43 L43 M43 N43

180 St SUR 186 D43 206 E43
. .226 K43 L43 L-N43 246 R43 S-T43 U43
...................266 V-W43
180A St SUR 186 D43 226 M43

181 St SUR ....
186 D43 206 J43 226 K43 L43 M43 V43
181A St SUR 226 M43 N43
181B St SUR 226 K43

182 St SUR 186 D43 206 E43 J43
........226 K43 M-N43 N43-44 266 V43
182A St SUR 186 D43 D44
. .206 E43 E44 226 K44 L44 M43-44 N43-44
182B St SUR 226 K44 N44

183 St SUR 226 L44 M44 266 V44
183A St SUR 226 L44 M44 N44

184 St SUR 206 E-F44 G44 H-J44
.........226 L44 N44 246 Q44 S-T44
.........266 W44 X44 Z44
184A St SUR 226 K44 L44 M44 N44
184B St SUR 226 K46 M44 N44

185 St SUR
.....206 F44 J44 226 K46 L44 M44 N44
185A St SUR
.....226 K46 L44 L-M44 M44 N44 P44
185B St SUR 226 M44

186 St SUR 186 D44 206 E44
.........226 L44 M44 N44 246 Q-R44
186A St SUR ..226 L44 L-M44 M44 N44

187 St SUR 206 E44 F44
.226 L44-45 L-M44 M44-45 N44-45
187A St SUR 226 L45 L-M45 M45 N44-45
187B St SUR 226 M45

188 St PTM 166 Y45
188 St SUR 186 D45
.....206 E45 E-F45 G45 H45 J45
.....226 K45 L45 M45 N45 N-P45
.....246 T45 266 Y45 Z45
188A St PTM 166 Y45 186 Z45
188A St SUR 226 L45 M45
188B St PTM 186 Z45

189 St SUR
.....206 E45 E-F45 F45 226 K45 M45 N45
189A St SUR 186 Z45
189A St SUR ..226 L45 M45 M-N45 N45
189B St PTM 186 Z45

190 St PTM 166 Y45 186 Z45
190 St SUR 186 D45 206 E45
.........226 K45 M45 M-N45
.....246 Q45 T45 U45 266 V45 Z45
190A St PTM 166 Y45 186 Z45
190A St SUR 226 M45
190B St SUR 226 M45

191 St PTM 166 Y45
191 St SUR
.....206 J45 226 K45 M45 266 V-W45
191A St PTM 186 Z45
191A St SUR 226 M45 M-N45
191B St PTM 166 Y45 186 Z45

192 St SUR ...206 E45-46 F45-46 H-J45
.226 L45-46 N45-46 246 Q45-46 T45 U45
.........266 V45 Y45 Z45
192A St PTM 186 A46 Z46
192A St SUR ..206 J46 226 K46 L46
192B St PTM 166 Y46 186 A46 Z46

193 St PTM 166 Y46 186 A46 Z46
193 St SUR 206 E46 226 K46
193A St PTM 186 A46 Z46
193A St SUR ...206 E46 226 K-L46 L46
193B St PTM 166 Y46 186 A46 Z46
193B St SUR 226 L46

194 St PTM 166 Y46
194 St SUR .206 E-F46 J46 226 L46 M46
.....246 S46 T46 266 W46 Y46 Z46
194A St PTM
.....166 Y46 186 A46 Z46 Z46
194A St SUR ...206 E46 226 K46 M46
194B St PTM 166 Y46 186 A46 Z46
194B St SUR 226 L-M46

195 St SUR .206 E46 226 L46 L-M46 M46
195A St PTM 186 A46 Z46
195A St SUR 226 M46 246 Q46
195B St PTM 186 A46 Z46
195B St SUR 206 H46 226 L-M46

196 St LGC ..226 M46 P46 246 Q46 Q46
196 St LGT 206 G-H46 J46
.........226 K46 K-L46 M46
.....246 R46 S-T46 U46 266 V-W46
196 St SUR 206 J46 226 K46
196A Ct LGT 226 L46
196A St LGC 226 M46 N-P46 P46 246 Q46
196A St LGT ..206 F46 J46 226 K46 M46
.....246 Q46 R46 S46 266 X46 267 X47
196A St PTM 186 A46
196B Pl LGT 226 K-L46

196B St LGC 226 P46
196B St LGT 186 D46 246 R46
196B St LGT 187 A47
196C St PTM 147 T47

197 St LGC 226 N-P46 P46 227 P47
.........246 Q46 247 Q47
197 St LGT 186 D46 206 G-H46 H46
.....207 G-H47 H47 J47 226 K46 L46
.........227 K47 L47 246 R46 S46
197A St LGT ....
.........226 N46 227 N47 P47 247 Q47
197A St LGT 246 Q46 T-U46
.....247 Q47 R47 S47 T-U47 267 W47
197B St LGC 227 P47
197B St LGT ....
.187 D47 207 E47 J47 227 K47 247 Q47
197B St PTM 187 A47
198 St LGC 227 N47 P47 247 Q47
198 St LGT 207 E47 F47 G47 J47
.........227 K47 L47 247 Q-R47 R47 S47
.........267 V47 Z47
198 St PTM 187 A47
198A St LGC 227 N47 247 Q47
198A St LGT 207 G47 H47
.........227 K47 247 Q47 R47 S47 267 X47
198B St LGC 227 P47 247 Q47
198B St LGT ....
.........187 D47 207 E47 J47 247 Q47
198C St LGC 247 Q47

199 St LGC 227 N47 P47 247 Q47
199 St LGT ....
.207 H47 227 K47 L47 247 S47 267 Z47
199A Cr LGT 247 R47
199A St LGC 227 N47 N-P47 P47 247 Q47
199A St LGT 187 D47 207 E47 J47
.........227 K47 247 Q-R47 S47
199B St LGT 187 D47

200 St LGC 227 M-P47 247 Q47
200 St MAP 187 Z47
200 St PTM 147 T47 167 U47
200 St (Carvolth Rd) LGT ...207 E-J47
.....227 K-L47 247 R-U47 267 V-Y47 Z47
200A St LGC .227 M47 N47 P47 247 Q47
200A St LGT ...207 E47 J47 247 R47
200B St LGT 227 P47
200B St LGT 207 J47 R47

201 St LGC 227 N47 P47 247 Q47
201 St LGT 187 D47 207 E47 J47
.........227 K47 L47 247 R-S47 T-U47
201 St MAP 187 Z47
201 St (Station Rd) LGT ....
.........187 D47 207 E47
201A St LGC .227 M47 N47-48 N-P47 P47
201A St LGT 247 R47 R-S47 S47
201A St MAP 187 A48
201B St LGT 207 J48 227 K48
201B St MAP 187 A47-48 Z48

202 St LGC 227 M48 247 Q47-48
202 St LGT 187 D48 207 E47 F48 J48
.227 M48 247 R-S47 S-T47 T47 U47 267 Y48
202 St MAP 167 Y48 187 Z48
202A St LGC 227 P48 247 Q47
202A St LGT ....
.....207 E47-48 J48 247 R48 R-S48 S48
202A St MAP 167 Y48 187 A48 Z48
202B St LGT 207 E-F48 227 K48
202B St MAP 167 Y48 187 A48 Z48

203 St LGC 227 N-P48 247 Q47
203 St LGT 187 D48 207 E48 E-F48
.........227 L48 L-M48 247 R48 S48
203 St MAP 167 X-Y48 187 A48 Z48
203A St LGC .227 M-N48 P48 247 Q48
203A St LGT .207 E-F48 F48 247 R48 S48
203B St LGT .207 E-F48 F48 J48 247 R48

204 St LGC 227 M48 N48 P48 247 Q48
204 St LGT 207 E48 G48 H-J48
.....227 K48 M48 247 R48 S48 T48 U48
.........267 Y48 Z48
204 St MAP 167 Y48 187 A48 Z48
204A St LGC 247 Q48
204A St LGT 207 E48 F48
.....227 K-L48 247 R48 S48 267 V48

204B St LGT 207 E48 F48 247 R48
204B St MAP 167 Y48 187 Z48

205 St LGC 227 N48 P48 247 Q48
205 St LGT ....
.....207 E48 227 K48 L48 L-M48 247 S-T48
205 St MAP 167 Y48 187 A48 Z48
205 St (Knich Rd) LGT 247 S-T48
205A St LGC 227 M48 P48 247 Q48
205A St LGT 187 D48
.....207 E48 F48 227 L48 247 R48 R-S48
205A St MAP 187 Z48
205B St LGC 227 P48
205B St LGT 207 E48 247 R48 R-S48
205B St MAP 167 Y48

206 St LGC ..227 M48 N48 P48 247 Q48
206 St LGT .207 E48 F48 F-G48 G48 J48
.227 K48 L48 247 R48 T48 U48 267 V48
206 St MAP 167 Y48 187 A48 Z48
206A St LGC ..227 M48 M48-49 247 Q48
206A St LGT ....
.207 E48 E48-49 J49 227 K49 247 R48 S48
206A St MAP 187 A48-49
206B St LGC 247 Q48-49
206B St LGT 207 E48 E-F48 G48-49
206B St MAP 187 A49 Z49

207 St LGC 227 N49 P49 247 Q49
207 St LGT ...207 E48-49 E49 F49 G49
.........227 K49 R49 S49
207 St MAP 187 A49 Z49
207A St LGC 227 P49 247 Q49
207A St LGT ....
.....207 E49 F49 G49 247 R49 T49
207B St LGC 227 P49 247 Q49
207B St LGT 207 F49 R49 S49

208 St LGC 227 N49 P49 247 Q49
208 St LGT 187 C-D49 207 E-G49
208 St MAP 167 Y49 187 A49 Z49
208 St (Alexander Rd) LGT ....
.........207 H-J49 227 K49
208 St (Berry Rd) LGT ....
.....247 R-U49 267 V-X49 Z49
208A St LGC 227 P49 247 Q49
208A St LGT ....
.....187 D49 207 E49 G48 247 Q49 R49
208B St LGC 247 Q49
208B St LGT 207 E49 G49

209 Cr LGT 207 E-F49
209 St LGC 227 N49 P49 247 Q49
209 St LGT ....
.207 E49 G49 H48 227 K49 247 Q49 R49 T49
209 St MAP 167 X49 Y49 187 A49 Z49
209A St LGC 227 P49 247 Q49
209A St LGT ....
.....207 E49 G49 J49 227 K49 247 Q49
209B St LGT 207 E49 E-F49 247 Q49

210 St LGC 247 Q49
210 St LGT 207 E49 F49 227 K49
.........247 Q49 S49 T49 U49 267 Z49
210 St MAP 167 X49 Y49 187 A49 Z49 Z49
210A St LGC 227 N-P49
210A St LGT 227 N49 247 Q49 Q-R49
211 St LGT 207 E49 G48 227 N49
211 St MAP ...167 Y49 187 A49 Z49 Z49
211A St LGT 207 E49-50 G50 H49
211B St LGT 207 F49-50 F50 H49
212 St LGT 187 C50
.....207 E50 E-F50 F-G50 H50 H-J50
.247 Q50 R50 T50 267 V-W50 W-X50 Z50
212 St MAP 167 Y50 187 A50 Z50
212A St LGT 207 E50 F50
212B St LGT 207 E50 E-F50 F50

213 St LGT ....
.....207 E-F50 F50 G50 J50 247 R50
213A Pl LGT 207 F50
213A St LGT 227 N50 247 R50

214 Pl LGT 207 F50
214 St LGT ....
.....207 E50 E-F50 F50 G50 227 P50
214 St MAP .167 Y50 Y50 187 Z50 Z50
214A St LGT ....
....207 E50 G50 227 M-N50 P50 247 Q50

214B St LGT 207 F50 G50

215 St LGT 207 E50 G50 227 P50 247 Q50
215 St MAP 167 Y50 187 A50
215A St LGT ....
.........207 E50 G50 227 P50 247 Q50
215B St LGT 207 E50 G50 247 Q50
216 St LGT 207 H-J50 227 K51
216 St MAP 167 W51 X50-51 Y50 Y51
.........187 A50-51 Z50 Z50-51 Z51
216 St (Johnston Townline Rd) LGT .
.........227 L-P50 247 Q-U50 267 V-Z50
216 St (Topham Rd) LGT ....
.........187 C-D50 207 E-G50
216A St LGT ....
.........227 P50 P50-51 P51 247 Q50 Q51
216B St LGT 207 E51

217 St LGT 207 E51 247 Q51
217 St MAP 167 Y51 187 Z51
217A St LGT ....
.........207 G51 227 N-P51 P51 247 Q51 Q51
217B St LGT 227 P51 247 Q51

218 St LGT 227 P51
218 St MAP 187 Z51
218A St LGT 227 P51 247 Q51

219 St LGT 227 P51 247 Q51
219 St MAP 167 Y51
219A St LGT 227 P51 247 Q51

220 St LGT ....
.207 E51 227 P51 247 Q51 U51 267 V51
220 St MAP 167 W51 Y51 187 Z51
220A St MAP 167 Y51

221 St LGT 227 P51 247 Q51-52
221 St MAP 167 Y51 187 Z51
221A St LGT ..227 P51 247 Q51 Q51-52

222 St LGT ....
.........207 E-F52 227 P52 247 Q52
222 St MAP ...167 Y52 Y52 187 Z52 Z52
222A St LGT 207 F-G52 227 P52
223 St LGT 227 P52 247 Q52
223 St MAP 167 Y52 187 A52 Z52
223A St LGT ....
.....207 F52 227 P52 P52 247 Q52 Q52
223B St LGT 227 P52

224 St LGT ...207 G52 227 K52 L52 M52
.........247 R52 S52 U52 267 V52 Z52
224 St MAP ....
...167 V52 W52 X52 Y52 187 A52 Z52 Z52
224 St (Biggar Rd) LGT ....
.........227 P52 247 Q-R52 267 W-Z52

225 St MAP 187 A52

226 St LGT 227 L-M52
226 St MAP ..167 X-Y53 Y53 187 Z52-53
227 Cr LGT 207 H53
227 St LGT 267 W-X53
227 St MAP .167 X-Y53 Y53 187 A53 Z53
227A St MAP 167 X-Y53
227B St MAP 167 X-Y53

228 St LGT ..227 L-M53 247 Q53 R53 T53
228 St MAP 167 W53 X53 X-Y53
.........187 A53 Z53
228A St LGT 267 W-X53
228A St MAP 167 W53 X53 Y53
228B St LGT 207 H53
228B St MAP 167 W53

229 La MAP 167 V53
229 St LGT 207 J53 227 K53
229 St MAP 167 V53 X53 Y53 187 A53 Z53
229B St MAP 167 V53

230 St LGT 227 L-M53 247 T53
230 St MAP ....
...167 V53 X53 Y53 Y53 187 A53 Z53
230A St LGT 227 K53
230B St MAP 187 A53-54

231 St LGT ...207 J53 227 K53 267 X53
231 St MAP ...167 X54 Y54 187 A54 Z54

Albion / Atlantic

Albion Way DEL ... 224 L28
Alden La CNV ... 123 M15
Alder CQT ... 145 S38
Alder Av CHL ... 213 J6
Alder Av HHS ... 155 Q-R19
Alder Crsg VAN 10 L36 162 U12
Alder Ct DNV ... 144 P23
Alder Dr LGT ... 248 S61
Alder La WHS ... 401 B3
Alder Pl HOP ... 118 E47
Alder Pl KNT ... 175 X21-22
Alder Pl PCQ ... 146 T42
Alder Pl SQM ... 301 K3
Alder Pl SUR ... 266 W39
Alder St ABT ... 250 U72
Alder St CNV ... 143 P-Q17
Alder St FRA ... 253 R5
Alder St MIS ... 210 J74
Alder St VAN ... 162 U12-13
Alder Way ANM ... 145 P33
Alder Bay Walk VAN ... 10 L35 162 U12-13
Alderbridge Way RMD ... 202 E11-14
Alderbrook Pl CQT ... 165 U38
Alderfeild Pl WVA ... 121 K3
Aldergrove-Bellingham Hwy LGT ... 268 Y60-61 Z61
Aldergrove-Bellingham Rd LGT ... 248 Q-R60 268 V-W60
Alderlynn Dr DNV ... 123 M-N20
Alderside Rd PMD 145 R32-33
Alderson Av CQT ... 165 X31-33
Alderview St ABT ... 250 U76
Alderwood Av PCQ ... 146 S41
Alderwood Cr BUR ... 163 X22
Alderwood Cr DEL ... 224 L30
Alderwood La DEL ... 224 L-M30
Alderwood Pl DNV ... 122 N14
Aldford Av DEL ... 204 E28
Aldous Ct BUR ... 164 W26
Aldrin Pl BUR ... 144 T26
Alea Ct ABT ... 249 T70
Alexander Av CHL ... 213 F6-7
Alexander Bay PMD ... 145 S35
Alexander Cr ABT ... 250 U76
Alexander Rd DEL ... 204 H23
Alexander St NEW ... 184 B29
Alexander St VAN ... 11 G41 143 S15
Alexandra Gt RMD ... 202 E13
Alexandra Rd RMD 202 E12-14
Alexandra St MIS ... 210 G73
Alexandra St SUR ... 245 T31
Alexandra St VAN ... 162 V-W12 W12
Alexandria Cr SUR ... 205 F32
Alexis Cr CHL ... 195 C19-20
Alexis Ct RMD ... 202 H14
Alexis Rd KNT ... 175 V23
Algoma Dr RMD ... 202 H14
Algonquin Dr RMD ... 202 H14
Algonquin Mews VAN ... 183 Z19-20
Alice St ABT ... 250 T72
Alice St NEW ... 184 A30
Alice St VAN ... 163 W17
Alice Lake Pl CQT ... 165 V36
Alken Rd FRA ... 254 Q-R15
Allan Rd DNV ... 123 L20
Allan St MIS ... 189 A69 Z69
Allandale Av PMD ... 145 T31
Allard Cr LGT ... 187 B49-50 B52 C48-49 C53 D52-53
Allard St CHL ... 213 F6
Allard St CQT ... 165 X32
Allcott Rd FRA ... 211 F-G82
Allen Av ABT ... 250 T-U75
Allen Dr DEL ... 263 Y17
Allen St NEW ... 165 Y31
Allen Way PTM ... 166 X-Y45
Alliance Dr RMD ... 222 L10
Alliance St ABT ... 250 U75
Allison Av HOP ... 118 D44
Allison Ct ABT ... 251 S79
Allison Ct RMD ... 202 H14
Allison Pl CHL ... 214 H-J15
Allison Pl NEW ... 184 Z29
Allison Rd UEL ... 161 T-U4
Allison St CQT ... 165 X31
Allison St RMD ... 202 H14
Allman St BUR ... 164 X-Y26
Allwood St ABT ... 250 T-U73
Alma Av CHL ... 233 N6
Alma St ABT ... 270 V76
Alma St VAN ... 142 T8 162 U8 V8 W8 X-Y8
Almond Pl BUR ... 164 X29
Almondel Ct WVA ... 121 K5
Almondel Pl WVA ... 121 K5
Almondel Rd WVA ... 121 K4-5
Alouette Blvd PTM ... 187 B47
Alouette Ct RMD ... 202 J12
Alouette Dr CQT ... 165 W36
Alouette Dr RMD ... 202 J12
Alouette Pl PTM ... 187 B47
Alouette Rd MAP ... 168 X57
Alpen Pl SUR ... 185 A34
Alpenwood La DEL ... 263 Z17
Alpha Av BUR ... 143 S-T22 163 U22
Alpha Dr BUR ... 143 T22
Alpha Lake Vlg WHS ... 401 H1
Alpine Av ABT ... 270 V73
Alpine Cr CHL ... 233 N8
Alpine Cr MAP ... 167 Y49
Alpine Cr WHS ... 401 F3
Alpine Ct CQT ... 165 V34-35
Alpine Ct DNV ... 123 J16
Alpine Ct MIS ... 210 H75
Alpine Dr ANM ... 125 N33
Alpine La CQT ... 145 Q38
Alpine Pl DEL ... 224 K30
Alpine Pl PMD ... 145 R36
Alpine Way WHS ... 401 B-C3
Alta Av ABT ... 270 V74-75
Alta Ct RMD ... 202 F11
Alta Lake Pl CQT ... 165 V36
Alta Lake Rd WHS ... 401 D2-3 F2 G1-2 H1
Alta Vista Rd WHS ... 401 F2-3
Altair Pl BUR ... 164 V29
Altamont Cr WVA ... 122 K8
Altamont Pl WVA ... 122 K8
Alton Pl SUR ... 205 G36
Altona Pl RMD ... 202 H14
Altringham Ct BUR ... 164 Y26-27
Alvin Narod Mews VAN ... 142 T13
Alvis Ct CQT ... 145 R37
Amadis Cr CHL ... 213 E5
Amazon Ct PCQ ... 166 U41
Amazon St PCQ ... 166 U41
Ambassador Cr WHS ... 401 E4
Amber Ct CQT ... 145 Q36
Amber Dr CHL ... 213 H5-6
Amberly Pl VAN ... 183 A20
Amberpoint Pl ABT ... 250 S71
Amberwood Pl BUR ... 164 U28
Amble Greene Blvd SUR ... 265 W33
Amble Greene Cl SUR ... 265 W33
Amble Greene Ct SUR ... 265 W33
Amble Greene Dr SUR ... 265 V-W33
Amble Greene Pl SUR ... 265 V-W33
Amble Wood Dr SUR ... 265 W33-34
Ambleside Cl PCQ ... 146 S41
Ambleside La WVA ... 122 M10-11
Amblewood Pl ABT ... 270 W76-77
Amess St NEW ... 164 X-Y30
Amethyst Av RMD ... 202 H14
Amherst Av DNV ... 143 Q21
Amicus Pl ABT ... 250 T74
Amiens Rd CHL ... 233 N5
Amundsen Pl RMD ... 202 G9
Anahim Dr RMD ... 202 J14 203 J15
Ancaster Cr VAN ... 183 A18
Anchor Bay DEL ... 223 N17
Anchor Pl CQT ... 165 U36
Ancient Cedars La WHS ... 401 H2
Anderson Av ABT ... 210 J78
Anderson Av CHL ... 193 C8
Anderson Av MIS ... 209 F67-68
Anderson Cr WVA ... 122 L-M12
Anderson Pl DEL ... 223 P20 243 Q20
Anderson Pl MAP ... 187 A50
Anderson Rd RMD 202 F12-13
Anderson St VAN ... 10 K35 162 U12
Anderson St WRK ... 265 W-X36
Anderson Way PCQ 166 V-W40
Andover Cr WVA ... 122 J12
Andover Pl WVA ... 122 J12-13
Andrews Av CHL ... 213 E8
Andrews Pl ABT ... 270 V76
Andrews Rd RMD ... 222 L10
Angela Av CHL ... 213 F7-8
Angela Dr PMD ... 145 T31-32
Angelo Av PCQ ... 166 U40
Angelus La SQM ... 301 E4
Anglers Pl VAN ... 182 A11
Anglesea Dr RMD ... 202 J14
Angus Cr ABT ... 251 R79
Angus Dr CHL ... 193 D8
Angus Dr VAN ... 162 V12 V-Y11 182 A-B11 Z11
Angus Pl HHS ... 155 R19
Angus Pl SUR ... 226 M41
Angus Campbell Rd ABT ... 271 W-Z79
Anita CHL ... 252 Q93
Anita Ct CNV ... 123 M19
Anita Dr PCQ ... 166 W39
Ann St VAN ... 163 X20
Annacis Hwy DEL ... 204 J27 224 K28 M28-29 P30
Annacis Pkwy DEL ... 184 C-D28
Annance Ct DEL ... 204 F26-27
Annapolis Pl RMD ... 202 J9
Anne Macdonald Way DNV ... 124 N24-25
Annieville Pl DEL ... 204 F29
Annis Rd CHL ... 214 E-G16
Anola Dr BUR ... 164 U23
Anora Dr ABT 250 U78 270 V78
Ansell Pl WVA ... 101 D4
Ansell St MAP ... 168 Y56
Anskar Ct CQT ... 165 U31
Anson Av CQT ... 145 T38
Anson Av RMD ... 182 C-D11
Anson Pl HOP ... 118 E46
Antelope Av MIS ... 210 H73
Antelope Cr MIS ... 210 H73
Anthony Ct NEW ... 184 A29
Antrim Av BUR ... 184 Z23
Antrim Rd SUR ... 185 B35
Antwerp La VAN ... 162 U8
Anvil Cr RMD ... 202 G8-9
Anvil Ct CQT ... 146 R39
Anvil Gn PCQ ... 165 Y38
Anvil Way SUR ... 205 H32-33 J32-33
Anvil Way (129A St) SUR ... 205 J33
Anvil Way (78 Av) SUR ... 205 H32
Anzio Dr VAN ... 163 V-W20
Apaloosa Pl SUR ... 226 M44
Apel Dr PCQ ... 146 S41
Apex Av DNV ... 124 N24 144 P24
Apex Ct ABT ... 249 S70
Apex Pl DNV ... 144 P24
Appel Rd KNT ... 175 Y21
Appian Way CQT ... 164 V30 165 V31
Appin Rd DNV ... 123 M-N20
Apple Grove Cl MAP ... 187 Z53
Appleby Ct MIS ... 210 G73
Appleby La MIS ... 210 F73
Appledale Pl VAN ... 183 Z20
Applehill Cr SUR ... 205 F33
Applewood Dr ABT ... 251 S80
Appleyard Ct PMD ... 145 S35
Appliance Science La UEL ... 161 U4
Approach Dr ABT ... 269 W69
Apps Ct MIS ... 210 G75
April Rd PMD ... 145 Q32-33
Aqua Dr VAN ... 183 A17-18 B17-18
Aqua Vista Trailer Pk FRA ... 211 F79
Aquarius Dr BUR ... 164 V29
Aquarius Mews VAN ... 11 J37-38 142 T13-14
Aquila Rd RMD ... 202 H-J14
Aragon Rd RMD ... 202 J14 203 J15
Araki Gt MIS ... 210 G76
Arbor Av VAN ... 183 Z20-21
Arbor St BUR ... 183 Z21
Arborlynn Dr DNV ... 123 N20
Arbour Pl CHL ... 193 D7
Arbour Pl DEL ... 204 G27
Arbroath St BUR ... 184 Z24 Z24-25
Arbury Av CQT ... 165 V34
Arbutus Av CHL ... 213 E-F8
Arbutus Av MIS ... 210 H74
Arbutus Div VAN ... 182 Z11
Arbutus Dr KNT ... 175 X21-22
Arbutus Dr SQM ... 301 K3
Arbutus Dr WHS ... 401 F3
Arbutus Pl CQT ... 145 P38
Arbutus Pl MAP ... 169 Y63
Arbutus Pl SUR ... 186 C40
Arbutus Pl WVA ... 101 G1
Arbutus Rd WVA ... 101 G1
Arbutus St ABT ... 250 U72
Arbutus St NEW ... 184 A29
Arbutus St VAN ... 10 J-L32 142 T11 162 U11 U-V11 Y11 182 Z11 Z11
Arbutus Wynd SUR ... 186 C40
Arcadia Rd RMD ... 202 E-F13
Arcadian Way ABT ... 250 R75
Archer St NEW ... 164 Y30 184 Z30
Archibald Rd WRK ... 265 W-X36
Archibald Way WHS ... 401 F3
Archimedes St VAN 163 X-Y20
Arcola St BUR ... 184 Z25 Z26
Arden Av BUR ... 164 U27
Arden Dr ABT ... 250 S-T78
Ardingley Av BUR ... 164 V24 V-W24
Argentia Dr RMD ... 202 J10 222 K10
Argo Pl BUR ... 164 V29
Argue St PCQ ... 165 Y38 166 Y39-40
Argyle Av (Ambleside) WVA ... 122 M10 M11
Argyle Av (Horseshoe Bay) WVA ... 101 G2
Argyle Dr VAN ... 163 X17 X-Y17 183 A17 Z17
Argyle Rd DNV ... 123 L19-20
Argyle St CQT ... 146 Q41
Argyll Cr SQM ... 301 E4
Argyll St ABT ... 250 S74
Aries Pl BUR ... 164 V29
Arlington Cr DNV ... 123 L15
Arlington Dr CHL ... 233 L-M5
Arlington St ABT ... 250 T-U75
Arlington St VAN ... 163 Y20 183 Z20
Armada St CQT ... 165 U36
Armitage St CHL ... 213 E8
Armour Ct DNV ... 123 J20
Armstrong Av ABT ... 250 Q78
Armstrong Av BUR ... 164 X-Y29
Armstrong Pl CHL ... 233 N8
Armstrong Rd CHL ... 194 D12
Armstrong Rd LGT ... 208 F-G56 G-H56
Armstrong St NEW ... 184 A30 B29-30
Armstrong St RMD ... 202 G13-14
Arnhem Rd CHL ... 233 M-N6
Arnold Rd ABT ... 271 Y86
Arnold Rd CHL ... 212 J94
Arpe Cr DEL ... 204 G27
Arpe Rd DEL ... 204 G27
Arran Pl SUR ... 205 F32
Arras Rd CHL ... 233 N6
Arrow La CQT ... 165 X31
Arrow St BUR ... 164 Y23
Arrow-Wood Cl PMD ... 145 R-S35
Arrow-Wood Pl PMD ... 145 S35
Arrowhead Rd SQM ... 301 B2
Arrowsmith Dr RMD ... 202 H14
Arrowsmith Pl CQT ... 146 Q39
Arrowsmith Pl RMD ... 202 H14
Arroyo Ct DNV ... 123 M22
Arthur Av BUR ... 184 A23
Arthur Dr DEL ... 243 Q16 S16-17
Arthur Pl CQT ... 165 U32
Arundel La CQT ... 165 X35-36
Arundel Rd DNV ... 123 K15
Arvida Dr RMD ... 202 H14
Arvida Gt RMD ... 202 H14
Arvin Ct BUR ... 144 T27
Asbeck La SUR ... 245 T31
Ascot Pl VAN ... 163 X20
Ascot St CQT ... 165 V-W34
Ascott Av ABT ... 250 S77
Ash Cr VAN ... 182 Z13
Ash Pl SQM ... 301 J4
Ash St ABT ... 250 T-U76
Ash St NEW ... 184 A28 B29
Ash St RMD ... 202 G-J13
Ash St VAN ... 162 U-V14 V13-14 W13 X13-14 Y13 ... 182 A13 A-B13 Z13
Ash St WRK ... 265 X-Y38
Ash Grove Cr BUR ... 164 U29
Ashbrook Ct RMD 202 H13-14
Ashbrook Pl CQT ... 165 U38
Ashburn St VAN ... 183 A18 Z18
Ashbury Ct MAP ... 187 Z50
Ashbury Pl CHL ... 233 M4
Ashbury Pl DEL ... 243 Q15
Ashby Dr CHL ... 233 M8
Ashby Pl RMD ... 202 H14
Ashby Pl SUR ... 205 G37
Ashcroft Av RMD ... 202 J14 203 J15
Ashcroft Dr ABT ... 250 S72
Ashdown Pl SUR ... 186 C40
Ashfeild Rd WVA ... 121 K3
Ashford Pl SUR ... 205 F36
Ashley Cl DNV ... 123 K-L20
Ashley Cr MAP ... 187 Z48
Ashley St CQT ... 165 W31
Ashley Way ABT ... 270 V74
Ashley Grove Ct BUR 164 U29
Ashmore Pl MIS ... 210 G73
Ashton Rd KNT ... 175 V-W18
Ashurst Av CQT ... 165 W35-36 X35-36
Ashwell Rd CHL ... 213 E-F5
Ashwood Dr PMD ... 145 Q35
Ashwood Dr RMD ... 202 H13-14
Ashwood Gt RMD ... 202 H14
Ashworth Av BUR ... 164 Y25 184 Z25
Ashworth Pl BUR ... 164 Y25
Aspen Av ABT ... 250 R74
Aspen Av VAN ... 162 X11
Aspen Cr WVA ... 121 J3
Aspen Ct MIS ... 210 H75
Aspen Ct PMD ... 145 R35
Aspen Ct WHS ... 401 G2
Aspen Dr WHS ... 401 G2
Aspen Dr WVA ... 121 J3
Aspen Pl BUR ... 164 X30
Aspen Pl CHL ... 213 E7-8
Aspen Pl MAP ... 169 Y63
Aspen Rd SQM ... 301 F1-2
Aspen St CQT ... 165 V31
Aspen Way DEL ... 223 N-P17
Aspenwood Dr PMD ... 145 Q-R35
Aspenwood Pl BUR ... 164 U28
Aspin Ct RMD ... 202 G-H14
Aspin Dr RMD ... 202 G-H14
Aspin Pl RMD ... 202 H14
Aster Ct CQT ... 145 R36
Aster Rd SUR ... 265 V38
Aster Ter MIS ... 210 G75
Astor Dr BUR ... 164 V30
Astoria Cr ABT ... 250 T72
Astoria Ct ABT ... 250 S-T72
Atchelitz Rd CHL ... 213 G-H4
Athabasca Dr RMD ... 202 H14 203 H15
Athletes Way VAN ... 11 K39-40 142 T14
Athlone St VAN ... 162 Y12
Atkins Av PCQ 165 V38 166 V39
Atkins St CQT ... 165 U33-34
Atkinson La ABT ... 251 S84
Atkinson Rd ABT ... 251 S83 S85 S86 252 S87-91
Atlantic Av CQT ... 145 S37

Atlantic / Benbow

Atlantic St VAN ... 11 J41 143 T15-16
Atlee Av BUR ... 164 W24
Atlin Pl CQT ... 165 W36
Atlin St VAN ... 163 W19
Atwater Cr ABT ... 250 S-T72
Atwood Cr ABT ... 251 Q81
Aubeneau Cr WVA ... 122 L-M12
Aubrey Pl VAN ... 163 W15
Aubrey St BUR ... 144 T24-25 T26-27
Auburn Dr RMD ... 202 H14 203 H15
Auburn Pl CHL ... 213 E8
Auburn Pl CQT ... 145 R37
Auburn Pl DEL ... 204 J29
Auburn St ABT ... 250 U72
Auchenway Rd FRA ... 254 Q11-12
Auckland St NEW ... 184 B28
Audley Blvd DEL ... 204 E27
Audrey Dr PCQ ... 166 W39
August Dr SUR ... 205 G37
Augusta Av BUR ... 144 T26 T26 164 U26
Augusta Pl CQT ... 145 P38 146 P39
Augusta Pl DEL ... 263 W16-17
Augusta St NEW ... 184 B28
Auguston Pkwy E ABT ... 251 Q81
Auguston Pkwy S ABT ... 251 Q80-81
Aurora Ct DEL ... 243 Q18
Aurora Pl ABT ... 250 T75
Aurora Pl MAP ... 167 Y54
Aurora Rd DNV ... 123 L15
Aurora St MAP ... 167 Y54
Austin Av ABT ... 250 S-T72
Austin Av CQT ... 165 W31-36
Austin Rd BUR ... 164 W30
Austin Rd CQT ... 165 W31
Austrey Av VAN ... 163 X19-20
Automall Dr ABT ... 249 S-T68
Automall Dr CNV ... 123 N15
Autumn Av ABT ... 250 U72-73
Autumn Dr WHS ... 401 B5
Autumn Pl WHS ... 401 B5
Avalon Av BUR ... 164 W28-29
Avalon Av CHL ... 193 C7
Avalon Cr ABT ... 270 V73
Avalon Dr PMD ... 145 S35
Avalon Pl WVA ... 121 J2-3
Avery Av VAN ... 182 A12
Aves Ter MIS ... 210 H71
Aviator Dr ABT ... 269 W-X69
Avison Way VAN ... 142 Q13
Avondale Av ABT ... 250 T75
Avondale Av VAN ... 162 X12
Avondale St BUR ... 163 V21
Avonlynn Cr DNV ... 123 N20
Axen Rd SQM ... 301 B1-2
Axford Bay PMD ... 145 R33
Ayleslynn Dr DNV ... 123 N20
Ayling St PCQ ... 146 S42
Aylmer Av RMD ... 182 C-D11
Ayr Av DNV ... 123 L15
Ayr Dr SQM ... 301 E4
Ayr Dr SUR ... 185 A37
Ayshire Dr BUR ... 144 T26-27
Azalea Cl ABT ... 250 S78
Azalea Pl MIS ... 210 J75
Azalea Pl PCQ ... 146 S40
Aztec St RMD ... 183 D15
Azure Blvd RMD ... 202 F11
Azure Ct CQT 145 Q38 146 Q39
Azure Gt RMD ... 202 F11
Azure Rd N RMD ... 202 F11
Azure Rd S RMD ... 202 F11

B

B St ABT ... 270 Y-Z78
Babcock Pl DEL ... 263 W17
Babich Pl ABT ... 250 T75
Babich St ABT ... 250 T75
Badger Av MIS ... 210 H73
Badger Pl CQT ... 145 Q38
Badger Pl DNV ... 124 M26
Badger Rd DNV ... 124 M26
Baffin Ct RMD ... 202 G9
Baffin Dr RMD ... 202 G9
Baffin Pl BUR ... 164 Y24
Bahr La SUR ... 245 T-U31
Bailey Cr HOP ... 118 H43
Bailey Cr SUR ... 184 D30
Bailey Ct PCQ 165 X38 166 X39
Bailey Pl MIS ... 210 G73
Bailey Rd CHL ... 233 L8 234 L9-10
Bailey St SQM ... 301 J1-2
Baillie St VAN ... 162 X13
Bainbridge Av BUR ... 164 V26
Baird Rd DNV ... 123 K-L19 L19
Bairdmore Cr RMD ... 202 G8-9
Baker Dr CHL ... 213 F7-8
Baker Dr CQT ... 165 U35
Baker Pl DEL ... 224 L30
Baker Pl MAP ... 188 C56
Baker Rd DEL ... 224 K-L30
Baker View St DNV ... 144 P26
Bakerview SUR ... 266 W39
Bakerview Av MIS 210 H73-74
Bakerview Dr RMD 202 J13-14
Bakerview Dr SUR ... 225 N36
Bakerview St ABT ... 250 U72 270 V72
Bakstad Rd FRA ... 231 M84
Balabanian Cir MAP ... 167 Y53
Balaclava St VAN ... 162 U-V9 W9 W-X9 X9 X-Y9 182 Z9
Balbirnie Blvd PMD ... 145 T31
Balboa Ct CQT ... 165 X35
Baldwin Rd ABT ... 250 T-U77
Baldwin St CQT ... 145 S37-38
Baldwin St VAN ... 163 W-X18
Balfour Av VAN ... 162 V-W12 V-W13
Balfour Dr ABT ... 250 S72
Balfour Dr CQT ... 165 W35-36
Balkan St VAN ... 163 W15
Ballam Rd CHL 193 A8 194 Z10
Ballantrae Ct PMD ... 145 T31
Ballantree Pl WVA ... 102 H13 122 J13
Ballantree Rd WVA ... 102 H13
Ballenas Ct CQT ... 146 R39
Balloch Dr SUR ... 205 E33
Balmoral Av CHL ... 233 L5
Balmoral Av CQT ... 165 U33-34
Balmoral Dr CQT ... 145 S-T35
Balmoral Pl PMD ... 145 S35
Balmoral Rd E DNV ... 123 K17
Balmoral Rd W DNV ... 123 K17
Balmoral St ABT ... 249 R68
Balmoral St BUR ... 184 Z25 Z26
Balmoral St VAN ... 183 Z17
Balsam Av CHL ... 213 E8
Balsam Av HHS ... 155 Q19
Balsam Av MIS ... 210 H75
Balsam Cr ABT ... 250 R74
Balsam Cr SUR ... 245 T33
Balsam Dr LGT ... 248 R-S56
Balsam Pl PMD ... 145 Q35
Balsam Pl SQM ... 301 J4
Balsam Pl VAN ... 162 Y10
Balsam St FRA ... 253 R5
Balsam St MAP ... 167 W-X54
Balsam St VAN ... 10 K-L32 162 U10 V10 X-Y10 Y10 182 Z10
Balsam St WRK ... 265 X-Y38
Balsam Way SQM ... 301 J4-5
Balsam Way WHS ... 401 D-E3
Baltic St CQT ... 165 X34
Bamberton Ct RMD ... 202 J11-12
Bamberton Dr RMD ... 202 J11-12
Bamfield Dr RMD ... 183 D15
Bamfield Gt RMD ... 183 D15
Banbury Av CQT ... 145 R-S37
Banbury Rd DNV ... 124 M-N26 N26
Banderas Bay SUR 266 V-W39
Banff Av BUR ... 164 W23
Banff Ct DNV ... 124 N25
Banff Pl ABT ... 250 S74
Banford Rd CHL ... 194 D11 214 E-J11
Bank St BUR ... 184 A25
Bank St MIS ... 230 K75
Banner Pl CQT ... 146 Q39
Bannister Dr MIS ... 210 G75
Banting Pl BUR ... 183 A21
Banting St CQT ... 165 U31-32
Barbell Pl BUR ... 184 Z23
Barber Dr CHL ... 193 D6
Barber La PMD ... 145 Q-R33
Barber St PMD ... 145 R33
Barberry Dr PCQ ... 166 U41
Barberry Pl PMD ... 145 R35-36
Barclay St MAP ... 187 A48
Barclay St VAN ... 10 F35 G36 142 R-S12 S13
Bargen Dr RMD ... 183 C-D15
Barkentine Pl RMD ... 222 K9
Barker Av BUR ... 163 W21 X22 Y21 Y21-22
Barker Av MAP ... 187 A49 Z49
Barker Cr BUR ... 163 X21-22
Barker Rd ABT ... 271 Y-Z85
Barkerville Ct RMD ... 202 J12
Barkley Dr DEL ... 224 K30
Barkley Pl DEL ... 224 K30
Barlynn Cr DNV ... 123 M19
Barmond Av RMD ... 202 H8-9
Barmston Pl DEL ... 204 J29
Barnard Dr RMD ... 202 E-F8
Barnard Pl RMD ... 202 E8
Barnard St VAN ... 182 A-B11
Barnes Dr RMD ... 183 C16
Barnes Rd DEL ... 204 E-F29
Barnes Rd PTM ... 166 X42
Barnet Hwy CQT ... 145 T36
Barnet Hwy PMD ... 145 S32
Barnet Rd BUR ... 144 R27 R-S30 S26
Barnett St MIS ... 210 H75-76
Barnfield Pl WHS ... 401 E3
Barnham Pl WVA ... 122 J13
Barnham Rd WVA ... 122 J13
Barnsdale St MAP ... 167 X53
Barnston Dr E SUR ... 186 D43 206 E43
Barnston Dr W SUR ... 186 D41
Barnston View Rd PTM ... 186 B46
Baron Pl CQT 145 T34 165 U34
Barr St MIS ... 190 D75 210 E75
Barrett St MIS ... 209 E69
Barrie Av BUR ... 184 Z23
Barritt Rd CHL ... 193 D5
Barrons Way ABT ... 270 W77
Barrow Rd CHL ... 212 J94
Barrow St DNV ... 143 Q20
Barrymore Dr DEL ... 204 J28
Bartlett Av CQT ... 165 U33
Bartlett Ct BUR ... 164 W30
Bartlett St CHL ... 193 D7
Bartlett St LGT ... 207 F54
Barton Av CHL ... 213 F5-6
Bashuk Pl RMD ... 202 H10
Basran Av NEW ... 184 D26
Bassani Av ABT ... 251 S79
Bassano Ter ABT ... 251 S79
Bassett Pl RMD ... 202 G11
Bassett Rd RMD ... 202 G11
Batchelor Bay Pl WVA 101 G1
Bateman Rd ABT ... 250 R76-78
Bates Rd ABT ... 229 P70 230 N71 249 Q70
Bates Rd DEL ... 204 J28
Bates Rd RMD ... 202 J12
Bath Rd RMD ... 183 C-D16
Bathgate Pl RMD ... 183 C-D16
Bathgate Way RMD 183 C-D16
Batt Rd FRA ... 231 M83
Battison St VAN ... 163 Y20
Battistoni Pl PCQ ... 145 T38 146 T39
Battle Av MAP ... 187 A48
Bauer St VAN ... 163 U17
Baxter Pl BUR ... 164 V29
Bay St DNV ... 143 Q20
Bay St LGT ... 207 F54
Bay St WRK ... 265 X36
Bay St WVA ... 101 G2
Bay Mill Rd PTM ... 186 B46
Bayard Pl SUR ... 226 M44
Baycrest Av CQT ... 146 R-S42
Baycrest Dr DNV ... 144 P26
Baydala Ct RMD ... 182 C14
Baynes Rd PTM ... 186 A45 Z45
Baynes St ABT ... 229 N-P63
Baynes St MIS ... 210 H77
Bayou Av LGT ... 248 S56
Bayridge Av WVA 121 K5-6 K6
Bayridge Cr WVA ... 121 K5
Bayridge Ct WVA ... 121 K5-6
Bayridge Pl WVA ... 121 K5-6
Bayshore Av CHL ... 233 N4
Bayshore Dr VAN ... 10 E35-36 142 R12-13
Bayshore Dr WHS ... 401 H1
Bayswater Av CQT ... 146 R40
Bayswater Pl CQT ... 146 R40
Bayswater St VAN ... 142 T10 162 U10
Baytree Ct BUR ... 164 X23
Bayview Dr BUR ... 144 S26
Bayview Dr DEL ... 263 X16
Bayview Pl DEL ... 263 X16
Bayview Pl LIO ... 101 B23
Bayview Rd LIO ... 101 B23-24
Bayview Sq CQT ... 165 U33
Bayview St RMD ... 222 L8-9
Bayview St SUR ... 245 U31
Beach Av PMD ... 145 Q32
Beach Av VAN ... 10 F33-34 G-H34 H-J35 142 R11-12 S12 S-T12 T12 T13
Beach Cr VAN ... 10 K36 11 K37 142 T13
Beach Ct CQT ... 165 U36
Beach Rd SUR 266 Y39-40 Z40
Beach St NEW ... 184 C27
Beach Grove Ct DEL ... 263 X18
Beach Grove Rd DEL ... 263 W-X18
Beach View Av WRK ... 265 X36-37
Beachview Dr DNV ... 144 P-Q26
Beacon Dr CQT ... 145 T36-37
Beacon La WVA ... 121 L3
Beacon Rd HOP ... 118 G43
Beaconsfield Rd DNV ... 123 K15-16
Beadnell Ct VAN ... 183 A20 Z20
Beagle Ct VAN ... 183 Z19
Beaman Dr KNT ... 175 W-X20
Beamish Ct BUR ... 163 X22
Beamish Ct VAN ... 183 A20
Bear Av HHS ... 155 P19-20
Bear Cr MIS ... 210 H73
Bear La WVA ... 121 L3
Bear Cave La WHS ... 401 G-H2
Bear Creek Dr SUR ... 205 H35
Bearcroft Dr RMD ... 183 D15
Beaton Rd ABT ... 230 M74-75 M78
Beatrice St VAN ... 163 W17 W-X17 Y17 183 A17 Z17
Beatrice St La PMD ... 145 R-S35
Beatty Dr MIS ... 230 K74
Beatty Rd ABT ... 229 M-N64
Beatty St VAN ... 11 J38 142 S-T14
Beatty Walk VAN ... 11 J38 142 T13-14
Beaufort Pl DNV ... 124 N26
Beaufort Rd CHL ... 233 K7
Beaufort Rd DNV ... 124 N25-26
Beaulynn Pl DNV ... 123 M-N20
Beaumaris Cl PCQ ... 166 U41
Beaumont Dr DNV ... 123 K15
Beaver Cr CHL ... 194 C9
Beaver Dr FRA ... 195 C20
Beaver Dr MIS ... 210 H72-73
Beaver Dr SUR ... 185 D31-32
Beaver La WHS ... 401 E3
Beaver Rd DNV ... 123 J17
Beaver St ABT ... 250 U73 270 V73
Beaverbrook Cr BUR ... 164 V29-30
Beaverbrook Dr BUR ... 164 V29
Beavis St HOP ... 118 F43
Beck Rd ABT ... 250 T-U77
Beckett Rd SUR ... 245 T32
Beckley St MAP ... 187 A48
Beckman Pl RMD ... 182 C14
Beckwith Rd RMD ... 182 C13
Bedard Cr PMD ... 145 T32
Bedford Ct DNV ... 122 L14
Bedford Dr SUR ... 185 A35-36
Bedford Pkwy CHL ... 233 M8
Bedford Pl ABT ... 250 U73 270 V73
Bedford Pl CHL ... 233 M5
Bedford St PCQ ... 165 U38
Bedford Tr LGT ... 207 E53
Bedingfield St PMD ... 145 Q33
Bedora Pl WVA ... 101 D4
Bedwell Bay Rd ANM 145 P32
Bedwell Bay Rd BEL ... 124 N29-30 P28-29
Bedwell Bay Rd PMD 145 P31
Beech Av ABT 250 U72 270 V72
Beech Av HOP ... 118 G42-43
Beech St PCQ ... 166 U41
Beech Nut Av CHL ... 233 K5-6
Beecham Rd RMD ... 202 F-G8
Beechcliffe Dr BUR ... 164 V25
Beecher St SUR ... 245 U31
Beechwood Av DEL 224 L-M30
Beechwood Cr DNV ... 122 N14
Beechwood Ct SUR ... 186 C40-41
Beechwood Dr ABT ... 270 V75-76
Beechwood Pl KNT ... 175 X20
Beechwood St DEL ... 224 L30
Beechwood St VAN ... 162 Y11 182 Z11 Z11
Beecroft Cr ABT ... 250 U77
Beedie Dr CQT ... 146 R40
Beedie Pl CQT ... 146 R40
Beedie St BUR ... 184 C23
Begbie St NEW ... 184 B29
Begbie Ter PCQ ... 166 X-Y39
Begg St VAN ... 143 T16
Begin St CQT ... 165 X33
Beharrell Rd ABT ... 230 K78 M-P78 231 L-M79
Behrner Dr SQM ... 301 K2
Belair Cr DEL ... 263 X16-17
Belair Dr CHL ... 193 C7
Belair Dr DEL ... 263 X16-17
Belair Dr RMD ... 202 H11-12
Belanger Dr ABT ... 251 R79
Belcarra Dr BUR ... 144 S25-26
Belcarra Bay Rd BEL ... 124 N-P28
Belden Rd BUR ... 164 V23
Belfast Av PCQ ... 166 W42
Belfriar Dr BUR ... 164 W30
Belgrave Av DNV ... 123 J15
Belgrave Way DEL ... 184 D27 204 E27
Bell Av BUR ... 164 V-W29
Bell Av MAP ... 188 D62 189 D63 D65
Bell Rd ABT 230 L-P77 250 Q77
Bell Rd CHL 193 B-C8 194 A-B9
Bell Rd FRA ... 211 E85
Bell Rd SUR ... 226 M-N40
Bell St MIS ... 169 Y69
Bell-Irving St RMD ... 202 E10
Bell Acres Rd FRA 254 Q13-14
Bella Vista St VAN ... 163 V17
Belle Pl PCQ ... 166 W39
Belle Isle Pl DNV ... 122 M13
Bellelynn Pl DNV ... 123 N20
Belleville Av BUR ... 163 X21
Belleville St NEW ... 184 A-B28
Bellevue Av CQT ... 145 T35
Bellevue Av WVA ... 122 L8 L-M9 M10-11
Bellevue Cr WRK ... 265 X36
Bellevue Dr CHL ... 213 F5
Bellevue Dr VAN 142 T7 161 T6
Bellflower Ct CQT 145 Q36-37
Bellflower Dr RMD ... 202 F9
Belloc St DNV ... 123 N22
Bellvue Cr ABT ... 270 V74
Bellvue Pl ABT ... 270 V73-74
Bellwood Av BUR ... 164 U23
Belmond Av ABT ... 250 U71-72
Belmont Av DNV ... 123 L15
Belmont Av VAN 142 T7 161 T6
Belmont St NEW ... 184 A28
Belrose Rd ABT ... 252 U90-91
Belvedere Dr DNV ... 123 J15
Belvista Cr DNV ... 123 J15
Belyea St NEW ... 184 B27
Bemi Rd DEL ... 224 K30
Ben Nevis Cr SUR ... 205 F33
Benbow Rd WVA ... 122 K7

Brentlawn / Canfield

Brentlawn Dr BUR 163 U22 164 U23
Brentwood Cr SUR 185 B34
Brentwood Dr CHL 193 C-D8
Breslay St CQT 165 U-V31
Breton Rd BUR 183 C22
Brett Av CHL 213 E6
Brett La MIS 210 G74
Brewster Dr CQT 145 R37
Brewster Dr E DEL 224 K30
Brewster Dr W DEL 224 K30
Brewster Pl ABT 250 U78 270 V78
Brewster Pl CHL 234 M9-10
Brian Dr CQT 146 R39-40
Briar Av VAN 162 W11
Briar Rd BUR 164 X29-30
Briarcliffe Dr CQT 145 R36
Briarlynn Cr DNV 123 M20
Briarwood Cr BUR 163 X22
Briarwood Cr DEL 224 M30
Briarwood Pl ABT 250 U78 251 U79
Briarwood Pl DEL 224 M30
Briarwood Pl PMD 145 R35
Brice Rd CHL 193 C8
Brickwood Cl MAP 187 A52
Bridal Falls Rd FRA 195 B23 C-D21
Bridge Rd KNT 175 Y21 195 A20 Z21
Bridge Rd SUR 185 B31
Bridge Rd WVA 122 M12-13 N12
Bridge St DEL 223 P16 243 Q16
Bridge St DNV 143 P21-22
Bridge St MIS 230 K74
Bridge St RMD 202 G14
Bridge Way VAN 143 R20-21
Bridgeport Rd RMD 182 C13-14 183 C15-16
Bridget Dr PCQ 166 W-X39
Bridgeview Dr SUR 185 A32-33
Bridgeview St ABT 250 Q-R74
Bridgewater Cr BUR 164 W30
Bridgeway St VAN 143 R20
Bridgewood Dr BUR 164 V26
Bridgman Av DNV 122 M14 M-N14
Bridgman Av PCQ 166 V40-41
Bridleridge Cr CHL 233 N-P7
Bridlewood Ct BUR 164 U26
Bridlewood Dr CHL 233 N-P7
Bridlington Dr DEL 204 H-J29
Brief St BUR 164 Y23 184 Z23
Brient Dr MIS 210 H78
Brigadoon Av VAN 183 Z17-18
Brigantine Dr CQT 165 Y34 185 Z34
Brigantine Rd DEL 223 N16-17
Brighton Av BUR 164 V-W28
Brighton Pl ABT 250 R72
Brighton Pl CHL 233 M5
Brighton Pl PTM 187 Z47
Brightwood Pl VAN 183 A18
Brinx Rd CHL 193 B7
Brio Entrance WHS 401 F3
Brisbane Av CQT 165 U33
Brisbane Cr BUR 144 R-S23
Brisbane Ct ABT 250 R72
Brisco Ct CQT 165 X35
Briskham St MIS 210 J73
Bristlecone Ct CQT 145 Q38
Bristol Dr ABT 250 T-U77
Bristol Dr KNT 175 X20-21
Bristol Pl SUR 225 K33
Bristol Island Rd HOP 118 F42
Bristol Slough Rd HOP 118 F41
Britannia Av SQM 301 H1-2
Britannia Dr RMD 222 L9-10
Briteside Rd CHL 234 P11
Brittania St PCQ 166 U40
Britton Av CHL 213 J7
Britton Dr PMD 145 R35
Britton St BUR 184 A26 Z26
Brixham Rd DNV 124 N23 144 P23
Broadmoor Blvd RMD 202 H11-12
Broadview Ct CQT 165 U33-34
Broadview Dr DNV 143 P22 144 P23
Broadway BUR 164 U24-25 U30 V26-27 V29
Broadway E VAN 163 U15-20
Broadway W VAN 162 U8-14
Broadway Av MIS 230 K75
Broadway E ABT 250 U73-74
Broadway St ABT 250 U73 270 V73
Broadway St CHL 193 D8 213 E-G8
Broadway St PCQ 166 W-X40
Broadway St RMD 222 K8-9
Brock St RMD 204 E24
Brock St VAN 163 W18
Brockton Cr DNV 124 N25
Brockton Pl DNV 124 N25
Brodie Pl DEL 223 P19
Brodie Rd DEL 223 P18-19
Bromfield Pl RMD 202 J14
Bromley Ct BUR 164 V25
Bromley Pl RMD 222 K12
Bromley St CQT 165 W36
Bromley St MAP 187 B48
Bronte Dr DNV 123 M-N22
Brookdale Ct ABT 249 S70
Brookdale Ct BUR 144 T23-24
Brookdale Pl DEL 224 K29
Brooke Pl DEL 204 F28
Brooke Rd DEL 204 F-G28
Brookeside Av WVA 121 K3
Brooklyn Av BUR 144 T25
Brookmere Av CQT 164 W30 165 W31
Brookmere Ct MAP 187 A52
Brookmount Dr PMD 145 T35
Brookridge Dr DNV 122 L14
Brooks Av CHL 213 F7-8
Brooks Av MAP 167 Y48
Brooks Cr SUR 226 M46
Brooks St VAN 163 Y20 183 Z20
Brooksbank Av CNV 143 P19
Brooksbank Av DNV 123 N19 143 P19
Brookside Av ABT 249 R69 R70 250 R71
Brookside Dr PMD 145 T35
Brookside Gr SUR 186 C39
Brookwood Pl CHL 214 H16
Broom Pl PCQ 146 S40
Broom St MIS 210 H75
Broome Rd SUR 265 V38
Brothers Pl SQM 301 F1
Broughton St VAN 10 G35 142 S12-13
Brown Av MAP 187 Z52 Z52-53
Brown Cr MIS 210 H74
Brown Rd FRA 231 M84
Brown Rd RMD 182 D13
Brown St DEL 223 K21
Brown St PCQ 166 V-W40
Browndale Rd RMD 182 D12
Browne Rd CHL 233 N-P2
Brownell Rd RMD 182 D12-13
Browngate Rd RMD 182 D12-13
Browning Pl DNV 143 P22
Brownlea Rd RMD 182 D12
Brownley Rd CHL 234 K14
Brownwood Rd RMD 182 D12
Bruce Av MAP 187 Z47-48
Bruce Av MIS 210 H74
Bruce Dr PTM 186 A46
Bruce Pl MAP 187 Z48
Bruce Rd CHL 234 P15
Bruce Rd FRA 234 P15
Bruce St DNV 143 P20
Bruce St VAN 163 X17 X-Y17 Y17
Bruce St WVA 101 G2
Brûlé Mews VAN 183 Z19-20
Brundige Av ABT 270 V74
Bruneau Pl LGT 249 T63
Brunette Av CQT 165 X32-33 X-Y34
Brunette Av NEW 165 Y31
Brunswick Dr RMD 222 L10
Brunswick Pl RMD 222 L10
Brunswick St VAN 163 U15
Brunswick Beach Rd LIO 101 A23
Bryan Pl SUR 205 F34
Bryant Ct BUR 184 Z25
Bryant Pl CHL 214 J15
Bryant St BUR 164 Y24 184 Z24 Z25
Brydon Cr LGC 227 N47
Brynlor Dr BUR 184 A24-25
Bryson Bay RMD 182 D14
Bryson Ct RMD 182 D14
Bryson Dr RMD 182 D14
Bryson Pl RMD 182 D14
Buchanan Av ABT 229 M65-66
Buchanan Av NEW 164 Y30
Buchanan Pl SUR 205 F32
Buchanan St BUR 163 U22 164 U23 U24 U25-26
Buchanan St RMD 222 L10
Bucketwheel VAN 11 L38 162 U13-14
Buckhorn Dr WHS 401 C3
Buckhorn Pl PMD 145 R35
Buckhorn Pl WHS 401 C-D3
Buckingham Av BUR 164 X25
Buckingham Dr ABT 251 R81
Buckingham Dr BUR 164 Y25-26 Y26
Buckingham Dr PMD 145 S-T35
Buckingham Pl BUR 164 X-Y26
Buckley Av SQM 301 H1 J2
Buckskin Pl SUR 226 L-M42
Bueckert Av MIS 210 J72
Buena Vista Av BUR 164 X29
Buena Vista Av WRK 265 X36-38 266 X39
Buffalo Dr BUR 164 V26
Buffalo Dr MIS 210 H72
Buffalo St BUR 164 V26
Buffer Cr ABT 249 T63-64
Bulkley St ABT 250 R-S78
Buller Av BUR 184 A24 B24 Z24
Buller St PMD 145 T34
Bunker Rd FRA 195 C20 C-D21
Bunting Av RMD 222 K10
Buntzen Creek Rd ANM 125 N33
Buoy Dr CQT 145 T36
Burbank Dr DEL 204 H28
Burbidge St CQT 165 Y35 185 Z35
Burdette St RMD 183 B18
Burdock St MIS 210 H74
Burford St BUR 184 Z25
Burgess Av ABT 229 M68-70
Burgess St BUR 184 Z27
Burhill Rd WVA 122 L13
Burian Dr CQT 165 W36
Burke St BUR 163 X21-22 X22
Burke Mountain St CQT 146 R-S41
Burkehill Pl WVA 121 K5
Burkehill Rd WVA 121 K5 K-L5
Burkeridge Pl WVA 121 K5
Burkholder Dr VAN 183 Z20
Burleigh Av PCQ 165 U38
Burley Dr WVA 122 L12 L-M12
Burley Pl WVA 122 L12
Burlington Av BUR 184 Z23
Burlington Dr CQT 145 S37-38
Burma St MIS 169 X-Y70
Burnaby St NEW 164 Y30
Burnaby St VAN 10 G34-35 142 S12
Burnaby Mountain Pkwy BUR 144 S-T26 T27
Burnage Rd DNV 122 L14
Burnett St MAP 187 A53 Z53
Burnfield Cr BUR 164 X26
Burnham Ct BUR 164 U-V26
Burnlake Dr BUR 164 W27-28
Burns Av DNV 124 M-N26
Burns Ct BUR 164 Y25 184 Z25
Burns Dr DEL 223 N19-20 224 P24-25
Burns Pl BUR 164 Y24
Burns Rd PCQ 166 U43
Burns St BUR 164 Y25
Burns St CQT 165 W-X32
Burnside Dr ABT 251 S79
Burnside Pl CQT 145 S36-37
Burnside Rd WVA 122 K11
Burnwood Av BUR 144 S26
Burnwood Dr BUR 144 T26
Burquitlam Dr VAN 183 A18
Burr Pl DEL 204 J29
Burr Pl DNV 143 P22
Burr St NEW 184 B28
Burrard Cr PMD 145 R-S32
Burrard Pl VAN 11 F38
Burrard St VAN 10 H36 K-L33 142 S13-14 T11 T12-13 162 U-V11
Burrill Av DNV 123 K20 K21
Burris St BUR 164 X26 Y25
Burrows Rd RMD 183 C17-18
Bursill St VAN 163 X19
Burton Av RMD 202 G9
Burton Ct CQT 165 U37
Bury Av PCQ 165 U-V38
Bury La WVA 122 K13
Busby Rd ABT 250 U75 270 V75
Buscombe St VAN 183 A15
Bush Ct MIS 210 G-H76
Bushby St NEW 184 A30
Bushnell Pl DNV 123 L20
Bustin Rd CHL 195 B18
Buswell St RMD 202 F12
Butchart St CHL 213 F8
Bute Cr CQT 146 S39
Bute St VAN 10 G36 H35 142 S12 S13
Butler Pl MIS 210 J73
Butler St VAN 163 Y20 183 A20 Z20
Buttermere Dr RMD 202 J12
Buttermere Pl RMD 202 J11
Butternut La PTM 187 Z47
Butternut St CQT 165 U37
Buxton Ct BUR 163 X22
Buxton St BUR 164 X23
Byng St CQT 165 W35
Byrne Rd BUR 184 B-C23
Byrne Rd BUR 184 B24
Byrnepark Dr BUR 184 A-B25
Byrnes Rd MAP 208 E61
Byron Pl DNV 123 N22
Byron Rd DEL 204 G28
Byron Rd DNV 123 N22
Byway WVA 121 K-L2
Bywell Ct VAN 183 A20-21

C

Cabeldu Cr DEL 224 L29
Cable Ct CQT 145 T36
Cabot Dr RMD 202 F-G9
Cactus Ct DNV 123 M22
Caddell Dr DEL 224 N30
Caddy Rd DNV 144 P26
Cade Barr St MIS 210 G-H75
Cadogan Rd RMD 202 H10
Caen Av CHL 233 N5
Caignou Rd KNT 195 Z20
Cairnmore Pl RMD 202 G8-9
Cairns Ct RMD 202 F10
Caithcart Rd RMD 182 D14 183 D15
Caithness Cr PMD 145 T31
Caithness Pl ABT 250 S74
Calais Cr CHL 233 N5
Calder Av DNV 123 K17 L17
Calder Ct RMD 202 G-H10
Calder Pl ABT 250 U77
Calder Rd RMD 202 G-H10
Calderwood Cr RMD 202 H10
Caldew St DEL 204 E27
Caledonia Av DNV 124 M26 M-N26 N26
Caledonia Dr SUR 185 B36
Calgary Av ABT 251 S79
Calgary Dr CQT 146 Q44
Caliente Pl CQT 146 R39
Callaghan Av MAP 187 A52
Callaghan Cl PTM 186 B46
Callaghan Cr ABT 251 Q80-81
Callaghan Dr WHS 401 H1
Calverhall St DNV 123 N19 143 P19
Calvert Dr DEL 223 P16
Calvin Cr MAP 167 X54
Calvin Ct BUR 144 T25
Camano St VAN 183 Z20
Camarillo Pl BUR 164 U26
Camaro Dr DEL 263 X16-17
Camberley Ct CQT 165 W36
Cambie Ct MIS 210 G78
Cambie Rd RMD 182 D12-14 183 D15-19
Cambie St ABT 249 T-U63
Cambie St VAN 11 G-H39 H38 142 S14 S-T14 T14 162 U-W14 X13-14 X-Y14 182 A-B14 Z14
Cambrai Av CHL 233 N5-6
Cambridge Ct DEL 263 Y16-17
Cambridge Dr CQT 165 V33
Cambridge Pl MIS 210 G-H77
Cambridge St ABT 250 T76
Cambridge St BUR 144 S23 S24
Cambridge St CHL 233 M5
Cambridge St PCQ 166 U39
Cambridge St VAN 143 S18 S18-19 S20
Cambridge Way PMD 145 S32
Camden Cr RMD 202 H10
Camden Ct ABT 271 V79
Camden Pl RMD 202 H10
Camel Ct MIS 210 H73
Camelback Ct CQT 145 P38
Camelback La CQT 145 P38
Camellia Ct ABT 250 T77
Camellia Ct CQT 145 R35-36
Camelot Av ABT 229 L67
Camelot Rd WVA 122 K11
Cameron Av MIS 210 E73-74
Cameron Av PCQ 166 W39-40
Cameron Av VAN 142 T8-9
Cameron Cr ABT 250 U78 251 U79
Cameron Ct MAP 188 B56
Cameron Ct RMD 183 D16
Cameron Dr RMD 183 D16 203 E16
Cameron St BUR 164 V30
Cameron St NEW 184 B28
Camino Ct BUR 164 V24
Camino Dr WHS 401 C3
Camlann Ct RMD 202 H9-10
Cammeray Rd WVA 122 K10-11
Camosun St VAN 162 U-V8 W-X8
Camp River Rd CHL 194 B10-15 195 A-B17
Campbell Av ABT 250 U76
Campbell Av DNV 123 K-L20
Campbell Av MAP 187 Z50
Campbell Av PCQ 166 X39-40
Campbell Av VAN 143 S-T16
Campbell Pl SUR 205 E-F32
Campbell Rd ABT 251 U84-86 252 U87-90
Campbell Rd CHL 214 E14-15
Campbell Rd PMD 145 R-S34
Campbell St MIS 190 Z75
Campbell St NEW 184 D27
Campion CQT 165 V37
Campion La PMD 145 R35-36
Campion St MIS 189 A69
Campobello Pl RMD 202 J9
Campus Rd UEL 161 T-U4
Camridge Pl WVA 122 K11
Camridge Rd WVA 122 K10
Camrose Av CHL 193 C7
Camrose Dr BUR 164 V26
Camsell Cr RMD 202 F10-11
Camwell Dr WVA 122 K11
Camwood Av MAP 187 Z49
Canada Pl VAN 11 F38 142 R-S14
Canada Rd FRA 272 Y94
Canada Way BUR 163 V22 164 V23 W23-24 X25-26 Y26-27 184 Z27
Canary Ct ABT 249 U68-69
Canary Dr SUR 185 B37
Canberra Av BUR 144 S23
Candia Pl WVA 101 H1
Candlewick Wynd DEL 263 W17
Candlewood Dr RMD 202 H9
Candow St CHL 193 D6
Canfield Cr DNV 123 L15

Duranleau / Express

Duranleau St VAN 10 K35 142 T12
Durant Dr CQT 145 R-S37
Durham Pl ABT 250 U78 270 V78
Durham Rd SUR 265 V38
Durham St NEW 184 Z28-29
Durham St E NEW 164 Y29 184 Z29
Durieu Rd FRA 190 Z79
Durieu St MIS 230 K74 K75
Durward Av VAN 163 X16
Duthie Av BUR 144 S-T26 164 U26
Duval Ct CQT 165 V34
Duval Rd DNV 123 L21
Dyck Rd DNV 123 K19-20
Dyer Rd FRA 195 C20
Dyke Access MIS 230 K73
Dyke Rd ABT 209 G-H64
Dyke Rd CHL 193 D5 213 E5
Dyke Rd CHL 233 N4-5
Dyke Rd FRA 195 B19 212 F91-92
Dyke Rd RMD 203 H19 204 F23-24 F25 222 L10 M11-14 223 L15
Dyke Rd SUR 184 B30
Dylan Pl RMD 202 J10-11

E

Eagle Av MAP 187 Z53
Eagle Cr CHL 194 C-D10
Eagle Cr MIS 210 H72
Eagle Cr PMD 145 Q-R33
Eagle Ct DNV 103 H15
Eagle Dr PMD 145 Q33
Eagle Dr WHS 401 E3
Eagle Is WVA 121 J2
Eagle La FRA 212 E91
Eagle Pass PMD 145 Q-R33
Eagle Pl SUR 185 B37
Eagle Rd FRA 211 F-G80
Eagle Spur FRA 211 G80
Eagle St ABT 270 V74-75
Eagle St HHS 155 P19-20
Eagle Ter MIS 210 H72
Eagle Way DEL 262 W15
Eagle Harbour Rd WVA 121 J2-3
Eagle Lake Access Rd WVA 101 G4-5 121 J5
Eagle Mountain Dr ABT 251 U79
Eagle Mountain Dr CQT 145 Q36
Eagle Ridge Cr WHS 401 F3 S-T21
Eagle Ridge Pl CHL 213 F2
Eagle Run Dr SQM 301 C2
Eaglecrest Dr ABT 251 U80
Eaglecrest Pl ABT 251 U80
Eaglecrest Rd ANM 125 N33
Eagleridge Dr CQT 145 S36
Eagleridge Dr WVA 101 H2 121 J2
Eagleridge Pl WVA 101 H2
Eagles Dr BUR 164 Y25
Eagles Dr UEL 161 V4
Eaglewind Blvd SQM 301 J1
Earl St CHL 233 M6-7
Earl Finning Way VAN 163 U16
Earles St VAN 163 X19 X-Y19
Earlmond Av RMD 202 H8-9
Earls Ct ABT 250 T76-77
Earls Ct PCQ 166 X39
Easmont Ct PCQ 166 U41
East Blvd VAN 162 V11 X-Y11 182 A11-12 Z11
East Ct BUR 144 T23
East Mall UEL 161 U-V4
East Rd ANM 145 P33 P-Q34
East Campus Rd BUR 144 S-T29
East Edwards St MIS 210 F-G78
East Hemlock Dr ANM 125 N33-34
East Lake Gt CQT 165 V37
East Whalley Ring Rd SUR 185 C34 C-D34 D34
Eastbrook Pkwy BUR 163 U-V22
Eastcot Rd WVA 122 L13
Easterbrook Rd RMD 202 E9
Easterbrook St CQT 165 V31-32
Eastern Av CNV 123 L17 M17 N17
Eastern Dr PCQ 165 X38 166 W39
Eastglen Cl SUR 186 B-C40
Eastglen Pl SUR 186 C40
Easthope Av RMD 222 L8
Eastlake Dr BUR 164 V28-29 V29
Eastlawn Dr BUR 144 T23
Eastleigh Cr LGC 227 N48-49
Eastleigh La DNV 124 M-N26
Eastman Dr RMD 202 J10
Eastmont Dr WVA 101 H1
Eastridge Rd DNV 124 M27
Eastview Ct ABT 250 T74
Eastview Pl ABT 250 T74-75
Eastview Rd CNV 123 M-N19
Eastview St ABT 250 T74
Eastwood St CQT 145 S38
Easy St WHS 401 D-E3
Eaton Pl DEL 204 F26
Eaton Way DEL 204 F25
Ebert Av CQT 164 V30 165 V31
Ebony St ABT 270 V76
Ebor Rd DEL 204 E29
Eburne Way RMD 183 B15
Ebury Pl DEL 204 G26
Echo Av HHS 155 P19-20
Echo Pl VAN 183 Z20
Echo Rd ABT 269 X67-68
Eckersley Rd RMD 202 F13
Eckert Av NEW 184 D26
Eckert St CHL 252 Q-R93
Edal St LGT 207 F53-54
Eddie Dr NEW 184 Z29
Eddington Dr VAN 162 W10-11
Eddystone Cr DNV 144 P23
Eden Av CQT 165 V33-34
Eden Cr DEL 263 X17-18
Eden Dr CHL 213 J6 233 K6
Eden Pl DEL 263 X17-18
Eden Pl WVA 122 M12
Edenvale Ct WVA 121 K3
Edenvale Pl WVA 121 K3
Edgar Av CQT 165 X31-32
Edgar Cr VAN 162 W10
Edge Pl VAN 183 B20
Edge St MAP 167 X52 Y52 187 Z52
Edge St MIS 210 H73
Edgedale Av MAP 187 A49-50
Edgehill Av ABT 249 T70
Edgemont Blvd DNV 122 K-L14 123 L15 L-M15
Edgemont Pl CHL 233 M8
Edgeview Pl ABT 270 V78
Edgewater Cr SQM 301 F1-2
Edgewater Dr SQM 301 F2
Edgewater La DNV 123 N21
Edgewater Pl CHL 195 C18
Edgewood Av ABT 270 W74
Edgewood Av CQT 165 W34-35
Edgewood Dr SUR 266 V40
Edgewood Pl DNV 122 K14
Edgewood Rd DNV 122 K14 123 K15 K16
Edgewood Hostel Access WHS 401 C3-4
Edinburgh Dr PMD 145 S-T35
Edinburgh Dr SUR 205 F33
Edinburgh Pl PMD 145 T35
Edinburgh Pl SUR 205 F33
Edinburgh St BUR 143 R21
Edinburgh St NEW 184 A27 B26-27
Edinburgh St PCQ 146 T39
Edinburgh St VAN 143 R20-21
Edison St BUR 164 V26
Edith St BUR 144 S26
Edmerston Rd FRA 253 S7
Edmonds Dr DEL 243 Q15
Edmonds St BUR 164 Y27 184 A25-26 Z26-27
Edmondson Rd CHL 194 A15
Ednor Cr BUR 144 T26
Edson Av BUR 183 A22
Edson Dr CHL 233 L6
Edson Pl ABT 251 S79
Education Rd UEL 161 U3
Edward Cr PMD 145 T35
Edward St CHL 213 E6 F6
Edwards Dr HOP 118 G43
Edwards Rd CHL 195 B-C19
Edwards Rd CHL 232 N94
Edwards Rd FRA 254 Q10-11
Edwards Rd SQM 301 B2-3
Edwards St CQT 146 Q-R43
Edwards St MIS 210 G78
Edworthy Way NEW 185 Z31
Eena Dr CHL 233 M3-4
Egan Pl DEL 223 P17
Egglestone Av MIS 210 G73-74
Eglinton St BUR 164 W23-24 W-X24
Egmont Av CQT 165 U31
Egret Ct RMD 222 K10
Ehkolie Cr DEL 262 X15 263 X16
Eider St MIS 210 H-J73
Eildon St PMD 145 T31
El Camino Dr CQT 146 Q-R39
El Casa Ct CQT 146 R39
Elan Pl CQT 145 R37
Elbow Pl PCQ 166 U42
Elder Av CHL 213 H6
Elder Rd HOP 118 G42
Eldon Rd DNV 122 K14
Eldorado Pl ABT 270 V76
Eldridge Rd ABT 251 S-T84
Eleanor Av ABT 270 V77
Eleanor St BUR 184 A-B24
Electronic Av PMD 145 S-T34
Elementary Rd ANM 145 P33
Elevator Rd SUR 204 E28-29
Elford St BUR 164 X-Y30
Elgey Rd FRA 195 B22
Elgin Av BUR 164 Y24 184 Z24
Elgin Av PCQ 166 U39
Elgin Dr CHL 193 C8
Elgin Pl BUR 164 Y24
Elgin Rd SUR 245 S35 S35-36
Elgin St NEW 184 A29
Elgin St PMD 145 T33
Elgin St VAN 163 W-X16 X16 Y16
Elgon Ct ABT 250 T77
Elinor Cr PCQ 165 W-X38
Elizabeth CHL 252 Q93
Elizabeth Av ABT 230 N75
Elizabeth Dr CQT 146 R39-40
Elizabeth Dr FRA 253 R6
Elizabeth St VAN 162 X14
Elizabeth Way DNV 122 L14
Elk Pl CQT 145 Q38
Elk Pl DEL 224 K30
Elk Ter MIS 210 H73
Elk Valley Pl VAN 183 Z20
Elk View Rd CHL 234 L10-11 L-M13 M-N15 M-N16
Elkford Dr ABT 250 S72
Elkhorn Av CQT 165 X35
Elkmond Rd RMD 202 J8
Elkwood Pl BUR 164 U28
Ellen St CHL 233 M4
Ellendale Dr SUR 185 B36
Ellerslie Av BUR 144 S25 164 V25
Ellerton Ct BUR 163 X22
Ellesmere Av N BUR 144 S24
Ellesmere Av S BUR 144 S-T24 164 U24
Ellice Av CQT 165 U31
Elliot Av ABT 270 V77-78
Elliot St DEL 223 P16 243 Q16
Elliot St NEW 184 A29-30
Elliott Av CHL 193 C8
Elliott St VAN 163 Y18 183 A18 Z18
Ellis Dr PCQ 166 U41
Ellis St DNV 144 P23
Elm CQT 145 S38
Elm Dr CHL 213 F7
Elm Rd KNT 175 X21
Elm St ABT 250 U76
Elm St PMD 145 S34-35
Elm St VAN 162 W-X10 X-Y10
Elm St WRK 265 X36-37
Elm Vlg SUR 206 F39
Elmbridge Way RMD 202 E11-12
Elmer St NEW 164 Y30
Elmgrove Dr BUR 163 W22 164 W23
Elmgrove Pl BUR 163 W22 164 W23
Elmhurst Dr VAN 183 Z19
Elmwood Dr ABT 250 S-T76
Elmwood Pl DNV 122 N14
Elmwood St BUR 163 W21
Elmwood St CQT 165 U31
Elsdon Bay PMD 145 Q33
Else Rd KNT 175 V18-19
Elsie Pl CHL 233 M3-4
Elsie Rd ABT 229 N65
Elsmore Rd RMD 202 G-H8
Elsom Av BUR 163 X-Y22
Elspeth Pl PCQ 166 W-X39
Elstree Pl DNV 123 L16
Elswick Pl CHL 233 M4
Eltham St MAP 187 A48
Elva Av CQT 165 W34
Elveden Row WVA 122 J12
Elwell St BUR 164 X28 Y26 Y27 184 Z25 Z26
Elwood Pl ABT 270 V78
Elwood Rd CHL 213 J6
Elwyn Dr BUR 164 X25
Emerald Av ABT 270 V73
Emerald Av HHS 155 R19-20
Emerald Dr CHL 193 C8
Emerald Dr DNV 123 K-L15
Emerald Dr WHS 401 A-B5
Emerald Pl RMD 202 F10
Emerald Pl WHS 401 B5
Emerald Rd HOP 118 E47
Emerson Ct DNV 124 N23
Emerson St ABT 250 T-U73 270 V73
Emerson St BUR 164 Y25
Emerson St CQT 165 U31
Emerson Way DNV 124 N23
Emery Pl DNV 123 M19-20
Emiry St MIS 210 F73
Emmerson Rd FRA 231 P83
Emory St NEW 184 A29
Empire Dr BUR 144 S23
Empress Av BUR 164 Y25 184 Z25
Empress Dr ABT 251 T80
Empress La ABT 251 T-U80
Empress La CHL 213 E7
Emwood Pl DEL 204 F30
Enderby Av DEL 263 W-X18
Enderby St ABT 270 V78
Endersby St BUR 164 Y29
Engineering Rd UEL 161 U-V4
English Av RMD 222 L8
English Pl SUR 225 K33
English St BUR 163 V22
English Bluff Ct DEL 262 Y15 263 Y16
English Bluff Rd DEL 262 X15 263 X16 Z16
Ennerdale Rd DNV 123 M19
Enterprise Av ABT 250 T75-76
Enterprise Dr CHL 213 H3-4
Enterprise Pl SQM 301 H1
Enterprise St BUR 164 V27
Enterprise Way SQM 301 H1
Enterprise Way SUR 226 M46
Entertainment Blvd RMD 203 J17 J18 223 K17
Entrance Ct CQT 146 S39
Eperson Rd RMD 202 G9
Epp Dr CHL 194 D9
Epping Ct BUR 164 W26
Epps Av DNV 124 N26
Epson Ct ABT 250 S77
Epson La ABT 250 S77
Epworth Ct ABT 251 T81
Erho Rd FRA 272 W94
Eric Dr CHL 193 C8 194 C9
Erickson Dr BUR 164 V30
Erickson St MIS 210 E77
Erin Av BUR 164 X29
Erin Pl DEL 263 Y16
Erin Way DEL 263 Y16
Errigal Pl WVA 122 K10
Errington Rd RMD 202 J12
Erskine Av MIS 210 J75
Erskine Pl PCQ 165 X38
Erskine St CQT 145 R37
Erwin Dr WVA 121 L4-5
Escola Bay PMD 145 Q33
Esmond Av BUR 143 R-S21 S-T21 T21 163 U21 V21
Esmond Av N BUR 143 R-S21
Esperanza Dr CQT 146 S39
Esperanza Dr DNV 103 H15
Esplanade E CNV 143 P17
Esplanade W CNV 123 N16 143 P16
Esplanade Av HHS 155 P18-20
Esplanade Av PMD 145 S33-34
Esplanade Av WVA 122 M11-12
Esquimalt Av WVA 122 M10-12 M12-13
Esquimalt Ter ABT 250 S73
Essendene Av ABT 250 U75-76
Essex Av PCQ 146 S42
Essex Dr ABT 270 V78
Essex Pl SUR 265 V38
Essex Rd DNV 123 K15
Estate Dr FRA 254 Q10
Estevan Ct ABT 251 T81
Estevan Pl WVA 121 K4
Ethel Av BUR 184 A26-27
Eton Cr ABT 250 S77
Eton St BUR 143 S21-22 144 S23
Eton St VAN 143 S18 S18-19 S20
Euclid Av VAN 163 X19-20
Euclid Ct CQT 165 X31
Eugene Cr SUR 225 P31
Euphrates Cr PCQ 166 V41
Eureka Av PCQ 166 X40
Eva Lake Rd WHS 401 G2
Evancio Cr RMD 202 H10
Evans Av VAN 143 T15-16
Evans Pkwy CHL 213 H5
Evans Pl DEL 204 H29
Evans Pl PCQ 146 T42 166 U42
Evans Rd CHL 213 H-J5 233 K-L5
Evans St MAP 167 Y51 187 Z51
Eveleigh St VAN 11 F37 142 S13
Evelyn Dr WVA 122 M12
Evelyn St DNV 123 K19-20 K20-21 K21
Everall St WRK 265 W-X37
Everett Cr BUR 144 T26
Everett Dr ABT 270 V78
Everett Rd ABT 270 V78
Everett St ABT 270 V78
Everglade Pl DNV 123 K-L16
Evergreen Av WVA 121 L5
Evergreen Cr ANM 145 Q34
Evergreen Dr KNT 175 W-X20
Evergreen Dr PMD 145 S32
Evergreen La DEL 243 Q16
Evergreen Pl DNV 123 K15-16 K-L16 L16-17
Evergreen St ABT 250 T71-72
Evergreen St CHL 193 C7
Evergreen St PCQ 146 S-T41
Everson Pl ABT 270 V78
Ewart St BUR 184 A24
Ewen Av NEW 184 C27-28 D26-27
Ewen Av RMD 222 L8
Ewen Rd RMD 203 F-G22
Ewert Av MIS 210 G78
Ewson St WRK 265 X38 266 X39
Exbury Av ABT 250 S78
Exbury Pl ABT 250 S78
Exegesis St RMD 202 F-G10
Exeter Av MAP 167 Y50 Y51
Exmouth Rd DNV 144 P23
Explorers Walk VAN 183 A20
Expo Blvd VAN 11 H39-40 J38 142 T14 T14 143 T15
Express St BUR 164 V27

Gostick / Haverman

Gostick Pl *CNV* 123 N15 143 P15
Gothard St *VAN* 163 W-X18
Goudy Pl *DEL* 243 Q19
Goundrey St *MIS* 210 F-G76
Gourlay Rd *FRA* 211 G86 212 G87
Government Rd *BUR* 164 W26-28
Government Rd *SQM* 301 A1 B1-2 C2 E3 F1-3 G1
Government St *BUR* 164 W28-30
Governor Ct *PCQ* 166 X39
Governors Ct *NEW* 184 Z30
Gower St *RMD* 202 J13-14
Goyer Ct *CQT* 165 W33
Grace Av *ABT* 230 M75
Grace Av *BUR* 164 W25
Grace Cr *DNV* 123 K15
Grace Rd *SUR* 184 C-D30
Grace St *MAP* 167 Y51
Gracemar Dr *CHL* 194 D10
Grade Cr *LGC* 227 P47 247 Q48-49
Grafton Ct *BUR* 164 Y23
Grafton St *BUR* 163 Y22 164 Y23
Graham Av *BUR* 184 Z27
Graham Cr *ABT* 209 J64 229 K64
Graham Ct *MIS* 210 G75
Graham Dr *CHL* 234 M-N13
Graham Dr *DEL* 263 Z16
Graham St *MAP* 189 A-B64
Graham St *PCQ* 146 T39
Granada Cr *DNV* 123 K16
Grand Blvd *CNV* 123 M18 N18
Grand St *MIS* 210 H-J74
Grand View Dr *CHL* 213 F2 G1-3
Grandview Cr *ABT* 250 T71
Grandview Hwy *BUR* 163 V21-22
Grandview Hwy *VAN* 163 V19-20
Grandview Hwy N *VAN* 163 U17
Grandview Hwy S *VAN* 163 V18
Grandview Viaduct *VAN* 143 T16 163 U16-17
Grandy Rd *RMD* 202 G11
Grange St *BUR* 163 Y21-22
Granite Av *ABT* 250 T72-73
Granite Ct *CQT* 145 Q36
Granite Ct *DNV* 124 M25
Granite Way *MAP* 168 W55
Grant Av *MAP* 188 B60
Grant Av *PCQ* 166 U39-40
Grant Ct *PCQ* 146 T41 166 U41
Grant Pl *BUR* 144 T25
Grant Pl *DEL* 204 E30
Grant Pl *PCQ* 146 T41 166 U41
Grant Rd *SQM* 301 C1-2
Grant St *ABT* 250 U72 270 V72
Grant St *BUR* 143 T21 T21-22 144 T24 T24-25 164 U24
Grant St *CHL* 193 C8
Grant St *CQT* 145 T31 165 U31
Grant St *PMD* 145 T33
Grant St *VAN* 143 T17-19
Grant McConachie Way *RMD* 182 C10-11
Grantham Pl *DNV* 143 P21
Granville Av *RMD* 202 F8-14
Granville Cr *RMD* 202 F11
Granville Seawalk N *VAN* 10 J35-36 142 T12
Granville St *NEW* 184 A29-30
Granville St *VAN* 10 J36 142 T13 162 U12
Grassmere St *BUR* 163 X22 164 X23
Grauer Bypass *RMD* 182 B11
Grauer Rd *RMD* 182 B-C12
Graveley St *BUR* 143 T21 T21 T22 163 U21 U22
Graveley St *DNV* 122 M13 M14
Graveley St *VAN* 143 T17-18 T19-20 T20
Graves St *MAP* 187 A49 Z49
Gray Av *ABT* 209 G63 G65
Gray Av *BUR* 183 A22 Z22
Gray Rd *FRA* 195 C21 D21
Gray St *MAP* 167 Y52
Graybar Rd *RMD* 204 F23
Grayson Av *CQT* 165 X31
Graystone Dr *ABT* 251 U80
Graystone La *ABT* 251 U80
Great Canadian Way *RMD* 182 C13
Great Northern Av *ABT* 249 U69
Great Northern Way *VAN* 11 L41 163 U15-16
Grebe Cr *MIS* 210 H73
Green Av *ABT* 250 T77
Green Av *MIS* 189 C-D69
Green Ct *BUR* 163 U22
Green Pl *DEL* 223 P17
Green Rd *KNT* 175 W20
Green Rd *PTM* 166 Y44
Greenacres MHP *FRA* 211 E-F79
Greenall Av *BUR* 183 A21 A-B21
Greenbriar Pl *PMD* 145 R35
Greenbriar Way *DNV* 122 K-L14
Greenbrier Pl *CQT* 145 R36
Greenbrook Dr *SUR* 206 G41
Greenbrook Pl *SUR* 206 G41
Greenchain *VAN* 11 L37 162 U13
Greencrest Dr *SUR* 245 S35
Greendale Ct *ABT* 249 S69
Greene Pl *MIS* 210 F73
Greene St *CQT* 165 U38
Greenfield Dr *RMD* 202 H13
Greenfield Gt *RMD* 202 H-J13
Greenford Av *BUR* 184 Z25
Greenhaven Ct *PTM* 187 Z47
Greenhill Ct *CQT* 145 R36-37
Greenhill Pl *DEL* 204 G29
Greenhill Rd *CHL* 234 P9
Greenlake Pl *BUR* 164 W28
Greenland Dr *DEL* 263 Z17
Greenland Dr *RMD* 183 D16
Greenland Pl *RMD* 183 D16
Greenleaf Ct *PMD* 145 P-Q35
Greenleaf Dr *PMD* 145 Q35
Greenleaf La *WVA* 121 J3
Greenleaf Rd *WVA* 121 J3
Greenlees Rd *RMD* 202 J12
Greenmount Av *PCQ* 146 S40
Greenmount St *CHL* 233 K-L5
Greenock Pl *DNV* 123 M20
Greenock Pl *SUR* 205 F32
Greensboro Pl *VAN* 182 Z14
Greenside Dr E *SUR* 226 M46
Greenside Dr W *SUR* 226 M46
Greenstone Ct *CQT* 145 Q36
Greentree La *DNV* 122 K-L14
Greentree Pl *BUR* 163 X22 164 X23
Greentree Rd *WVA* 121 K2-3
Greenway Av *DNV* 123 J-K16
Greenway Dr *SUR* 206 G41
Greenwell St *MAP* 167 Y53 187 Z53
Greenwood Dr *CHL* 213 J7 233 K7
Greenwood Dr *HOP* 118 E46
Greenwood Dr *MIS* 189 B70
Greenwood Pl *BUR* 164 V26
Greenwood Pl *WVA* 122 J12
Greenwood Rd *WVA* 122 J12-13
Greenwood St *BUR* 164 V25 V26-27
Greenwood Way *SQM* 301 D-E4
Greer Av *VAN* 10 J-K33 142 T11
Greer Pl *PCQ* 145 T38 146 T39
Greer St *ABT* 270 W75
Greer St *LGT* 207 E53
Greta St *BUR* 183 Z22
Grewall Cr *MIS* 210 H75
Greylynn Cr *DNV* 123 M20
Greystone Dr *BUR* 144 T26-27 164 U27
Greystone Pl *PMD* 145 R35
Griffen Rd *MAP* 187 B54
Griffin Dr *CHL* 233 K7
Griffin Pl *DNV* 123 L15
Griffith Pl *NEW* 164 Y30
Griffith Rd *ABT* 270 V77
Griffiths Av *BUR* 164 Y25 184 A25 Z25
Griffiths Dr *BUR* 184 A25-26
Griffiths Way *VAN* 11 H-J39 142 T14
Grigg Rd *CHL* 194 D14
Grimmer St *BUR* 184 Z23
Grizzly Pl *CQT* 145 Q38
Groat Av *RMD* 202 J9
Grosvenor Av N *BUR* 144 S23
Grosvenor Av S *BUR* 144 S23
Grosvenor Cr *BUR* 144 S23
Grosvenor Pl *ABT* 250 U77
Grosvenor Pl *CQT* 146 R40
Grosvenor Rd *SUR* 185 B34-35
Grosvenor Sq *DEL* 184 D27-28
Grouse Av *MIS* 210 H72
Grouse Ct *ABT* 250 U73
Grouse Walk *VAN* 163 X15
Grousewoods Cr *DNV* 103 H15
Grousewoods Dr *DNV* 103 H15
Grousewoods Pl *DNV* 103 H15
Grove Av *BUR* 144 S-T25
Grove Av *CHL* 233 N8
Grove Av *DEL* 223 P17
Grove Av *MIS* 210 G71-72
Grove Cr *DEL* 263 W18
Grove Cr *SUR* 185 D32
Grove Pl *DEL* 263 W18
Grove Pl *DNV* 123 M22
Groveland Ct *WVA* 122 J11
Groveland Pl *WVA* 122 J-K12
Groveland Rd *WVA* 122 J12
Grover Av *CQT* 165 U31-34
Groveridge Wynd *DEL* 263 Z17
Guelph St *VAN* 163 U-V15
Guest St *PCQ* 166 X39
Guest Ter *MIS* 210 H71
Guest Wynd *PMD* 145 R33-34
Guilby St *CQT* 165 W-X31
Guildford Dr *PMD* 145 S35-36
Guildford Dr *SUR* 185 C37
Guildford Way *CQT* 145 S36-38
Guilford Dr *ABT* 250 U77 270 V77
Guilford Dr *SQM* 301 K2-3
Guiltner St *CQT* 165 U-V31
Gulf Pl *WVA* 121 K2
Gulf View Wynd *DEL* 263 Z16
Gunderson Rd *DEL* 204 E29
Gunn Av *MIS* 209 G68-70
Gurney Rd *FRA* 253 R7
Gwillim Cr *VAN* 183 Z20-21

H

Habgood St *WRK* 266 W39 X39
Hachey Av *CQT* 165 X33
Hacienda Pl *ABT* 270 V73
Hacienda Pl *CHL* 233 M4
Hack-Brown Rd *CHL* 214 G16
Hadden Dr *WVA* 122 K-L13
Hadden St *LGT* 207 F53
Haddon Ct *RMD* 202 J10
Haddon Dr *RMD* 202 J10
Haddon Pl *RMD* 202 J10
Haddon Rd *SUR* 185 B33
Hadway Dr *HHS* 155 R19-20
Haffner Ter *MIS* 210 G73
Haggart St *VAN* 162 W10
Haida Dr *ABT* 250 S73
Haida Dr *VAN* 163 V20
Haig Dr *CHL* 213 J5-6
Haig Hwy *KNT* 175 X21-22
Haig St *MIS* 210 J73
Haig St *VAN* 182 A12
Haig Station Rd *HOP* 118 D43
Hailey St *CQT* 165 U-V32
Hale Rd *PTM* 146 T46 166 V-W46
Haley Rd *CHL* 234 N-P14
Haley St *MAP* 167 W53
Halifax Av *PCQ* 146 S41
Halifax Pl *SUR* 225 N35
Halifax St *BUR* 163 U21-22 164 U23 U23-26
Hall Av *BUR* 184 Z26
Hall Av *RMD* 182 D14
Hall Pl *CHL* 213 H7-8
Hall Pl *DEL* 204 G30
Hall Pl *RMD* 182 D14
Hall Rd *FRA* 195 C21
Hall Rd *SUR* 225 K34
Hall St *MAP* 187 Z51
Hall St *MIS* 189 D67
Hallam Ct *CQT* 146 Q39
Hallert Rd *ABT* 230 P72 P76-78 231 P79
Halley Av *BUR* 163 W22 X-Y22
Halligan St *BUR* 184 Z25-26
Halnor Av *MAP* 168 Y57
Halss Cr *VAN* 162 X-Y7 Y8
Halstead Pl *SUR* 185 D36
Halston Ct *BUR* 164 W29-30
Halston Ct *WVA* 122 K9
Hamber Ct *DNV* 124 N25
Hamber Pl *DNV* 124 N25
Hamber St *RMD* 202 F8
Hambry St *BUR* 184 Z24
Hamilton Av *CNV* 123 M-N15
Hamilton Pl *PCQ* 146 T42
Hamilton Rd *KNT* 175 X-Y17
Hamilton Rd *RMD* 204 F25
Hamilton St *CHL* 193 D5-6
Hamilton St *NEW* 184 A27 A27-28 B26 B26-27
Hamilton St *PCQ* 146 S42 T42
Hamilton St *VAN* 11 H38 J37 142 S-T14 T13
Hamlin Dr *DEL* 224 L29
Hamm St *ABT* 269 Y-Z69
Hammarskjold Dr *BUR* 144 S-T24
Hammersmith Gt *RMD* 223 K15
Hammersmith Way *RMD* 223 K-L15
Hammond Av *CQT* 165 W33-34
Hammond Rd *MAP* 187 A48 Z47
Hammond Rd *PTM* 186 Z46 187 Z47
Hammond St *MIS* 210 F74
Hamon Cr *ABT* 270 V78
Hamon Dr *ABT* 270 V78
Hampshire Ct *SUR* 246 T39
Hampshire Pl *ABT* 250 U77 270 V77
Hampshire Rd *DNV* 123 K15
Hampstead Cl *DEL* 204 F25
Hampstead Pl *BUR* 164 X-Y25
Hampton Blvd E *SUR* 225 L32
Hampton Blvd N *SUR* 225 L32
Hampton Ct *SUR* 225 L32
Hampton Dr *CQT* 145 P38
Hampton Gn *CQT* 145 P38 146 P39
Hampton Gt *CQT* 145 P38
Hampton Pl *UEL* 161 V5
Hampton St *MAP* 187 A-B48
Handel Av *VAN* 183 A20
Handley Av *RMD* 182 D11
Handley Cr *PCQ* 146 T42
Handsworth Rd *DNV* 122 J14 123 J15 J15-16
Hanes Av *CNV* 123 N15
Haney By-Pass *MAP* 187 A52 A-B53
Haney Pl *MAP* 187 Z52
Hankin Dr *RMD* 202 E8
Hanna Ct *BUR* 184 A25
Hansard Cr *CQT* 145 T37
Hansen Rd *SUR* 185 B34-35
Hansom Rd *FRA* 254 Q11
Happy Valley La *WVA* 121 L2-3
Harbour Av *DNV* 143 P-Q20 Q20
Harbour Av *MIS* 230 K75
Harbour Dr *CQT* 165 U33-34
Harbour Pl *PMD* 145 R34
Harbour Rd *DNV* 143 Q21
Harbour St *PCQ* 166 X40
Harbour Stroll *DEL* 223 P16
Harbour View Pl *SQM* 301 J-K2
Harbourgreene Dr *SUR* 265 V31
Harbourside Dr *CNV* 143 P15
Harbourside Pl *CNV* 143 P15
Harbourview Rd *BUR* 144 R23
Harder *CHL* 232 P94 252 Q94
Hardie Av *WRK* 265 X36-37
Hardwick St *BUR* 164 W23-24
Hardy Cr *DNV* 123 N22
Hardy Pl *DEL* 204 F29
Hardy Rd *DEL* 204 E-F29
Hardy Rd *KNT* 155 T18 175 U18
Hardy St *MAP* 167 Y50
Hare Av *CHL* 232 P92
Harford St *CHL* 193 D7 213 E7
Hargitt Pl *MIS* 210 F73-74
Hargitt St *ABT* 230 L76
Harken Dr *BUR* 163 X22
Harkness Ct *MAP* 167 Y51
Harley Ct *BUR* 163 Y22 164 Y23
Harmony Bay *SUR* 266 V-W39
Harmony Ct *ABT* 250 S71
Harmony Ct *WHS* 401 G2
Harmony Pl *SUR* 265 V-W38
Harms St *MIS* 210 G75
Haro St *VAN* 10 E35 G36 142 R12 S13
Harold Rd *DNV* 123 L19 L20
Harold St *VAN* 163 Y20
Harper Ct *BUR* 163 X21
Harper Dr *ABT* 250 U78 251 U79
Harper Rd *CQT* 146 P-Q41
Harper Rd *SUR* 185 B34
Harrier Dr *CQT* 145 S36
Harriet St *VAN* 163 W16
Harris Av *CQT* 165 X32
Harris Av *DNV* 124 N26
Harris Pl *DEL* 263 X16-17
Harris Pl *DNV* 124 N26
Harris Rd *ABT* 229 N64-65 N67-70 230 N71-78 231 N79
Harris Rd *PTM* 146 T45-46 166 U45-46 V45-46 X46 186 A46 Z46
Harris Rd *SQM* 301 E3
Harris St *MIS* 210 G73
Harrison Av *CQT* 165 U31
Harrison Av *RMD* 203 E15-16
Harrison Dr *VAN* 183 A17-18
Harrison St *CHL* 193 D6
Harrison St *MAP* 187 A53
Harrogate Dr *DEL* 204 G27-28
Hart St *CQT* 165 X31
Hartford Pl *DNV* 144 P23
Hartley Av *CQT* 165 Y34-35
Hartley St *VAN* 183 B19
Hartman Av *MIS* 210 E76
Hartnell Pl *ABT* 250 R78
Hartnell Rd *RMD* 223 K15-16
Harvard Dr *PMD* 145 S31-32
Harvard Pl *CHL* 213 G6
Harvest Dr *ABT* 251 S79-80
Harvest Dr *DEL* 243 Q17-18
Harvey St *NEW* 184 Z30
Harvie Rd *SUR* 206 F45 G-H44 H-J43
Harwood Av *CQT* 146 R39
Harwood Cr *ABT* 250 R-S74
Harwood Pl *ABT* 250 R74
Harwood St *VAN* 10 G34 H35 142 S12
Hashizume Ter *MIS* 210 G73
Hastings Pl *PCQ* 145 T38 146 T39
Hastings St *BUR* 143 S21-22 144 S23-26
Hastings St *NEW* 184 A30
Hastings St *PCQ* 146 T39 166 U39
Hastings St E *VAN* 11 H41 143 S16-20
Hastings St W *VAN* 11 F37 G39 142 R13 S14
Haszard St *BUR* 164 X25-26 Y25
Hatton Av *BUR* 144 T26
Haven Pl *SUR* 265 V31
Haverhill Pl *DNV* 123 L20
Haverman Rd *ABT* 229 P64-67

Haversley / Hunt

Haversley Av CQT 165 W33-35
Haviland St DEL 223 P16 243 Q16
Hawkins Rd ABT 229 P69
Hawkins Pickle Rd FRA 211 E83-86
Hawks Av VAN 143 S-T16
Hawkstream Dr SUR 205 H35
Hawksview Pl ABT 251 S80
Hawser Av CQT 145 T36
Hawstead Pl WVA 122 J13
Hawthorn Dr PMD 145 P-Q35
Hawthorne CHL 194 C13
Hawthorne Av ABT 270 W74-75
Hawthorne Av MIS 210 G74
Hawthorne Av PCQ 165 V38 166 V39
Hawthorne Pl DEL 243 Q18
Hawthorne Pl KNT 175 X20
Hawthorne Pl WHS 401 F3
Hawthorne St MAP 187 Z54
Hawthorne Ter BUR 184 A25 Z25
Hayashi Ct RMD 222 K-L9
Hayes St WVA 121 L6
Hayle Pl SUR 225 K33
Hayne Ct RMD 182 D14
Hayseed Cl DNV 123 M22
Hayton Rd ABT 230 L77
Hayward Connector MIS 209 F67
Hayward La CQT 145 R37
Hayward Pl DEL 204 F30
Hayward Pl MIS 209 F67
Hayward Rd KNT 195 Z20
Hayward St MIS 189 C-D67 209 E-F67
Haywood Av WVA 122 L10-11 L11 L9-10
Hazel Cr MIS 210 G74
Hazel Ct DEL 223 P17
Hazel Ct SUR 186 C40
Hazel Dr CQT 146 P40
Hazel St BUR 163 Y22 164 Y23
Hazel St CHL 193 D8 213 E8 F8
Hazel St HOP 118 D44
Hazelbridge Way RMD 182 D12 202 E12
Hazellynn Pl DNV 123 M20
Hazelmere St BUR 164 Y26
Hazelnut Gr KNT 175 W20
Hazelnut Pl BUR 164 X29
Hazelton St VAN 143 T19-20
Hazelwood Av ABT 250 S76-77
Hazelwood Cr BUR 163 X21-22
Hazelwood St MAP 187 B48
Headland Cl WVA 121 K3
Headland Ct WVA 121 K3
Headland Dr WVA 121 J-K4 K3
Headland Pl WVA 121 K3
Health Sciences Rd UEL 161 U4
Hearthstone Ct ABT 250 R77-78
Heath Cr CQT 145 S36-37
Heath Cr DEL 204 J29
Heath Rd KNT 175 W-X21
Heathdale Ct BUR 144 T23-24
Heathdale Dr BUR 144 T23 164 U23
Heather Av HOP 118 G42
Heather Av MIS 210 H-J75
Heather Av PCQ 146 S40
Heather Dr ABT 270 V76-77
Heather Pl PMD 145 R35
Heather Pl RMD 202 J13
Heather St CHL 193 D7-8
Heather St RMD 202 G-H13
Heather St VAN 162 U-X13 182 A13 B13 Z13
Heatherstone Pl ABT 251 U80
Heatley Av VAN 143 S-T16
Hebb Av VAN 163 V19
Hecate Pl VAN 183 Z20-21
Heckbert Pl CQT 165 U37
Hedge Av BUR 184 Z27
Hedgestone Ct CQT 145 Q-R38
Hedley Av BUR 184 A25 Z25
Hedley St ABT 250 S72
Heffley Cr CQT 145 S38
Helc Pl SUR 245 T38
Helen Dr PCQ 165 X38
Helen Dr SUR 185 D32
Helm Pl WHS 401 G2
Helmcken St VAN 11 H37 142 S-T13
Helston Cr SUR 225 K32
Hemlock Av HOP 118 E44
Hemlock Av MAP 167 U54
Hemlock Av SQM 301 J-K3
Hemlock Cr ABT 250 U76
Hemlock Cr PCQ 146 T42
Hemlock Ct VAN 10 K36
Hemlock Dr ANM 125 N33
Hemlock Pl PMD 145 R36
Hemlock St ABT 250 U72 270 V72
Hemlock St CHL 193 D7
Hemlock St FRA 253 R5
Hemlock St MIS 210 H-J71
Hemlock St VAN 162 U-V12
Hendecourt Pl DNV 123 L19
Hendecourt Rd DNV 123 L19
Henderson Av CHL 193 D6 213 E6
Henderson Av CQT 165 X31-32
Henderson Av DNV 123 K-L20
Henderson Rd FRA 272 Z90-92
Henderson St MIS 210 F-G74
Hendon St ABT 250 S77
Hendry Av DNV 123 N18-19
Hendry Pl NEW 184 D27
Hengestone Ct ABT 250 S77-78
Henley Av ABT 250 T-U77
Henley Av CHL 193 D6
Henley St NEW 184 A27
Henlow Rd WVA 122 J12
Hennepin Av VAN 183 Z20
Henning Dr BUR 163 U21
Henry Av MIS 210 G78
Henry St CHL 233 K7
Henry St PMD 145 T33
Henry St VAN 163 W-X16
Herar La MIS 210 G76
Herbert Rd RMD 202 H-J12
Hereford Pl SUR 226 M41
Heritage Blvd DNV 143 P21
Heritage Dr ABT 249 S69
Heritage Dr CHL 233 K6
Heritage Mountain Blvd PMD 145 R-S35
Heritage Peaks Tr WHS 401 H2
Hermitage Dr RMD 202 J9 222 K9
Hermon Dr VAN 163 U20
Hermosa Av DNV 123 K16
Hermosa Dr DEL 204 H28
Heron Av ABT 249 T70
Heron Pl VAN 183 A20
Heron Pl WHS 401 F3
Heron St MIS 210 H72
Heron Bay Cl DEL 223 P16
Herring Pl PTM 187 Z47
Herrmann St CQT 165 U37
Herron Av CHL 193 D6
Hersham Av BUR 164 Y26 184 Z26
Hertford St BUR 163 X21
Hess Rd FRA 211 D-E85
Hesslea Cr ABT 229 K63
Hett Creek Dr PMD 145 Q34
Hewitt St BUR 144 T26
Heywood St CNV 143 P19
Hialeah Ct CQT 145 S37
Hiawatha Dr WVA 122 M-N12
Hibbard Av CQT 165 U32
Hibiscus Ct ABT 251 U79
Hickey Dr CQT 165 W35-36
Hickory Ct BUR 164 W23
Hickory Dr PMD 145 P35
Hickory La ABT 251 U79
Hickory St PCQ 146 T41
Hideaway Bay SUR 266 W39
Hidhurst Pl WVA 122 K13
Hie Av CQT 165 X34
Hiebert St CHL 213 E8
Higgins Ct MAP 167 Y51
Higginson Cr ABT 270 W76
Higginson Rd CHL 233 K6-8
High Dr ABT 250 S-T78
High St WRK 265 W36 X36
High St, The CQT 145 S38
High Park Av SUR 246 S39-40
High Point Dr WHS 401 H2
High Rock Passage WVA 121 K-L2
High View Pl PMD 145 T32
Highbury St VAN 142 T8 162 U-W8 W8 X8 X-Y8
Highfield Cr ABT 250 U77
Highfield Dr BUR 144 R-S24
Highgate St VAN 163 X18
Highland Av ABT 250 S74
Highland Blvd DNV 123 K15
Highland Cr ANM 125 N33
Highland Dr CHL 252 R93
Highland Dr CQT 146 Q40-41
Highland Dr WVA 122 J12 K11-12 K12
Highland Pl DNV 123 K15-16
Highland Pl WVA 122 J11-12
Highland Way PMD 145 S35-36
Highlands Way N SQM 301 E4
Highlands Way S SQM 301 E-F4
Highlawn Dr BUR 143 T22 163 U22 164 U23
Highroad Cr CHL 233 N8
Highview Pl LIO 101 C23-24
Highview Pl MAP 167 Y51
Highview St ABT 270 W75
Highway WVA 121 L3-4
Hilary Pl DNV 123 N21
Hilda St BUR 184 Z27
Hill Av BUR 164 X27 Y28
Hill Av MAP 188 D55-56
Hill Av MIS 210 H74
Hill Dr BUR 184 A25
Hill Dr DNV 124 M23
Hill St NEW 184 A27
Hill-Tout St ABT 250 U71
Hilland Av MAP 168 Y58
Hillcrest Av ABT 250 U72-73
Hillcrest Av DNV 122 K14
Hillcrest Av MIS 210 J71-72
Hillcrest Dr CHL 194 C-D10
Hillcrest Dr WHS 401 G2-3
Hillcrest La WHS 401 G2
Hillcrest St CQT 165 V-W35
Hillcrest St WVA 121 K-L6
Hillier St CHL 193 D6
Hillkeep Pl CHL 213 G1
Hillman Rd FRA 211 D85
Hillside Av CQT 165 Y34
Hillside Cr DEL 224 L29
Hillside Dr ABT 250 U75
Hillside Pl BUR 164 U28
Hillside Rd SUR 225 N31
Hillside Rd WVA 122 J12
Hillside St MAP 167 Y52
Hillview Cr ABT 270 V78
Hillview Ct SUR 246 T42
Hillview Pl SUR 246 T42
Hillview St BUR 164 V25-26
Hilton Dr CHL 213 G7
Hilton Rd SUR 185 B33-34 B34
Hinch Cr MAP 167 Y52-53
Hinkley Rd CHL 214 J14 234 K15
Hipwell Dr CHL 233 M5
Hirschman Rd FRA 254 Q10
Hitchingpost Cr LGT 248 Q57
Hixon Ct DNV 124 M25
Hixon Pl DNV 124 M25
Hockaday Pl CQT 146 Q39
Hockaday St CQT 146 Q39
Hockin Rd HOP 118 G43
Hocking Av CHL 213 F6-7
Hodgins Av CHL 213 E5-6
Hodgson Rd FRA 212 D92-93
Hodson Pl MIS 210 H75
Hoffmann Way PTM 186 B46
Hogarth Dr RMD 202 J11
Hogarth Pl RMD 202 J11 222 K11
Hogberg Rd FRA 231 N-P82
Holborn St CQT 165 W32
Holdom Av N BUR 144 S24
Holdom Av S BUR 144 S-T24 164 U24
Holdsworth Pl CQT 146 R39-40
Holiday Av MIS 210 H72
Holland Av ABT 270 V75
Holland Av PCQ 166 W42
Holland St NEW 184 B27
Holland St VAN 162 X-Y8
Hollis Pl BUR 184 A23
Hollister Pl MIS 210 G76
Holly CQT 145 S38 146 S39
Holly CQT 165 V-W37
Holly Av NEW 184 C28
Holly Dr PMD 145 Q35
Holly Rd KNT 175 W18-19
Holly St ABT 250 U72 270 V72
Holly St BUR 184 Z26
Holly St CHL 213 E8
Holly St MAP 167 Y50 187 A50 Z50
Holly Park Ct DEL 243 Q19
Holly Park Dr DEL 243 Q19
Holly Park La SUR 185 C36-37
Holly Park Pl DEL 243 Q19
Holly Park Wynd DEL 243 Q19
Hollybank Dr RMD 202 J10
Hollyberry Ct ABT 270 V76
Hollybridge Way RMD 202 E11
Hollybrook St CQT 146 R40
Hollycroft Dr RMD 202 J10
Hollycroft Gt RMD 202 J10
Hollyfield Av RMD 202 J10
Hollyhock La VAN 183 A20
Hollymount Dr RMD 202 J10 222 K10
Hollymount Gt RMD 202 J10
Hollywell Dr RMD 202 J10
Hollywood Av ABT 250 U73
Hollywood Dr RMD 202 J10
Holmbury Pl WVA 122 K-L12
Holmes St BUR 164 X30
Holmes St NEW 164 X30
Holstein St SUR 226 M41
Holt Av RMD 202 F10
Holt Rd (120A St) SUR 205 F31
Holyrood Av MAP 187 A53
Holyrood Rd DNV 123 L17
Homer Mews VAN 10 K36 142 T13
Homer Pl CHL 213 F5
Homer St VAN 11 H38 J37 142 S14 T13
Homestead Cr ABT 250 S71
Homesteader Ct PCQ 165 Y38
Homesteader Way PCQ 165 Y38
Homeview St ABT 250 U75
Homfeld Pl PCQ 166 V-W40
Honeydew Dr PTM 187 Z47
Honeyman St DEL 223 K21
Honeysuckle Dr CHL 213 F-G1
Honeysuckle La CQT 145 R36
Honeysuckle Pl DNV 103 H15
Hong Kong Dr CHL 233 N5-6
Hood Av MIS 210 G73
Hood Rd FRA 233 P8 253 Q8
Hood Rd SQM 301 E3
Hood St MAP 187 Z50
Hooge Rd CHL 233 N1
Hopcott Rd DEL 203 J20
Hope Pl HHS 155 R19
Hope Rd ABT 269 W-X68
Hope Rd DNV 122 M14
Hope Rd SQM 301 B1
Hope St HOP 118 D-E44
Hope St PMD 145 T32-33 T34
Hope River Rd CHL 193 C8 D7-8 194 C9-10
Hopedale Av ABT 250 T72
Hopedale Rd CHL 213 J1 233 K-M1
Hopedale Rd E CHL 233 N1
Hopedale Rd W CHL 233 N1
Horizon St ABT 270 V75
Horley St VAN 163 X19
Horn St ABT 250 S74
Hornby Dr DEL 224 P26-29
Hornby St CQT 146 R-S39
Hornby St VAN 10 H-J36 142 S-T13
Horne St BUR 164 W29
Horne St MIS 210 H74-75 J75 230 K75
Horseshoe Pl RMD 223 L15
Horseshoe Way RMD 223 K-L15
Horstman La WHS 401 E5 S23
Horstman Pl WHS 401 E5 S-T23
Hoskins Pl DNV 123 L20
Hoskins Rd DNV 123 J-K20 K-M20
Hoskins St DEL 203 H-J22
Hosmer Av VAN 162 V11
Hosmer Ct CQT 165 U38
Hospital La UEL 161 U4
Hospital Pl SQM 301 J-K2
Hospital St NEW 164 Y30
Hospital St WRK 265 W38
Hot Springs Rd HHS 155 P-Q19
Hot Springs Rd KNT 155 S-T19 175 U-V19
Hoult St NEW 164 X-Y30
Housman Pl RMD 222 K11
Housman St RMD 202 J11 222 K11
Houston St LGT 207 F53
Howard Av N BUR 144 S23-24
Howard Av S BUR 144 S23-24 T23 T23 164 U23
Howard Cr CHL 213 F8
Howard Ct WVA 121 K3
Howard Pl DEL 224 L29
Howard St RMD 202 E14
Howay St NEW 184 A28
Howe St VAN 11 G38 H37 142 S13-14
Howe Sound La WVA 121 L2-3
Howell Ct RMD 183 D15
Howell Rd FRA 212 F-G88
Howes St NEW 184 D26-27
Howey Rd SUR 185 B34
Howie Av CQT 165 W32-33
Howison Av MAP 187 Z51
Howse Pl CQT 165 W33
Hoy St CQT 145 T37 165 U37 U38
Hoy St VAN 163 W20 X20
Hoylake Av VAN 183 A18
Huber Dr PCQ 146 S42
Hubert St BUR 184 Z26
Huckleberry La DNV 103 H15
Huckleberry La PMD 145 R34-35
Huckleberry Pl CHL 213 F-G2
Huckleberry Pl DNV 103 H15
Hudson Av MIS 169 Y67
Hudson Av RMD 182 C11
Hudson Ct WVA 122 K9
Hudson Rd CHL 233 M8 234 M9
Hudson St CQT 145 R-S37
Hudson St VAN 162 V-W12 X-Y12 182 A-B12 Z12
Hudson Bay St HOP 118 E44-45
Hudson Bay St LGT 207 F54
Huff Blvd DEL 224 K29
Huggins Av ABT 250 T75
Hugh St PMD 145 T34
Hughes Pl PCQ 146 T39
Hughes Ter MIS 210 H75
Hull Ct CQT 145 T36
Hull St VAN 163 V17-18
Hum-Lu-Sum Dr VAN 162 Y8
Humber Cr PCQ 166 W39
Humber Pl DEL 204 F26-27
Humberside Av SUR 246 S39
Hume Av DEL 223 K21
Hume St NEW 184 D26
Humm St VAN 183 Z18
Hummel St BUR 164 U25
Hummingbird Dr ANM 145 Q34-35
Hummingbird Dr RMD 222 K10
Hummingbird Pl SUR 185 B37
Hummingbird Pl VAN 183 A20
Humphries Av BUR 164 Y26 184 Z26
Humphries Ct BUR 184 Z27
Humphries Pl BUR 164 Y25
Humphrys Dr HOP 118 H42
Hunt St RMD 222 K8

Hunter / Kenmore

Hunter Ct *BUR* ... **164** V-W27
Hunter Pl *MAP* ... **187** Z49
Hunter Pl *SQM* ... **301** J2
Hunter Pl *SUR* ... **226** M44
Hunter Rd *DEL* ... **263** X17
Hunter St *BUR* ... **164** W27-28
Hunter St *DNV* ... **143** P20
Huntingdon Cr *DNV* ... **124** N26 **144** P26
Huntingdon Rd *ABT* ... **269** X70 Y63-66 **270** X71-75
Huntington Pl *PCQ* ... **165** U38
Huntleigh Cr *DNV* . **144** P23-24
Huntleigh Ct *DNV* ... **144** P24
Huntley Av *SUR* ... **205** E33
Hurd St *MIS* ... **210** H-J72
Hurdle Cr *SUR* ... **205** J32
Hurndall Cr *CHL* ... **213** F8
Huron Dr *CQT* **145** T35 **165** U35
Huron Mews *VAN* ... **183** Z19
Huron St *CHL* ... **213** J6
Hurst Av *VAN* ... **183** Z20-21
Hurst Cr *ABT* ... **250** S77
Hurst Pl *VAN* ... **183** Z20
Hurst St *BUR* . **183** Z21 Z21-22
Huston Rd *CHL* ... **234** N13
Huston Rd *DEL* ... **203** H22
Hutcherson La *DEL* .. **243** Q17
Hutchinson Pl *PCQ* ... **166** W39-40
Huxley Av *BUR* ... **163** W22
Hyack Dr *VAN* ... **183** A20
Hyannis Dr *DNV* ... **124** M23
Hyannis Pt *DNV* ... **123** M22
Hyatt Pl *ABT* ... **250** U77
Hycrest Dr *BUR* ... **164** U25
Hycrest Pl *ABT* ... **250** U77
Hycroft Rd *WVA* ... **101** F-G1
Hycroft St *PMD* ... **145** R34-35
Hyde St *BUR* ... **164** V24
Hyde St *MIS* ... **210** H74
Hyde Buker Rd *FRA* ... **211** H81 H-J80
Hyde Park Pl *CQT* ... **146** R40
Hyfield Dr *FRA* ... **231** L83
Hylan Av *ABT* ... **250** U72-73
Hyland Creek *LGT* **207** F50-51
Hyland Dr *DEL* ... **224** L30
Hyland Pl *DEL* ... **224** L30
Hyland Rd *SUR* ... **225** K-L34 L35 L37
Hymar Dr *CHL* ... **193** C8
Hynes St *MAP* **188** B62 **189** B63
Hypwell Pl *CHL* ... **233** M5
Hythe Av N *BUR* ... **144** S23
Hythe Av S *BUR* ... **144** S23

I

Idylwood Pl *WHS* ... **401** C2-3
Ihles Av *MIS* ... **210** F75
Ikwikus Rd *WVA* .. **122** M-N13
Immel St *ABT* ... **250** S-T77
Imperial Av *LGC* ... **227** N48
Imperial Av *PCQ* ... **166** W39
Imperial Av *WVA* ... **101** G1
Imperial Dr *RMD* ... **222** L10
Imperial Gt *DEL* ... **263** W16
Imperial Pl *ABT* ... **250** U71
Imperial St *ABT* ... **250** U71
Imperial St *BUR* ... **164** Y26 ... **183** Z21-22 **184** Z23-24 Z26
Imperial St *CHL* ... **194** C10
Indian Rd *ABT* ... **251** T83
Indian Fort Dr *SUR* .. **265** V31
Indian Reserve Rd *DNV* ... **144** P24
Indian River Cr *DNV* . **124** M25
Indian River Dr *DNV* ... **124** L27-28 L-M26 M-N25
Industrial Av *ABT* ... **250** S76
Industrial Av *LGC* **227** M47 N48
Industrial Av *PCQ* ... **166** W40
Industrial Av *VAN* ... **11** K41 **163** U15
Industrial Rd *KNT* . **175** W-X22
Industrial Rd *SUR* ... **185** A31
Industrial Way *ABT* .. **270** Y77
Industrial Way *CHL* ... **212** H94 J93 **213** H1-2
Industrial Way *SQM* . **301** H1-2
Ingersoll Av *PMD* . **145** T31-32
Ingleside Ct *BUR* ... **164** V27
Ingleton Av *BUR* ... **143** R21 S-T21 **163** U21 V21 W21
Inglewood Av *WVA* ... **122** L10-12 L12-13 L9-10
Inglewood Cr *CHL* .. **193** D7-8
Inglewood Pl *DEL* ... **224** M30
Inglewood Pl *WVA* ... **122** L13
Inglis Dr *RMD* ... **202** E10
Inkman Rd *KNT* ... **175** W20
Inlet Cr *DNV* ... **124** N25
Inlet Dr *BUR* ... **144** S26
Inlet St *CQT* ... **145** S38
Inman Av *BUR* .. **163** W21 X21
Inman Cl *BUR* ... **163** W21
Innsbruck Dr *WHS* ... **401** H2
Innsmoor Pl *BUR* .. **164** X-Y27
Insley Av *CHL* ... **233** L5
Institute Rd *DNV* ... **123** L20
Inter-Provincial Hwy *ABT* ... **232** N-P89 **252** Q-U89 **272** V89
International Av *ABT* . **270** Z77
International Pl *RMD* . **203** E17
Invergarry Av *BUR* **144** S25 T25
Inverness Pl *PCQ* ... **146** T42
Inverness Pl *SUR* ... **205** F33
Inverness St *ABT* ... **250** S74
Inverness St *PCQ* .. **146** S-T42
Inverness St *VAN* ... **163** V-X16 X-Y16 **183** A16 Z16
Ioco Rd *PMD* ... **145** Q31-32 R34 S35
Iona Dr *UEL* ... **161** T3-4
Iona Pl *SUR* ... **205** E31
Ireland Av *MIS* ... **210** G77
Irene Av *CHL* ... **233** L6
Irene Pl *DNV* ... **123** J21
Iris *CQT* ... **165** V37
Iris Av *BUR* ... **164** W24
Iris Pl *CHL* ... **233** M5
Iris Pl *SUR* ... **265** V38
Irmin St *BUR* ... **183** A21 A21-22 A22 A22 ... **184** A23 A23 A24
Iron Ct *DNV* ... **124** M-N25
Ironwood *CQT* ... **146** S39
Ironwood Ct *PMD* . **145** R35-36
Ironwood Pl *DEL* ... **263** Y18
Ironwork Passage *VAN* ... **10** L36 **162** U13
Irvine Av *PCQ* ... **166** V39
Irvine St *CQT* ... **165** U38
Irving St *BUR* . **164** Y23 Y23-24
Irving St *MAP* **167** Y48 **187** Z48
Irwin Rd *DEL* ... **244** Q-R28
Isa La Av *CHL* ... **253** Q5
Isaac Cr *MAP* . **167** Y51 Y51-52
Isabel Pl *VAN* ... **182** A11
Island Av *VAN* ... **183** A17
Island Park Walk *VAN* ... **10** K34-35 L35 **142** T12 **162** U12
Isleview Pl *LIO* ... **101** B23
Isleview Rd *WVA* ... **101** F1
Israel Av *MIS* ... **210** H71
Ito Pl *MIS* ... **210** H74
Ivanhoe St *VAN* ... **163** X-Y19
Ivar Pl *BUR* ... **164** W-X23
Iverson Cr *DEL* ... **204** G27
Iverson Rd *FRA* **272** W-X93 Y90
Ivy Av *BUR* ... **183** B21
Ivy Av *CHL* ... **233** K7
Ivy Av *CQT* ... **165** V31
Ivy Ct *ABT* ... **250** S78
Ivy Ct *MIS* ... **210** H75
Ivywood Pl *DEL* ... **224** M30
Izon Ct *MAP* ... **167** Y52

J

Jacana Av *PCQ* ... **166** X39-40
Jack Adams Rd *MAP* **187** B47
Jack Bell Dr *RMD* ... **183** D16 **203** E16
Jackson Av *VAN* ... **11** G-J41 **143** S-T15
Jackson Cr *NEW* ... **164** Y29
Jackson Rd *MAP* .. **188** C-D57
Jackson St *ABT* . **270** V74 W74
Jackson St *CHL* ... **213** E5-6
Jackson St *CQT* ... **165** X31
Jackson Way *DEL* ... **263** X18
Jacobs Rd *PMD* ... **145** R34
Jacobs Rd *WVA* ... **122** N13
Jacobsen St *MIS* ... **189** C-D69
Jacobson Way *RMD* ... **223** K15-16
Jacombs Rd *RMD* ... **183** D16 **203** E16
Jade Ct *RMD* ... **202** F10
Jade Dr *ABT* ... **251** U79
Jade Manor *DEL* ... **223** P17
Jade Pl *CQT* ... **145** Q36
Jade Pl *FRA* ... **195** D20
Jade Tree Ct *VAN* ... **183** A20
James Av *CQT* ... **165** X32
James Pl *DEL* ... **204** F28-29
James Rd *PMD* ... **145** T34-35
James Rd E *DNV* . **123** L17-18
James St *ABT* ... **250** U73
James St *BUR* ... **163** Y21-22
James St *CHL* ... **214** E9
James St *MIS* ... **210** J74
James St *VAN* ... **162** X14 **163** W15 X15
James Walk *VAN* ... **162** X14
Jamieson Ct *NEW* **184** A30 Z30
Jamison Rd *FRA* .. **231** K82-83
Jane St *PCQ* ... **165** U38
Jane St *PMD* ... **145** T33-34
Janis St *CHL* ... **233** M5
Janovick Rd *FRA* ... **272** W94
Janzen Av *MIS* ... **210** G73-74
Janzen Rd *CHL* ... **232** L94
Janzen St *ABT* ... **250** U71-72
Japonica Pl *CQT* ... **145** Q37
Jardine St *NEW* ... **184** D26
Jarvis St *CQT* ... **165** U32
Jaskow Dr *RMD* ... **202** H10
Jaskow Gt *RMD* ... **202** H10
Jaskow Pl *RMD* ... **202** H10
Jasmine Ct *CQT* ... **145** R36
Jasper Av *MIS* ... **210** H77
Jasper Cr *VAN* ... **183** A17
Jasper Ct *ABT* ... **250** U73
Jasper Ct *CQT* ... **165** W34
Jasper Dr *CHL* ... **213** J5
Jasper Ter *MIS* ... **210** H77
Jay Cr *SQM* ... **301** D4
Jay Cr *SUR* ... **185** B37
Jay Pl *SQM* ... **301** D4
Jean Ct *ABT* ... **250** T71
Jedburgh Pl *SUR* . **205** F32-33
Jefferson Av *CQT* ... **164** U30
Jefferson Av *WVA* ... **122** L10 L11 L11-12 L9-10
Jellicoe St *VAN* ... **183** A-B19
Jennings St *MIS* ... **210** G74
Jenny Lewis Av *LGT* . **207** E53
Jensen Av *PCQ* ... **146** T40
Jensen Dr *RMD* ... **203** E15-16
Jensen Gt *RMD* ... **183** D16 **203** E16
Jensen Pl *BUR* ... **164** W27
Jericho Cir *VAN* **142** T7 **162** U7
Jericho Rd *RMD* ... **182** C-D10
Jerome Pl *DNV* ... **123** J-K21
Jersey Av *BUR* ... **163** X-Y21
Jersey Dr *SUR* ... **226** M41
Jervis Cr *ABT* ... **250** S-T72
Jervis Ct *ABT* ... **250** S-T72
Jervis Mews *VAN* ... **11** F37 **142** R13
Jervis St *PCQ* **145** T38 **165** U38
Jervis St *VAN* ... **10** G36 **142** R13 S12 S12-13
Jesmond Av *RMD* .. **202** H-J8
Jesperson Rd *CHL* ... **194** A12
Jess Rd *CHL* ... **194** Z11
Jewel Av *CHL* ... **233** L6
Jewel Ct *ABT* ... **251** U79
Jibset Bay *DEL* ... **223** N16
Jimmie Rd *CHL* ... **213** F4-5
Jinkerson Rd *CHL* ... **234** M9
Joan St *ABT* ... **250** T72
Joanita Pl *ABT* ... **229** K64
Joe Sakic Way *BUR* . **164** V25
Joffre Av *BUR* **183** A21 B21 Z21
John Pl *CHL* ... **233** K7-8
John St *VAN* ... **163** W15
Johnson Av *RMD* ... **202** F8
Johnson Ct *CQT* ... **145** R37
Johnson Rd *FRA* .. **212** D-F88
Johnson Rd *HOP* ... **118** D48
Johnson Rd *KNT* ... **175** X22
Johnson St *CHL* ... **193** D8
Johnson St *CQT* ... **145** Q-T37
Johnson Wynd *DEL* . **204** G27
Johnston Rd *WRK* . **265** W-X37
Johnston St *NEW* ... **184** C27
Johnston St *VAN* ... **10** K35 **142** T12 **162** U12
Jones Av *CNV* . **123** L16 M-N16
Jones Av *DNV* ... **123** L16
Jones Dr *CHL* ... **194** C-D11
Jones Rd *FRA* ... **211** G85
Jones Rd *RMD* .. **202** G12-13
Jones Ter *MIS* ... **210** F-G77
Jonquil Ct *ABT* ... **251** U79
Jordan Dr *BUR* ... **164** U25
Jordan La *WHS* ... **401** H1
Jordan Pl *ABT* ... **271** V79
Jordan St *CQT* ... **145** R37
Joshua Pl *ABT* ... **271** V79
Joyce Av *ABT* ... **270** V72
Joyce Dr *FRA* ... **253** R6
Joyce St *CQT* ... **165** W32
Joyce St *VAN* . **163** X20 Y19-20
Joyner Pl *PTM* **186** A46 **187** A47
Jubilee Av *BUR* .. **184** A23 Z23
Jubilee Ct *DNV* ... **124** N25
Judd Ct *CQT* ... **165** U38
Judd Rd *SQM* ... **301** C1-3
Judd Ter *MIS* ... **210** F73
Judith Av *CHL* ... **233** L6
Judith St *MIS* ... **210** G74
Julian Av *CQT* ... **145** R38
Junction Av *ABT* . **249** T63-64
June Cr *PCQ* ... **165** X38
Juneau St *BUR* ... **163** U22
Juniper *CQT* ... **146** S39
Juniper Av *PCQ* ... **146** T41
Juniper Cr *ABT* ... **250** S76
Juniper Cr *SQM* ... **301** J3
Juniper Dr *RMD* ... **202** H11
Juniper Gt *RMD* ... **202** H11
Juniper Pl *DEL* ... **263** Y17
Juniper Pl *HHS* ... **155** Q19
Juniper Pl *PMD* ... **145** R36
Juniper Pl *WHS* ... **401** F3
Juniper St *CHL* ... **193** D7
Juniper St *MIS* ... **210** H-J74
Jura Cr *SQM* ... **301** E4-5
Justice Way *ABT* .. **250** T-U72

K

K St *HOP* ... **118** C43
K de K Ct *NEW* ... **184** B-C29
Kadenwood Dr *WHS* **401** H1-2
Kadlec Ct *WVA* ... **122** J-K9
Kadota Dr *DEL* ... **263** X16
Kahana Pl *ABT* ... **251** U79
Kahu Ct *ABT* ... **271** V79
Kaiser St *CQT* ... **145** S36-37
Kalamalka Cr *RMD* .. **202** F11
Kalamalka Dr *CQT* ... **165** V37
Kaleigh Ct *ABT* ... **251** R79
Kalmar Rd *SUR* .. **185** B34-35
Kalodon Rd *SQM* ... **301** E-F3
Kalyk Av *BUR* ... **163** V-W21
Kalyna Dr *KNT* ... **175** X20
Kamloops Pl *PCQ* ... **146** T41
Kamloops St *NEW* **184** B27-28
Kamloops St *VAN* .. **143** R-T18 ... **163** U18 U-V18 V18 W18
Kamloops St N *VAN* ... **143** R-S18
Kanaka La *MAP* ... **188** B55
Kanaka St *LGT* ... **207** E53
Kanaka Way *MAP* ... **187** B54 **188** A-B55
Kanaka Creek Rd *MAP* ... **188** B55
Kaptey Av *CQT* ... **165** X34-35
Karen Cr *WHS* ... **401** H2
Karen Dr *CHL* ... **213** F8
Karen Dr *FRA* ... **253** R6
Karen St *BUR* ... **164** U25
Karley Cr *CQT* ... **146** R39
Karp Ct *CQT* ... **165** W33
Karr Pl *DEL* ... **204** G27
Karrman Av *BUR* ... **164** Y29
Karson Rd *CHL* ... **252** S93
Kartner Rd *RMD* ... **203** E-F20
Kaslo Ct *ABT* ... **270** W75
Kaslo St *VAN* ... **143** R-T19 **163** U-W19
Kaslo St N *VAN* ... **143** R-S19
Kaslo Ter *ABT* ... **270** W75
Kathleen Av *BUR* ... **163** Y22
Kathleen Dr *CHL* ... **233** M5
Kathleen Pl *WHS* ... **401** H1-2
Kathryn St *MAP* ... **169** Y63
Katzie Rd *MAP* ... **186** B46 **187** B47
Katzie Rd *PTM* ... **186** A46
Kaw Rd *HOP* ... **118** D48
Kawkawa Lake Rd *HOP* ... **118** D48 E45-47
Kawtin Rd *WVA* ... **122** N13
Kay Av *ABT* ... **270** V74
Kaylela Pl *DNV* ... **143** P20
Kaymar Dr *BUR* ... **183** A21
Ke Kait Pl *VAN* ... **162** Y8
Kearns Av *MAP* ... **188** D62 **208** E62
Keary St *NEW* **164** Y30 **165** Y31
Keats Ct *ABT* ... **270** W74-75
Keats Rd *DNV* ... **123** N22
Keats St *ABT* ... **270** W75
Kebet Way *PCQ* .. **166** X40-41
Keefer Av *RMD* ... **202** G13
Keefer Pl *VAN* ... **11** H39-40
Keefer St *VAN* ... **11** H39-41 ... **142** S14 **143** S15-16 S16
Keeping Rd *ABT* ... **251** Q82
Keets Dr *CQT* ... **165** U-V37
Keeves Pl *MIS* ... **169** X68-69
Kehler St *CHL* ... **252** Q93
Keil Cr *WRK* .. **265** X38 **266** X39
Keil St *WRK* . **265** W38 **266** W39
Keith Dr *CQT* ... **146** R40
Keith Dr *VAN* ... **163** U-V16
Keith Pl *CQT* ... **146** R39-40
Keith Pl *WVA* ... **122** M13
Keith Rd *DNV* ... **123** M15
Keith Rd (Ambleside) *WVA* ... **122** M11-13
Keith Rd (Cypress Park) *WVA* ... **121** J3 J-K3 K4 K-L4
Keith Rd (Horseshoe Bay) *WVA* ... **101** G2
Keith Rd E *CNV* ... **123** N17 **143** P17 P17-18
Keith Rd E *DNV* . **143** P19-21
Keith Rd W *CNV* . **123** N16-17
Keith Rd W *DNV* .. **122** M14
Keith St *BUR* ... **183** B21 **184** A23-24
Keith Wilson Rd *CHL* ... **232** N92-94 **233** M3-6
Kelleher St *ABT* ... **210** J77 **230** K77
Kelley Cr *CHL* ... **253** Q6
Kelly Av *PCQ* . **165** V38 **166** V39
Kelly Dr *DEL* ... **243** Q15
Kelly Pl *DEL* ... **243** Q15
Kelly Rd *ABT* ... **251** T83
Kelly Rd *BEL* ... **124** N29
Kelly St *NEW* ... **164** Y30
Kelmer Cr *ABT* ... **270** V76
Kelmore Rd *RMD* ... **202** H8-9
Kelowna St *VAN* ... **143** T19
Kelso Ct *CQT* ... **165** W34
Kelvin St *CQT* ... **165** U32
Kelvin Grove Way *LIO* **101** C23
Kemi Pl *MAP* ... **167** Y52
Kemp St *BUR* ... **163** Y22
Kempley Ct *ABT* ... **270** W75
Kemprud St *ABT* .. **250** Q-R75
Kempson Cr *DEL* ... **224** L29
Kempton Pl *VAN* .. **183** Z18-19
Kemsley Av *CQT* ... **165** U31
Kendal Pl *DNV* ... **122** K14
Kendale Ct *BUR* ... **164** U25
Kendale Pl *ABT* ... **270** V73
Kendale Pl *DEL* ... **204** E29
Kendale View *DEL* ... **204** E29
Kendale Way *DEL* ... **204** E29
Kendrick La *MAP* ... **167** Y53
Kendrick Loop *MAP* ... **167** Y52-53
Kendrick Pl *MAP* ... **167** Y53
Keneng Ct *CQT* ... **165** V33
Kenmore Dr *SUR* ... **205** E34

N

Normandy / Parker

Normandy Rd VAN 162 U7-8
Norquay St VAN 163 W-X18
Norrish Av CHL 213 F7
Norrish Av MIS 210 H77
North Av MAP 187 Z52
North Dr SUR 266 V39
North Pl SUR 266 V39
North Rd CQT 164 U-W30
North Bend St CQT 165 Y36
North Bluff Rd WRK 265 W36-37
North Burgess Av ABT 229 M69-70
North Dyke Rd RMD 182 A8-9
North Fraser Cr BUR 183 A-B22
North Fraser Ct BUR 183 C22
North Fraser Way BUR 183 B21-22 184 C24-25 C-D23
North Nicomen Rd FRA 212 D90 D91
North Parallel Rd ABT 232 P88 251 R85-86 T83 252 Q87 271 V80-81
North Railway Av MIS 210 J74-75
North Service Rd RMD 182 C10
North Sward Rd FRA 190 D78 210 E78
Northbrook Ct BUR 183 B21
Northcliffe Cr BUR 144 S25-26
Northcote Cr MIS 210 J75
Northcote St MIS 210 J75
Northcrest Dr SUR 245 T-U35
Northdale Ct ABT 250 S71
Northern Av CQT 145 S37-38
Northern St VAN 11 K41 143 T15
Northey Rd RMD 182 D13
Northglen Cl SUR 186 C39-40
Northglen Pl SUR 186 C39
Northlands Blvd WHS 401 E-F4 S21
Northlands Dr DNV 124 N23
Northlawn Dr BUR 143 T22 144 T23
Northmount Av MIS 210 H74
Northpark Cr SUR 225 M31
Northpark Pl SUR 225 M31
Northridge Dr SQM 301 J3
Northumberland Av VAN 183 A20
Northview Cr DEL 224 K29
Northview Cr SUR 246 T40
Northview Ct BUR 163 X22
Northview Pl ABT 250 T75
Northview Pl DEL 224 K-L29
Northview St CHL 193 D6
Northwood Dr WVA 121 J4
Norton Ct DNV 124 N25
Norton Ct RMD 204 E24-25
Norum Cr DEL 204 F28
Norum Pl DEL 204 F28
Norum Rd DEL 204 F28-29
Norwood Av DNV 123 K17 K-L17
Norwood Ct CQT 125 N38
Nottingham Pl PCQ 166 X39
Nottingham Rd DNV 123 K20
Nottman St MIS 210 G74
Nova Scotia Av PCQ 166 X39
Novak Dr CQT 146 R40
Nowell St CHL 213 E-F7
Nugget St PCQ 166 X39-40
Nulelum Way DEL 263 V-W16
Nurseries Rd UEL 161 W5
Nursery St BUR 164 X26
Nuthatch Pl DNV 103 H15
NW Marine Dr UEL 161 S-T4 T-U3

O

O'Byrne Rd FRA 254 Q16 255 Q17
O'Flaherty Gt PCQ 165 X-Y38
O'Hara La SUR 245 T31
Oak CQT 165 V-W37
Oak Av ABT 250 U72
Oak Bay SUR 266 W39
Oak Ct ANM 125 N32
Oak Gt SUR 186 C40
Oak La MIS 210 J74
Oak Pl DEL 243 Q16-17
Oak Pl SQM 301 C3
Oak St CHL 193 D7
Oak St FRA 253 R-S5
Oak St NEW 184 A29
Oak St VAN 162 V-Y13 182 A-B13 Z13
Oak Ter PTM 166 Y46
Oakdale Rd BUR 164 Y23
Oakdale St PCQ 146 S41-42
Oakglen Dr BUR 164 X-Y23
Oakhill Dr ABT 250 U78
Oakhill Pl BUR 164 Y25
Oakland Pl BUR 164 Y23
Oakland St BUR 164 Y23-25
Oakland St NEW 184 A29
Oakmond Rd RMD 202 H8
Oakmount Cr BUR 164 Y23
Oakridge Cr ABT 270 V71
Oaktree Ct BUR 164 X23
Oakview St CQT 165 U32
Oakwood Cr DNV 122 N13-14
Oakwood Dr KNT 175 X20
Oban Pl SUR 205 E33
Oben St VAN 163 X-Y20
Oboe Pl WHS 401 E3
Ocean Pl WVA 121 J2
Ocean Breeze Pl SUR 265 V31-32
Ocean Cliff Dr SUR 265 V32
Ocean Forest Dr SUR 265 V32
Ocean Forest Pl SUR 265 V32
Ocean Park Rd SUR 265 V-W31 V-W32
Ocean Surf Pl SUR 265 V-W32
Ocean Tide Ct SUR 265 V31
Ocean View La SQM 301 J2-3 K3
Ocean Wind Dr SUR 265 V32
Oceanview Pl LIO 101 C23
Oceanview Rd LIO 101 C23-24
Odd St HOP 118 E44
Odell St MAP 189 D63
Odlin Cr RMD 182 D13
Odlin Pl RMD 182 D13
Odlin Rd RMD 182 D13-14
Odlum Ct WVA 101 G1
Odlum Dr VAN 143 T17
Officers La CHL 233 M6
Ogden Av VAN 10 J33 142 T11
Ogden St CQT 145 T37 165 U37
Ogilvie Cr PCQ 146 T39
Ogilvie St HOP 118 E45
Ogilview Dr HOP 118 E47
Ohashi Ct MIS 210 G-H73
Ohman Rd FRA 193 Z1-2
Okanagan Dr ABT 250 S73
Olafsen Av RMD 183 C15
Old Bridge Ct VAN 10 K36
Old Bridge St VAN 10 K35 162 U12
Old Bridge Walk VAN 10 K36
Old Clayburn Rd ABT 250 T77 251 R-S79
Old Dollarton Rd DNV 143 P-Q21
Old Gravel Rd WHS 401 H1
Old Hope-Princeton Way HOP 118 F44-46
Old Lillooet Rd DNV 143 P20
Old Marine Dr UEL 161 W4
Old McLellan Rd SUR 226 M-N40
Old Milk La WHS 401 G2
Old Orchard Rd CHL 212 G94 H93-94
Old Riverside Rd ABT 250 S74
Old Yale Rd ABT 250 T71 U72 U76-77 U78 271 V79-80
Old Yale Rd CHL 195 C18-20
Old Yale Rd HOP 118 G41-42 H42-43
Old Yale Rd LGC 227 N-P49
Old Yale Rd LGT 227 P49-50 247 Q51-52 Q-R53 R54 248 R55 T61
Old Yale Rd SUR 184 B30 B30 185 B31 B-C31 B-C32 C32 C-D33 D34
Old Yale Rd E SUR 226 K43
Oldfield Av RMD 183 D15
Olds Dr CHL 213 G7
Olive Av BUR 163 Y21-22
Olive Ter WHS 401 H2
Olive Way ABT 270 V76
Oliver Av MAP 208 E61
Oliver Cr CHL 233 M5
Oliver Cr VAN 162 W10
Oliver Dr RMD 204 E24
Oliver Rd CQT 146 R44
Oliver St MIS 230 K71-72
Oliver St NEW 184 A29
Olsen Rd SQM 301 D3
Olsen Rd SUR 184 B30 185 B31
Olson Av HOP 118 E45
Olson Av MIS 209 F70 210 F71-72
Olund Cr MAP 187 A53
Olund Rd ABT 229 M-P69 249 Q69 Q70
Olympia Pl ABT 250 U78 270 V78
Olympic St VAN 162 X-Y8
Omineca Av PCQ 166 U42
Omineca Ct ABT 251 S79
Oneida Dr CQT 145 T35
Onslow Pl WVA 122 J-K13
Ontario Av CHL 213 E6
Ontario Pl VAN 162 Y14 163 Y15
Ontario St DEL 243 Q21
Ontario St NEW 184 B28-29
Ontario St VAN 11 K-L40 142 T14 162 U14 V-Y14 182 A14 Z14
Onyx Pl ABT 249 S69
Opal Pl ABT 270 V73
Opal Pl RMD 202 F10
Oranda Av CQT 165 W35
Orchard Dr ABT 250 U78 270 V78
Orchard La PTM 187 Z47
Orchard La WVA 122 K9
Orchard Pl ABT 250 U78
Orchard Rd CHL 213 F-G4
Orchard Way WVA 122 K9-10 L9-10
Orchid CQT 165 V37
Orchid Cr MIS 210 H74
Orchid Ct MIS 210 H74
Orchid Dr MIS 210 H74
Orchid Pl MIS 210 H74
Orchill Rd WVA 101 H1-2
Oriole Av MIS 210 J72
Oriole Av PCQ 146 T41
Oriole Cr ABT 250 T73
Oriole Dr SUR 185 B37
Oriole Pl PCQ 146 T41
Orion Pl ABT 250 U78
Orion Pl BUR 164 V29
Orkney Ct CQT 165 V-W35
Orkney Pl DNV 124 N23
Orkney Way SQM 301 E4
Orland Dr CQT 165 V34
Orlohma Pl DNV 124 N25
Ormidale St VAN 163 Y20
Orr Dr PCQ 165 Y38
Orr Rd CHL 213 H5
Ortona Av UEL 161 U5
Ortona Cr VAN 162 U8
Ortona La VAN 162 U8
Orwell St DNV 143 P20 Q20
Osborne Av NEW 184 Z28
Osborne Rd CHL 193 C8
Osborne Rd FRA 254 Q12-13
Osborne Rd E DNV 123 L17-18
Osborne Rd W DNV 123 L17
Osborne St PCQ 146 T39
Osgoode Dr RMD 202 H12
Osgoode Pl RMD 202 H12
Osler St VAN 162 V12-13 W13 X13 Y13 182 A12-13 Z13
Osmond Av RMD 202 H9
Osoyoos Cr UEL 161 V5
Osprey Ct DNV 144 P24-25
Osprey Ct RMD 222 L10
Osprey Dr RMD 222 K-L10
Osprey Dr E ABT 249 T70
Osprey Dr W ABT 249 T69
Osprey Pl PCQ 146 T42
Osprey Pl WHS 401 F3
Osprey St MIS 210 H72
Ospring St MAP 187 A48 A-B47
Ostler Ct DNV 124 N26
Othello Rd HOP 118 E48
Ottaburn Rd WVA 122 K-L11
Ottawa Av WVA 122 L10-11 L11-12 L9-10
Ottawa Pl WVA 122 L10
Ottawa St DEL 243 Q21
Ottawa St PCQ 166 V41
Ottenbreit Rd KNT 175 Y21
Otter Pl RMD 202 H11
Otter St ABT 250 U73 270 V73
Oughton Dr PCQ 166 W39
Oval Dr CHL 193 C8
Ovens Av NEW 184 Z28-29
Overstone Dr WVA 101 H1
Owen St MAP 187 Z49
Owen St MIS 210 G78
Owl Ct DNV 103 H15
Owl St HOP 118 G-H43
Oxbow Way CQT 146 R39-40
Oxenham Av WRK 265 W-X36 X38
Oxford Av ABT 250 T76
Oxford Connector PCQ 166 U39-40
Oxford Dr PMD 145 S32
Oxford Pl CQT 146 R40
Oxford Rd CHL 233 K6
Oxford St BUR 143 S21-22 144 S23
Oxford St CQT 146 Q-R40
Oxford St DNV 143 Q20
Oxford St NEW 184 B28
Oxford St PCQ 146 S-T40 166 U40
Oxford St VAN 143 S18-19 S20
Oxford St WRK 265 W-X36
Oxley St N WVA 121 K6 122 K7
Oxley St S WVA 121 L6
Oxtoby Pl CQT 145 T37
Oyama Ct UEL 161 U-V5
Oyama St MIS 210 H71
Ozada Av CQT 146 S39

P

Pacemore Av RMD 202 G8-9
Pacific Av WRK 265 X37-38 266 X39
Pacific Blvd VAN 11 J37-39 142 T13-14 143 T15
Pacific Ct DEL 262 X15
Pacific Dr DEL 262 X15
Pacific Hwy SUR 206 G-H42 226 P42 246 Q42 266 V-W42
Pacific Pl ABT 250 T71
Pacific Pl DEL 262 X15
Pacific Pl WRK 266 X39
Pacific St CQT 145 S37
Pacific St VAN 10 H35 142 S-T12
Packard Av CQT 145 S37
Paco Rd SQM 301 F4
Paddock Dr CQT 145 P38
Page Rd ABT 230 L75-78 231 L79
Page Rd DNV 123 K20
Page Rd FRA 195 C22
Paige Pl CHL 233 K5
Painted Cliff Rd WHS 401 E5 F4 S23
Paisley Av CHL 213 F5
Paisley Av PCQ 146 S42
Paisley Pl SQM 301 E4-5
Paisley Rd DNV 122 L14
Paitsmauk Rd WVA 122 N13
Pakenham Pl MIS 210 H77-78
Palace Ct ABT 250 T76
Palace Pl BUR 164 Y25-26
Paladin Ter PCQ 165 Y38 166 Y39
Palermo St CQT 145 T35
Palisade Cr PCQ 165 Y38 166 Y39
Palisade Ct PCQ 165 Y38 166 Y39
Palisade Dr DNV 123 J16
Palliser Av CQT 165 X34-35
Palm CQT 165 V37
Palm Av BUR 184 Z23
Palm Cr ABT 250 T71
Palmberg Rd RMD 203 J17 223 K17
Palmdale St CQT 145 T37 165 U37
Palmer Av CQT 145 T35-36
Palmer Dr WHS 401 E3
Palmer Pl CHL 214 G-H16
Palmer Rd RMD 202 H-J9
Palmer Rolph St MAP 188 A-B59
Palmerston Av WVA 122 K-L8 L10 L11 L11-12 L9-10
Palmtree La PTM 186 A46
Palomino Cr SUR 226 M43
Pandora Av ABT 270 V73
Pandora Dr BUR 144 S26
Pandora Pl ABT 270 V73
Pandora St BUR 144 S23-24
Pandora St BUR 144 S26
Pandora St CHL 213 E-F5
Pandora St VAN 143 S17-19 S20
Panorama Dr ABT 270 V78
Panorama Dr CQT 145 Q36-37
Panorama Dr DNV 124 M26-27 M-N26
Panorama Dr PMD 145 Q35
Panorama Dr SUR 225 M-N37
Panorama Pl LIO 101 C23
Panorama Pl PMD 145 Q35
Panorama Pl SQM 301 J2-3
Panorama Rd CHL 214 H-J15
Panorama Rd LIO 101 C23
Panorama Ridge WHS 401 F-G3
Papuc Pl DEL 224 K30
Par Rd WHS 401 E-F3
Paradise Av CQT 165 X35
Paradise Bay SUR 266 W39
Paradise Pl ABT 250 R78
Paramount Cr ABT 270 V71
Parana Dr PCQ 166 U41-42
Parana Pl PCQ 166 U41-42
Parapet Ter PCQ 166 X39
Pare Ct CQT 165 X34
Park Av HOP 118 E47
Park Av LGC 227 N48
Park Av WRK 265 W35
Park Cr CQT 145 T35 165 U35
Park Cr NEW 184 Z29
Park Cr SQM 301 E3-4
Park Ct DEL 243 Q19
Park Dr ABT 250 U76
Park Dr FRA 253 S5-6
Park Dr SUR 185 B34-35 B35 266 W39
Park Dr VAN 182 A12 Z12
Park Dr (101B Av) SUR 185 D31
Park Dr (124A St) SUR 185 D32
Park Dr (Chilliwack) CHL 213 F5-6
Park Dr (Squiaala IR) CHL 213 F-G4
Park La MAP 167 W51
Park La VAN 10 E34 142 R11-12
Park La WVA 122 L7-8
Park Pl RMD 202 F13
Park Pl SUR 185 B35
Park Rd FRA 212 D92
Park Rd PTM 166 Y46
Park Rd RMD 202 F12 F13
Park Row NEW 184 A29
Park St CNV 143 P-Q17
Park St HOP 118 E44-45
Park St KNT 175 W21
Park St MIS 210 J73
Park Way SQM 301 B1-2
Parkcrest Dr BUR 164 U24
Parkdale Dr BUR 164 U24-25 U25
Parkdale Pl PMD 145 R34-35
Parke Rd FRA 212 D91
Parker Pl WRK 265 W38

Robson / Sandstone

Robson Ct RMD 202 F9
Robson Dr ABT ...250 R-S77
Robson Dr CQT 145 Q38 146 Q39
Robson Dr RMD 202 F8-9
Robson Pl DEL 263 Z16
Robson Rd BEL 124 N28
Robson Rd SUR 184 D29 204 E29
Robson St CHL 193 D6 213 E6
Robson St VAN ...10 E35 F36 ..11 H37-38 142 R12-13 R-S13
Rochdale Dr RMD ...222 K14
Roche Pl DNV 144 Q25
Roche Point Dr DNV 124 N25 144 P25 P-Q25
Rochester Av CHL ...233 K5
Rochester Av CQT 164 W30 165 W31-33
Rochester St BUR ..164 W30
Rock Ridge Dr MAP .168 W55
Rockbank Pl WVA 121 K4
Rockcliff Rd DNV .124 M-N26
Rockcress Pl CQT ...145 Q37
Rockend Pl WVA 121 K5
Rocket Way CQT 165 Y35
Rockford Pl DEL 224 K29
Rockhill Pl ABT 249 S-T70
Rockland Av ABT .270 V75-76
Rockland Rd E DNV .123 K17
Rockland Rd W DNV 123 K16-17
Rockland Wynd WVA .101 G1
Rocklin St CQT 146 S42
Rockpoole Dr VAN 182 A14 Z14
Rockridge La CQT ..145 Q37
Rockridge Pl MIS ...210 H77
Rockridge Pl WVA ..121 K4-5
Rockridge Rd WVA 121 K4 K4-5
Rockview Pl WVA 121 K6 122 K7
Rockwell Dr ABT 271 V79
Rockwell Dr HHS 155 P20
Rockwell La ABT 271 V79
Rockwood Ct CQT ..145 Q37
Rockwood Dr CHL ...233 N7
Rockwood Pl CHL ...233 N7
Rod Rd SQM 301 C1
Roderick Av CQT 165 X31 X32
Rodger Av PCQ ..166 X39-40
Rodgers St CHL 213 F8
Rodman Av MIS ..210 F71-72
Roe Dr PMD 145 Q32-33
Rogate Av CQT 165 X36
Roger Av BUR 163 W22
Rogers Av ABT 250 S72
Rogers Av CNV 143 P16
Rogers Av CQT 185 Z35
Rogers Av MAP 167 Y53
Rogers La CNV 143 P16
Rogers St VAN 143 S16
Rogerson Dr CQT ...165 U35
Rolinde Cr CHL 213 F8
Rolley Cr MAP 188 D61
Rolley Rd MAP 208 E59
Rolley Lake St MIS 169 Y68 189 Z68
Rolls St MIS 210 H77
Rolston Cr VAN 10 J36 142 T13
Romaniuk Dr RMD 202 H10-11
Romaniuk Pl RMD 202 H10-11
Ronayne Rd DNV 123 L19
Rondeau St CQT 165 U33
Rondoval Cr DNV ...123 J17
Rook Cr MIS 210 H-J72
Roosevelt Cr DNV ...123 N15
Roper Av WRK 265 X36-38 266 X39
Rora Dr SUR 186 C43
Rosalie Ct CQT 146 Q39
Rosamond Av RMD .202 H8-9
Roscoe Rd ABT 271 V81
Rose CQT 165 V37
Rose Av MIS 210 G74
Rose Cr WVA 121 K5
Rose Rd CHL 194 B11
Rose St VAN 143 T18
Rosebank Cr RMD ..222 K12
Rosebank Ct RMD ..222 K12
Rosebank Pl CHL ...194 B10
Roseberry Av BUR 183 A21 A-B21 Z21
Roseberry Rd CHL ...233 L5
Rosebery Av WVA ...101 G1-2 122 K10 K7-8 K8-9
Rosebrook Rd RMD 202 J13 222 K13
Rosebury La VAN ...182 Z13
Rosebury Walk VAN ..182 Z13
Rosecroft Cr RMD 202 J12-13
Rosedale Dr VAN 183 A18
Rosedale Ferry Rd FRA 195 A19-20
Rosedene Cr RMD 202 J12-13
Rosedene Ct RMD ...202 J13
Roseglen Ct BUR .164 V26-27
Rosehill Dr RMD 202 J13 222 K12-13
Rosehill Wynd DEL .263 Y-Z17
Roseland Gt RMD ...222 K13
Roselea Cr RMD 202 J13 222 K13
Roselea Pl RMD 222 K13
Roselynn Way PCQ ..166 X39
Rosemary Av RMD ..222 K13
Rosemary Heights Cr SUR 245 S37-38 T38
Rosemary Heights Dr SUR 245 S-T38
Rosemont Dr VAN 183 A19-20 Z19
Rosepark Pl CHL ...195 D17
Rosetta Av MIS 210 F74
Rosetti Ct RMD 202 J11 222 K11
Rosevale Av KNT 175 X21
Rosevale Rd RMD ...202 J13
Rosewell Av RMD 202 J12 222 K12
Rosewood Av HOP 118 G42-43
Rosewood Cr DNV ...122 N14
Rosewood Dr ABT 250 U75-76
Rosewood Dr DEL ..224 M30
Rosewood Pl MAP ..187 Z49
Rosewood Pl SUR ...186 C40
Rosewood Rd CHL ..195 C18
Rosewood St BUR 164 Y27 184 Z26
Rosewood St MAP ..187 Z49
Rosewood St PCQ ..166 U41
Roslin Pl SUR 205 F34
Roslyn Av BUR 184 A23
Roslyn Blvd DNV 144 P26 P-Q26
Ross Av CQT 165 V33
Ross Cr WVA 121 L4
Ross Dr NEW 184 A30
Ross La WVA 121 L4
Ross Pl SUR 205 E32
Ross Rd ABT 209 H67 J67 229 M-P67 249 Q-U67 269 V-Z67
Ross Rd CHL 234 M10-11
Ross Rd DEL 203 J21
Ross Rd DNV 123 L19-21
Ross Rd FRA 212 E90
Ross Rd HOP 118 C43
Ross Rd SQM 301 A1-2 B2
Ross St VAN ....163 W-X16 X-Y16 Y16 Y16 ....183 A16 Z16 Z16
Rosser Av BUR 143 S-T22 163 U22
Rosser Av N BUR ...143 S22
Rossland Pl ABT 250 U73
Rossland St VAN 143 T19
Rossmore Ct CQT ...165 X34
Rosswood Pl BUR ...164 U28
Rotary St CHL 193 D7
Rothbury Pl BUR 164 V26
Rothsay St MAP 188 Z62
Roundhouse Dr ABT .249 T63
Roundhouse Mews VAN 11 J-K37 142 T13
Rousseau St NEW 165 Y31
Routley Av PCQ ..166 X39-40
Rowan Av BUR 164 X24
Rowan Pl RMD 183 D16
Rowan Rd FRA 211 F84
Rowat Av CHL 213 F6-7
Rowland St PCQ 165 V38
Rowling Pl RMD 204 E24
Rowling St RMD 204 E24
Roxburgh Cr VAN ...162 X12
Roxburgh Rd SUR ...185 A36
Roxbury Rd DNV 124 N27
Roxham St CQT 165 W32
Roxton Av CQT 146 R41
Roy Av CHL 233 K7
Roy St BUR 164 U23-24
Roy Vickers Ct ABT .251 Q81
Royal Av DNV 123 L18
Royal Av NEW 184 A-B29
Royal Av WRK 265 X37-38
Royal Av WVA 101 G2
Royal Av E NEW 184 A30
Royal Cr ABT 250 T72
Royal Cr MAP 187 Z52
Royal Cr SUR 184 D29-30 204 E29
Royal Ct ABT 250 T72
Royal Ct PCQ 165 X38 166 X39
Royal St ABT 250 T72
Royal St LGT 207 F54
Royal Oak Av BUR ...164 V23 W-Y23 184 A23 Z23
Royal Oak Dr DEL ...263 X17
Royalmore Av RMD .202 H8-9
Royalwood Blvd FRA 195 C20
Roycroft Ct BUR 164 V26
Ruby Av DNV .122 K14 123 K15
Ruby Pl CHL 213 J5
Ruby St VAN 163 X20
Ruckle Ct DNV 144 P24
Ruddick Av MIS 189 Z69
Rufus Av CNV 123 N19
Rufus Dr CNV 123 M-N19
Rugby St BUR 164 X25
Ruger Pl CHL 233 M6
Rumble Av VAN 183 A21
Rumble St BUR 183 A21-22 184 A24
Runnel Dr CQT 145 T36
Runnymede Av CQT .165 V32
Runnymede Rd DNV 123 K16-17
Rupert St DNV 143 P20
Rupert St HOP 118 D44
Rupert St VAN ....143 S-T20 .....163 U-X20 X-Y19 183 Z19
Rush Ct DNV 123 J20
Rushmoor Rd RMD ..202 J12
Ruskin Cr MIS 189 C66
Ruskin Pl DNV 123 J-K16
Ruskin Pl RMD ...202 J12-13
Ruskin Rd RMD ...202 J12-13
Russ Baker Way RMD 182 C12 D11
Russell Av BUR 184 Z24
Russell Av DNV 124 N26
Russell Av WRK 265 W36 W37 W38
Russell Ct DNV 124 N26
Russell Dr DEL 204 F29
Russell Rd CHL 234 M9
Russell Rd FRA 231 M82
Russet Pl ABT 250 U77 270 V77
Russet Pl WVA 122 K9
Russet Way WVA 122 K9
Ruth Cr DNV 123 K20
Rutherford Cr DNV .123 K-L18
Ruthina Av DNV 123 J15
Rutland Ct CQT 164 V30
Rutland Rd WVA 121 K4
Rutley Rd FRA 195 C20
Ruttan Rd FRA 211 F81
Ryall Cr DEL 224 K-L29
Ryall Pl DEL 224 K-L29
Ryan Cr RMD .202 J13 222 K13
Ryan Ct RMD 202 J13
Ryan Pl RMD 202 J13
Ryan Rd RMD 202 J12-13
Ryan St MIS 210 J75
Rydal Av DNV 122 K14
Ryder St HOP 118 F45
Ryder Lake Rd CHL 234 L-M11 M12-13

S

S E Marine Dr VAN 183 A15-17 A19 A-B18
S W Marine Dr VAN 162 Y9-10 182 A11 A13-14 B12-13 183 A15
Saab Pl ABT 249 S69
Saanich St ABT ...250 S-T73
Saba Rd RMD 202 F12
Sable Av RMD 202 J8-9
Sache St CHL 195 D17-18
Saddle La VAN 183 Z19
Saddle St ABT 250 S-T77
Saddle St CQT 145 T37 165 U37
Saddlehorn Cr LGT 248 Q56 Q56-57
Safflower Cr CHL 233 L6
Saffron Ct BUR 164 U29
Sage Av MIS 210 H74
Sail Pl CQT 145 T36-37
Sailes Av LGT 207 E-F53
St. Albans Av DNV ...123 K17
St. Albans Rd RMD 202 G-H13
St. Albert Av PCQ ...166 U40
St. Alice St HHS 155 P19
St. Andrew's Way WHS 401 E3
St. Andrews Al WHS .401 T21
St. Andrews Av CNV 123 M-N17 143 P17
St. Andrews Av DNV 123 K-L18
St. Andrews Ct ABT 251 S79-80
St. Andrews Dr SUR .185 A36
St. Andrews Pl DEL 263 W16-17
St. Andrews Pl WVA 102 H13 122 J13
St. Andrews Rd WVA 102 H13 122 J12-13 J13
St. Andrews St LGT 207 F53 F53-54
St. Andrews St NEW 184 A-B28
St. Andrews St PMD 145 T32-34
St. Anne Av MAP 187 A52
St. Anne St PCQ 146 T40
St. Annes Dr DNV ...122 L14
St. Anthony's Way MIS 209 F-G67
St. Anton Way WHS ..401 F3
St. Brides Ct RMD 202 J9
St. Brides Pl RMD 202 J9
St. Catherines St VAN 163 U-W16 X16 X-Y16 Y16
St. Charles Pl BUR ..184 Z24
St. Christophers Rd DNV 123 L19
St. Clair Pl VAN 162 Y8
St. David St CHL 193 D7
St. Davids Av CNV ...143 P17
St. Denis Av DNV 123 N20 143 P20
St. Denis Pl WVA 122 L10
St. Denis Rd WVA ...122 L10
St. Edwards Dr RMD 182 C-D14
St. Florians Ct DNV 123 K17-18
St. Gallen Way ABT ..250 U78
St. George St HOP 118 F44-45
St. George St NEW ..184 A29
St. George St PMD 145 T32-34
St. George St VAN ...143 T16 ....163 U16 U-V15 V-W15 ....W15 X15 Y15 Y15 ....183 A15 Z15 Z15
St. Georges Av CNV 123 M-N17 143 P17
St. Georges Av DNV 123 K-L17
St. Georges Av WVA ..101 H1
St. Georges Cr WVA ..101 H1
St. Giles Rd WVA 102 H13 122 J13
St. Ives Cr DNV 123 L16
St. James Cr WVA ...122 K13
St. James Rd W DNV 123 L16-17
St. James St PCQ ...166 U40
St. John St DEL ...243 Q-R21
St. Johns Pl RMD 202 J9
St. Johns St PMD .145 T33-34
St. Julien Mews VAN .183 Z19
St. Kilda Av DNV 123 L18
St. Laurence St CQT .165 U34
St. Lawrence St VAN 163 W-X18
St. Margarets St VAN 163 X18 Y18
St. Marys Av DNV 123 K17 L17
St. Marys Pl DNV .123 K17-18
St. Marys St NEW ...184 A29
St. Matthews Way ABT 270 V77-78
St. Michael St PCQ ..166 U40
St. Moritz Cr WHS 401 F3
St. Moritz Way ABT ..250 U78
St. Olaf Av ABT 230 M75
St. Patrick St NEW ..184 A29
St. Patricks Av CNV .143 P17
St. Pauls Av DNV 123 K17
St. Regis La VAN 11 G38 142 S14
St. Stephens Pl DNV 123 M19-20
St. Thomas Pl PCQ ..146 T42
St. Thomas St PCQ 146 S42 T42
St. Vincents Ct RMD ..202 J9
St. Vincents Pl RMD ..202 J9
Salal Cr CQT 145 Q36-37
Salal Dr VAN 162 U11
Salal Pl SUR 205 E33
Salerno St VAN 162 U8
Salisbury Av BUR ...184 Z25
Salisbury Av PCQ 146 T39 T40
Salisbury Dr SUR 186 C41
Salish Ct BUR .164 V-W29 W30
Salish Dr VAN 162 X7 Y7-8
Salish Rd BEL 124 N28
Salish Rd MAP 186 B46 187 B47
Salish Rd PTM 186 A46
Salish Way CHL 233 K7
Salmo Cr UEL 161 V5
Salmonberry Dr CHL .213 G1
Salsbury Av MIS 210 G73
Salsbury Dr VAN 143 S-T17 T17
Salt La LGC 227 N48
Salt St VAN .11 K39-40 142 T14
Salt Spring Av CQT ..146 S39
Salter St NEW 184 C28 D26 D27 204 E26
Salton Rd ABT ..270 V76 W76
Saltspring Ct RMD ...202 G8
Salvador Ct DNV 123 J16
Samara Ct BUR 163 X22
Sampson La WVA 101 E3
Samson Dr NEW 184 B29
Samtree Pl ABT 251 T81
Samuel Ct ABT 250 S72
Samuels Ct CQT ...146 R-S39
San Antonio Pl CQT 165 X-Y35
San Juan Pl CQT 165 X35
San Lucas Ct CQT ..165 X35
San Remo Dr PMD .145 R-S34
Sand Rd CHL ..252 R92 R-S91
Sandalwood Cr ABT .270 V75
Sandbar Pl DEL 263 Y19
Sandberg St ABT ..230 K-L78
Sandborne Av BUR ..184 A25
Sandell St BUR 163 X-Y21
Sanders St BUR 164 Y23
Sanderson Way BUR 163 W22
Sandhurst Pl WVA .122 J-K11
Sandiford Dr RMD ...202 J10
Sandiford Pl RMD ...202 J10
Sandlewood Cr BUR 164 W30
Sandlewood St PCQ .166 U41
Sandollar Pl DEL ..263 Y17-18
Sandon Dr ABT ...250 U77-78
Sandon Pl ABT 250 U78
Sandown Pl DNV .122 M13-14
Sandpiper Av MAP ..187 Z54
Sandpiper Ct CQT ...146 Q39
Sandpiper Ct RMD ..222 K10
Sandpiper Dr ABT 249 S69 T70
Sandpiper Dr MIS ...210 H72
Sandpiper Pl ABT ...249 T70
Sandpiper Pl DEL .224 K29-30
Sandpiper Pl MIS ...210 H72
Sandra Way PCQ ...166 X39
Sandringham Av NEW 184 Z28
Sandringham Cr DNV 123 K-L17
Sandringham Dr ABT 251 T80-81
Sandstone Cr CQT ..145 Q36
Sandstone Ct CQT 145 Q35-36

Sandstone / Simpson

Sandstone Dr *ABT* **271** V79
Sandy Hill Cr *ABT* **251** R-S79
Sandy Hill Rd *ABT* **251** R-S79
Sangara Av *ABT* **209** J66-67
Sangster Pl *NEW* **184** Z29
Santa Monica Dr *DEL* **204** H27-28
Santa Monica Pl *DEL* **204** H28
Santiago St *CQT* **165** X35
Sapper St *NEW* **184** Z30
Sappers Way *CHL* **233** M5-6
Sapperton Av *BUR* **164** X30
Sapphire Dr *CHL* **213** H-J5
Sapphire Pl *ABT* **249** S68
Sapphire Pl *CQT* **145** Q36
Sapphire Pl *RMD* **202** F10
Sapporo Dr *WHS* **401** H2
Sarajevo Dr *WHS* **401** H2
Saran Way *ABT* **270** X-Y77
Saratoga Ct *BUR* **163** X22
Saratoga Dr *DEL* **263** W16-17
Sardis Cr *BUR* **164** Y23
Sardis St *BUR* **163** X21-22 X-Y22 **164** Y23
Sargent Ct *CQT* **165** V34
Sarita Av *DNV* **103** H15 **123** J15
Sarita Pl *DNV* **123** J15
Sarnia St *NEW* **184** A30
Sasamat La *DNV* **124** J-K29
Sasamat Pl *VAN* **142** T7 **162** U7
Sasamat St *VAN* **142** T7 **162** U-V7
Saskatchewan St *PCQ* **166** X39
Satchell St *ABT* **209** J66 **229** K-L66
Saturna Cr *ABT* **250** S-T72
Saturna Dr *BUR* **164** V29
Saturna Dr *WRK* **265** W36
Saturna Pl *RMD* **202** G8
Sauder La *UEL* **161** U3
Saunders Rd *RMD* **202** J12-14
Saunders St *MIS* **190** D74
Sauve Ct *DNV* **123** K19
Sauve Pl *DNV* **123** K19
Savage Rd *DEL* **222** P11 **242** Q11
Savage Rd *RMD* **183** B18
Savary Av *CQT* **146** R39
Saville Cr *DNV* **123** K16
Savoy Rd *CHL* **252** R-S92
Savoy St *DEL* **243** Q15
Saw-Cut *VAN* **11** L37 **162** U13
Sawyer Av *MIS* **210** J72
Sawyer Pl *PCQ* **145** T38 **146** T39
Sawyer's Rd *PTM* **186** B46
Sawyers La *VAN* **11** L37 **162** U13
Saxbee Ct *ABT* **270** V78
Sayers Cr *MAP* **169** X-Y63
Scales Pl *VAN* **163** X20-21
Scantlings *VAN* **10** L36 **162** U13
Scarboro Av *VAN* **183** A17-18 A18
Scarborough Cr *PCQ* **166** W39
Scarborough Dr *DEL* **204** J28-29
Sceptre Cr *RMD* **202** J8-9
Schaefer Av *RMD* **202** H11-12
Schaefer Gt *RMD* **202** H11-12
Scheldt Rd *CHL* **233** M-N6
Schmidt Cr *MAP* **187** Z49-50
Schneider Rd *ABT* **271** Y-Z84
School Av *MIS* **189** D68-69
School Av *VAN* **163** X-Y19 Y20
School Gn *VAN* **10** L36 **162** U13
School La *CHL* **233** K7
School Rd *HOP* **118** G43
School Rd *LGT* **207** F53
School St *CHL* **213** E-F6
School St *NEW* **164** Y30
Schoolhouse St *CQT* **165** U-W33 X33
Schooner Ct *RMD* **222** K10
Schooner St *CQT* **165** Y34 **185** Z34
Schooner Way *DEL* **223** N16-17
Schou St *BUR* **164** V23
Schroeder Av *ABT* **229** K68
Schweyey Rd *CHL* **213** E-F4
Science Rd *BUR* **144** T28-29
Scotchbrook Rd *RMD* **202** H13
Scotia St *VAN* **11** K41 L41 **163** U15 V15
Scotsdale Av *RMD* **202** J9
Scotsdale Pl *RMD* **202** J9
Scott Av *MIS* **210** J72
Scott Cr *SQM* **301** K2
Scott Dr *HOP* **118** F45
Scott Pl *PCQ* **146** T39
Scott Rd *DNV* **123** L20 L21
Scott Rd *KNT* **175** W22-23
Scott Rd *SUR* **184** D30 **185** B-C31 C31
Scott St *ABT* **229** P66
Scott St *NEW* **164** Y29
Scratchley Cr *RMD* **183** D15
Sea Av N *BUR* **144** S24
Sea Av S *BUR* **144** S24
Sea Island Way *RMD* **182** C13
Sea Ridge Bays *SUR* **265** V38
Sea Shell La *DNV* **144** P-Q26
Sea to Sky Hwy *LIO* **101** A23
Sea To Sky Hwy *SQM* **301** D-E3 G-H2
Sea to Sky Hwy *WHS* **401** F-G3 H1 S-T21
Sea To Sky Hwy *WVA* **101** G2
Seabay Rd *RMD* **203** J15
Seabird Island Rd *KNT* **175** U22-23 V23
Seabreeze Walk *VAN* **10** J35-36 **142** T12
Seabright Rd *RMD* **203** J15
Seabrook Cr *RMD* **203** J15
Seacastle Dr *RMD* **203** J15
Seacliff Rd *RMD* **203** J15
Seacote Rd *RMD* **203** H-J15
Seacrest Ct *PMD* **145** T31
Seacrest Dr *SUR* **245** U31
Seacrest Rd *RMD* **203** J15
Seafair Dr *RMD* **202** H8
Seafield Cr *RMD* **203** J15
Seafield Cr N *RMD* **203** J15
Seafield Cr S *RMD* **203** J15
Seaforth Cr *CQT* **165** X34
Seaforth Dr *VAN* **163** V20
Seaforth Way *PMD* **145** T32
Seagrave Rd *RMD* **203** J15
Seagull Pl *VAN* **183** A20
Seaham Cr *RMD* **203** J15
Seahaven Dr *RMD* **203** J15 **223** K15
Seahaven Pl *RMD* **203** J15
Seaholm Cr *CHL* **193** C8
Seahurst Pl *RMD* **223** K15
Seahurst Rd *RMD* **223** K15
Seal Way *ABT* **250** U73
Sealily Pl *RMD* **203** J15
Sealord Pl *RMD* **203** J15
Sealord Rd *RMD* **203** J15
Seameadow Ct *RMD* **203** H-J15
Seamount Rd *RMD* **203** J15 **223** K15
Seaport Av *RMD* **203** J15
Seascape Cl *WVA* **101** D4
Seascape Ct *WVA* **101** D4
Seascape Dr *WVA* **101** D4
Seascape La *WVA* **101** D4
Seascape Pl *WVA* **101** D4
Seascape Rd *WVA* **101** D4
Seashell Dr *DEL* **263** Y19
Seashell Pl *DEL* **263** Y19
Seaside Bay *SUR* **266** W39
Seaside Pl *WVA* **121** K2
Seaton Av *CQT* **165** U-V31
Seaton Ct *RMD* **203** J15
Seaton Pl *MAP* **187** Z51
Seaton Pl *RMD* **203** J15
Seaton Rd *RMD* **203** J15
Seavale Rd *RMD* **203** J15
Seaview Dr *PMD* **145** T31-32
Seaview Pl *LIO* **101** B-C23
Seaview Pl *WVA* **121** J2
Seaview Rd *DEL* **263** Z19-20
Seawalk *VAN* **11** F37-38
Seaward Ct *RMD* **203** J15 **223** K15
Seaward Gt *RMD* **223** K15
Seaway Rd *RMD* **203** J15 **223** K15
Sechelt Dr *CQT* **146** S39
Sechelt Dr *DNV* **123** M22 **124** M23
Sechelt Ter *ABT* **250** S73
Secret Ct *CQT* **146** S39
Sedge Ct *CQT* **145** Q36
Sedgemond Pl *RMD* **202** J8
Sefton St *PCQ* **146** S40 T40 **166** U40
Seguin Dr *CQT* **165** X33
Selby Rd *DNV* **123** K20
Seldon Rd *ABT* **250** Q-R75
Selkirk Av *ABT* **251** S79
Selkirk Av *MAP* **187** Z51-52 Z52
Selkirk Bay *SUR* **266** V39
Selkirk Cr *CQT* **165** U34
Selkirk Dr *SUR* **185** B34
Selkirk St *CHL* **233** L5
Selkirk St *VAN* **162** V-W12 X12 Y12 Y12 **182** A12 A-B12 Z12
Sellers Av *BUR* **184** Z24
Selma Av *BUR* **164** Y23
Selman St *CQT* **165** W31
Selonas Dr *CHL* **233** L6
Semana Cr *VAN* **162** X7
Semiahmoo Av *WRK* **265** X38
Semiahmoo Pl *SUR* **245** U37
Semiahmoo Rd *SUR* **185** C-D33
Semiahmoo Tr *SUR* **245** T36
Semisch Av *CNV* **123** N16 **143** P16
Semlin Ct *RMD* **202** F8
Semlin Dr *RMD* **202** F8
Semlin Dr *VAN* **143** S-T18 T18 **163** U18 V17-18
Semlin Pl *ABT* **250** R-S77
Senda Ct *MIS* **169** Y67
Seneca Ct *ABT* **250** S78
Seney Pl *LGT* **207** F53
Seniac St *VAN* **163** Y20
Senkler Rd *BEL* **124** M30
Sennok Cr *VAN* **162** X7
Sentinel Dr *ABT* **250** U77
Sentinel Dr *WVA* **122** L-M12
Sentinel La *WVA* **122** L12
Sentinel Rd *PMD* **145** S34-35
Sentinel St *MAP* **187** Z48
Sepass Pl *CHL* **213** J7
Seppos Way *WHS* **401** E3
Sequoia Dr *SUR* **205** H37-38
Sequoia Rd *BUR* **164** X29-30
Serl Rd *ABT* **250** U76 **270** V76
Service St *BUR* **164** Y24
Sesame St *CHL* **213** J7 **233** K7
Settebello Dr *WHS* **401** E4
Settlers Ct *PCQ* **165** X-Y38
Seux Rd *FRA* **190** Z79
Severn Dr *RMD* **202** J13
Seville Pl *RMD* **202** J8
Sexsmith Rd *RMD* **182** C-D13
Seymour Av *WRK* **265** X36
Seymour Blvd *DNV* **143** P21
Seymour Ct *DNV* **143** P21
Seymour Ct *NEW* **184** Z30
Seymour Dr *CQT* **165** U35
Seymour Mews *VAN* **10** J-K36 **142** T13
Seymour St *PCQ* **165** U38 **166** U39
Seymour St *VAN* **11** H37 **142** S14 T13
Seymour View *ANM* **145** P34
Seymour River Pl *DNV* **143** P21
Shackleton Dr *RMD* **202** G9
Shackleton Gt *RMD* **202** G9
Shadbolt Av *ABT* **251** Q80-81
Shadbolt La *WVA* **122** K9
Shafton Pl *WVA* **122** K10
Shaftsbury Av *PCQ* **145** T38
Shaftsbury Pl *PCQ* **145** T38 **146** T39
Shakespeare Av *DNV* **123** L19
Shakespeare Pl *SUR* **205** G33
Shale Ct *CQT* **145** Q-R36
Shaman Cr *DEL* **262** X15
Shamrock Dr *CHL* **193** C-D7
Shamrock Pl *WVA* **122** K9
Shanghai Alley *VAN* **11** H40 **142** S14 **143** S15
Shannon Cr *DNV* **123** K-L16
Shannon Ct *CQT* **165** U34
Shannon Dr *ABT* **270** V76
Shannon Pl *SUR* **226** N43
Shannon Rd *RMD* **182** B8
Shannon Way *DEL* **263** Y16
Sharon Dr *WVA* **121** K-L6
Sharon Pl *WVA* **121** K5-6
Sharpe Av *RMD* **204** E-F24
Sharpe Rd *PTM* **167** V-W48
Sharpe St *CQT* **165** U37
Sharpe St *MIS* **210** J75
Sharpe St *NEW* **184** B27
Sharpewood Pl *CQT* **146** Q-R39
Shasta Ct *CQT* **165** U34
Shaughnessy Pl *CQT* **146** R39
Shaughnessy St *CQT* **146** R39-40
Shaughnessy St *PCQ* **146** S-T39 **166** U-V39
Shaughnessy St *VAN* **182** A13 B13
Shavington St *CNV* **143** P19
Shaw Av *CHL* **213** J6
Shaw Av *CQT* **165** W31-32
Shaw St *MIS* **189** B-D70
Shaw St *NEW* **184** B28
Shawna Way *CQT* **165** W35
Shawnee Pl *VAN* **183** Z19
Shawnigan Dr *CHL* **233** M6
Shawnigan Pl *RMD* **202** J11
Shearwater Dr *ABT* **251** Q-R79
Sheaves Ct *DEL* **204** G27
Sheaves Pl *DEL* **204** G27
Sheaves Rd *DEL* **204** G-H27
Sheaves Way *DEL* **204** H27
Sheena Pl *ABT* **251** R79
Sheffield Dr *KNT* **175** X21
Sheffield Pl *DEL* **224** K29
Sheffield Way *CHL* **213** J6 **233** K6
Shefield Way *ABT* **250** U76
Shelby Ct *BUR* **164** W23-24
Sheldon Av *MIS* **210** J74
Sheldon Rd *FRA* **254** Q13
Sheldrake Ct *MAP* **168** X55
Shell Rd *RMD* **183** C-D15 **203** E15 J15 **223** K15
Shellbridge Gt *RMD* **182** D14
Shellbridge Way *RMD* **182** D14 **183** D15
Shelley Av *ABT* **270** W75
Shelley Pl *DEL* **224** L28-29
Shelley Rd *DNV* **123** N22
Shellmont St *BUR* **164** U27-28
Shelter Cr *CQT* **146** S39
Shepherd Dr *RMD* **182** D14 **202** E14
Shepherd St *BUR* **163** Y22 **164** Y23
Shepherd Way *DEL* **204** F28-29 G28-29
Sherban Ct *BUR* **164** U24
Sherbrooke St *NEW* **164** Y30 **165** Y31
Sherbrooke St *VAN* **163** X-Y16 Y16 **183** A16 Z16 Z16
Sheridan Av *CQT* **165** X34
Sheridan Dr *PTM* **147** S-T48
Sheridan Pl *ABT* **250** R-S78
Sheridan Rd *RMD* **202** J11
Sheriff St *CQT* **165** U32
Sherlaw Rd *CHL* **234** N11 P12
Sherlock Av *BUR* **144** T26 **164** U25-26 U26
Sherman St *CQT* **145** R37
Sherman St *WVA* **121** K-L5
Sherritt Ct *BUR* **144** T25-26
Sherwood Av *CQT* **165** X32
Sherwood Blvd *DEL* **263** Z17-18
Sherwood Cr *ABT* **270** V72
Sherwood Dr *CHL* **233** N7
Sherwood La *WVA* **122** L-M10
Sherwood Pl *DEL* **263** Z17
Shetland Pl *SUR* **226** M43-44
Shief Joseph St *CNV* **123** N16
Shields Av *RMD* **202** G14
Shikaze Ct *MIS* **210** H74
Shiles St *NEW* **164** Y30 **184** Z30
Shiloh Ct *CQT* **165** U38
Shiloh Pl *CQT* **165** U37-38
Shimek St *MIS* **210** G78
Shinglebolt Cr *PTM* **186** B46
Shirley Av *BUR* **184** Z24
Shirley Av *DNV* **123** J15
Shoesmith Cr *MAP* **168** X55-56
Shoesmith Loop *MAP* **168** W-X55
Shone Rd *DNV* **124** N25
Shook Av *MIS* **211** G79-80
Shook Rd *FRA* **211** E-F79 G79-80
Shook St *MIS* **211** G-H79
Shore Cr *ABT* **270** V76
Shore Rd *FRA* **211** F80
Shoreline Cir *PMD* **145** R31-32
Shorepine Walk *VAN* **10** L35 **162** U12
Short Rd *ABT* **270** Y-Z74
Short Rd *FRA* **195** D21
Short St *BUR* **184** Z23-24
Short St *PMD* **145** S-T32
Shrewsbury Dr *CHL* **212** G94
Shuswap Av *CQT* **165** Y36
Shuswap Av *RMD* **222** K8-9
Shuswap Ct *ABT* **250** S73-74
Shuswap Ter *ABT* **250** S73
Shuttle St *ABT* **249** T63
Si-Lu Dr *VAN* **162** Y8
Sicamous Av *CQT* **165** X35
Sicamous Pl *CQT* **165** X35
Sidaway Rd *RMD* **203** F-J16 **223** K16
Sidegrove Ct *ABT* **250** S71
Sidley St *BUR* **184** Z23 Z24
Sidney St *CHL* **193** D6
Sidney St *VAN* **163** W17-18 W18
Sidoni Av *ABT* **249** T70
Sidoni Pl *ABT* **249** T70
Siemens Rd *CHL* **234** P15
Siemens Rd *FRA* **254** Q15
Sierpina Dr *RMD* **202** H13
Sierpina Pl *RMD* **202** H13
Sierra Dr *BUR* **144** S25-26
Sierra Pl *ABT* **270** V78
Siesta Bay *SUR* **266** W39
Signal Ct *ABT* **249** T-U63
Signal Ct *CQT* **165** U36
Silica Pl *CQT* **145** P35-36
Sills Av *RMD* **202** G13
Silver Av *BUR* **163** Y22 **183** Z22
Silver Av *CHL* **213** J7 **233** K6
Silver Cr *MIS* **209** F67
Silver Way *ABT* **251** S-T83
Silver Fox Ter *MIS* **210** H72
Silver Lake Pl *CQT* **165** V37
Silver Skagit Rd *HOP* **118** G-H42
Silver Springs Blvd *CQT* **145** R38
Silver Valley Rd *MAP* **167** V54 W53
Silverado Pl *DEL* **263** W17
Silverberry Ct *CQT* **145** Q36
Silverdale Av *MIS* **209** G67-68 H69-70 **210** H-J71
Silverdale Pl *DNV* **123** K16
Silverdale Pl *MIS* **210** H72
Silverglen Dr *MIS* **209** E67
Silverhill Av *MIS* **209** E68-70
Silverhope Rd *HOP* **118** G-H42
Silversmith Pl *RMD* **223** K15
Silverthorne Pl *PTM* **187** A47
Silverthorne Rd *CHL* **233** L6
Silverthrone Dr *CQT* **145** Q38 **146** Q39
Silvertree Ct *ABT* **250** T-U75
Silverview Rd *HOP* **118** G43
Silverwood Cr *DNV* **122** N13-14
Sim Rd *ABT* **210** J78 **230** K77 K78 L76
Simmons Rd *CHL* **233** P1 **253** Q1
Simon Av *ABT* **250** T73-74
Simon St *MIS* **210** J72
Simon Fraser Ct *PMD* **145** S31
Simon Pierre Rd *MAP* **187** B47
Simpson Av *VAN* **142** T7 **161** T6
Simpson Rd *ABT* **249** U63 U66-67 U69
Simpson Rd *CHL* **233** L3-4
Simpson Rd *RMD* **183** C15

Texaco / VanHorne

Texaco Dr *BUR* **144** R27-28
Texada St *CQT* **146** S39
Thacker Av *CQT* **165** U37-38
Thacker Av *HOP* **118** D44-45
Thacker Mountain Rd *HOP* **118** D-E45
Thames Cr *PCQ* **166** V41
Thames Ct *DNV* **123** K20
Thames Ct *UEL* **161** V5
Thames Pl *PCQ* **166** U-V41
Thea Dr *PCQ* **166** W39
Thellaiwhaltun Av *VAN* **162** Y8
Theology Mall *UEL* **161** T4
Theresa La *CHL* **213** F-G5
Thermal Dr *CQT* **165** U35
Therrien St *CQT* **165** W-X33
Theta Ct *DNV* **124** N25-26
Thetford Pl *WVA* **122** K13
Thetis Pl *RMD* **202** F11
Thimbleberry Ct *CQT* **145** Q36
Thirlmere Dr *RMD* **202** J11
Thistle *CQT* **165** W37
Thistledown Pl *DEL* **263** Y17-18
Thom Creek Dr *CHL* **234** M9
Thomas Av *CQT* **165** X33 X34
Thomas Av *MIS* **190** Z74
Thomas Dr *RMD* **202** J10
Thomas Pl *RMD* **202** J10
Thomas Rd *CHL* **233** M6-7
Thomas St *BUR* **164** W25
Thompson Av *CQT* **165** U31
Thompson Av *MIS* **210** J75 **230** K75
Thompson Cr *WVA* **122** K7
Thompson Gt *RMD* **184** D25
Thompson Pl *WVA* **122** K7
Thompson Rd *PTM* **147** T49-50
Thompson Rd *RMD* **184** D25 **204** E25
Thompson Rd (Bridal Falls) *FRA* **195** D20
Thompson Rd (Nicomen Island) *FRA* **211** G85
Thomson Rd *ANM* **145** P33-34
Thor Ct *CQT* **146** Q39
Thor Rd *FRA* **254** Q16 **255** Q17
Thorburn Way *PTM* **186** B46
Thoreau Av *ABT* **250** S77
Thormanby Cr *RMD* **202** G8-9
Thorncliffe Dr *DNV* **123** L15
Thorne Av *MAP* **187** A48 A49
Thorne St *BUR* **184** C25
Thornhill Dr *VAN* **183** A17
Thornhill Pl *ABT* **250** S71-72
Thornhill St *CHL* **233** M8
Thornton Av *MAP* **167** Y50
Thornton Pl *ABT* **250** R78
Thornton Pl *MAP* **167** Y50
Thornton Rd *CHL* **234** N9
Thornton St *VAN* **11** J-K41 **143** T15
Thornwood Pl *BUR* **164** W23
Thorpe Rd *RMD* **183** D15
Thorpe St *MIS* **210** G73
Thrasher St *MIS* **210** H73
Three Cedars Dr *VAN* **183** A20
Threshold Dr *ABT* **269** W69
Thrift Av *WRK* **265** W36-38 **266** W39
Thrift St *CQT* **165** X31-32
Thrush Av *MIS* **210** J71-72
Thrush Pl *VAN* **183** A20
Thunderbird Blvd *UEL* **161** U-V4
Thunderbird Cr *BUR* **164** V28
Thunderbird Ct *DEL* **224** K29-30
Thunderbird Ridge *SQM* **301** D-E5
Thurlow St *VAN* **10** G36 H35-36 **142** R13-14 S12-13
Thurston Cl *PMD* **145** S35-36
Thurston Pl *ABT* **250** S71
Thurston St *BUR* **163** X21
Thurston Ter *PMD* **145** S35-36
Thyme *CQT* **165** W37
Tiber Cl *PCQ* **166** U-V41
Tiber Pl *PCQ* **166** U41
Ticehurst La *PCQ* **165** U38 **166** U39
Tide Pl *CQT* **165** U37
Tidewater Bay *DEL* **223** N17
Tidewater Pl *VAN* **182** A11
Tidewater Way *LIO* **101** C23
Tiffany Blvd *RMD* **202** F10
Tiffany Pl *RMD* **202** F10
Tiffin Cr *RMD* **202** F9
Tigris Cr *PCQ* **166** V41-42
Tilbury Av *CHL* **233** L6
Tilbury Pl *SUR* **186** B-C41
Tilbury Rd *DEL* **203** J20
Tillicum St *BUR* **184** C-D23
Tilston Ct *CQT* **165** U33
Tilston St *CHL* **213** F8
Tilton Rd *RMD* **202** E9-10
Timber Ct *BUR* **164** U28
Timber Ct *CQT* **145** P-Q38
Timber La *WHS* **401** C3
Timber Ridge *WHS* **401** H1
Timbercrest Dr *PMD* **145** R35
Timbercrest Pl *PMD* **145** R34-35
Timberfeild Dr *WVA* **121** J-K3
Timberfeild La *WVA* **121** J3-4
Timberfeild Pl *WVA* **121** J-K3
Timberlake St *MIS* **210** J75 **230** K75
Timberland Rd *SUR* **184** B-C30
Timberlane Dr *ABT* **251** U80 **271** V79 V80
Timberline Pl *CHL* **194** C10-11
Timberline Pl *DNV* **123** J15
Timbertop Dr *LIO* **101** B24
Timbervalley Rd *DEL* **263** Z17-18
Timberwood Av *MIS* **210** J75 **230** K75
Timothy Av *CHL* **233** M6
Tims Av *ABT* **250** T72
Tims St *ABT* **250** T72
Tina Way *PCQ* **166** X39
Tindall Ter *MIS* **210** G78
Tinmore Pl *RMD* **202** H8-9
Tipping Rd *RMD* **183** B16
Tipton St *CQT* **165** V33
Tisdall St *VAN* **162** Y13 Y13 **182** Z13 Z13
Toad Hollow *WHS* **401** D-E3
Toba Dr *CQT* **146** S39
Toba Pl *VAN* **183** Z21
Tobena Rd *HOP* **118** G41-42
Tobermory Way *SQM* **301** D-E5
Tobruck Av *CNV* **123** N15
Todd Cr *SUR* **205** J35
Todd Ct *ABT* **250** T78
Todd Pl *DEL* **224** L30
Todd St *VAN* **163** W-X19
Toderick St *VAN* **163** Y20 **183** Z20
Tolbooth La *VAN* **183** A20
Tollcross Rd *DNV* **124** N23 **144** P23
Tolmie Av *CQT* **165** W35
Tolmie Av *RMD* **202** F8
Tolmie Rd *ABT* **232** M-P90 **252** Q-T90
Tolmie St *VAN* **142** T7 **161** U6 V6 **162** U7 V7
Tom Berry Rd *HOP* **118** G42-43
Tom Thomson Ct *ABT* **251** Q80
Tomahawk Av *WVA* **122** M-N12
Tompkins Cr *DNV* **124** M23
Toni Sailer La *WHS* **401** E4
Topaz Ct *CQT* **145** Q36
Topaz Dr *CHL* **213** H-J6
Topaz Pl *RMD* **202** F10
Topaz St *ABT* **270** V73
Topley Av *CHL* **193** C7-8
Topper Ct *MIS* **210** H75
Topper Dr *MIS* **210** H75
Torbet Pl *SQM* **301** D5
Toronto Pl *PCQ* **146** S40-41
Toronto Rd *UEL* **161** U4-5
Toronto St *PCQ* **146** S-T41 **166** U41
Torquay Av *DNV* **123** M20
Tory Av *CQT* **146** R39
Totem Ct *BUR* **163** U21-22
Tourney Rd *DNV* **123** J20
Tournier Pl *CHL* **233** N7
Tower Ct *PCQ* **166** X-Y39
Tower Dr *KNT* **175** W-X22
Tower Rd *BUR* **144** T29
Tower Rd *CHL* **193** B7
Tower St *ABT* **269** W69
Tower Hill Cr *WVA* **122** K8
Town Rd *ABT* **252** T91 U90-91
Town Centre Blvd *CQT* **145** S38
Townley St *CQT* **165** U-V32
Townley St *VAN* **162** W10
Townline Rd *ABT* **249** Q-T70 **269** V-W70 Y-Z70
Townsend Pl *NEW* **184** A29
Townshipline Av *MIS* **210** E71-72
Townshipline Rd *ABT* **229** P64-68 **230** P71-78
Townshipline Rd *LGT* **228** P62 **229** P63
Tracey St *ABT* **270** W71
Trafalgar St *ABT* **250** T74
Trafalgar St *VAN* **142** T10 **162** U-W10 W-X10 Y10
Trail's End La *WHS* **401** H2
Tralee Cr *DEL* **263** Y16
Tralee Pl *DEL* **263** Y16
Tranmer Rd *KNT* **175** X-Y22
Tranquille Pl *RMD* **202** F11
Trapp Av *BUR* **184** C25 C25-26
Trapp Rd *NEW* **184** C26
Trattle St *LGT* **207** F53
Travers Av *WVA* **122** L7
Treetop Dr *ABT* **251** S80
Treetop La *DNV* **123** M22
Treetop La *WHS* **401** E3
Treetops Dr *PMD* **145** R34
Trembath Av *MIS* **210** J72
Trenant St *DEL* **223** P16
Trent Av *CQT* **165** V34
Trent St *CHL* **233** L5
Trenton Pl *DNV* **123** K16
Trenton Rd *PCQ* **166** W42
Trenton St *PCQ* **166** W42
Trepassey Dr *RMD* **202** J9 **222** K9
Trestle Av *ABT* **249** T63-64
Tretheway Dr *BUR* **164** V25
Trethewey Av *CHL* **213** F6-7
Trethewey Cr *MAP* **188** A60
Trethewey St *ABT* **250** S-T73
Triangle Rd *RMD* **203** J17-18
Tricouni Pl *WHS* **401** H1
Triggs Rd *SUR* **186** C-D43
Trillium Pl *CQT* **145** R36
Trillium Pl *DNV* **123** N22 **124** N23
Trim Rd *DEL* **242** R12
Trimaran Dr *RMD* **222** K9
Trimaran Gt *RMD* **222** K9
Trimble St *VAN* **142** T7 **162** U-V7
Trinity St *ABT* **250** U75-76
Trinity St *BUR* **143** R21
Trinity St *CQT* **165** W35
Trinity St *VAN* **143** R18-19 R20
Trites Rd *RMD* **222** L10
Trites Rd *SUR* **225** N35
Triumph St *BUR* **143** S21-22 **144** S23
Triumph St *VAN* **143** S18-19 S20
Trolley Pl *VAN* **163** W18
Trounce Alley *VAN* **11** G39-40 **142** S14
Trudy Ct *BUR* **144** T26
Trudy's Ldg *WHS* **401** B4
Trumond Av *RMD* **202** H8
Trumpeter Dr *RMD* **222** K10
Trunk Rd *PTM* **167** X47
Truro Dr *RMD* **202** J9
Trutch Av *CHL* **213** F5
Trutch Av *RMD* **202** F8
Trutch St *VAN* **162** U-V9
Tsatsu Shores Dr *DEL* **262** X15
Tsawwassen Dr N *DEL* **262** V-W15
Tsawwassen Dr S *DEL* **262** W-X15
Tsawwassen Beach Rd *DEL* **262** X-Y15 Y15 Y-Z15
Tuam Pl *VAN* **183** Z20
Tuaq Dr *VAN* **183** A20-21
Tucker Av *RMD* **202** F9
Tuckwell Ter *MIS* **210** H75
Tudor Av *DNV* **123** K15-16
Tudor Ct *ABT* **250** S77
Tudor Ct *DEL* **263** Y17
Tugboat Pl *VAN* **182** A11
Tulameen Pl *PCQ* **166** U42
Tulip Cr *ABT* **250** U73
Tulip Dr *SUR* **265** V-W38
Tulloch Rd *SUR* **245** T-U32
Tully Cr *PTM* **187** A-B47
Tulsy Cr *SUR* **205** G33
Tulsy Cr E *SUR* **205** G33-34
Tulsy Pl *SUR* **205** G33
Tum-Tumay-Whueton Dr *PMD* **144** P28-30
Tum Tum Rd *HOP* **118** H42-43
Tumberry Cr *VAN* **162** Y14 **182** Z14
Tunbridge Av *MIS* **210** F73-74
Tunis Pl *SUR* **205** G38
Tuohey Av *PCQ* **145** T38
Tupper Av *CQT* **165** X32
Tupper Blvd *MIS* **210** G74
Tupper St *CHL* **213** E6
Tupper St *VAN* **162** V-W14
Turbine Av *ABT* **269** W69
Turnberry La *CQT* **125** N37 **145** P37 P38
Turnbuckle Wynd *DEL* **223** P16
Turner Av *CQT* **146** Q39
Turner Pl *DEL* **204** H29
Turner St *ABT* **250** S-T76
Turner St *HOP* **118** F44
Turner St *MIS* **210** J71
Turner St *RMD* **204** E24
Turner St *VAN* **143** S-T18 S-T19 S-T20
Turner Creek Dr *PMD* **145** R34-35
Turnill St *RMD* **202** G13
Turquoise Dr *RMD* **202** F10
Turret Cr *CQT* **145** R36
Turtle Head Rd *BEL* **124** N27-28
Tuttle Av *RMD* **182** D14
Tuxedo Dr *PMD* **145** T31-32
Tuxedo Pl *PMD* **145** T31
Tuyttens Rd *KNT* **175** X20 X-Y19
Tweedsmuir Av *RMD* **202** J12
Tweedsmuir Dr *ABT* **251** S-T79
Twigg Pl *RMD* **183** B15
Twigg Rd *RMD* **183** B16
Twin Creek Pl *WVA* **122** J9-10
Twintree Pl *RMD* **202** F10-11
Tye Ct *BUR* **144** T24
Tyee Ct *WVA* **122** N12
Tyee Dr *WVA* **122** N12
Tyler *CHL* **252** Q94
Tyler Av *PCQ* **166** V-W39
Tyler St *MIS* **210** F-H72
Tyndale Cr *BUR* **164** V26-27
Tyndale Pl *BUR* **164** V27
Tyndall St *CQT* **164** U30
Tyne Pl *SUR* **266** V39
Tyne St *VAN* **163** Y20 **183** Z20
Tynehead Dr *SUR* **186** D40 D41-42
Tyner Av *MAP* **167** Y48-49
Tyner St *PCQ* **166** V39
Tyrol Cr *WHS* **401** F3
Tyrol Ct *WVA* **122** K10
Tyrol Pl *WVA* **122** K10-11
Tyrol Rd *WVA* **122** K11
Tyson Pl *RMD* **202** F-G9
Tyson Rd *CHL* **233** L-M5
Tytahun Cr *VAN* **162** X7-8

U

Udy Rd *ABT* **231** P83 **251** Q83
Udy Rd *RMD* **202** G11
Ullsmore Av *RMD* **202** H8
Ulster St *BUR* **164** Y26
Ulster St *PCQ* **146** S41 T41
Ultra Ct *CQT* **165** U35
Una Way *PCQ* **166** X39
Underhill Av *BUR* **164** U-V28
Underhill Dr *CHL* **232** L93-94
Underhill Dr *DEL* **263** X-Y16
Underwood Av *DNV* **123** J20-21
Underwood Pl *DNV* **123** J20-21
Ungless Way *PMD* **145** S35
Union Av *ABT* **250** U71-72
Union St *BUR* **143** T21-22 **144** T23 T25-26
Union St *PMD* **145** R-S32
Union St *VAN* **11** J41 **143** T15-16 T16
Union Bar Rd *HOP* **118** D-E46
United Blvd *CQT* **165** X-Y36 Y32-34
University Blvd *SQM* **301** E5
University Blvd *UEL* **161** U3-6
University Cr *BUR* **144** S-T29
University Dr E *BUR* **144** S29 T28-29
University Dr W *BUR* **144** S27-28
University La *LGT* **207** J52
University High St *BUR* **144** T29
Unsworth Rd *CHL* **233** K-L4 L-M3
Upland Cr *ABT* **250** T71
Upland Dr *DEL* **263** W16-17
Upland Dr *VAN* **183** Z17-18
Upland Pl *DEL* **263** W16
Upland Rd *SUR* **225** L36
Uplands Ct *CQT* **145** R36
Uplands Dr *ANM* **125** N33
Uplands Dr *CHL* **233** M7-8
Uplands Dr *HOP* **118** H42
Uplands Dr *LGC* **247** Q49
Uplands Rd *CHL* **233** M8
Upper Levels Hwy *CNV* **123** M16-17
Upper Beach Rd *SUR* **266** Y40
Upper Bellevue Av *WVA* **122** L8-9
Upper Canyon Rd *DEL* **224** K28-29
Upper Levels Hwy *DNV* **123** N19
Upper Levels Hwy *WVA* **101** H2-3 H3 **121** J3 K6 **122** K7-8 L11-13
Upper Maclure Rd *ABT* **249** T70 **250** T71
Upper Prairie Rd *CHL* **214** E-F14 H-J14
Upper Roper Av *WRK* **265** X36
Upper Sumas Mountain Rd *FRA* **231** K81-82 M-P82
Upton Rd *DNV* **123** L20
Ursus Cr *SUR* **205** F34

V

Valdez Ct *CQT* **146** S39
Valdez Dr *ABT* **250** S72
Valdez Rd *VAN* **162** V-W9
Vale Ct *DNV* **123** L15
Valemont Cr *ABT* **250** U71
Valemont St *CHL* **193** D8
Valencia Av *DNV* **123** J-K16
Valencia Ct *ABT* **270** V73
Valens St *PCQ* **166** W40
Valley Cr *ANM* **125** M-N33
Valley Dr *SQM* **301** K2
Valley Dr *VAN* **162** V-W10 W10-11 W-X11
Valley Dr *WHS* **401** B-C3
Valley Rd *ABT* **250** S75-76
Valley Rd *DNV* **123** J-K20
Valleyview Ct *CQT* **145** Q-R37
Valleyview Rd *CHL* **233** N7-8
Valleyvista Dr *CQT* **145** Q37
Valmont Way *RMD* **183** B18
Valour Dr *PMD* **145** T31
Vance Rd *FRA* **253** R-S6
Vancouver St *NEW* **184** A29-30
Vancouver St *SQM* **301** K1
VanDyke Pl *RMD* **183** B-C17
Vanessa Ct *CQT* **165** V31
Vanguard Rd *RMD* **183** D15
VanHorne Way *RMD* **182** B-C13

Vanier / Westhaven

Vanier Av *CQT* 165 W33
Vanier Pl *RMD* 183 D16
Vanmar St *CHL* 233 K7
Vanness Av *VAN* 163 W18-19 X19-20
Vanson Av *BUR* 164 W27
Vantage Pl *ABT* 249 S70 250 S71
Vantage Pl *DEL* 203 J22
Vantage Way *DEL* 203 J21-22
VanVelzen Av *MIS* 210 J72
Vardon Pl *DEL* 263 W18
Varley La *WVA* 122 K9
Varley St *BUR* 164 Y26
Vasey Rd *DEL* 223 M18
Vauxhall Pl *RMD* 183 C16
Vedder Pl *PCQ* 146 T42 166 U42
Vedder Rd *CHL* 213 H-J6 233 K-N6
Vedder Way *ABT* 270 V77-78
Vedder Mountain Rd *CHL* 233 N-P5 P4
Vedder Mountain Rd *FRA* 233 P1 P2 253 Q1
Vega Ct *BUR* 164 V29
Velma Av *CHL* 213 H7-8
Venables St *BUR* 143 T21-22 144 T23
Venables St *VAN* 143 T17-18 T18-20
Venice Av *CQT* 165 W35
Ventura Av *ABT* 250 T-U74
Ventura Cr *DNV* 123 J16-17
Venture St *BUR* 164 V27
Venture St *DEL* 223 K21
Venture Way *SUR* 205 G38 206 G39
Vera Rd *FRA* 253 V2
Verbena Dr *CHL* 233 K-L7
Verbena Pl *CQT* 145 R36
Verdon Way *ABT* 250 R73
Verdun Pl *RMD* 183 C17
Veres Ter *MIS* 210 G75
Vermilyea Ct *RMD* 202 E9-10
Vernon Av *MIS* 210 F74-75
Vernon Dr *VAN* 143 S-T16 T16 163 U16
Vernon Ter *ABT* 250 S78
Verona Pl *DNV* 123 K16
Veterans Way *ABT* 250 T73
Vicars St *CHL* 213 F5
Viceroy Pl *RMD* 183 B-C18
Vickers Way *RMD* 183 C16
Vickery St *MIS* 210 F72
Victor Dr W *CHL* 195 C19
Victor La *FRA* 212 E91
Victor St *CHL* 213 E7
Victor St *CQT* 165 V31
Victoria Av *CHL* 213 E6-7
Victoria Av *WRK* 265 X37-38
Victoria Div *VAN* 163 V17
Victoria Dr *CQT* 146 R42-43
Victoria Dr *PCQ* 146 S41-42
Victoria Dr *VAN* 143 S-T17 163 U-V17 W-Y17 183 A17 Z17 Z17
Victoria Pl *PCQ* 146 S41
Victoria St *ABT* 250 T-U72
Victoria St *DEL* 243 R21-22
Victoria St *NEW* 184 B29
Victoria St *SQM* 301 J-K1
Victory Blvd *ABT* 270 V76
Victory Dr *PMD* 145 T31
Victory St *BUR* 183 Z21 Z22 Z22 184 Z23
Vidal St *WRK* 265 W37 X37
Vienna Cr *DNV* 123 K16
View Av *MIS* 210 J73-74
View Cr *DEL* 263 W17
View Ct *PMD* 145 S32
View Pl *SQM* 301 J2-3
View St *PMD* 145 S32
Viewcrest Av *MIS* 210 G71-72
Viewgrove Pl *ABT* 270 V78
Viewlynn Dr *DNV* 123 M20
Viewmount Dr *PMD* 145 T35
Viewmount Pl *ABT* 250 S71
Viewmount Pl *PMD* 145 T35
Viewpoint Pl *CHL* 233 M8
Viewridge Pl *WVA* 121 K5-6
Viking Pl *RMD* 183 C17
Viking Way *RMD* 183 C-D17
Villa Rosa Pl *CHL* 233 M4
Village Dr *BUR* 163 W22 164 W23
Village Dr *SQM* 301 E-F5
Village Glen *ABT* 251 U80 271 V80
Village Gn *BUR* 184 Z25
Village Gn *WHS* 401 F4
Village Gn *WHS* 401 T21
Village Gt *KNT* 175 X20
Village Knoll *ABT* 251 U80
Village La *WHS* 401 T21
Village St *CHL* 233 M6
Village Stroll *WHS* 401 T21
Village Gate Blvd *WHS* 401 F3-4 T21
Village Gate Sq *WHS* 401 T21
Village Greens Wynd *DEL* 263 W17
Vimy Av *CHL* 233 N6
Vimy Cr *VAN* 163 V20
Vimy Rd *KNT* 175 X21
Vincent St *PCQ* 146 S-T40 166 U40
Vine Av *WRK* 265 W35 W36-37 W38 266 W39
Vine St *VAN* 10 K-L32 142 T11 162 U-V11 W11 X10 Y10
Vine Maple Dr *SUR* 245 T33-34
Vinedale Rd *DNV* 123 M18-19
Vinemaple Pl *CQT* 145 Q-R37
Vines St *CHL* 213 F5
Vineway St *PCQ* 146 T42
Vinewood Pl *BUR* 164 U28
Vinewood St *ABT* 270 V75
Viney Rd *DNV* 123 L19
Vinmore Av *RMD* 202 H8
Vinson Creek Rd *WVA* 122 J11
Vintner St *PMD* 145 T32-33
Viola Pl *MIS* 210 G74
Viola St *CHL* 233 N6
Violet *CQT* 165 W36
Vipond Pl *BUR* 183 Z22
Virginia Cr *DNV* 123 K15
Virtual Way *VAN* 163 U19
Viscount Pl *CHL* 213 G7
Viscount Pl *NEW* 184 D27
Viscount Way *RMD* 183 C16
Vishloff St *MIS* 210 F73
Vista Cr *BUR* 184 Z26
Vista Cr *SQM* 301 J3
Vista Ct *ABT* 250 S71
Vista Ct *CQT* 165 U35
Vista Dr *WRK* 265 X38
Vista Pl *DEL* 204 H28
Vista Pl *WVA* 121 K3-4
Vista Ridge Dr *MAP* 167 V53
Vistaview Ct *CQT* 145 Q-R37
Vivaldi Pl *VAN* 183 A20
Vivian Dr *VAN* 183 A18-19
Vivian Pl *PCQ* 166 X39
Vivian St *VAN* 163 Y19 183 Z19
Voight Rd *CHL* 234 P14
Volkoff La *UEL* 161 U3-4
Vonda Way *CQT* 146 R40
Vosburgh Av *MIS* 210 H77
Voyageur Way *RMD* 183 C15
Vulcan St *NEW* 165 Y31
Vulcan Way *RMD* 183 B-C17 C16
Vye Rd *ABT* 270 X76-78 271 X79-86 272 X87

W

Waddell Av *PCQ* 166 W39
Waddington Pl *CQT* 145 Q-R38
Wade Rd *DEL* 224 L30
Wade Ter *MIS* 210 H71
Wadham Dr *DEL* 204 G-H28
Wagner Dr *ABT* 249 S70 250 S71
Wagner Dr *RMD* 202 H13
Wagner Gt *RMD* 202 H13
Wagner Pl *ABT* 250 S71
Wagon Wheel Cir *CQT* 165 U37
Wagon Wheel Cr *LGT* 227 N54
Wagtail Av *RMD* 222 K10
Wain Pl *SQM* 301 B-C2
Wakefield Ct *BUR* 163 W21
Wakefield Ct *LGT* 227 L47
Wakefield Dr *LGT* 226 L46 227 L47
Wakely Ct *BUR* 164 V28
Walalee Dr *DEL* 262 X15
Walden St *ABT* 250 S77
Walden St *CHL* 214 E9
Walden St *VAN* 163 W-X15 X15
Wales St *VAN* 163 X-Y18 183 Z18
Walford St *RMD* 182 C-D13
Walker Av *BUR* 164 Y25 184 Z26
Walker Av *DEL* 263 Z16
Walker Cr *ABT* 270 V77-78
Walker Rd *KNT* 175 X20
Walker St *CQT* 165 W32 W-X31
Walker St *VAN* 163 W18
Wall St *VAN* 143 R19 R-S18
Wallace Av *DEL* 263 Z16-17
Wallace Cr *SUR* 205 E32
Wallace Cr *VAN* 162 U8
Wallace Ct *CQT* 145 T37
Wallace Dr *CHL* 233 P6 253 Q6
Wallace Dr *SUR* 185 A-B36
Wallace Pl *DEL* 263 Z17
Wallace Pl *VAN* 162 Y8
Wallace Rd *RMD* 202 J10
Wallace St *ABT* 230 M-N75
Wallace St *HOP* 118 E44-45
Wallace St *MIS* 189 D70
Wallace St *VAN* 142 T8 162 U8 V-X8 Y8 182 Z8
Wallace Wynd *PMD* 145 T31
Waller Ct *RMD* 202 J9
Waller Dr *RMD* 202 J9
Walls Av *CQT* 165 W32-33
Walmsley Av *ABT* 270 X71-72
Walmsley Ct *BUR* 164 Y26
Walmsley St *NEW* 184 A28-29
Walnut Av *CHL* 232 P94
Walnut Av *HHS* 155 Q19
Walnut Av (Abbotsford) *ABT* 250 T76
Walnut Av (Huntingdon) *ABT* 270 Y-Z77
Walnut Cl *SUR* 186 B40
Walnut Cr *CQT* 165 V34
Walnut Cr *MAP* 187 Z48
Walnut Dr *HOP* 118 G42-43
Walnut Pl *CQT* 165 V34
Walnut Pl *DEL* 223 P17
Walnut St *VAN* 10 J-K33 142 T11
Walnut Grove Dr *LGT* 207 F-G49
Walpole Cr *DNV* 123 N22 124 N23
Walsh Av *ABT* 250 U74-75
Walter Pl *BUR* 164 V23
Walter Rd *ABT* 251 T-U81
Walter Florence Rd *PTM* 187 B47
Walter Gage Rd *UEL* 161 T4 U3
Walter Hardwick Av *VAN* 11 K39-40 142 T14
Walters St *ABT* 210 J77
Walters St *CHL* 213 F8
Waltham Av *BUR* 164 Y24 184 Z24
Walton Av *CQT* 145 R37-38
Walton Rd *RMD* 202 F10
Walton Way *PMD* 145 R33
Waneta Pl *VAN* 163 V19
Wansford Dr *DEL* 204 H-J29
Wanstead St *MAP* 187 A48 B47-48
Warbler Av *RMD* 222 K10
Warbler La *CQT* 146 Q39
Ward Rd *ABT* 251 R83
Ward St *NEW* 164 Y30
Ward St *VAN* 163 X18 X18-19
Wardance St *WVA* 122 N12-13
Wardle St *HOP* 118 D44
Wardmore Pl *RMD* 202 H8
Wardrop St *MIS* 210 J73 230 K73
Ware St *ABT* 250 U74 270 V74
Waresley St *MAP* 187 A48
Waring Rd *FRA* 212 F87
Warren Pl *DEL* 204 F30
Warren Pl *LGT* 227 K-L47
Warren St *BUR* 163 X21
Warren St *NEW* 184 A29
Warrenton Av *CQT* 165 W35
Warrick St *CQT* 165 X35 Y35
Warwick Av *PCQ* 166 W39 W40
Warwick Av N *BUR* 144 S24
Warwick Av S *BUR* 144 S24 164 U24
Warwick Pl *PCQ* 166 V-W39
Warwick Rd *DEL* 204 J28-29
Wasco St *CQT* 165 U34
Washington Dr *PMD* 145 R-S32
Waska St *LGT* 207 E53
Water Av *HOP* 118 D-E44
Water La *WVA* 121 L3
Water St *PMD* 145 R32 R35
Water St *VAN* 11 G39-40 142 S14
Water Florence Rd *MAP* 187 B47
Waterford Dr *VAN* 182 A14 Z14
Waterford Pl *CQT* 145 Q38
Waterford Pl *SUR* 205 G33-34
Waterfront Rd E *VAN* 11 F-G39 G41 143 S15-16
Waterfront Rd W *VAN* 11 F-G39 G41 142 S14 143 S15
Waterleaf Pl *ABT* 251 U80 271 V80
Waterleigh Dr *VAN* 182 A14
Waterloo Dr *PMD* 145 S31-32
Waterloo St *VAN* 142 T9 162 U-V9
Waterside Av *VAN* 183 A17
Waterton Cr *ABT* 251 R79
Waterton Dr *RMD* 222 K12
Watkins Av *CQT* 146 Q40
Watkins Rd *FRA* 193 Z2
Watkins Ter *MIS* 210 H71
Watling St *BUR* 183 Z21 Z21-22 Z22 184 Z23
Watson Ct *DEL* 204 F29
Watson Dr *DEL* 204 F29
Watson Pl *DEL* 204 F29
Watson Rd *ABT* 249 Q63
Watson Rd *BEL* 124 M-N30
Watson Rd *CHL* 233 M4-6
Watson St *VAN* 163 V15 W15
Watson Way *WHS* 401 G2
Watt St *MIS* 190 B75-76 D76
Wavell La *ABT* 270 V76
Waverley Av *BUR* 183 A22 Z22
Waverley Av *VAN* 163 Y16 Y17-18 Y19-20
Waverly Pl *SUR* 205 E33
Wavertree Rd *DNV* 123 K15-16
Waxberry Cr *MIS* 210 H75
Wayburne Cr *LGT* 227 L47
Wayburne Dr *BUR* 163 W22 W-X22 164 V23 W23
Wayne Dr *DNV* 123 L16
Wayside La *WHS* 401 G2
Weare St *DEL* 243 Q15
Weather Ct *BUR* 164 X25-26
Weatherby St *WRK* 265 W38
Weatherhead Ct *MIS* 210 H75
Weaver Cr *MIS* 210 G78
Weaver Ct *VAN* 183 Z20
Weaver Dr *DEL* 263 Y16
Webb Av *CHL* 213 J6
Webb Ct *ABT* 250 U78
Webber Av *VAN* 163 W15
Webster Av *CQT* 164 V30 165 V31
Webster Ct *ABT* 270 V71
Webster Rd *CHL* 233 N4
Webster Rd *DEL* 204 H23
Webster Rd *RMD* 202 F9-10
Webster St *MAP* 188 Z59
Wedge La *WHS* 401 E3
Wedgeview Pl *WHS* 401 C2-3
Wedgewood Dr *CHL* 193 C8
Wedgewood St *BUR* 164 Y27 Y27-28 184 Z27
Wedgewood St *PCQ* 146 S41
Weeden Dr *CHL* 233 N7
Weeden Pl *CHL* 233 N7
Welch Av *MIS* 190 B73
Welch St *DNV* 122 N14
Welch St *WVA* 122 N13
Welcher Av *PCQ* 165 V38 166 V39
Weldon Ct *PMD* 144 T30
Wellburn Dr *DEL* 223 N-P17
Wellington Av *CHL* 213 E6
Wellington Av *VAN* 163 W19 X20
Wellington Av *WVA* 101 G1-2
Wellington Cr *DNV* 123 L15
Wellington Cr *RMD* 182 C-D11
Wellington Cr *SUR* 185 A36
Wellington Ct *CQT* 146 R40
Wellington Dr *DNV* 123 K17-18 K18-20
Wellington Dr *SUR* 185 A36
Wellington Pl *DNV* 123 K18
Wellington Pl *WVA* 101 G2
Wellington Rd *DEL* 242 S14
Wellington St *NEW* 184 A30
Wellington St *PCQ* 146 S-T40 166 U40
Wellmond Rd *RMD* 202 H8
Wells Pl *SUR* 205 E-F32
Wells Rd *CHL* 213 J5-6
Wells Rd *KNT* 175 W17
Wells St *MIS* 210 F75
Wells-Gray Av *ABT* 251 T79
Wells-Gray Ct *ABT* 251 S-T79
Wells-Gray Pl *ABT* 251 S-T79
Wells Gray Pl *NEW* 164 Y30
Wells Line Rd *ABT* 271 W82-86 272 W87-89
Wellsgreen Pl *DEL* 263 Z17
Welsh St *NEW* 184 A-B29
Welsley Dr *BUR* 164 Y26
Welton St *MIS* 210 J74
Welwyn St *VAN* 163 V-W17 W17
Wembley Dr *DNV* 123 L20-21
Wembley Pl *DNV* 123 L20-21
Wenda Pl *SQM* 301 D3
Wendel Pl *DNV* 123 L19
Wenonah St *VAN* 163 W18
Wentworth Av *DNV* 123 K15-16
Wentworth Av *WVA* 122 K9
Werks Dr *VAN* 183 Z20
Wesbrook Cr *UEL* 161 T-U4
Wesbrook Mall *UEL* 161 T-U4 V4-5 W5
Wesley Dr *DEL* 262 X15 X-Y15
Wesley Pl *DEL* 262 X15
Wessex St *VAN* 163 Y20
West Blvd *VAN* 162 X-Y11 182 Z11
West Mall *UEL* 161 U3 V4
West Rd *BEL* 124 N-P29
West Rd *RMD* 182 C12
West St *MAP* 187 Z47
West Beach Av *WRK* 265 X36
West Campus Rd *BUR* 144 S28
West Edwards St *MIS* 210 F-G78
West Point Pl *VAN* 162 U7
West Railway St *ABT* 250 U76 270 V76
West Vista Ct *WVA* 121 K3
West Whalley Ring Rd *SUR* 185 B-C33 C33 C34 D33-34
Westbank Pl *VAN* 183 Z20
Westbury Av *ABT* 270 V75
Westbury La *VAN* 182 Z13
Westbury Walk *VAN* 182 Z13
Westcot Pl *WVA* 122 L12
Westcot Rd *WVA* 122 L12
Westcott St *RMD* 222 L10
Westdean Cr *WVA* 122 L10
Westerly St *ABT* 250 U71
Western Av *CNV* 123 L-M17
Western Cr *UEL* 161 T4
Western Dr *PCQ* 166 W-X39
Western Pkwy *UEL* 161 T-U4
Western Pl *PCQ* 165 X38
Western St *VAN* 11 K40-41 143 T15
Westfield Av *MAP* 187 A48-49
Westham La *DEL* 243 Q16-17
Westham Island Rd *DEL* 222 P10 242 Q10 Q11-12
Westhaven Ct *WVA* 121 J3
Westhaven Pl *WVA* 121 J3
Westhaven Rd *WVA* 121 J3

Street Index

222 pgs
6 pt